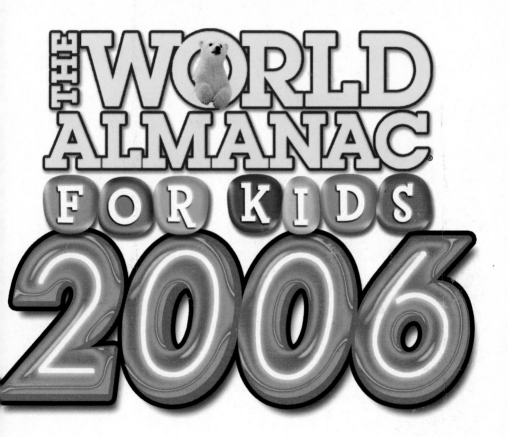

THE WORLD ALMANAC FOR KIDS 2006

WORLD ALMANAC BOOKS
A Division of World Almanac Education Group, Inc.
A WRC Media Company

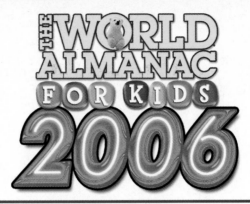

EDITOR: Kevin Seabrooke

CURRICULUM CONSULTANT:
Eric S. Elkins, M.A., Youth Content Editor, Denver Newspaper Agency

CONTRIBUTORS: Elizabeth Barden, Laura C. Girardi, Joseph Gustaitis, Richard Hantula,
Raymond P. Hill, Emily Keyes, Carol Moran, Donna Mulder, Amy Perry,
Sean Price, Kerria Seabrooke, Lori Wiesenfeld
Consultant: Lee T. Shapiro, Ph.D. (Astronomy)

KID CONTRIBUTORS: Brooke Duvall, Melissa Gagliardi, Sabina Latifovic,
Maya Master Park, Kristyn Romaine, Shelby Thigpen

Thanks to all the kids who wrote to us with their great ideas!

DESIGN: Bill SMITH STUDIO
Creative Director: Brian Kobberger **Project Director:** David Borkman
Design: Roxanne Daner, Geron Hoy, Ron Leighton, Marina Terletsky
Photo Research: Scott Haag **Production:** James Liebman

WORLD ALMANAC BOOKS

Director of Sales and Marketing	Editorial Director	Managing Editor	Director of Desktop Publishing
Chuck Errig	William McGeveran Jr.	Zoë Kashner	Elizabeth J. Lazzara

Editorial Staff: Erik C. Gopel, Senior Editor;
Sarah Janssen, Vincent G. Spadafora, Associate Editors

WORLD ALMANAC EDUCATION GROUP
Chief Executive Officer, WRC Media Inc.: Martin E. Kenney Jr.
General Manager/Publisher: Ken Park
Director of Purchasing and Production/Photo Research: Edward A. Thomas
Director of Indexing Services: Marjorie B. Bank; Index Editor: Walter Kronenberg
Marketing Coordinator: Julia Suarez.

The World Almanac For Kids 2006
Copyright © 2005 by World Almanac Education Group, Inc.
The World Almanac and The World Almanac For Kids are registered trademarks of World Almanac Education Group, Inc.
Softcover ISBN-13: 978-0-8868-7960-0; ISBN-10: 0-88687-960-4
Hardcover ISBN-13: 978-0-8868-7961-7; ISBN-10: 0-88687-961-2
Smyth-sewn edition: ISBN 13: 978-0-8868-7970-9; ISBN-10: 0-88687-970-1

Printed in the United States of America
The softcover and hardcover editions are distributed to the trade in the United States by St. Martin's Press.
The Smyth-sewn edition is distributed by World Almanac Education, (800) 321-1147.
WORLD ALMANAC® BOOKS
An Imprint of World Almanac Education Group, Inc.
512 Seventh Avenue
New York, NY 10018
E-Mail: Waforkids@waegroup.com
Web site: www.worldalmanacforkids.com
The addresses and content of Web sites referred to in this book are subject to change.
Although The World Almanac For Kids carefully reviews these sites, we cannot take responsibility for their content.

CONTENTS

8

FACES & PLACES

10th ANNIVERSARY

10 Years of Favorites

The very first *World Almanac for Kids* came out 10 years ago. Since then, millions of kids have read editions of this book. The famous faces below have all appeared in *The World Almanac for Kids*. Who are they and when did the event described occur? (Hint: There's one event for each year 1995 through 2001.)

I became the first African-American U.S. Secretary of State in _____. I am _____.

At age 11, I had just finished my first season of *All That* in _____. I am _____.

My group first started singing together in _____. I am _____.

The same year I started to be "in the middle," I appeared in a movie with "my dog" in _____. I am _____ _____.

The first American edition of my novels about muggles and wizards was published in _____. I am _____.

My team won the World Cup in Los Angeles in front of 90,000 fans in _____. I am _____.

I made my first major-league appearance as a Yankee in _____. I am _____.

ANSWERS ON PAGES 335-338. FOR MORE PUZZLES GO TO WWW.WORLDALMANACFORKIDS.COM

9

HIGH NOTES IN·MUSIC

KELLY

Kelly Clarkson, the original American Idol, can still hit the high notes. In 2005, her song "Since U Been Gone" reached #1.

ALICIA

Alicia Keys continues to rock the music awards. In 2005, she snapped up three more Grammys for her work on *The Diary of Alicia Keys*—bringing her total number of Grammy awards up to nine!

USHER

Everyone wants to hear Usher's *Confessions*. It was the best-selling album of 2004! Usher Raymond also walked away with four Grammys and three Soul Train Awards in 2005.

LINDSAY

You know Lindsay Lohan from her hit movies *Parent Trap*, *Confessions of a Teenage Drama Queen*, and *Herbie: Fully Loaded* but her album *Speak* reached #4 on the Billboard Charts.

TUBE FAVORITES

SCOWELL

American Idol's toughest judge, Simon Cowell (center), with judges Randy Jackson and Paula Abdul.

HEAVEN

7th Heaven's Camden family sticks together no matter what. Did you know that 14-year-old Mackenzie Rosman (Ruthie Camden—at left) has been on the show since she was five years old?

VERSATILE SPONGE

Few actors can successfully make the transition from TV to the movies, but that was not a problem for animated ocean-dweller SpongeBob SquarePants. His performance in 2004's *SBSP* movie was really deep.

SUPERTEEN

Tom Welling uses his superhero talent to play a teenaged Clark Kent on *Smallville*.

MOVIE MAGIC

QUEEN

Keisha Castle-Hughes, 15, plays the role of Queen Apailana in 2005's *Star Wars Episode III: Revenge of the Sith*, the final of six Star Wars films since 1977. Keisha's debut performance in *Whale Rider* earned her an Academy Award nomination in 2004.

UNFORTUNATE

Jim Carrey with Emily Browning and Liam Aiken in *Lemony Snicket's A Series of Unfortunate Events*. Not as dark as the books, but still pretty scary.

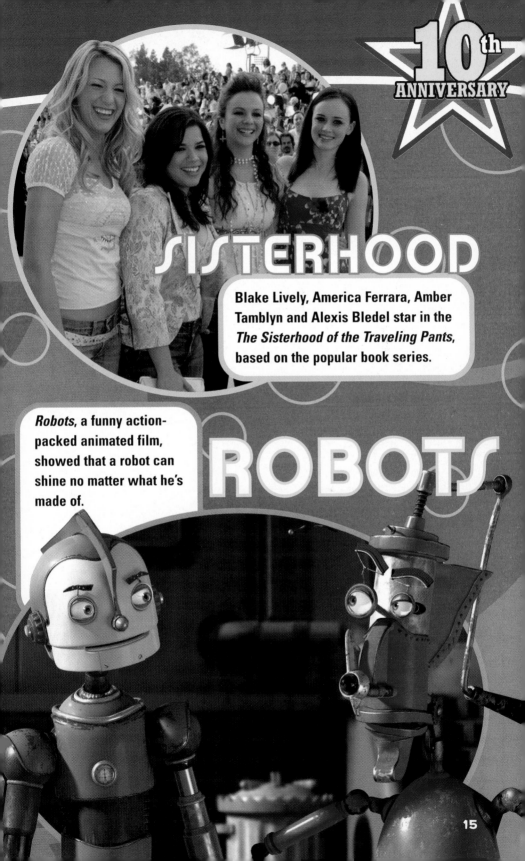

SISTERHOOD

Blake Lively, America Ferrara, Amber Tamblyn and Alexis Bledel star in the *The Sisterhood of the Traveling Pants*, based on the popular book series.

ROBOTS

Robots, a funny action-packed animated film, showed that a robot can shine no matter what he's made of.

SEEKING ITALIAN GOLD

OH YES

At the 2006 Winter Olympics in Turin, Italy, short-track speedskater Apolo Anton Ohno hopes to add gold medals to ones he's already won at the 2002 Olympics and 2005 World Championships.

BODES WELL

Bode Miller won the 2005 World Cup skiing championship, the first American to earn that title since Phil Mahre in 1983.

SASHA-Y ON ICE

Skater Sasha Cohen was fourth at the 2002 Olympics, when she was just 17. She placed second in the 2005 World Championship. How will she do at the 2006 Olympics?

WINNERS

9-8, AND COUNTING

In spring 2005, Tiger Woods won his ninth major golf tournament and Annika Sorenstam won her eighth. The way these two are playing, those numbers may be higher by the time you read this.

BRADY BUNCH OF TITLES

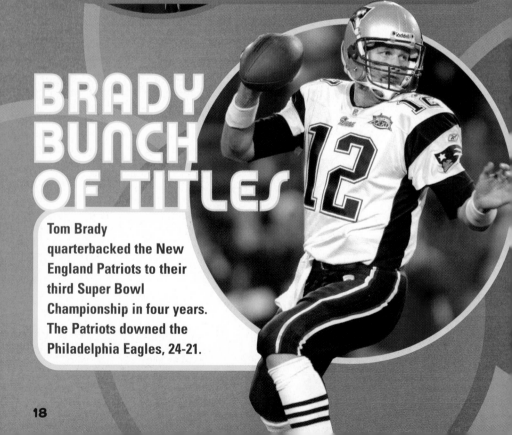

Tom Brady quarterbacked the New England Patriots to their third Super Bowl Championship in four years. The Patriots downed the Philadelphia Eagles, 24-21.

GOAL-A-GAME

Eddie Johnson, 20, after scoring his eighth goal in eight games for the U.S. national soccer team, which was working to qualify for the 2006 World Cup in Germany.

COACH!

This win really counted! Coach Roderick Jackson from Birmingham, AL, won his case before the Supreme Court in spring 2005. Jackson, a high school teacher, had gone to court because he was fired from his girls' basketball coaching job after protesting that his team was not getting fair treatment compared to the boys' team.

IN THE NEWS

SOFT T. REX

In spring 2005 scientists announced that for the first time they had discovered "soft tissue," including blood vessels, from a dinosaur—a Tyrannosaurus Rex!

BRAVE VOTERS

An Iraqi woman holds up her hand to show a purple finger, indicating she has just voted in Iraq's January 30 elections despite threats and violence from insurgents.

POPE JOHN PAUL II

The leader of the Roman Catholic Church died on April 2, 2005 at the age of 84. The charismatic Polish pontiff served as pope for 26 years. German Cardinal Joseph Ratzinger, 78, a close advisor to John Paul, was selected as his successor and chose the name of Pope Benedict XVI.

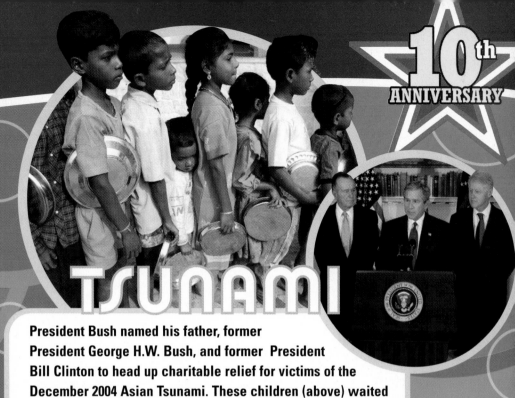

TSUNAMI

President Bush named his father, former President George H.W. Bush, and former President Bill Clinton to head up charitable relief for victims of the December 2004 Asian Tsunami. These children (above) waited for food in January in the Indian city of Madras.

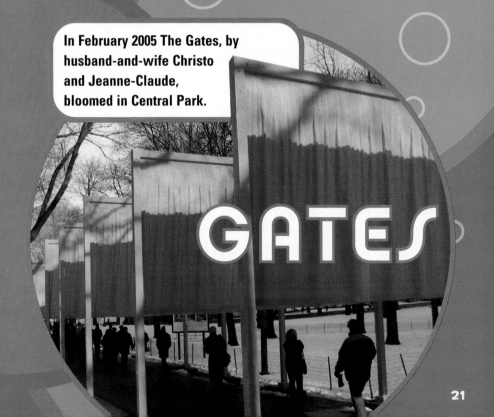

In February 2005 The Gates, by husband-and-wife Christo and Jeanne-Claude, bloomed in Central Park.

GATES

10 YEARS OF THE WORLD ALMANAC FOR KIDS

The World Almanac for Kids 1996

was the first-ever World Almanac written just for kids. This 2006 edition marks our 10th Anniversary! The people on these pages were in the 1996 book. Find out what they were up to back then and what they are doing today.

Michelle Kwan

Then: Michelle was just 15 years old in 1995—and she had already skated in the World Championships the year before. (She finished in 8th place.)

Now: Today, Michelle is a champion skater. She's won the world title in figure skating five times since 1995 and won her 9th U.S. Championship in 2005.

Steve Fossett

Then: Fossett became the first person to make a solo flight across the Pacific Ocean in a balloon, in 1995.

Now: Fossett broke another record in 2005—this time in a plane. He became the first person to fly around the world alone without stopping or refueling. His journey was 23,000 miles long and took 67 hours.

Major League Baseball

Then: Baseball teams were playing their first season back after the strike of 1994. It became a record-breaking year when Cal Ripkin, Jr. matched legendary player Lou Gehrig's record for consecutive games played—playing 2,131 consecutive games.

Now: The Boston Red Sox, in October, 2004, won their first World Series since 1918. After a come-from-behind victory against the New York Yankees in the American League championship, they swept the Cardinals in four games.

Nelson Mandela

Then: Mandela was the president of South Africa, having won the nation's first election open to people of all races, in 1994. Mandela had spent over 25 years of his life in prison fighting for equality for blacks in his country.

Now: Mandela retired from public life at age 85. In January 2005, he spoke out about his son's death from AIDS. He wanted people to understand that AIDS sufferers deserve care and respect.

Supreme Court of the United States

Then: The members of the Supreme Court were Chief Justice Rehnquist, and Associate Justices Ginsburg, Souter, Thomas, Breyer, Scalia, Stevens, O'Connor, and Kennedy.

Now: In early 2005, the membership of the Supreme Court was still exactly the same. However, Chief Justice Rehnquist was in poor health, and 3 justices were over age 70, so changes in the Court were expected.

Mary-Kate and Ashley Olsen

Then: In 1995, the twins were only nine years old. They were just finishing up their role playing Michelle Tanner on the TV show *Full House*.

Now: Today, both girls are students at New York University. But they are still very much involved in show business. They produce movies starring themselves, and sell products like CDs and clothing through Dualstar, their company. Some estimate that they are worth $40 million each!

Hilary Rodham Clinton

Then: As wife of President Bill Clinton, she was the first lady. Mrs. Clinton worked on issues like health care, women's rights, and children's issues.

Now: Today, Hilary Rodham Clinton is the only First Lady to ever be elected to the U.S. Senate. She is serving as a senator from New York State.

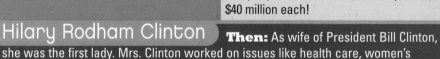

Yasir Arafat, Shimon Peres, and Yitzhak Rabin

Then: Palestinian leader Yasir Arafat (right), Israeli Prime Minister Yitzhak Rabin (left), and former Israeli leader Shimon Peres shared the Nobel Peace Prize in 1994 for building a path to peace in the Middle East. In 1995, Rabin was assassinated by a right-wing Jewish extremist. Then, after a breakdown in peace talks in 2000, clashes between Israelis and Palestinians increased.

Now: A few months after Arafat died in 2004, Israeli Prime Minister Ariel Sharon, with Peres as his deputy, was making new plans for peace with the Palestinians, working with Palestinian leader Mahmoud Abbas.

Animals

What is the most popular dog?   page 34

Animal Facts

Frogs can't swallow unless they close their eyes. Frog eyes bulge not only on the outside but on the inside of their faces as well. Since the underside of their eyes protrudes into the mouth cavity, they have to use their eyes to push the food down their stomach.

Cats purr about 26 cycles per second, the same frequency as an idling diesel truck engine. Although purring is usually a sign of contentment, it can also mean the opposite. Cats can purr when frightened, when trying to calm a potential enemy, when injured, when giving birth, and even when dying. Scientists think that purring releases a calming substance in the brain called endorphins, which would explain why cats purr when in pain.

Pink elephants can be found only in storybooks, but you can see a **pink walrus** in real life! When a walrus is warm, its skin turns pink. There are plenty of other unusually colored animals, too. Horses can be found in white, black, gray, chestnut, creamy gold, and brown. And there are red foxes, orange tigers, and Belgian Blue or Estonian Red cattle.

The **American bison,** also called the American buffalo, is the heaviest land mammal in North America. Bison range from 5 to 6.5 feet long and can weigh up to 2,200 pounds. They once numbered an estimated 20 to 30 million, but today there are only 250,000 left in the United States. Of those, only 16,000 roam in the wild.

Unlike other marine animals, **sea otters** don't have a layer of blubber to keep them warm. Instead, warm air trapped in their fur keeps them nice and toasty in the water. Sea otters have the thickest fur of any mammal, with about 100,000 hairs per square inch.

All About... HORSES

The dog may be man's best friend, but horses have been more important to human history than any other domestic animal. Until the invention of the internal combustion engine, horses and horse-drawn vehicles were the best way to plow the soil, as well as to transport goods, people, and messages long distances. These useful animals also proved to be very valuable in warfare, with mounted cavalry having a great advantage over troops on foot.

Horses are believed to have been domesticated between 3000 and 4000 B.C. in Europe and Asia. Once the size of large ponies, they were used at first mainly for meat and possibly for milk. Then, as people settled in permanent villages and learned to grow grain, they ate the horses less and less and found other uses for the animals. Horses filled many roles: pulling plows, stagecoaches, mail coaches, and wagons. Even the first trains were pulled by horses on steel tracks.

The Persians were among the first to put the quick-footed animal to use as a communications tool. In the 5th century B.C., Persian officials used horses with riders to relay messages to far-off lands. And, centuries later in the 1800s, Pony Express riders were expected to ride 75 miles a day through "snow, rain, heat, and darkness" to deliver messages. It was very hazardous, but only one delivery was ever lost! The Pony Express greatly speeded up communications in the United States.

Today, there are nearly 6 million horses in the United States. But horses are not actually native to the Americas. They were brought over by Spanish explorers, and later left to roam free. Some tens of thousands of wild horses, like mustangs, roam the American West. However, ranchers claim they damage the land, so the U.S. government captures hundreds of them each year and puts them up for adoption.

The smallest horse in the world is located in Kittreu, North Carolina. "Black Beauty" is only 13.75 inches tall and weighs just over 41 lbs.

BIGGEST, SMALLEST, FASTEST
IN THE WORLD

WORLD'S BIGGEST ANIMALS

MARINE MAMMAL: blue whale (100 feet long, 200 tons)

LAND MAMMAL: African bush elephant (12 feet high, 4–7 tons)
  TALLEST MAMMAL: giraffe (18 feet tall)

REPTILE: saltwater crocodile (20 feet long, 1,150 pounds)

SNAKE: anaconda (27 feet, 9 inches long, 500 pounds)
  LONGEST SNAKE: reticulated python (26–32 feet long)

FISH: whale shark (45 feet long, 10 tons)

BIRD: ostrich (9 feet tall, 345 pounds)

INSECT: stick insect (15 inches long)

WORLD'S FASTEST ANIMALS

MARINE MAMMAL: killer whale (35 miles per hour)

LAND MAMMAL: cheetah (70 miles per hour)

FISH: sailfish (68 miles per hour)

BIRD: peregrine falcon (150 miles per hour)

INSECT: dragonfly (36 miles per hour)

FASTEST SNAKE: black mamba (14 mph)

WORLD'S SMALLEST ANIMALS

MAMMAL: bumblebee bat (1.1 to 1.3 inches)

FISH: stout infantfish (0.25 inches)

BIRD: bee hummingbird (2.2 inches)

SNAKE: thread snake and brahminy blind snake (4.25 inches)

LIZARD: Jaragua sphaero lizard (0.63 inches)

INSECT: fairy fly (0.01 inches)

How Fast Do Animals Run?

Some animals can run as fast as a car. But a snail needs more than 30 hours just to go 1 mile. If you look at this table, you will see how fast some land animals can go. Humans at their fastest are still slower than many animals. The record for fastest speed for a human for a recognized race distance is held by Michael Johnson, who won the 1996 Olympic 200 meter dash in 19.32 seconds for an average speed of 23.16 mph.

MILES PER HOUR

Animal	Miles per hour
Cheetah	70
Antelope	60
Lion	50
Elk	45
Zebra	40
Rabbit	35
Reindeer	32
Cat	30
Elephant	25
Wild turkey	15
Squirrel	12
Snail	0.03

HOW LONG DO ANIMALS LIVE?

Most animals do not live as long as human beings do. A monkey that's 14 years old is thought to be old, while a person at that age is still considered young. The average life spans of some animals are shown here. The average life span of a human in the United States today is about 75 to 80 years.

Galapagos tortoise . 200+ years
Box turtle . . . . 100 years
Gray whale . . . . 70 years
Alligator . . . . 50 years
Chimpanzee . . . . 50 years
Humpback whale . . . . . 50 years
African elephant . . . 35 years
Bottlenose dolphin . . . . 30 years
Gorilla . . . . 30 years
Horse . . . . 20 years
Black bear . . . . 18 years
Tiger . . . . 16 years
Lion . . . . 15 years
Lobster . . . . 15 years
Cat (domestic) . . . . 15 years
Cow . . . . 15 years
Tarantula . . . . 15 years
Dog (domestic) . . . . 13 years
Camel (bactrian) . . . . . . 12 years
Moose . . . . 12 years
Pig . . . . 10 years
Squirrel . . . . 10 years
Deer (white-tailed) . . . . . 8 years
Goat . . . . 8 years
Kangaroo . . . . 7 years
Chipmunk . . . . 6 years
Beaver . . . . 5 years
Rabbit (domestic) . . . . . . 5 years
Guinea pig . . . . 4 years
Mouse . . . . 3 years
Opossum . . . . 1 year
Worker bee . . . . 4-5 weeks
Adult housefly . . . . . . 3-4 weeks

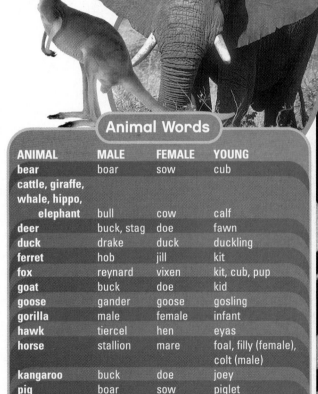

Animal Words

ANIMAL	MALE	FEMALE	YOUNG
bear	boar	sow	cub
cattle, giraffe, whale, hippo, elephant	bull	cow	calf
deer	buck, stag	doe	fawn
duck	drake	duck	duckling
ferret	hob	jill	kit
fox	reynard	vixen	kit, cub, pup
goat	buck	doe	kid
goose	gander	goose	gosling
gorilla	male	female	infant
hawk	tiercel	hen	eyas
horse	stallion	mare	foal, filly (female), colt (male)
kangaroo	buck	doe	joey
pig	boar	sow	piglet
rabbit	buck	doe	kit, bunny
swan	cob	pen	cygnet
tiger	tiger	tigress	cub
turkey	gobler, tom	hen	chick or puult
woodchuck	he-chuck	she-chuck	kit or cub

Life on Earth

This time line shows how life developed on Earth. The earliest animals are at the bottom of the chart. The most recent are at the top of the chart.

	YEARS AGO		ANIMAL LIFE ON EARTH
CENOZOIC	10,000–PRESENT		Human civilization develops.
	1.8 MILLION TO 10,000		Large mammals like mammoths, sabre-toothed cats, and giant ground sloths develop. Modern human beings evolve. This era ends with an ice age.
	65 TO 1.8 MILLION		Ancestors of modern-day horses, zebras, rhinos, sheep, goats, camels, pigs, cows, deer, giraffes, camels, elephants, cats, dogs, and primates begin to develop.
MESOZOIC	144 TO 65 MILLION		In the Cretaceous period, new dinosaurs appear. Many insect groups, modern mammal and bird groups also develop. A global extinction of most dinosaurs occurs at the end of this period.
	206 TO 144 MILLION		The Jurassic is dominated by giant dinosaurs. In the late Jurassic, birds evolve.
	248 TO 206 MILLION		In the Triassic period, marine life develops again. Reptiles also move into the water. Reptiles begin to dominate the land areas. Dinosaurs and mammals develop.
PALEOZOIC	290 TO 248 MILLION		A mass extinction wipes out 95% of all marine life.
	354 TO 290 MILLION		Reptiles develop. Much of the land is covered by swamps.
	417 TO 354 MILLION		The first trees and the forests appear. The first land-living vertebrates, amphibians and wingless insects appear. Many new sea creatures also appear.
	443 TO 417 MILLION		Coral reefs form. Other animals such as the first known freshwater fish develop. Relatives of spiders and centipedes develop.
	542 TO 443 MILLION		Animals with shells (called trilobites) and some mollusks form. Primitive fish and corals develop. There is also evidence of the first primitive land plants.
PRECAMBRIAN	3.8 BILLION TO 542 MILLION		First evidence of life on Earth. All life is in water. Early single-celled bacteria and achaea appear, followed by multicelled organisms, including early animals.
	4.6 BILLION		Formation of the Earth.

Animal Kingdom

The world has so many animals that scientists looked for a way to organize them into groups. A Swedish scientist named Carolus Linnaeus (1707–1778) worked out a system for classifying both animals and plants. We still use it today.

The animal kingdom is separated into two large groups—animals with backbones, called **vertebrates**, and animals without backbones, called **invertebrates**.

These large groups are divided into smaller groups called **phyla**. And phyla are divided into even smaller groups called **classes**. The animals in each group are classified together when their bodies are similar in certain ways.

Vertebrates
Animals With Backbones

FISH	Swordfish, tuna, salmon, trout, halibut
AMPHIBIANS	Frogs, toads, mud puppies
REPTILES	Turtles, alligators, crocodiles, lizards
BIRDS	Sparrows, owls, turkeys, hawks
MAMMALS	Kangaroos, opossums, dogs, cats, bears, seals, rats, squirrels, rabbits, chipmunks, porcupines, horses, pigs, cows, deer, bats, whales, dolphins, monkeys, apes, humans

Invertebrates
Animals Without Backbones

PROTOZOA	The simplest form of animals
COELENTERATES	Jellyfish, hydra, sea anemones, coral
MOLLUSKS	Clams, snails, squid, oysters
ANNELIDS	Earthworms
ARTHROPODS	
Crustaceans:	Lobsters, crayfish
Centipedes and Millipedes	
Arachnids:	Spiders, scorpions
Insects:	Butterflies, grasshoppers, bees, termites, cockroaches
ECHINODERMS	Starfish, sea urchins, sea cucumbers

Homework Help

How can you remember the animal classifications from most general to most specific? Try this sentence:

King **P**hilip **C**ame **O**ver **F**rom **G**reat **S**pain.
K = Kingdom; **P** = Phylum; **C** = Class; **O** = Order; **F** = Family; **G** = Genus; **S** = Species.

BIRDS

Birds are warm-blooded animals, with feathers and wings. Unlike mammals, (except for the duck-billed platypus), birds lay eggs. Feathers provide insulation for birds, allowing them to maintain a high body temperature. Their long wing feathers also help them to get the lift necessary for flight. A streamlined body, a lightweight skeleton of hollow bones, and very efficient circulatory and respiratory systems also aid them in their airborne journeys. Birds usually fly pretty fast— between 20 and 30 miles per hour. They are able to fly even faster, but save their top speed for emergencies. Ducks have been known to fly over 60 miles an hour when being pursued by predators.

Not all birds can fly, however. The largest of all living birds, the ostrich, has lost this ability. Ostriches can grow to be over 9 feet tall and weigh up to 330 pounds. No wonder they can't get off the ground!

The smallest bird is the bee hummingbird, which is only about a half-inch long, and is often mistaken for an insect.

There are more than 9,000 species of birds in the world and they can be found in just about every type of environment.

Among the best-known birds are the birds of prey, such as hawks, eagles, ospreys, falcons, and owls. They have hooked beaks, strong talons or claws on their feet, and keen eyesight and hearing. The larger hawks and eagles prey on small mammals, such as rodents; ospreys and many eagles eat fish; falcons eat mostly insects; and owls eat everything from insects to fish and mammals.

More than half of all birds are perching birds. They have an unusual arrangement of toes and leg tendons that allows them to balance like an acrobat on small twigs or telephone wires. Songbirds make up most of this group, which includes sparrows, finches, warblers, crows, blackbirds, thrushes, and swallows.

Another type of bird is the aquatic bird, which gets most of its food from the water. Some of these birds, such as the albatross, spend much of their time over the open ocean, far away from land. Others, like penguins, live on the land. Some aquatic birds, such as loons, prefer lakes; pelicans and some others switch between salt water and fresh water. Waterfowl, which include ducks, geese, and swans, often breed on freshwater lakes and marshes and make their homes in marine habitats.

All About... SHARKS

Sharks are among the oldest animals on Earth; they have ruled the seas for over 400 million years. The two largest kinds of fish are sharks, and both are threatened species. At more than 40 feet long (about the size of a bus!), **whale sharks** are the biggest fish of all. But they are harmless to humans. With their huge mouths, they swim along slowly near the surface, filtering tiny plankton out of the water. The second-largest shark, the **basking shark**, also eats plankton.

▲ *Whale shark*

The basking shark grows to about 33 feet long. Both of these slow-moving fish are easy targets for harpoon fishermen and can also get tangled in commercial fishing nets.

When most people picture a shark, they think of the streamlined "mackerel" sharks—like the **great white** (which is actually rare)—or "requiem" sharks like the **silky shark**. But many sharks don't look the way you might imagine. Sharks live in many different parts of the ocean and have developed specialized shapes, teeth, fins, and coloring to fit their habitats. The 350+ species are divided into eight orders. The common names of these types of sharks are: angelsharks, sawsharks, dogfish and cookiecutter sharks, ground sharks, mackerel sharks, carpet sharks, horn sharks, and frilled and cow sharks. About half of all sharks grow only to around 40 inches long. One of the smallest kinds is the 7-inch **pygmy spiny shark**.

Unlike a tuna or salmon, sharks have no bones. A shark's skeleton is made up of a tough, flexible material called **cartilage**. Sharks can see, hear, smell, taste, and feel — they also have a sixth sense. Through tiny pores in their heads, they can pick up electrical impulses that every animal emits. This ability, combined with strength and razor-sharp teeth, makes them excellent hunters.

▲ *Horn shark*

However, sharks have a big enemy of their own: humans. People kill 30 to 70 million sharks each year. The great white may be the top predator of the sea, but its fins, jaws, and teeth are valuable in international markets. Many other types of sharks are also killed for their fins. Shark fin soup is a big favorite in parts of Asia, and it can sell for up to $90 a bowl in Hong Kong. Shark meat is growing in popularity in the U.S. Other shark parts are used to make health and beauty aids. Some people also hunt sharks for sport. Because sharks reproduce slowly, these killings are a serious problem, and the future of the shark is threatened in many parts of the world.

▲ *Silky shark*

did you know? *Sharks like the great white are considered the fiercest creatures in the sea. One of the gentlest creatures in the sea is the manatee, also known as the sea cow. Found in central Florida and along the Gulf of Mexico and Caribbean coasts, the manatee can live in salt or fresh water, and grows to about 1,300 pounds. These mammals are called sea cows because they live in herds and graze on underwater plants. Manatees are considered an endangered species.*

BUTTERFLIES

Butterflies belong to the insect order Lepidoptera, which is Greek for "scaly wing." Butterfly wings are made of tiny scales that create beautiful colors and striking patterns. The dark colors help the butterfly keep warm by absorbing heat from sunlight. Because they are cold-blooded, butterflies cannot produce their own body heat. There are about 20,000 species of butterflies and they can be found in every part of the world, except in Antarctica.

During their lifetimes butterflies change form three times—from egg to caterpillar to chrysalis to butterfly. This is called metamorphosis. When the caterpillar hatches from the egg, all it wants to do is eat. It gains so much weight that it has to shed its skin four or five times. The last shed produces a hard case called a **chrysalis** or pupa. Some species wrap themselves in silk before they change to a chrysalis for extra protection. Though it's not visible, a dramatic change takes place inside the chrysalis. The caterpillar turns into a butterfly. Some species make the change in few days; others may take years!

Butterflies spend most of their time finding food, escaping from predators, and looking for a mate. An adult butterfly drinks flower nectar for food. A butterfly's mouth (proboscis) is actually a long tube that stays rolled up until needed and then is used like a straw. Butterflies may also be seen feeding on rotting fruit, tree sap, and mud puddles.

Poisonous butterflies, with their bright colors, warn predators like bats, mice, wasps, birds, and lizards to stay away. Other butterflies use camouflage to hide in plain sight. And still others that are nonpoisonous try to copy the look of poisonous types to fool predators into leaving them alone.

Monarch butterflies make an amazing journey each year. Because they cannot survive the winter in a cold climate, they travel thousands of miles from southern Canada to central Mexico. In autumn millions of monarchs fly south and roost in huge numbers in trees in mountainous areas of California and Mexico. Then in the spring they must fly north again to find the right food in plentiful supply. Most lay eggs and die during the journey. Then their offspring continue the trip north. This tiny creature—weighing only 1/50 of an ounce—can travel 20 mph and reach an altitude of 10,000 feet!

FUN FACTS

- Butterflies range in size from 1/25 inch to 10 inches.
- Butterflies can see red, green, and yellow.
- Butterflies cannot fly if their body temperature is less than 86 degrees.
- Some species need up to seven years to become adults. Most of this time they spend as a chrysalis.
- The brimstone butterfly has the longest adult life span: nine to ten months.
- Butterflies can get drunk on the juice of rotten fruit that sometimes contains alcohol. Sipping this juice, they can even become too drunk to fly!

REPTILES & AMPHIBIANS

Reptiles and amphibians are **vertebrates**, which means they have backbones. They are also **ectotherms**, which means they can't regulate their own body temperature. They need sunlight to warm them up and shade to cool them down if they get too hot. They get sluggish and don't move around too much in cold weather. In winter, some species hibernate.

Kinds of REPTILES

Reptiles have been around for millions of years and once were the most common vertebrate animals on Earth. Today, they are divided into **four main groups**: turtles and tortoises; lizards and snakes; crocodiles and alligators; and the tuatara. (A tuatara looks like a lizard, but it isn't. It's a species left over from a group of reptiles as old as dinosaurs. Tuatara live only in New Zealand and are in danger of becoming extinct.)

Some reptiles, like crocodiles and alligators, spend most of their time in water. Some turtles (like snapping turtles), snakes (like anacondas), and lizards (like marine iguanas) spend a lot of their time in water as well. But most species live on land. All have a scaly skin to protect them. Reptiles are found in all habitats except polar ice and tundra.

Reptiles usually lay their eggs in nests or holes dug in the ground. But some snakes, like rattlesnakes, let the eggs hatch inside the body and give birth to live babies.

Female alligators and crocodiles are very good mothers. They guard the nest and even help the hatchlings get a start in life. Some snakes do this too! But most reptiles lay their eggs and leave. The hatchlings, which are perfect miniature copies of their parents, are on their own. Baby rattlesnakes even have a supply of venom!

Kinds of AMPHIBIANS

Amphibians are cold-blooded animals that live part of their lives in water and part on land. They are divided into **three main groups**: salamanders, newts, and mudpuppies; caecilians; and frogs and toads. (Caecilians are sometimes called "rubber eels" and look like worms or small snakes without scales.) The skin of most amphibians is soft and moist. And though they are protected by mucus that comes out of the skin, amphibians usually must live near water or moist places to help keep them from drying out.

Unlike reptiles (or humans!), amphibians start life looking very different from their parents. A young amphibian is called a larva. It changes into an adult through a process called **metamorphosis**. The tadpole is a good example of a frog larva. It starts out with gills to breathe underwater and a tail for swimming. As it grows up, it develops lungs, legs, and a different mouth. Its eyes move up on its head. When it loses its tail, it is an adult frog, and will spend much of its time on land. Other amphibians go through similar changes.

What Are Groups of Animals Called?

Here are some, often odd, names for animal groups.

BEARS: *sleuth* of bears
CATTLE: *drove* of cattle
CROCODILES: *bask* of crocodiles
CROWS: *murder* of crows
ELKS: *gang* of elks
FISH: *school* of fish
FOXES: *skulk* of foxes
GEESE: *flock* or *gaggle* of geese
GNATS: *cloud* of gnats
HARES: *down* of hares
HAWKS: *cast* of hawks
KITTENS: *kindle* or *kendle* of kittens
LEOPARDS: *leap* of leopards

LIONS: *pride* of lions
MINNOWS: *shoal* of minnows
MONKEYS: *troop* of monkeys
MULES: *span* of mules
NIGHTINGALES: *watch* of nightingales
OYSTERS: *bed* of oysters
OWLS: *parliament* of owls
PEACOCKS: *muster* of peacocks
SHARKS: *shiver* of sharks
TROUT: *hover* of trout
RAVENS: *unkindness* of ravens
WHALES: *pod* of whales
WOLVES: *pack* of wolves

Pets At The Top

TOP TEN DOG BREEDS

Here are the ten most popular U.S. dog breeds with the numbers of dogs registered by the American Kennel Club in 2004:

#	Breed	Number	#	Breed	Number
1	Labrador retriever	146,693	6	Dachshund	40,770
2	Golden retriever	52,550	7	Boxer	37,741
3	German shepherd	46,046	8	Poodle	32,671
4	Beagle	44,555	9	Shih tzu	28,958
5	Yorkshire terrier	43,522	10	Chihuahua	24,850

WHO AM I?

My name means "barker" in Russian. I was the first living creature sent into orbit. I rode into space in the Soviet spacecraft Sputnik II on November 3, 1957. I became famous all over the world as I orbited the globe at an altitude as high as 1,000 miles. Sadly, no plans were made for my return voyage. I died in space about a week after I went into orbit.

Answer: Laika

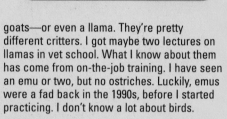

Large Animal Veterinarian

Dr. Derek Vandrey, large animal veterinarian
Washington, Virginia

Did you grow up around a lot of animals?

My uncle out in California had a horse farm, but I grew up in the suburbs in Maryland. I was a city kid, but I didn't like it. My parents had me taking riding lessons when I was 8 years old.

Did you think you would grow up to be a veterinarian?

Yes. When I was about 8 I wanted to be a vet, along with a fighter pilot, engineer, fireman, and all the other stuff you want to be when you're a kid.

By the time I was 11, I was at the barn everyday either taking riding lessons or mucking (cleaning) out stalls. I also hung around whenever the horse doctor was at the stable where I worked. In high school, I knew for sure that I wanted to be a vet. James Herriot's books, like *All Creatures Great and Small,* were an inspiration to me. Of course, he always put a happy spin on it. There are a lot of things that turn out well and are funny. It's not easy though. Large animal vets can be on-call 24 hours a day, seven days a week.

What kind of animals do you work with?

I work with all large animals, usually ones you might find on a farm. I work with horses mostly, and cows, but you never know what is going to come up. It could be pigs, sheep, goats—or even a llama. They're pretty different critters. I got maybe two lectures on llamas in vet school. What I know about them has come from on-the-job training. I have seen an emu or two, but no ostriches. Luckily, emus were a fad back in the 1990s, before I started practicing. I don't know a lot about birds.

What do you spend most of your time doing on a regular day?

One thing you do as a large animal vet is spend a lot of time getting lost. The patients don't come to us, so I travel all over back country roads trying to find my appointments. The work is pretty seasonal. In the spring, for instance, I work with a lot of horses and cattle giving birth. Dairy work is year-round, doing checkups and monthly pregnancy checks. I deliver a lot of calves.

What do you like best about your job?

I do a lot of different things, but I get a lot of satisfaction anytime something difficult goes well, whether it's a successful surgery or a good birth for a horse or cow. It always makes you feel good.

What's the hardest thing about your job?

Any kind of situation where you have something wrong with an animal and you can't figure out what it is is really hard. Making a diagnosis can be tough. Any situation is challenging when you're first learning.

What advice would you give to a kid who wants to become a veterinarian?

It is very important to get some experience watching and hanging out with a vet.

Art

What color is the opposite of red?   page 40

Through Artists' Eyes

Artists look at the world in new ways. Their work can be funny or sad, beautiful or disturbing, realistic or strange.

▶ Throughout history, artists have painted pictures of nature (called **landscapes**), pictures of people (called **portraits**), and pictures of flowers in vases, food, and other objects (known as **still lifes**). Today many artists create pictures that do not look like anything in the real world. These are examples of **abstract art.**

▶ **Photography**, too, is a form of art. Photos record both the commonplace and the exotic, and help us look at events in new ways.

▶ **Sculpture** is a three-dimensional form made from clay, stone, metal, or other material. Sculptures can be large, like the Statue of Liberty, or small, like The Little Mermaid, at right. Some are realistic. Others have no form you can recognize.

Out-There Artwork!

People all over the world go to museums to see art everyday, while on field trips, on vacation, or just having fun. But what happens when the museum is itself a work of art—one that may disappear the next day?

The Nomadic Museum (below), designed by architect Shirgeru Ban, was constructed on New York City's Pier 54 in March 2005. It stays true to its name: the Nomadic Museum can travel the world because it can be packed into itself! Its walls are made out of 148 multicolored shipping containers arranged in a checkerboard pattern. Recycled paper tubes form an arched ceiling, and a curtain made from a million recycled Sri Lankan paper tea bags drapes 40 feet above visitors' heads.

Inside the museum, artist Gregory Colbert exhibits his photographs in a 45,000-square-foot space—the size of two football fields. Nothing seems anchored in the Nomadic Museum. Colbert's unframed photographs hang from the ceiling on invisible wires. There is also a "floating library" with Colbert's books projected onto the walls.

The Nomadic Museum has planned stops in Los Angeles, Beijing, and Paris. Who knows where else it might roam.

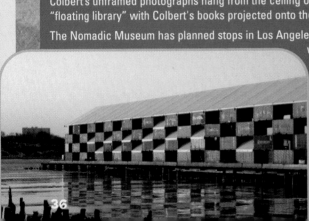

Schools of Art

The style of a painting depends on many choices by the artist. What kind of paint and what colors to use. What brushes to use and how to make the strokes. How to use light and shadow. When a group of artists paint in a similar way, and sometimes paint the same kind of thing (a portrait or landscape), it is called a movement or "school" of painting. Here are some famous painters and the "schools" of art they belong to.

Detail from Toros en un Pueblo *by Goya*

Francisco de Goya (1746-1828), a **ROMANTIC** painter, started his career painting scenes of upper-class amusements for Spanish nobility. After he became a court painter for King Charles III, Goya painted portraits of the royal family that shocked the world—they showed royalty as unattractive people! After Napoleon invaded Spain, Goya painted scenes that showed the horror of war. Goya is considered by many to be the "father of modern art," influencing all artists who came after him with his original style.

Breezing Up by Homer

Winslow Homer (1836-1910), a **NATURALIST** painter, often painted landscapes but was most famous for his paintings of the sea. He was interested in the effects of light, but also wanted his scenes to look as much like real life as possible.

Edgar Degas (1834-1917), was one of the great **IMPRESSIONIST** painters. Like other impressionists, this French artist turned away from classical subjects and painted portraits of average people and everyday social interactions. He became particularly famous for his paintings of dancers, which showed them as muscular athletes exerting themselves. This true-to-life effect was unusual for his time.

Dancers by Degas

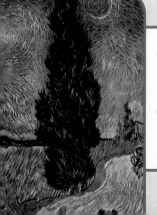

Vincent van Gogh (1853-1890) was one of the most famous **POSTIMPRESSIONISTS**, so called because they came after the impressionists. They changed reality in their paintings to create an emotional effect. After them, **EXPRESSIONISTS**, like Edvard Munch (1863-1944), distorted reality much more, and paintings of **ABSTRACT EXPRESSIONISTS**, like Jackson Pollock (1912-1956), often do not show anything we can recognize at all. The colors and brush strokes of these paintings are meant to create a mood or reaction in the person who views them.

◀ *Cyprus Road by Van Gogh*

Photography

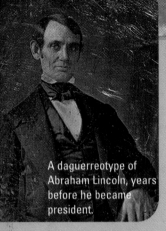

A daguerreotype of Abraham Lincoln, years before he became president.

When cameras were invented in the 19th century, they forever changed the way people viewed the world. Joseph Nicéphore Niépce, a French inventor, is said to have taken the first real photograph. However, the print was not permanent and faded after a short time. In 1837, the French painter Louis Daguerre was the first to create or "fix" a permanent photographic image on a surface using a machine he invented. Such an image was later called a daguerreotype.

CAMERA

You can think of a camera as basically a box with a hole that holds film. Its main job is to expose light-sensitive film to light. A lens isn't even essential. But, cameras can also be extremely complex machines with many adjustable parts. And modern digital cameras are different because they don't use film. Instead, images are shot onto electronic light sensors.

FILM

Celluloid film has microscopic chemical grains on its surface that react to light. When exposed, the grains become darker. To get a picture, the film must be developed—a chemical process by which the light-sensitive grains are "fixed," so that they no longer react to light. After the film is developed, a negative is produced.

THE NEGATIVE

If you look at a film negative, you'll notice that the colors look strange. Areas that are light in reality look dark on negative film. To make an accurate print, light must be flashed through the negative so that an image is projected onto photosensitive paper. This is done in a darkroom. Photosensitive paper is coated with light-sensitive chemicals and works just like film. It needs to be exposed to light and then fixed. Once this is done, you have a picture.

Photography as Art

Any good camera can record a clear image. But is it art or just a snapshot?

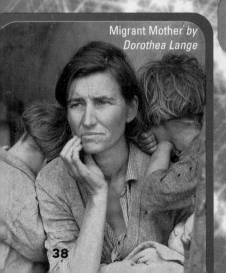

Migrant Mother by Dorothea Lange

One of the most famous great photographers is Ansel Adams. In 1941, he began making large photo murals for the U.S. Department of the Interior. He's famous for black and white pictures of nature, especially Yosemite National Park in California. Adams helped found the world's first museum collection of photographs at the Museum of Modern Art in New York City in 1940. He also founded the California School of Fine Arts in San Francisco in 1946. It was the first art school to teach photography as a profession.

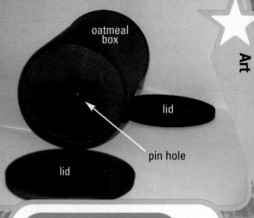

oatmeal box

lid

pin hole

lid

MATERIALS:

- A cylindrical oatmeal box
- 2 oatmeal box lids
- Dull black paint (not shiny) or marker
- Black electrical tape
- Roll of 100 or 200 speed
  4" x 5" or 2" x 3" sheet film*
- Black construction paper
- No. 10 sewing needle
- Scissors or a small knife
- 2 index cards
- Ruler

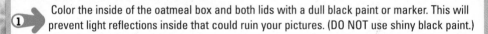

MAKE YOUR OWN CAMERA

① Color the inside of the oatmeal box and both lids with a dull black paint or marker. This will prevent light reflections inside that could ruin your pictures. (DO NOT use shiny black paint.)

② On the bottom, cut a hole about ½ to 1 inch in diameter right in the middle. Don't worry if it looks uneven or if it's too big or small. You can correct these problems later. Just make sure that it's in the middle.

③ Take the black construction paper and cut it to match the size of the two index cards. Sandwich this piece between the two cards. Tape them together at the edges.

④ Using the sewing needle (ASK AN ADULT FOR HELP), poke a hole through the middle of the index card/paper sandwich. Stick the needle in about halfway. Make sure the hole is as round as possible by spinning the needle. Do your best to keep it straight and not to make the hole on an angle. This could warp the image.

⑤ Measure and cut a 3-inch square around the pinhole. Try to center the pinhole. This will make positioning it on the camera body easier. Discard the index cards so that you are left only with a construction paper square with the pinhole in the middle.

⑥ Tape the square OVER the outside bottom of the oatmeal box so that it covers the hole you previously made. Using a ruler, try to measure out the exact center of the bottom and position the pinhole over it. Once positioned, tape the edges of the square. Remember to tape them well enough so that no light can get through, except through the pinhole itself.

⑦ Place one of the lids over the pinhole.

⑧ Here's the hard part. In a dark closet, attach the sheet film to the middle of the inside part of the remaining lid. If you are using 4 x 5 film, you may need to cut the edges with scissors to fit. Try to tape it flat to the surface of the lid. Also, try not to touch the middle of the film too much. Once attached, place the lid over the oatmeal box. Your "camera" is now "loaded."

⑨ Find something you want to photograph. Position the camera, using either blocks or whatever you have available to steady it. When ready, remove the lid that's over the pinhole. After 2 seconds, cover the pinhole again. Your film has been exposed. Bring your film to a film developer and have your image processed.

*Make sure your local film developer can develop sheet film. It may be easier to use photographic paper. Ask an adult for advice.

Color Wheel

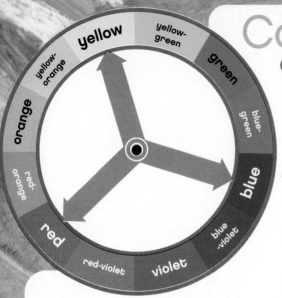

This color wheel shows how colors are related to each other.

Primary colors The most basic colors are RED, YELLOW, and BLUE. They're called primary because you can't get them by mixing any other colors. In fact, the other colors are made by mixing red, blue, or yellow. Arrows on this wheel show the primary colors.

Secondary colors ORANGE, GREEN, and VIOLET are the secondary colors. They are made by mixing two primary colors. You make orange by mixing yellow and red, or green by mixing yellow and blue. On the color wheel, GREEN appears between BLUE and YELLOW.

Tertiary colors When you mix a primary and a secondary color, you get a tertiary, or intermediate, color. BLUE-GREEN and YELLOW-GREEN are intermediate colors.

More Color Terms

Values the lightness or darkness of a color is its value.

▶ **Tints** are light values made by mixing a color with white. PINK is a tint of RED.

▶ **Shades** are dark values made by mixing a color with black. MAROON is a shade of RED.

Complementary colors
are contrasting colors that please the eye when used together. These colors appear opposite each other on the wheel and don't have any colors in common. RED is a complement to GREEN, which is made by mixing YELLOW and BLUE.

Cool Colors
are mostly GREEN, BLUE, and PURPLE. They make you think of cool things like water and can even make you feel cooler.

Warm Colors
are mostly RED, ORANGE, and YELLOW. They suggest heat and can actually make you feel warmer.

Analagous colors
the colors next to each other on the wheel are from the same "family." BLUE, BLUE-GREEN, and GREEN all have BLUE in them and are analagous colors.

Birthdays

Who shares your birthday?

JANUARY

Shannon Lucid

1 J.D. Salinger, *author,* 1919
2 Kate Bosworth, *actress,* 1983
3 J.R.R. Tolkien, *author,* 1892
4 Louis Braille, *teacher/ inventor,* 1852
5 Warrick Dunn, *football player,* 1975
6 Early Wynn, *baseball player,* 1920
7 Liam Aiken, *actor,* 1990
8 Elvis Presley, *singer,* 1935
9 Dave Matthews, *musician,* 1967
10 George Foreman, *boxer,* 1949
11 Mary J. Blige, *singer,* 1971
12 Andrew Lawrence, *actor,* 1988
13 Orlando Bloom, *actor,* 1977
14 Shannon Lucid, *astronaut,* 1943
15 Rev. Martin Luther King Jr., *civil rights leader,* 1929
16 Albert Pujols, *baseball player,* 1980
17 Zooey Deschanel, *actress,* 1980
18 A.A. Milne, *author,* 1882
19 Drea de Matteo, *actress,* 1972
20 Buzz Aldrin, *astronaut,* 1930
21 Jam Master Jay, *DJ,* 1965
22 Beverly Mitchell, *actress,* 1981
23 John Hancock, *leader of U.S. Revolution,* 1737
24 Mischa Barton, *actress,* 1986
25 Alicia Keys, *singer,* 1981
26 Wayne Gretzky, *hockey player,* 1961
27 Wolfgang Amadeus Mozart, *composer,* 1756
28 Elijah Wood, *actor,* 1981
29 Oprah Winfrey, *TV personality,* 1954
30 Christian Bale, *actor,* 1974
31 Jackie Robinson, *baseball player,* 1919

FEBRUARY

1 Langston Hughes, *poet,* 1902
2 Judith Viorst, *author,* 1931
3 Norman Rockwell, *artist,* 1894
4 Oscar de la Hoya, *boxer,* 1974
5 Hank Aaron, *baseball player,* 1934
6 Ronald Reagan, *40th U.S. president,* 1911
7 Ashton Kutcher, *actor,* 1978
8 Alonzo Mourning, *basketball player,* 1970
9 David Gallagher, *actor,* 1985
10 Emma Roberts, *actress,* 1991
11 Thomas Edison, *inventor,* 1847
12 Judy Blume, *author,* 1938
13 Randy Moss, *football player,* 1977
14 Rob Thomas, *musician,* 1972
15 Matt Groening, *cartoonist,* 1954
16 Jerome Bettis, *football player,* 1972
17 Michael Jordan, *basketball player,* 1963
18 Vanna White, *TV personality,* 1957
19 Nicolaus Copernicus, *astronomer,* 1473
20 Stephon Marbury, *basketball player,* 1977
21 Charlotte Church, *singer,* 1986
22 Drew Barrymore, *actress,* 1975
23 Dakota Fanning, *actress,* 1994
24 Steve Jobs, *computer innovator,* 1955
25 Justin Berfield, *actor,* 1986
26 Johnny Cash, *musician,* 1932
27 Josh Groban, *singer,* 1981
28 Lemony Snicket (Daniel Handler), *author,* 1970
29 Ja Rule, *rapper,* 1976

Thomas Edison

MARCH

Cy Young

1 George Eads, *actor,* 1967
2 Dr. Seuss, *author,* 1904
3 Jessica Biel, *actress,* 1982
4 Patricia Heaton, *actress,* 1958
5 Jake Lloyd, *actor,* 1989
6 Shaquille O'Neal, *basketball player,* 1972
7 Laura Prepon, *actress,* 1980
8 Freddy Prinze Jr., *actor,* 1976
9 Bobby Fischer, *chess champion,* 1943
10 Matt Kenseth, *race car driver,* 1972
11 Benji and Joel Madden, *musicians,* 1979
12 Samm Levine, *actor/comedian,* 1982
13 Danny Masterson, *actor,* 1976
14 Albert Einstein, *physicist,* 1879
15 Sean Biggerstaff, *actor,* 1983
16 Lauren Graham, *actress,* 1967
17 Mia Hamm, *soccer player,* 1972
18 Queen Latifah, *rapper/ actress,* 1970
19 Bruce Willis, *actor,* 1955
20 Mr. (Fred) Rogers, *TV personality,* 1928
21 Johann Sebastian Bach, *composer,* 1685
22 Reese Witherspoon, *actress,* 1976
23 Jason Kidd, *basketball player,* 1973
24 Peyton Manning, *football player,* 1976
25 Kate DiCamillo, *author,* 1964
26 Keira Knightley, *actress,* 1985
27 Sarah Vaughan, *singer,* 1924
28 Vince Vaughn, *actor,* 1970
29 Cy Young, *baseball player,* 1867
30 Norah Jones, *musician,* 1979
31 Ewan McGregor, *actor,* 1971

APRIL

1 Randy Orton, *wrestler*, 1980
2 Hans Christian Anderson, *author*, 1805
3 Amanda Bynes, *actress*, 1986
4 Jamie Lynn Spears, *actress*, 1991
5 Pharrell Williams, *musician*, 1973
6 Bret Boone, *baseball player*, 1969
7 Jackie Chan, *actor*, 1954
8 Kofi Annan, *UN secretary general*, 1938
9 Dennis Quaid, *actor*, 1954
10 Mandy Moore, *singer/actress*, 1984
11 Joss Stone, *singer*, 1987
12 Beverly Cleary, *author*, 1916
13 Thomas Jefferson, *3rd U.S. president*, 1743
14 Sarah Michelle Gellar, *actress*, 1977
15 Emma Watson, *actress*, 1990
16 Charlie Chaplin, *actor/director*, 1889
17 Jennifer Garner, *actress*, 1972
18 Alia Shawkat, *actress*, 1989
19 Hayden Christensen, *actor*, 1981
20 Andy Serkis, *actor*, 1964
21 Queen Elizabeth II, *British queen*, 1926
22 Jack Nicholson, *actor*, 1936
23 George Lopez, *actor/comedian*, 1961
24 Kelly Clarkson, *singer*, 1982
25 Renee Zellweger, *actress*, 1969
26 Tom Welling, *actor*, 1977
27 Coretta Scott King, *civil rights activist*, 1927
28 Harper Lee, *author*, 1926
29 Dale Earnhardt, *racecar driver*, 1951
30 Kirsten Dunst, *actress*, 1982

Harper Lee

MAY

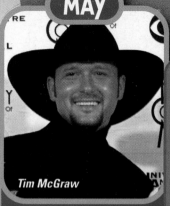

Tim McGraw

1 Tim McGraw, *musician*, 1967
2 David Beckham, *soccer player*, 1975
3 James Brown, *singer*, 1933
4 Dawn Staley, *basketball player*, 1970
5 Brian Williams, *TV news anchor*, 1959
6 Martin Brodeur, *hockey player*, 1972
7 Breckin Meyer, *actor*, 1974
8 Enrique Iglesias, *singer*, 1975
9 Candice Bergen, *actress*, 1946
10 Kenan Thompson, *actor*, 1978
11 Jonathan Jackson, *actor*, 1982
12 Tony Hawk, *skateboarder*, 1968
13 Stevie Wonder, *singer*, 1950
14 George Lucas, *filmmaker*, 1944
15 Emmitt Smith, *football player*, 1969
16 Billy Martin, *baseball player/manager*, 1928
17 Sugar Ray Leonard, *boxer*, 1956
18 Chow Yun-Fat, *actor*, 1955
19 Kevin Garnett, *basketball player*, 1976
20 Cher, *singer/actress*, 1946
21 Ashlie Brillault, *actress*, 1987
22 Sir Arthur Conan Doyle, *author*, 1859
23 Jewel, *singer*, 1974
24 Billy Gilman, *singer*, 1988
25 Mike Myers, *actor*, 1963
26 Lenny Kravitz, *singer*, 1964
27 André 3000, *musician*, 1975
28 Jim Thorpe, *Olympic champion*, 1888
29 John F. Kennedy, *35th president*, 1917
30 Manny Ramirez, *baseball player*, 1972
31 Clint Eastwood, *actor/director*, 1930

JUNE

1 Justine Henin-Hardenne, *tennis player*, 1982
2 Wayne Brady, *comedian/actor*, 1972
3 Lalaine (Varaga-Paras), *actress*, 1987
4 Angelina Jolie, *actress*, 1975
5 Richard Scarry, *author/illustrator*, 1919
6 Bjorn Borg, *tennis player*, 1956
7 Allen Iverson, *basketball player*, 1975
8 Kanye West, *musician*, 1977
9 Natalie Portman, *actress*, 1981
10 Judy Garland, *actress*, 1922
11 Shia LaBeouf, *actor*, 1986
12 Anne Frank, *diary writer*, 1929
13 Ashley and Mary-Kate Olsen, *actresses*, 1986
14 Donald Trump, *entrepreneur*, 1946
15 Ice Cube, *rapper/actor*, 1969
16 Phil Mickelson, *golfer*, 1970
17 Venus Williams, *tennis player*, 1980
18 Paul McCartney, *musician*, 1942
19 Lou Gehrig, *baseball player*, 1903
20 Nicole Kidman, *actress*, 1967
21 Prince William of Great Britain, 1982
22 Carson Daly, *TV personality*, 1973
23 Jason Mraz, *singer*, 1977
24 Solange Knowles, *singer/actress*, 1986
25 Linda Cardellini, *actress*, 1975
26 Derek Jeter, *baseball player*, 1974
27 Tobey Maguire, *actor*, 1975
28 John Elway, *football player*,
29 Theo Fleury, *hockey player*, 1968
30 Michael Phelps, *Olympic champion*, 1985

Derek Jeter

JULY

Lindsay Lohan

1 Liv Tyler, *actress,* 1977
2 Lindsay Lohan, *actress,* 1986
3 Tom Cruise, *actor,* 1962
4 George Steinbrenner, *Yankees owner,* 1930
5 "Goose" Gossage, *baseball player,* 1951
6 George W. Bush, *43rd U.S. president,* 1946
7 Lisa Leslie, *basketball player,* 1972
8 Beck (Hansen), *musician,* 1970
9 Tom Hanks, *actor,* 1956
10 Jessica Simpson, *singer,* 1980
11 E.B. White, *author,* 1899
12 Bill Cosby, *comedian/actor,* 1937
13 Harrison Ford, *actor,* 1942
14 Woody Guthrie, *folk musician,* 1912
15 Rembrandt, *artist,* 1606
16 Will Farrell, *actor,* 1967
17 Jason Jennings, *baseball player,* 1978
18 Vin Diesel, *actor,* 1967
19 Topher Grace, *actor,* 1978
20 Sir Edmund Hillary, *Everest climber,* 1919
21 Robin Williams, *actor/comedian,* 1952
22 Keyshawn Johnson, *football player,* 1972
23 Daniel Radcliffe, *actor,* 1989
24 Anna Paquin, *actress,* 1982
25 Matt LeBlanc, *actor,* 1967
26 Kate Beckinsale, *actress,* 1973
27 Alex Rodriguez, *baseball player,* 1975
28 Jim Davis, *cartoonist,* 1945
29 Martina McBride, *singer,* 1966
30 Arnold Schwarzenegger, *actor/governor,* 1947
31 J.K. Rowling, *author,* 1966

AUGUST

1 Francis Scott Key, *writer of national anthem,* 1779
2 James Baldwin, *writer,* 1924
3 Tom Brady, *football player,* 1977
4 Barak Obama, *U.S. Senator,* 1961
5 Neil Armstrong, *astronaut,* 1930
6 M. Night Shyamalan, *filmmaker,* 1970
7 Charlize Theron, *actress,* 1975
8 Dustin Hoffman, *actor,* 1937
9 Deion Sanders, *football/baseball player,* 1967
10 Antonio Banderas, *actor,* 1960
11 Hulk Hogan, *wrestler,* 1953
12 Pete Sampras, *tennis player,* 1971
13 Annie Oakley, *markswoman,* 1860
14 Halle Berry, *actress,* 1966
15 Debra Messing, *actress,* 1968
16 Vanessa Carlton, *singer,* 1980
17 Robert De Niro, *actor,* 1943
18 Mika Boorem, *actress,* 1987
19 Bill Clinton, *42nd U.S. president,* 1946
20 Todd Helton, *baseball player,* 1973
21 Carrie-Anne Moss, *actress,* 1967
22 Bill Parcells, *football coach,* 1941
23 Kobe Bryant, *basketball player,* 1978
24 Rupert Grint, *actor,* 1988
25 Regis Philbin, *TV personality,* 1931
26 Macaulay Culkin, *actor,* 1980
27 Alexa Vega, *actress,* 1988
28 Shania Twain, *singer,* 1965
29 John McCain, *U.S. senator,* 1936
30 Andy Roddick, *tennis player,* 1982
31 Hideo Nomo, *baseball player,* 1968

Barak Obama

Jesse James

SEPTEMBER

1 Rocky Marciano, *boxer,* 1923
2 Keanu Reeves, *actor,* 1964
3 Charlie Sheen, *actor,* 1965
4 Beyoncé Knowles, *singer/actress,* 1981
5 Jesse James, *outlaw,* 1847
6 Mark Chesnutt, *singer,* 1963
7 Mark Prior, *baseball player,* 1980
8 Pink, *singer,* 1979
9 Adam Sandler, *actor,* 1966
10 Roger Maris, *baseball player,* 1934
11 Harry Connick Jr., *musician/actor,* 1967
12 Emily Rossum, *actress,* 1986
13 Roald Dahl, *author,* 1916
14 Larry Brown, *basketball coach,* 1940
15 Prince Harry of Great Britain, *1984*
16 Alexis Bledel, *actress,* 1981
17 Rasheed Wallace, *basketball player,* 1974
18 Lance Armstrong, *cyclist,* 1971
19 Jimmy Fallon, *actor,* 1974
20 Guy Lafleur, *hockey player,* 1951
21 Luke Wilson, *actor,* 1971
22 Swin Cash, *basketball player,* 1979
23 Ray Charles, *musician,* 1930
24 Jim Henson, *puppeteer,* 1936
25 Barbara Walters, *journalist,* 1931
26 Serena Williams, *tennis player,* 1981
27 Avril Lavigne, *singer,* 1984
28 Hilary Duff, *actress/singer,* 1987
29 Bryant Gumbel, *TV personality,* 1948
30 Elie Wiesel, *author,* 1928

OCTOBER

1 Julie Andrews, *actress,* 1935
2 Kelly Ripa, *TV personality/ actress,* 1970
3 Gwen Stefani, *singer,* 1969
4 Susan Sarandon, *actress,* 1946
5 Parminder Nagra, *actress,* 1975
6 Helen Wills-Moody, *tennis player,* 1905
7 Simon Cowell, *TV personality,* 1959
8 Matt Damon, *actor,* 1970
9 John Lennon, *musician,* 1940
10 Dale Earnhardt Jr., *racecar driver,* 1974
11 Michelle Trachtenberg, *actress,* 1985
12 Marion Jones, *Olympic champion,* 1975
13 Paul Simon, *singer,* 1941
14 Usher, *singer,* 1978
15 Emeril Lagasse, *TV chef,* 1959
16 John Mayer, *musician,* 1977
17 Evel Knievel, *daredevil,* 1938
18 Jean-Claude Van Damme, *actor,* 1960
19 John Lithgow, *actor,* 1945
20 Viggo Mortensen, *actor,* 1958
21 Carrie Fisher, *actress,* 1956
22 Ichiro Suzuki, *baseball player,* 1973
23 Tiffeny Millbrett, *soccer player,* 1972
24 Monica, *singer,* 1980
25 Pablo Picasso, *artist,* 1881
26 Hillary Rodham Clinton, *U.S. senator,* 1947
27 Kelly Osbourne, *TV personality,* 1984
28 Julia Roberts, *actress,* 1967
29 Winona Ryder, *actress,* 1971
30 Diego Maradona, *soccer player,* 1960
31 Peter Jackson, *director,* 1961

NOVEMBER

Jenna and Barbara Bush

1 Lyle Lovett, *singer/actor,* 1957
2 Nelly, *rapper,* 1974
3 Roseanne, *actress,* 1952
4 Laura Bush, *first lady,* 1946
5 Ryan Adams, *musician,* 1974
6 James Naismith, *basketball inventor,* 1861
7 Marie Curie, *scientist,* 1867
8 Courtney Thorne-Smith, *actress,* 1967
9 Nick Lachey, *singer,* 1973
10 Eve, *rapper/actress,* 1978
11 Leonardo DiCaprio, *actor,* 1974
12 Anne Hathaway, *actress,* 1982
13 Robert Louis Stevenson, *author,* 1850
14 Condoleezza Rice, *secretary of state,* 1954
15 Zena Grey, *actress,* 1988
16 Marg Helgenberger, *actress,* 1958
17 Tom Seaver, *baseball player,* 1944
18 Owen Wilson, *actor,* 1968
19 Gail Devers, *Olympic champion,* 1966
20 Ming-Na Wen, *actress,* 1967
21 Ken Griffey Jr., *baseball player,* 1969
22 Jamie Lee Curtis, *actress,* 1958
23 Billy the Kid, *outlaw,* 1859
24 Scott Joplin, *composer,* 1868
25 Jenna and Barbara Bush, *Pres. Bush's daughters,* 1981
26 Charles Schulz, *cartoonist,* 1922
27 Jimi Hendrix, *musician,* 1942
28 Jon Stewart, *TV host,* 1962
29 Louisa May Alcott, *author,* 1832
30 Ben Stiller, *actor,* 1965

DECEMBER

1 Woody Allen, *actor/director,* 1935
2 Britney Spears, *singer,* 1981
3 Brendan Fraser, *actor,* 1968
4 Jay-Z, *rapper,* 1969
5 Frankie Muniz, *actor,* 1985
6 Otto Graham, *football player/coach,* 1921
7 Emily Browning, *actress,* 1988
8 Annasophia Robb, *actress,* 1993
9 Clarence Birdseye, *frozen food pioneer,* 1886
10 Raven-Symone, *actress,* 1985
11 Rita Moreno, *actress,* 1931
12 Frank Sinatra, *singer/actor,* 1915
13 Jamie Foxx, *actor,* 1967
14 Craig Biggio, *baseball player,* 1965
15 Adam Brody, *actor,* 1979
16 Ludwig van Beethoven, *composer,* 1770
17 Eugene Levy, *actor,* 1946
18 Steven Spielberg, *director/producer,* 1947
19 Kevin McHale, *basketball player,* 1957
20 Rich Gannon, *football player,* 1965
21 Samuel L. Jackson, *actor,* 1948
22 Diane Sawyer, *journalist,* 1945
23 Scott Gomez, *hockey player,* 1979
24 Ryan Seacrest, *DJ/TV personality,* 1974
25 Clara Barton, *American Red Cross founder,* 1821
26 Ozzie Smith, *baseball player,* 1954
27 Louis Pasteur, *scientist,* 1822
28 Denzel Washington, *actor,* 1954
29 Jude Law, *actor,* 1972
30 LeBron James, *basketball player,* 1984
31 Henri Matisse, *artist,* 1869

Hillary Rodham Clinton

Clara Barton

Books

Who wrote "The Chronicles of Narnia"? page 48

Book Awards, 2004–2005

NEWBERY MEDAL
For the author of the best children's book
*2005 winner: **Kira-Kira**, by Cynthia Kadohata*

CALDECOTT MEDAL
For the artist of the best children's picture book
*2005 winner: **Kitten's First Full Moon**, illustrated and written by Kevin Henkes*

CORETTA SCOTT KING AWARD
For artists and authors whose works encourage expression of the African-American experience
2005 winner:
AUTHOR AWARD: *Remember: The Journey to School Integration*, by Toni Morrison ▶
ILLUSTRATOR AWARD: *Ellington Was Not a Street*, illustrated by Kadir Nelson

NEWBERY MEDALS OF THE LAST TEN YEARS

10th ANNIVERSARY

How many of these Newbery Medal winners have you read?

2005: *Kira-Kira*, Cynthia Kadohata

2004: *The Tale of Despereaux: Being the Story of a Mouse, a Princess, Some Soup, and a Spool of Thread*, Kate DiCamillo, illustrated by Timothy Basil Ering

2003: *Crispin: The Cross of Lead*, Avi

2002: *A Single Shard*, Linda Sue Park

2001: *A Year Down Yonder*, Richard Peck

2000: *Bud, Not Buddy*, Christopher Paul Curtis

1999: *Holes*, Louis Sachar

1998: *Out of the Dust*, Karen Hesse

1997: *The View from Saturday*, E.L. Konigsburg

1996: *The Midwife's Apprentice*, Karen Cushman

1995: *Walk Two Moons*, Sharon Creech

did you know?

A world without Potter-mania? It's almost impossible to imagine now, but in 1995 the first Harry Potter book was just a sheaf of papers that J.K. Rowling was sending out to London literary agents. It took a whole year for her agent to find a publisher in 1996. The first HP book was published in England in September of 1997 as Harry Potter and the Philosopher's Stone. *Here in America, the title was changed to* Harry Potter and the Sorcerer's Stone *when it was published in 1999. Now the whole world breathlessly waits for each new book.* Harry Potter and the Half-Blood Prince, *the sixth book in the series, is due out July 16, 2005.*

Books to Read

There are two major types of literature: fiction and nonfiction. A FICTION book includes people, places, and events are often inspired by reality, but are mainly from an author's imagination. NONFICTION is about real things that actually happened, and should be totally accurate. Nonfiction may be about how something works, or the history of an event or a person's life.

Within these two groups there are smaller subgroups called genres (ZHAN-ruz).

FICTION

▶ Mysteries and Thrillers

These adventure stories will keep you up late, as you follow a main character who must uncover a secret.

Try These *Chasing Vermeer*, by Blue Balliet; *The Westing Game* by Ellen Raskin.

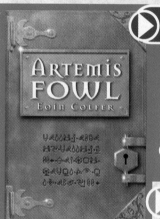

▶ Fantasy and Science Fiction

This genre is one of the most popular for teen readers. You've heard of the Harry Potter fantasy books, but there are thousands of books for kids and teens in this genre.

Try These *Artemis Fowl*, by Eoin Colfer; *The Hitchhiker's Guide to the Galaxy*, by Douglas Adams.

▶ Myths and Legends

These made-up stories go way back. Some are from 19th Century America, others are from ancient Greece and Africa.

Try These *The Once and Future King*, by T.H. White, the story of King Arthur; *The Children's Homer: The Adventures of Odysseus and the Tale of Troy*, by Padraic Colum.

▶ Historical Fiction

If you think history is just about facts, this is the genre for you. Authors take exciting historical events, and put the most interesting fictional characters right in the middle of them.

Try These *Bud, Not Buddy*, by Christopher Paul Curtis, a story about the Great Depression that's actually funny; *Number the Stars*, by Lois Lowry, a story about a child's escape from the Nazis during World War II.

▶ Realistic Fiction

Do you like stories that might have happened to you? Realistic fiction is about real-life situations that teens and kids deal with every day.

Try These *Because of Winn Dixie*, by Kate DiCamillo, about a girl who moves to Florida with her father (made into a 2005 film by the same name); *Slam!*, by Walter Dean Myers follows a hot-shot teen basketball star's troubled life.

NONFICTION

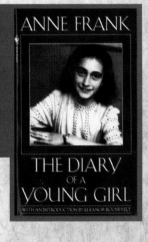

▶ Biographies, Autobiographies, and Memoirs

Do you like reading all about the details of a real person's life? This genre is for you.

Try These *A Boy*, by famous author Roald Dahl; *The Diary of Anne Frank*, by Anne Frank, who hid from Nazis before dying in the Holocaust; *To Be a Slave*, a collection of true personal stories collected by Julius Lester.

▶ History

Books in this genre can be about an event, an era, a country, or even a war.

Try These *The 1963 Civil Rights March*, by Scott Ingram; *George Washington, Spymaster: How the Americans Outspied the British and Won the Revolutionary War*, by Thomas B. Allen.

▶ Reference

Books that supply facts and practical information on one topic or many, including almanacs, atlases, dictionaries, and encyclopedias.

Try These *The World Almanac 2005, Roget's Student Thesaurus, Merriam-Webster's Collegiate Dictionary*.

▶ Self-Help

This popular genre can help you deal with any sort of personal problem, from study habits, to divorce in your family, to questions you have about growing up.

Try These *The 7 Habits of Highly Effective Teens*, by Sean Covey; *Chicken Soup for the Teenage Soul*, by Jack Canfield, Mark Victor Hasen, and Kimberly Kirberger.

ALL ABOUT... BOOKS

I f a Roman emperor wanted to read a book, he had to unroll it. Books were written on long **scrolls** (kind of like a roll of paper towels) that you unrolled as you went along. This was clumsy, especially if you were looking for a certain passage. Around A.D. 100 the **codex** was invented. It was made up of a stack of pages stitched together at the side and protected by a cover. The codex was easier to carry around, to store, and to search through. Books we read today look something like a codex.

In the Middle Ages books were made by monks who copied them by hand onto prepared animal skins called **parchment**. The monks often decorated the pages with beautiful color illustrations called "illuminations." Books were scarce and very expensive, and few people who were not priests or monks could read.

A big change came with the use of paper and printing, which were first invented in China. **Paper** came into Europe through the Muslim world and was common by the 14th century. Johann Gutenberg of Germany perfected **printing** in the 1450s. Once books no longer had to be copied by hand and could be printed on paper, they became less expensive and reading became more common.

At first, books were still not easy to make and not cheap. Each letter was on a separate piece of type, and a typesetter had to put each letter into place individually. Once all the letters for the page were in place, they were covered with ink and printed, one page at a time, by hand on a press. By the 19th century, however, steam-powered presses could print out hundreds of pages at a time. Another invention was the **linotype** machine, which stamped out individual letters and set them up much faster than a typesetter could. Now books had become truly affordable, and the skill of reading was something that everyone was expected to learn. Today, with the use of computers, books can be easily transferred into electronic files, and read as e-books.

WHO AM I?

I was born November 29, 1898, in Belfast, Ireland. My father was a lawyer and my mother died when I was a boy. My brother and I escaped into our imaginations, exploring made-up worlds. I served briefly in World War I, then went to Oxford University and later became an English professor. In 1950, I published *The Lion, the Witch, and the Wardrobe*, a book about kids in England who find a magical land through the back of a wardrobe (a kind of cabinet). By 1956, all seven books of "The Chronicles of Narnia" had been published. A film version of *The Lion, the Witch, and the Wardrobe* was scheduled to be in theaters by late 2005.

Answer: Clive Staples (C.S.) Lewis

Librarian

Joyce Kasman Valenza, Teacher-Librarian, Springfield Township High School in Pennsylvania

Is this something you thought you might do for a living someday?

I was the kind of kid who read all the time. I stayed up way past bedtime with a flashlight under my blanket. I loved to share my books. I loved to talk about books. I practically breathed books. My first job was working as a page, shelving books at Brooklyn Public Library.

What was your favorite book as a kid?

When I was around 12 I fell in love with *A Tree Grows in Brooklyn.* Though I grew up not far from Francy and her family, theirs was a whole different place and time, a struggle I never experienced myself.

What do you do on a typical day?

I think of myself as a scout on the Web for teachers and for students. I am always looking for new, high-quality information resources and technologies. Very often my own homework is to create Web pages to guide students in their research. For instance, I just worked on a pathfinder to lead students and teachers to streaming video collections on the Web. I teach students how to access, analyze, evaluate, and effectively communicate information. I help students as they put research papers together, and I also guide students as they develop presentations, movies, and websites based on their research. This is an exciting time to be a librarian.

What do you like best about your job?

Every single day my job is different. One day I am working mostly with physics classes; the next day many students are researching Shakespeare's *Hamlet* and several will need my help getting information about colleges and advice on where to find the right prom dresses.

Whom would you encourage to go into this type of work?

Today's teacher-librarian needs to enjoy using and creating information resources of all kinds. A librarian needs to enjoy working with people—students, teachers, parents, administrators. This is *not* a quiet job. Today's school libraries are buzzing with students working together in groups using and presenting in all types of media.

Do you like the Harry Potter books?

I wait for and eat up each new Harry Potter book as eagerly as a student. I love to get lost in the magic and adventure of real kids doing extraordinary things. I relate to Hermione—I was that kind of student. I do not relate to Madam Pince, the Hogwart's librarian. I would be far more helpful to young wizards!

Buildings

Why are some buildings "missing" a floor? page 51

TALLEST *BUILDINGS* IN THE WORLD

Here are the world's tallest buildings, with the year each was completed. Heights listed here don't include antennas or other outside structures.

◄TAIPEI 101, Taipei, Taiwan (2004) **Height**: 101 stories, 1,671 feet

PETRONAS TOWERS 1 & 2, Kuala Lumpur, Malaysia (1998) **Height**: each building is 88 stories, 1,483 feet

SEARS TOWER, Chicago, Illinois (1974) **Height**: 110 stories, 1,450 feet

JIN MAO TOWER, Shanghai, China (1998) **Height**: 88 stories, 1,380 feet

TWO INTERNATIONAL FINANCE CENTRE, Hong Kong, China (2003) **Height**: 88 stories, 1,362 feet

CITIC PLAZA, Guangzhou, China (1997) **Height**: 80 stories, 1,283 feet

WORLD'S TALLEST WHEN BUILT

The New York World Building
NY. Built 1890. Height: 309 feet. Torn down 1955.
• Home of the *New York World* newspaper, which started *The World Almanac* in 1868.

Metropolitan Life Insurance Tower
NY. Built 1909. Height: 700 feet.

Woolworth Building
NY. Built 1913. Height: 792 feet.

Chrysler Building
NY. Built 1930. Height: 1,046 feet.

Empire State Building
NY. Built 1931. Height: 1,250 feet.

World Trade Center Towers 1 & 2
NY. Built 1973. Height: 1,368 feet and 1,362 feet. Destroyed in September 2001.

THE TALLEST TOWERS

The world's **tallest free-standing structure** is the 1,815-foot **CN Tower** in Toronto, Canada. It is not exactly a *building* since it does not have stories. "Free-standing" means it supports its own weight and is not attached to anything. Brave visitors can walk across the glass floor at the 1,122-foot level!

The **tallest structure** is the **KVLY-TV tower** in Fargo, North Dakota. It's 2,063 feet tall (including the 113-foot antenna) and made of steel. The tower is anchored and supported by more than 7.5 miles of steel wires.

◄ CN Tower

A Short History of Tall Buildings

For over 4,000 years, the world's tallest structure was the 480-foot-tall Great Pyramid at Giza. Next to top the list was the cathedral spire in Cologne, Germany (513 ft., built in 1880), then the Washington Monument in Washington, D.C. (555 ft., 1884). These buildings all had thick stone walls, with not much space inside.

The biggest challenge to building tall was gravity. Whether made of mud, stone, brick, timber, or concrete, most buildings had load-bearing walls. This meant that the walls had to support their own weight, the roof, the floors, and everything in the building. The higher the walls, the thicker they needed to be, and too many windows would weaken the building.

By the 1880s, three **key factors in the evolution of tall buildings** were in place:

A NEED FOR SPACE Crowded cities had less space for building, and land got expensive. To create more space, buildings had to go up instead of out.

BETTER STEEL PRODUCTION Mass-producing steel made more of it available for construction. Long beams could be connected to make **columns**. These were braced with horizontal beams called **girders**. The columns and girders formed a strong three-dimensional grid called a **superstructure**. This type of building was lighter than a similar one made of stone or brick and its weight was directed down the columns, which were supported by a solid **foundation**.

THE ELEVATOR Too many stairs! The first elevator, powered by steam, was installed in a New York store in 1857. Electric elevators came along in 1880.

The first American "skyscraper" was built in Chicago in 1885. Though it was only 10 stories and 138 feet tall, the **Home Insurance Building** was the first tall building to have a metal superstructure and many windows.

As buildings got taller, a new problem sprang up—**wind**. Too much movement could damage buildings or make the people inside uncomfortable. Some tall buildings, like New York's Citicorp Center, actually have a counter-weight near the top. A computer controls a 400-ton weight, moving it back and forth to lessen the building's sway.

In California and Japan, **earthquakes** are a big problem and special techniques are needed to make tall buildings safer from quakes.

Are you superstitious? A lot of people believe that the number 13 is unlucky. So when buildings are constructed, often there will not be a floor numbered 13—the numbering will skip from 12 to 14. Even if the owner and the architect of the building aren't superstitious, they may omit the 13th floor to play it safe. They won't want potential tenants to avoid the floor. (There is a similar superstition in China—but for any floor with a 4 in it.) So, the next time you're riding in an elevator, look very carefully at the buttons for the floors. It's possible that you won't see a 13!

Where's the 13?

It's Not All About...TALL!

When it comes to buildings, the tall ones grab people's attention. But many other buildings are interesting and fun to look at. Here are a few really cool buildings.

KINGDOM CENTRE, Riyadh, Saudi Arabia

The first thing you notice about this unique skyscraper is its "missing" piece, which is visible from nearly all of Riyadh, the capital of Saudi Arabia. The building is covered in reflective glass, except for the opening, which is lined with aluminum and lit up at night with changing colored lights. A 200-foot observation bridge spans the top of the triangular hole. Because the city has a law against buildings with more than 30 floors, the designers made the top third of the Kingdom Centre just a decorative steel skeleton. That way they could build it as high as they wanted.

30 ST MARY AXE, London England

This 41-story office building is hard to miss in London's financial district. That's not because of its height, but because of its circular shape. Many Londoners call it "the gherkin" (because it resembles this cucumber used for pickling). The building was built with the environment in mind. It uses half the power a similar sized building would ordinarily use, because its outside layer is designed to stay cool in summer and heat up in winter. Also, the many windows keep lighting cost down.

THE GLASS HOUSE,
New Canaan, Connecticut

When architect Philip Johnson designed his own home in 1949, he created something beautiful and unique. What makes this house special is the structure: it is a steel frame with outside walls made of clear glass. This makes the house totally see-through. (Johnson did enclose the bathroom in brick!) In an interview, Johnson said, "It's the only house in the world where you can watch the sun set and the moon rise at the same time."

BURJ AL ARAB HOTEL, Dubai, United Arab Emirates

If you think the unusual design of this luxury hotel looks like a ship under full sail—you're right. British architect Tom Wills-Wright started with the idea of a dhow (an ancient Arab sailing vessel) and transformed it into this modern image. Built in 1999, the Burj al Arab (meaning "Tower of the Arabs") sits on an artificial island just off shore in the Persian Gulf.

Bridges

There are four main bridge designs: beam, arch, truss, and suspension.

BEAM

The beam bridge is the most basic kind. A log across a stream is a simple style of beam bridge. Highway bridges are often beam bridges. The span of a beam bridge, or the length of the bridge without any support under it, is short compared to other designs. That's why long beam bridges need many supporting poles, called piers.

ARCH

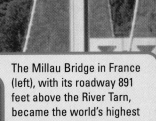

You can easily recognize an arch bridge, because it has arches holding it up from the bottom. The columns that support the arches are called abutments. Arch bridges were invented by the ancient Greeks.

TRUSS

The truss bridge uses mainly steel beams, connected in triangles to increase strength and span greater distances.

SUSPENSION

On suspension bridges, the roadway hangs from smaller cables attached to a pair of huge cables running over two massive towers. The weight of the roadway is held up by the towers. The ends of the giant cables are anchored firmly into solid rock or huge concrete blocks.

Magnifique!

The Millau Bridge in France (left), with its roadway 891 feet above the River Tarn, became the world's highest road suspension bridge when it opened in December 2004. The top of its highest tower reaches a height of 1,125 feet, making it taller than the Eiffel Tower. The roadway is held in place by relatively thin cables that fan out from the tops of the bridge's seven towers. The architect of the Millau, Norman Foster, described his design as having "the delicacy of a butterfly."

Camping

How long is the Appalachian Trail?   page 56

Let's Go to Camp!

Do you want to learn how to do something completely new? Or maybe you want to improve at something you already know how to do, in sports, art, music, dance, or drama. Or, maybe you just want to have a lot of fun and make new friends!

These are a few of the reasons why more than 10 million kids and adults in the U.S. go to camp each year.

Camp Is for Everyone

No matter where or who you are, there is probably a camp near you. Here are some kinds of camps:

Resident Camp: Usually for kids age 7 or older. Campers stay overnight, usually in cabins, tents, or tepees. Stays can last a few days, a week, or more.

Day Camp: For kids as young as 4. Many of the same activities as a resident camp, but everyone goes home at the end of the day.

Specialty Camp: Helps kids learn a special skill, like horseback riding, water skiing, or dancing, to name just a few.

Special Needs Camp: Each year, more than a million kids with special needs go to summer camp.

THE AMERICAN CAMP ASSOCIATION®

The American Camp Association is a resource for parents and kids to help them find the right camp to fit any need and budget. For more information, visit

WEB SITE **www.CAMPParents.org**

Camping Is Fun

Instead of going away to camp by yourself, you could try camping with your family. It can be loads of fun. Activities you might enjoy on a camping trip include hiking, biking, fishing, tubing, rafting, canoeing, sailing, horseback riding, and swimming. You don't have to go far to enjoy nature every day. Just step out of the tent and you're there. If the weather is nice—and there aren't too many bugs—you can even sleep out under the stars.

Sometimes there is water right on the site, but sometimes you may have to walk to a water source. Bathhouses with showers and toilets are usually nearby. There's often a small store in case you forgot something, like firewood, matches, or a can opener (or marshmallows!).

Private campgrounds or national chains like KOA or Jellystone Park usually have a lot more facilities. They often have spaces for trailers or motor homes. They may also rent cabins. They may have playgrounds, swimming pools, game equipment, and a fully stocked store. Some even have water slides!

The most serious campers hike far out into the wilderness using only what they can carry in and on their backpacks—including tents, sleeping bags, and food. In New York State's Lake George, you can camp on islands that you can only get to by boat.

Top Ten Family Hikes

1. Boston—Lizzy's Trail
2. Chicago—Illinois & Michigan Canal
3. Cleveland—Ohio & Erie Canal Trail
4. New York—Long Path
5. Orlando—Florida Trail
6. Pittsburgh—Great Allegheny Passage
7. Portland—Horsetail & Ponytail Falls
8. St. Louis—KATY Trail
9. San Francisco area— Point Reyes National Seashore
10. Washington, DC—C&O Canal

For more information about hiking and trails in the U.S. visit the American Hiking Society on the Web at **WEB SITE** *www.americanhiking.org*

Take a Hike

There is no better way to learn about and experience nature firsthand than to walk through it. There are many fascinating varieties of plants and animals to learn about. Not only is it good exercise, hiking also brings you to spectacular views, beautiful streams, and lakes.

Most established trails in national and state parks are well maintained and safe for a day's hike. But there are some ground rules you should always follow: To begin with, never go hiking alone. And don't go hiking without permission from your parents or without adult supervision.

Key rules for all hikers, kids or adults:

1. Tell someone where you are going.
2. Have a map of the trails you plan to take.
3. Stay on the marked trails.
4. If you plan to go a long way, it's also a good idea to know the predicted weather and to have a cell phone—but don't count on the phone to bail you out of trouble. It might not get reception where you are, and rescue workers might not be able to get to you easily.

America's Most Popular Trail

The Appalachian Trail (AT) is one of America's most beautiful and historic treasures with its scenic views and well-kept campgrounds. It runs some 2,174 miles—from Springer Mountain in Georgia to Mt. Katahdin in Maine. Blazed over several decades, it was completed in 1937 and is one of the oldest long-distance hiking trails in the U.S.

Each year, nearly 600 people manage to hike the AT from end to end, which can take anywhere from four to six months. Each night, hikers camp out in tents or in a special shelters with a roof and three walls. However, it's not necessary to hike the whole trail at once to experience its beauty. Most people only do short day hikes or spend a few days walking a section. There are also many shorter trails that branch off from the AT.

The first Saturday in June is the American Hiking Society's "National Trails Day." Across the country people get together to work on trails and learn more about the outdoors. Find out more at **WEB SITE** *www.americanhiking.org/events/ntd*

Computers

What's a FAQ? page 58

Computers perform tasks by using programs called **software**. **Programs** tell the computer what to do when the user enters certain information or commands. This is called **input**.

The computer then processes the information and gives the user the results **(output)**. The computer can also save, or store, the information.

The machines that make up a computer system are kinds of **hardware**. The largest and most powerful computers are called **mainframes**. Most people are more familiar with personal computers (PCs). These can be used at a desk **(desktops)**, carried around **(laptops)**, worn on your belt **(wearable computers)**, or even held in your hand **(hand-held)**.

SOFTWARE

KINDS OF SOFTWARE When you write on a computer you use a type of software called a word processing program. This program can be selected by using the **keyboard** or a **mouse**.

Other common types of software include programs for doing math, keeping records, playing games, and creating pictures.

ENTERING DATA In a word processing program, you can input your words by typing on the **keyboard**. The backspace and delete keys are like erasers. You can also press special **function keys** or click on certain symbols **(icons)** to center or underline words, move words around, check spelling, print out a page, and do other tasks.

HARDWARE

INSIDE THE COMPUTER The instructions from the program you use are carried out inside the computer by the **central processing unit**, or **CPU**. The CPU is the computer's brain.

SEEING THE RESULTS The **monitor** and **printer** are the most commonly used output devices in a computer system. When you type a story, the words show up on a **monitor**, which is like a TV screen. Your story can be printed on paper by using a **printer**.

If you print out a story, you can mail it to a friend. But if you are both connected to the Internet, you can e-mail it from your computer to your friend's computer.

COMPUTER *TALK*

BIT The smallest unit of data.

BLOG Short for "Web log." It's a personal journal or diary that people put on a website for others to read.

BOOT To start up a computer.

BROWSER A program to help get around the Internet.

BUG OR GLITCH An error in a program or in the computer.

BYTE An amount of data equal to 8 bits.

CHIP A small piece of silicon holding the circuits used to store and process information.

COOKIE Some websites store information, like your passwords and other preferences, on your computer's hard drive. When you go back to that site later, your browser sends the information (the "cookie") to the website.

DATABASE A large collection of information organized so that it can be retrieved and used in different ways.

DESKTOP PUBLISHING The use of computers to design and produce magazines, newspapers, and books.

DOWNLOAD To transfer information from a host computer to a personal computer through a network connection or modem.

ENCRYPTION The process of changing information into a code, especially passwords, or financial or personal information, to keep others from reading it.

FAQ "Frequently Asked Questions" is a document often found on a Web site, containing answers to common questions users ask.

GIG OR GIGABYTE (GB) An amount of information equal to 1,024 megabytes, or (in some situations) 1 thousand megabytes.

HTTP Hypertext Transfer Protocol is the method of file exchange used on the World Wide Web.

HTML The abbreviation for HyperText Markup Language, a computer language used to make web pages.

INTERNET A worldwide system of linked computer networks.

K Stands for *kilo,* or "thousands," in Greek. For example, "6K" is shorthand for 6,000 bytes.

MEGABYTE (MB) An amount of information equal to 1,048,516 bytes, or (in some situations) 1 million bytes.

NETWORK A group of computers linked together so that they can share information.

PDA OR PERSONAL DIGITAL ASSISTANT A handheld computer that can store addresses, phone numbers, and other information that's useful to have handy.

PIXEL OR PICTURE ELEMENT The smallest unit of an image on a computer monitor. It can be used to measure the size of an image.

RAM OR RANDOM ACCESS MEMORY Memory your computer uses to open programs and store your work until you save it to a hard drive or disk. Information in RAM disappears when the computer is turned off.

ROM OR READ ONLY MEMORY Memory that contains permanent instructions for the computer and cannot be changed. The information in ROM stays after the computer is turned off.

SPAM Electronic junk mail.

THREAD A series of messages and replies that relate to a specific topic.

URL OR UNIFORM RESOURCE LOCATOR The technical name for a website address.

VIRUS A program that damages other programs and data. It gets into a computer through the Internet or shared disks.

WI-FI OR WIRELESS FIDELITY Technology that allows people to link to other computers and the Internet from their computers without wires.

Today's electronic devices not only do many different things, they are often small enough to hold in your hand or carry in your pocket. Here are some of the coolest gadgets around.

SONY PSP It has a super-sharp 4.3-inch flat-panel LCD display. Many PlayStation games are available for the PSP. But it does do other things, like play movies on a Universal Media Disc.

AIR FLO New controllers that are air-cooled by tiny fans. Gamers' palms will be sweaty no more with NYKO'S nifty gadgets that come in wired and wireless models to go with the most popular console games.

DVD JR This Samsung gadget, expected to go on sale in 2005, has a 2.5-inch color screen (TFT or thin film transistor). It plays movies on 3-inch DVDs. Popular movies and cartoons are available in this format and the battery for the DVD Jr. lasts over two hours—long enough to play a whole movie. ▶

Computer **Games**

BACKYARD SKATEBOARDING Atari, for Windows. This kid-friendly game lets you choose your skater, including a kid version of Andy MacDonald, and explore a neighborhood park. It includes lots of mini-games like paper delivery and remote-control car racing.

BARBIE FASHION SHOW Vivendi Universal, for Windows. You are the designer! You choose the colors, the lines, the fabrics, even the model's hairstyles. You can print your creations and even post them on Barbie.com.

ZOO TYCOON 2 Microsoft, for Windows. This sim game is still a great place to build the ultimate zoo and now it has a new zoom feature and 3-D graphics.

ROLLER COASTER TYCOON 3 Atari, for Windows. This sim thrill game that lets you build your own rollercoasters and theme park is back better than ever with a new "Coaster Cam" that lets you "ride" your creations.

ZOO VET Legacy Interactive, for Windows and Mac. You are the head vet at the zoo in this sim game and it's up to you to heal the sick animals. Your work is judged by a master doctor and if you do well, you're rewarded with a trophy.

ALL ABOUT... MICROSOFT

If your computer has Windows, if you surf the Web on Internet Explorer, or if you write your papers in Word, then you have a Microsoft program. You might also know Bill Gates, the company's cofounder and former chairman, who is the wealthiest individual in the world, worth more than $40 billion.

What you may not know is that Gates never thought his love of computers would make him any money. He started programming computers as a hobby when he was just 13. He was planning a career in law when he and Microsoft cofounder Paul Allen rewrote BASIC (Beginner's All-purpose Symbolic Instruction Code), a computer programming language, for a personal computer.

Gates and Allen founded Microsoft in 1975 to market their new programs. Microsoft released MS-DOS, an operating system, in 1981 and the widely used Office (which includes programs like Word and Excel) in 1989. And though the company was slowed down by lawsuits and competitors in the 1990s, its products are still wildly popular. Microsoft had a recent success when it released the Xbox, a gaming system, in 2001.

Bill Gates served as chief executive officer (CEO) of Microsoft until 2000. He became the youngest self-made billionaire ever in 1987 (at 31 years old). He also puts his name on largest charitable foundation in the United States, The Bill and Melinda Gates Foundation, which has given billions of dollars of assistance to the needy around the world.

For more about Microsoft visit **WEB SITE** www.microsoft.com/museum/musstudent.mspx

WORD *CIRCUIT*

Complete the circuit by filling the words into the blanks, starting from the "C" in computer and finishing with the "R." Each new word begins with the last letter of the word before it. We've given you the first and last letters. The one we've given you shows that the words are spelled backwards on the bottom section of the circuit.

```
C  ooki E_____ N_____ K_____ D_____ P
O                                                        __
M                                                        __
P                                                        __
U                                                        __
T                                                        L
E                                                        __
R  etn E_____ D_____ T_____ R_____ P_____
```

Laptop	Desktop	Keyboard	Database	Reboot	Cookie
Encryption	Network	Portal	Printer	Thread	Enter

ANSWERS ON PAGES 335-338.
FOR MORE PUZZLES GO TO
WWW.WORLDALMANACFORKIDS.COM

Dinosaurs

When did Pangea break up? page 62

Dinosaurs last roamed the Earth some 65 million years ago. So how do we know so much about them?

Fossils: Clues to Ancient Life

Paleontologists are scientists who use fossils to study the past. **Fossils** are the remains of long-dead animals (like dinosaurs) or plants. Most fossils are formed from the hard parts of an animal's body, such as bones, shells, or teeth. Some fossils are **imprints**, like the outline of a leaf, or dinosaur footprints. Most fossils are found in **sedimentary rocks,** which form from the mud or sand (sediment) at the bottom of oceans, rivers, and lakes. Fossils have also been found in ice and tar. Insects that lived millions of years ago are sometimes found preserved in amber (hardened tree sap).

EARLY DISCOVERIES

▶ In 1824 British geologist William Buckland recognized some fossils as part of a giant extinct reptile. He named this first dinosaur **Megalosaurus,** from the Greek words *megalos* ("big") and *sauros* ("lizard").

▶ In 1842 Sir Richard Owen used the Greek words *deinos* ("terrible") and *sauros* to coin the term "dinosaur."

▶ The partial skeleton of a **Hadrosaurus** was found in New Jersey in 1858. This was the first major dinosaur discovery in North America. The remains were made into a full dinosaur skeleton, the first ever displayed, at the Philadelphia Academy of Natural Sciences.

▶ Discovered in Germany in 1861, the **Archaeopteryx** is a link between dinosaurs and birds. It had bones, teeth, and a skull like a dinosaur's. But it also had feathers and could probably fly.

News Flash!
Dino soft tissue found.
see page 20

Recent Dino News

Two recent discoveries in China are changing scientists' views of life 130 million years ago. One major new find was the fossil of an early relative of the fearsome **Tyrannosaurus Rex**. This fossil showed that the dinosaur had feathers, or something like feathers. In fact, Tyrannosaurs share many physical features with modern birds, including a wishbone, wrists that swivel, and three forward-pointing toes. The new find suggests that T-Rex may have had a fluffy coat during its development.

Another important discovery was announced by scientists at New York's Museum of Natural History. A dinosaur fossil discovered in China was found in an unique place—inside the stomach of a mammal. *Repenomamus robustus* (above right) was a possum-like mammal about 3 feet long. Before it died, it ate a baby psittacosaur, a plant-eating dinosaur. This new evidence shows that early mammals may have preyed on dinosaurs.

Apatosaurus

Deceptive lizard
Plant-eating
Length: 70+ feet
Period: Jurassic
Found in: Western U.S.

Velociraptor

Speedy thief
Meat-eating
Length: 6 feet
Period: Cretaceous
Found in: Asia

Hadrosaurus

Big lizard
Plant-eating
Length: 30 feet
Period: Cretaceous
Found in: Asia,
Europe, North and
South America

WHEN DID DINOSAURS LIVE?

Dinosaurs roamed the Earth during the Mesozoic Era, which is divided into three periods:

TRIASSIC PERIOD
from 248 to 206 million years ago

✦ **Pangea**, Earth's one big continent, began to break up in this period.

✦ The earliest known mammals, such as the tiny, rat-like **Morganucodon**, began to appear.

✦ Evergreen plants were the most common vegetation.

✦ One of the earliest known dinosaurs, **Eoraptor**, was a meat eater only about 40 inches long. **Herrersaurus**, also a meat eater, was about 10 feet long.

✦ Long-necked **plesiosaurs** and dolphin-like **ichthyosaurs**—both big reptiles that were not dinosaurs—ruled the sea.

JURASSIC PERIOD
from 206 to 144 million years ago

✦ Flowering plants appeared.

✦ Plant-eating **sauropods**, like **Apatosaurus** and **Brachiosaurus**, were the biggest land creatures ever! These dinosaurs were eaten by meat eaters like **Allosaurus** and **Megalosaurus**.

✦ **Archaeopteryx** was born— the earliest link between dinosaurs and birds.

✦ Flying reptiles called **pterosaurs**, close relatives of the dinosaur, dominated the sky.

CRETACEOUS PERIOD
from 144 to 65 million years ago

✦ The climate was warm, with no polar ice caps.

✦ Meat-eating **theropods** like **Tyrannosaurus Rex** and **Giganotosaurus** walked on two legs.

✦ All dinosaurs and other reptiles such as **ichthyosaurs** and **pterosaurs** became extinct by the end of this period. It may have been because a huge asteroid or comet hit the Earth. This would have filled the atmosphere with dust and debris, blocking most of the sun's light and heat. As a result many plants and animals would have died out.

DINOSAUR WORLD

Tyrannosaurus Rex ("T-Rex")

King of the tyrant lizards
Meat-eating • Length: 40 feet
Period: Cretaceous
Found in: Western U.S., Canada, Asia

Triceratops

Three-horned face • **Plant-eating**
Length: 30 feet • **Period:** Cretaceous
Found in: North America

Stegosaurus

Plated lizard • **Plant-eating**
• **Length:** 30 feet • **Period:** Jurassic
• **Found in:** North America

Camptosaurus

Bent lizard • **Plant-eating**
Length: 20 feet • **Period:** Jurassic-Cretaceous
Found in: North America and Western Europe

DINO SPOTTING

Some of the best places to see dinosaurs and fossils in North America are the Academy of Natural Sciences (Philadelphia), the American Museum of Natural History (New York City), the Fernbank Museum of Natural History (Atlanta), the Field Museum of Natural History (Chicago), the National Museum of Natural History (Washington, D.C.), and the Royal Tyrrell Museum of Natural History (Drumheller, Alberta, Canada). Or you can visit the University of California at Berkeley's virtual Museum of Paleontology at **WEB SITE** www.ucmp.berkeley.edu

Dino Maze

Two of these dinosaurs were enemies. The third was actually from a different era. Look back at pages 62–63 to find out who they were.

START

ANSWERS ON PAGES 335-338. FOR MORE PUZZLES GO TO WWW.WORLDALMANACFORKIDS.COM

FINISH

Disasters

What disaster happened at Chernobyl? page 66

Disasters come in many forms and sizes. There are natural ones like earthquakes, floods, and hurricanes. And there are human-related ones like airplane crashes, shipwrecks, and explosions. One of history's most famous disasters was the sinking of the luxury steamship *Titanic* (when it hit an iceberg in the Atlantic Ocean) in 1912; 1,503 people died.

ALL ABOUT . . . Famous Big City Fires

One of the earliest major fires happened in ancient Rome in A.D. 64. Legend has it that the blaze was set by the Emperor Nero, who played his fiddle while the city burned. Many historians doubt this story. (One thing they do know is that he didn't play a violin, which hadn't been invented yet.) Here are some other big city fires in history:

1666: **The Great Fire of London** It began in a bakery on September 2, lasted for several days, and destroyed over 13,000 houses. Only four dead were officially counted.

1871: **The Great Chicago Fire** Coming on a windy October 8 at the end of a hot, dry spell, it wiped out an area of 3 square miles in the center of the city, killing at least 300 people and destroying over 18,000 buildings. The story goes that it began when a cow kicked over a lantern in the barn of Catherine O'Leary. When Chicago rebuilt, they called it the "The Second City," a nice name that lives today.

1904: **Baltimore Fire** This fire started February 7. Eighty-six blocks of the business district were affected, 1,500 buildings burned, and 2,500 businesses were damaged or destroyed. Remarkably, only four people died, all firefighters.

1906: **San Francisco Earthquake and Fire** A massive earthquake early on the morning of April 18 set off a series of destructive fires. The death toll was over 3,000, and damage was estimated at $500 million.

Disasters

about major earthquakes, volcanoes, and tsunamis, see pages 93–95.

Aircraft Disasters

Date	Location	What Happened?	Deaths
May 6, 1937	Lakehurst, NJ	German zeppelin (blimp) *Hindenburg* caught fire as it prepared to land	36
Aug. 12, 1985	Japan	Boeing 747 jet collided with Mt. Ogur. Japan's worst single-aircraft disaster in history	520
Nov. 12, 1996	India near New Dehli	Boeing 747 and a cargo plane collided in midair	349
Nov. 12, 2001	New York City	Airbus A-300 crashed just after takeoff from JFK Airport	265

Explosions and Fires

Date	Location	What Happened?	Deaths
June 15, 1904	New York City	*General Slocum*, wooden ship carrying church members across East River, caught fire	1,021
Mar. 25, 1911	New York City	Triangle Shirtwaist Factory caught fire, workers were trapped inside	146
Nov. 28, 1942	Boston, MA	Fire swept through the Coconut Grove nightclub; patrons panicked. Deadliest nightclub fire in U.S. history	491
Dec. 3, 1984	Bhopal, India	A pesticide factory explosion spread toxic gas; worst industrial accident in history	15,000+

Rail Disasters

Date	Location	What Happened?	Deaths
Jan. 16, 1944	León Prov., Spain	Train crashed in the Torro Tunnel	500
March 2, 1944	Salerno, Italy	Passengers suffocated when train stalled in tunnel	521
Feb. 6, 1951	Woodbridge, NJ	Commuter train fell through a temporary overpass	84
June 6, 1981	Bihar, India	Train plunged off of a bridge into the river. India's deadliest rail disaster ever	800+

 **WORST NUCLEAR POWER ACCIDENT** *On April 26, 1986, an explosion occurred at one of the reactors at a nuclear power plant near Chernobyl, USSR (now Ukraine). The explosion destroyed the reactor's protective covering, and radioactive material leaked into the air for the next ten days. High levels of radiation were detected as far away as Italy and Norway. At least 31 people died immediately after the disaster and thousands more have died from illnesses caused by radiation exposure. More than 135,000 people had to be evacuated from the area within 1,000 miles of the plant.*

Date	Location	What Happened?	Deaths
April 14, 1912	near Newfoundland	Luxury liner *Titanic* collided with iceberg	1,503
May 7, 1915	Atlantic Ocean, near Ireland	British steamer *Lusitania* torpedoed and sunk by German submarine	1,198
Jan. 30, 1945	Baltic Sea	Liner *Wilhelm Gustloff* carrying German refugees and soldiers sunk by Soviet sub. Highest death toll for a single ship	6,000-7,000
Aug. 12, 2000	Barents Sea	Explosions sank Russian submarine *Kursk;* multiple rescue attempts failed	118
Sept. 26, 2002	Atlantic Ocean near The Gambia	Senegalese ferry capsized	1,863

Storms and Floods

Date	Location	What Happened?	Deaths
Mar. 11-14, 1888	Eastern U.S.	20–50 inches of snow buried the eastern U.S.	400
Sept. 8, 1900	Galveston, Texas	Hurricane came from the Gulf of Mexico	8,000+
Mar. 18, 1925	MO, IL, IN	"Great Tri-State Tornado" tore 3½-hour path through 13 counties. Deadliest tornado in U.S. history	689
Aug. 1931	China	Vast flooding on the Huang He River. Highest death toll from a flood	3,700,000
1939	Northern China	River flooding	200,000
Nov. 13, 1970	Bangladesh	Cyclone with 140 mph winds; the deadliest storm on record	300,000
Oct. 27-29, 1998	Honduras, Nicaragua, Guatemala, El Salvador	Hurricane Mitch ravaged several Central American nations. Deadliest hurricane on record, also most people made homeless	11,000+
Dec. 1999	Venezuela	Flooding and mudslides devastated the capital (Caracas) and surrounding areas	9,000+
Sept. 16-26, 2004	Dominican Rep., Haiti, Florida	Hurricane Jeanne damaged areas still stinging from earlier storms	1,500+

Galveston, Texas

MASSIVE FLOOD. *The worst U.S. flood happened on June 1, 1889, in Johnstown, Pennsylvania. At about 4 o'clock in the afternoon, people in this small city heard a rumble and then a "roar like thunder." Fourteen miles upriver, the old South Fork Dam had broken and a huge wall of water—sometimes as high as 60 feet—came crashing down on the city at 40 miles per hour. The official death toll reached nearly 2,200, but many victims were never found.*

67

Environment

Do all mosquitoes suck blood? page 72

SHARING *the* EARTH

We share the planet with trees, flowers, insects, birds, fish, and many other plants and animals. Each species (type) of animal or plant has its place on Earth, and each one is dependent on many others. Plants give off oxygen that animals need to breathe. Insects and birds pollinate plants and spread their seeds. **Animals** eat plants and are in turn eaten by larger animals. When plants and animals die, they become part of the soil in which new plants take root and grow.

People and the Environment

In **prehistoric times**, people killed animals for food and built fires to cook food and keep themselves warm. They cut down trees for fuel, and their fires released pollution into the air. But there were so few people that their activities had little impact on the environment.

In **modern times**, the world's population has grown very quickly. In 1850 there were around a billion people in the world. By 2005 there were about 6.4 billion in the world, including 295 million in the U.S. By 2050, according to United Nations estimates, there will be 8.9 billion people. Today, our activities have a big impact on the environment.

People are becoming more aware that human activities can seriously damage the planet and the animals and plants on it. Sometimes this damage can be reversed or slowed down. But it is often permanent. On the following pages you'll learn about the damage, and about some things that can be done to help clean up and protect our planet.

Every April 22, the world celebrates **Earth Day** to help make people more aware of environment problems and ways they can help. There are many projects kids can get involved in. One example is the Earth Day Groceries Project, a cool Internet project your school or class can do for fun. Have your teacher borrow paper bags from a local grocery store. Each kid decorates a bag with pictures and messages about helping the environment. Then the bags go back to the store, where they will be used for shoppers' groceries on Earth Day.

WEB SITE For more information, go to *www.earthdaybags.org*

You can learn more about the environment at
WEB SITE www.epa.gov/students

ENDANGERED SPECIES

When a species becomes extinct, it reduces the variety of life on Earth. In the world today, 7,266 known species of animals (and even more plant species) are threatened with extinction, according to the International Union for Conservation of Nature and Natural Resources. Humans have been able to save some endangered animals and are working to save more.

Some Endangered Animals

GORILLA The biggest dangers facing the gorilla are habitat loss, being hunted for meat, and the Ebola virus. There are only about 700 African mountain gorillas left in the world. (There are none in any zoos.) Believe it or not, that number is a 17% increase from 10 years ago, when they were on the brink of extinction. This type of gorilla is the most well-known, because of the studies of Dian Fossey in the 1960s and 70s.

ELEPHANT The largest living land mammals, weighing up to 6 tons, elephants can be found in Africa and Asia. Habitat loss and being hunted for the ivory in their tusks are the two greatest threats to elephants. In the wild, there are between 300,000 and 600,000 African elephants and between 35,000 and 50,000 Asian elephants.

FACTORS THAT CAN MAKE A SPECIES ENDANGERED:

▲ *Deforestation in the Amazon rain forest*

HABITAT DESTRUCTION. As human populations grow, they need places to live and work. People build houses and factories in areas where plants and animals live. Filling in wetlands and clearing forests (**deforestation**) are examples of this threat.

OVERHARVESTING. People may catch a kind of fish or hunt an animal until its numbers are too low to reproduce fast enough. Bison or buffalo once roamed over the entire Great Plains until they were almost hunted into extinction in the 19th century. They are now protected by law, and their numbers are increasing.

ALIEN SPECIES are plants and animals that have been moved by humans into areas where they are not naturally found. They may have no natural enemies there and can push out native species. Red fire ants, zebra mussels, and kudzu are examples of alien species.

POLLUTION in the air, water, and land can affect plants and animals. It can poison them or make it hard for them to grow or reproduce. Factories are not the only source. Oil, salt, and other substances sprayed or spilled on roads can wash into streams, rivers, and lakes. Acid rain damages and kills trees, especially in the mountains where acidic clouds and fog often surround them

HOME SWEET BIOME

A "**biome**" is a large natural area that is the home to a certain type of plant. The animals, climate, soil, and even the amount of water in the region also help distinguish a biome. There are more than 30 kinds of biomes in the world. But the following types cover most of Earth's surface.

Forests

Forests cover about one-third of Earth's land surface. Pines, hemlocks, firs, and spruces grow in the cool **evergreen** forests farthest from the equator. These trees are called **conifers** because they produce cones.

Temperate forests have warm, rainy summers and cold, snowy winters. Here **deciduous trees** (which lose their leaves in the fall and grow new ones in the spring) join the evergreens. Temperate forests are home to maple, oak, beech, and poplar trees, and to wildflowers and shrubs. These forests are found in the eastern United States, southeastern Canada, northern Europe and Asia, and southern Australia.

Still closer to the equator are the **tropical rain forests,** home to the greatest variety of plants on Earth. About 60 to 100 inches of rain fall each year. Tropical trees stay green all year. They grow close together, shading the ground. There are several layers of trees. The top, **emergent layer** has trees that can reach 200 feet in height. The **canopy,** which gets lots of sun, comes next, followed by the **understory.** The **forest floor,** covered with roots, gets little sun. Many plants cannot grow there.

Tropical rain forests are found mainly in Central America, South America, Asia, and Africa. They once covered more than 8 million square miles. Today, because of destruction by humans, fewer than 3.4 million square miles remain. More than half the plant and animal species in the world live there. Foods such as bananas and pineapples first grew there. Woods such as mahogany and teak also come from rain forests. Many kinds of plants there are used to make medicines.

When rain forests are burned, carbon dioxide is released into the air. This adds to the **greenhouse effect** (see page 77). As forests are destroyed, the precious soil is easily washed away by the heavy rains.

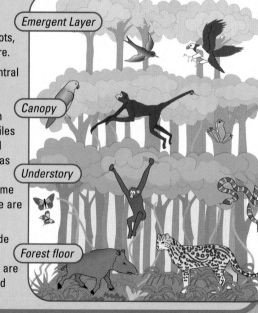

Emergent Layer

Canopy

Understory

Forest floor

Tundra & Alpine Region

In the northernmost regions of North America, Europe, and Asia surrounding the Arctic Ocean are plains called the **tundra.** The temperature rarely rises above 45 degrees Fahrenheit, and it is too cold for trees to grow there. Most tundra plants are mosses and lichens that hug the ground for warmth. A few wildflowers and small shrubs also grow where the soil thaws for about two months of the year. This kind of climate and plant life also exists in the **alpine** region, on top of the world's highest mountains (such as the Himalayas, Alps, Andes, and Rockies), where small flowers also grow.

WHAT IS THE TREE LINE? On mountains in the north (such as the Rockies) and in the far south (such as the Andes), there is an altitude above which trees will not grow. This is the **tree line** or **timberline.** Above the tree line, you can see low shrubs and small plants.

Deserts

The driest areas of the world are the **deserts.** They can be hot or cold, but they also contain an amazing number of plants. Cactuses and sagebrush are native to dry regions of North and South America. The deserts of Africa and Asia contain plants called euporbias. Date plants have grown in the deserts of the Middle East and North Africa for thousands of years. In the southwestern United States and northern Mexico, there are many types of cactuses, including prickly pear, barrel, and saguaro.

▲ *Arizona desert*

Grasslands

▲ *Grassland in Alberta, Canada*

Areas that are too dry to have green forests, but not dry enough to be deserts, are called **grasslands.** The most common plants found there are grasses. Cooler grasslands are found in the Great Plains of the United States and Canada, in the steppes of Europe and Asia, and in the pampas of Argentina. The drier grasslands are used for grazing cattle and sheep. In the **prairies,** where there is a little more rain, wheat, rye, oats, and barley are grown. The warmer grasslands, called **savannas,** are found in central and southern Africa, Venezuela, southern Brazil, and Australia. Most savannas have moist summers and cool, dry winters.

Oceans

Coral reef ▶

Covering two-thirds of the earth, the **ocean** is by far the largest biome. Within the ocean are smaller biomes that include **coastal areas, tidal zones,** and **coral reefs.** Found in relatively shallow warm waters, the reefs are called the "rain forests of the ocean." Australia's Great Barrier Reef is the largest in the world. It is home to thousands of species of plant and animal life.

What Is BIODIVERSITY?

The Earth is shared by millions of species of living things. The wide variety of life on Earth, as shown by the many species, is called "**biodiversity**" (**bio** means "life" and **diversity** means "variety"). Human beings of all colors, races, and nationalities make up just one species, *Homo sapiens*.

Species, Species Everywhere

Here is just a sampling of how diverse life on Earth is. The numbers are only estimates, and more species are being discovered all the time!

ARTHROPODS (1.1 million species)
  insects: 750,000 species
    moths & butterflies: 165,000 species
    flies: about 122,000 species
    cockroaches: about 4,000 species
  crustaceans: 44,000 species
  spiders: 35,000 species

FISH (24,500 species)
  bony fish: 23,000 species
  skates & rays: 450 species
  sharks: 350 species
  seahorses: 32 species

BIRDS (9,000 species)
  perching birds: 5,200-5,500 species
  parrots: 353 species
  pigeons: 309 species
  raptors (eagles, hawks, etc.): 307 species
  penguins: 17 species
  ostrich: 1 species

MAMMALS (9,000 species)
  rodents: 1,700 species
  bats: 1,000 species
  monkeys: 242 species
  whales and dolphins: 83 species
  cats: 38 species
  apes: 21 species
  pigs: 14 species
  bears: 8 species

REPTILES (8,000 species)
  lizards: 4,500 species
  snakes: 2,900 species
  tortoises & turtles: about 294 species
  crocodiles & alligators: 23 species

AMPHIBIANS (5,000 species)
  frogs & toads: 4,500 species
  newts & salamanders: 470 species

PLANTS (260,000 species)
  flowering plants: 250,000 species
  bamboo: about 1,000 species
  evergreens: 550 species

Fascinating Bio Facts

▶ There are about a thousand species of coral. The calcium carbonate skeletons of corals form large reefs. In tropical waters, they can grow from 1 inch to 2 feet per year, creating huge ecosystems. It took an estimated 5 million years for Australia's 1,250-mile Great Barrier Reef to form.

▶ Whales, dolphins, and porpoises are the only mammals that spend their entire lives in water.

▶ Only female mosquitoes suck blood from animals and humans. They need blood to produce eggs. Male mosquitoes feed on plant sap instead.

▶ Some species of bamboo can grow as much as 12 inches in a single day.

The World's ENERGY

One important way we interact with our environment is by extracting energy from natural resources and putting it to use in industry and everyday life.

Who **Produces** and **Uses** the **MOST ENERGY?**

The United States produces about 18% of the world's energy—more than any other country—but it also uses 24% of the world's supply. The table below on the left lists the world's top ten energy producers and the percent of the world's production that each nation was responsible for in 2002. The table on the right lists the world's top energy users and the percent of the world's energy that each nation consumed.

Top Energy Producers		Top Energy Users	
United States	18%	United States	24%
Russia	11%	China	10%
China	10%	Russia	7%
Saudi Arabia	5%	Japan	5%
Canada	4%	Germany	3%
Australia	3%	India	3%
India	3%	Canada	3%
Iran	3%	France	2%
Norway	3%	United Kingdom	2%
United Kingdom	3%	Brazil	2%

WHERE *DOES* U.S. ENERGY *COME FROM?*

In 2003, nearly 86% of the energy used in the U.S. came from fossil fuels (39.5% from petroleum, 23.4% from natural gas, and 23% from coal). The rest came mostly from hydropower (water power), nuclear energy, and renewable resources such as geothermal, solar, and wind energy, and from burning materials such as wood and animal waste.

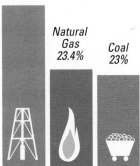

Petroleum 39.5%

Natural Gas 23.4%

Coal 23%

Nuclear power 8.1%

Hydro-power 2.8%

Other 3.4%

The field of energy production has a lot of slang. Here are a few terms that energy workers use:

► *A "wildcat" is a well drilled in an area where oil has not previously been found.*

► *A "can" is a building where a nuclear reactor is located.*

► *A "roughneck" is a nickname for an oil rig worker.*

► *A "doghouse" is a small building on an oil or gas rig used for an office.*

Sources of ENERGY

FOSSIL FUELS

Fuels are called "fossil" because they were formed from ancient plants and animals. The three basic fossil fuels are **coal, oil,** and **natural gas.** Most of the energy we use today comes from these sources. **Coal** is mined, either at the Earth's surface or deep underground. Pumpjacks pump **oil,** or petroleum, from wells drilled in the ground. **Natural gas,** which is made up mostly of a gas called methane, also comes from wells. Natural gas is a clean-burning fuel, and it has been used more and more. Oil and coal create more air pollution.

All fossil fuels have one problem: they are gradually getting used up. In the case of oil, many industrial and other countries lack oil resources or need much more oil than they have, so they depend on importing large amounts from oil-rich countries. Also, oil only exists in some countries. Countries without oil must import large amounts from oil-rich countries.

▼ *A pumpjack*

Hoover Dam, on the Colorado River about 30 miles southeast of Las Vegas, Nevada, provides power for 1.3 million people.

NUCLEAR ENERGY

A nuclear power plant

Nuclear power is created by releasing energy stored in the nucleus of an atom. This process is nuclear **fission,** which is also called "splitting" an atom. Fission takes place in a **reactor,** which allows the nuclear reaction to be controlled. Nuclear power plants release almost no air pollution. Many countries today use nuclear energy.

Nuclear power does cause some safety concerns. In 1979 a nuclear accident at Three Mile Island in Pennsylvania led to the release of some radiation. A much worse accident at Chernobyl in Ukraine in 1986 led to the deaths of thousands of people (see page 66 for more information).

WATER POWER

Water power is energy that comes from the force of falling or fast-flowing water. It was put to use early in human history. **Water wheels,** turned by rivers or streams, were common in the Middle Ages. They were used for tasks like grinding grain and sawing lumber.

Today water power comes from waterfalls or from dams. As water flows from a higher to a lower level, it runs a turbine—a device that turns an electric generator. This is called **hydroelectric power (hydro** = water). Today, over half of the world's hydroelectric power is produced in five countries: Brazil, Russia, Canada, China, and the United States.

A "farm" of wind turbines

WIND ENERGY

People have used the wind's energy for a long time. **Windmills** were popular in Europe during the Middle Ages. Later, windmills became common on U.S. farms. Today, huge high-tech windmills with propeller-like blades are grouped together in **"wind farms."** Dozens of wind turbines are spaced well apart (so they don't block each other's wind). Even on big wind farms, the windmills usually take up less than 1% of the ground space. The rest of the land can still be used for farming or for grazing animals.

Wind power is a rapidly growing technology that doesn't pollute or get used up like fossil fuels. By 2003, there was nearly four times the generating capacity in the U.S. as there had been in 1996. Unfortunately, the generators only work when the wind blows.

GEOTHERMAL ENERGY

Geothermal energy comes from the heat deep inside the Earth. About 30 miles below the surface is a layer called the **mantle.** This is the source of the gas and lava that erupt from volcanoes. Hot springs and geysers, with temperatures as high as 700 degrees, are also heated by the mantle. Because it's so hot, the mantle holds great promise as an energy source, especially in areas where the hot water is close to the surface. Iceland, which has many active volcanoes and hot springs, uses lots of geothermal energy. About 85% of homes there are heated this way.

BIOMASS ENERGY

Burning wood and straw (materials known as **biomass**) is probably the oldest way of producing energy. It's an old idea, but it still has value. Researchers are growing crops to use as fuel. Biomass fuels can be burned, like coal, in a power plant. They can also be used to make **ethanol,** which is similar to gasoline. Most ethanol comes from corn, which can make it expensive. But researchers are experimenting with other crops, like "switchgrass" and alfalfa.

A biomass power plant provides energy for Burlington, Vermont. It turns wood chips, solid waste, and switchgrass into a substance similar to natural gas.

SOLAR POWER

Energy directly from sunlight is a promising new technology. Vast amounts of this energy fall upon the Earth every day—and it is not running out. Energy from the sun is expected to run for some 5 billion years. Solar energy is also friendly to the environment. One drawback is the need for space for the solar panels which are large. Also, energy can't be gathered when the sun isn't shining.

A solar power plant

A solar cell is usually made of silicon, a **semiconductor.** It can change sunlight into electricity. The cost of solar cells has been dropping in recent years. Large plants using solar-cell systems have been built in several countries, including Japan, Saudi Arabia, the United States, and Germany.

THE AIR WE

The Earth's air is made up of different gases: about 78% nitrogen, 21% oxygen, and 1% carbon dioxide, water vapor, and other gases. All humans and animals need air to survive. Plants also need it. They use sunlight and the carbon dioxide in air to make food, and then give off oxygen.

Humans breathe more than 3,000 gallons of air a day. Because air is so basic to life, it is important to keep it clean. Air pollution causes health problems and may bring about acid rain, smog, global warming, and a breakdown of the ozone layer.

What is Acid Rain?

Acid rain is a kind of air pollution caused by chemicals in the air. Eventually these chemicals can make rain, snow, or fog more acidic than normal. The main source of these chemicals is exhaust from cars, trucks, buses, waste incinerators, factories, and some electric power plants, especially those that burn fossil fuels, such as coal. When these chemicals mix with moisture and other particles, they create sulfuric acid and nitric acid. The wind often carries these acids many miles before they fall to the ground in rain, snow, and fog, or even as dry particles.

Acid rain can harm people, animals, and plants. It is especially harmful to lakes. Thousands of lakes in Canada, Finland, Norway, and Sweden have been declared "dead." Not even algae can live in them. Birds and other species that depend on the lakes for food are also affected. Acid rain can also affect crops and trees. Buildings, statues, and cars are also damaged when acid rain destroys metal, stone, and paint.

What is the Ozone Layer?

Our atmosphere is made up of different layers. One layer, between 6 and 30 miles above the Earth, is made up of ozone gas. This **ozone layer** protects us from the Sun's harshest rays, called **ultraviolet** or **UV rays.** These rays can cause sunburn and skin cancer.

When old refrigerators, air conditioners, and similar items are thrown away, gases from them (called **chlorofluorocarbons,** or CFCs) rise into the air and destroy some of the ozone in this layer. Most countries no longer produce CFCs, but the gas can stay in the atmosphere for years—destroying ozone and adding to the greenhouse effect.

Each August, a **hole in the ozone layer** forms over Antarctica (it usually closes by December). Since it was discovered in the 1980s, it has doubled to about the size of North America. It sometimes extends over southern Chile and Argentina. On some days, people in Punta Arenas, Chile (the world's southernmost city), may limit their sun exposure to no more than 20 minutes between noon and 3 P.M. Other days, they don't go out at all!

What is Smog?
The brownish haze seen mostly in the summer and especially around big cities is **smog**. The main ingredient in smog is ozone. When ozone is high up in the atmosphere, it helps protect us from the Sun's stronger rays. But near the ground, ozone forms smog when sunlight and heat interact with oxygen and particles produced by the burning of fossil fuels. Smog makes it hard for some people to breathe, especially those with asthma. "Ozone Alerts" are not just for Los Angeles (famous for its smog). Many cities in the U.S. issue them through newspapers, TV, and radio stations to let people know when the air can be unhealthy for outdoor activities.

WEB SITE For more information visit *www.epa.gov/airnow/aqikids*

BREATHE

What is Global Warming

The average surface temperature on Earth was 57.9°F in 2004. Since accurate record keeping began in 1880, we know that it is an average of about 1°F higher than it was 100 years ago. Globally, 2004 was the fourth hottest on record so far, behind 1998, 2002, and 2003. The 10 hottest years on record have all been since 1990. (For the U.S., 2004 was the sixth wettest year and the 24th hottest, with an average temperature of 53.5°F). This gradual rise is called global warming. On that much, scientists agree. What they can't agree on is the cause. Some think it is just part of a natural cycle of warming and cooling. But most scientists believe that an increase in certain gases in the air generated by human activity plays a big role.

The **greenhouse effect** is a natural process, needed for life to exist on Earth. Certain gases in the atmosphere act like the glass walls of a greenhouse: they let the rays of the Sun pass through to the Earth's surface but hold in some of the heat that radiates from the Sun-warmed Earth. These naturally occurring greenhouse gases include water vapor, carbon dioxide, methane, nitrous oxide, and ozone. Without these gases, Earth's average temperature would be much colder.

Heat from the Sun

Most heat is trapped in atmosphere

Carbon dioxide, other gases from cars and factories trap extra heat.

Some heat escapes

Human activity is putting more of these "greenhouse gases" into the air. As cities have grown in size and population, people have needed more and more electricity, cars, and manufactured things of all kinds. As industries have grown, more greenhouse gases have been produced by the burning of fossil fuels such as oil, coal, and natural gas. The increases in these gases make the greenhouse "glass" thicker, causing more heat to be trapped than in the past.

It doesn't seem like much, but a slight warming could cause changes in the climate of many regions. If the climate changed enough, plants and animals would not be able to survive in their native habitats. Many scientists think average temperatures could rise as much as 6°F over the next 100 years. This warming could cause a lot of ice near the North and South Poles to melt, making more water go into the oceans and causing flooding along coasts.

WATER, WATER EVERYWHERE

Earth is the water planet. More than two-thirds of its surface is covered with water, and every living thing on it needs water to live. Water is not only part of our life (drinking, cooking, cleaning, bathing); it makes up 75% of our brains and 60% of our whole bodies! Humans can survive for about a month without food, but only for about a week without water. People also use water to cool machines in factories, to produce power, and to irrigate farmland.

HOW MUCH IS THERE TO DRINK? Seawater makes up 97% of the world's water. Another 2% of the water is frozen in ice caps, icebergs, glaciers, and sea ice. Half of the 1% left is too far underground to be reached. That leaves only 0.5% of **freshwater** for all the people, plants, and animals on Earth. This supply is renewable only by rainfall.

WHERE DOES DRINKING WATER COME FROM? Most smaller cities and towns get their freshwater from **groundwater**—melted snow and rain that seeps deep into the ground and is drawn out from wells. Larger cities usually rely on lakes or **reservoirs** for their water. Some areas of the world with little fresh water are turning to a process called **desalinization** (removing salt from seawater) as a solution. But this process is slow and expensive.

THE HYDROLOGICAL CYCLE: WATER'S ENDLESS JOURNEY Water is special. It's the only thing on Earth that exists naturally in **all three physical states**: solid (ice), liquid, and gas (water vapor). It never boils naturally (except around volcanoes), but it evaporates (turns into a gas) easily into the air. These unique properties send water on a cycle of repeating events.

clouds
rain
evaporation
snow
ocean

HOW DOES WATER GET INTO THE AIR? Heat from the sun causes surface water in oceans, lakes, swamps, and rivers to turn into water vapor. This is called **evaporation**. Plants release water vapor into the air as part of the process called **transpiration**. Animals also release a little bit when they breathe.

HOW DOES WATER COME OUT OF THE AIR? Warm air holds more water vapor than cold air. As the air rises into the atmosphere, it cools and the water vapor **condenses**—changes back into tiny water droplets. These droplets form clouds. As the drops get bigger, gravity pulls them down as **precipitation** (rain, snow, sleet, fog, and dew are all types of precipitation).

WHERE DOES THE WATER GO? Depending on where the precipitation lands, it can: **1.** evaporate back into the atmosphere; **2.** run off into streams and rivers; **3.** be absorbed by plants; **4.** soak down into the soil as ground water; **5.** fall as snow on a glacier and be trapped as ice for thousands of years.

Why We Need **Wetlands**

Wetlands are—you guessed it—**wet lands**. They are wet (covered with water, or with water at or near the surface) at least part of every year. Bogs, swamps, and marshes are all kinds of wetlands.

Wetlands have at least three important functions:

▶ **Storing water.** They absorb water like giant sponges and hold it in, releasing it slowly. During floods an acre of wetland can hold in 1.5 million gallons of water.

▶ **Cleaning up water.** They slow water flow down and let harmful sediments drop to the bottom. Plant roots and tiny organisms remove human and animal waste.

▶ **Providing habitats.** They are home to huge numbers of plants, fish, and wildlife. More than one-third of all threatened and endangered species in the U.S. live only in wetlands.

There are about 100 million acres of wetlands left in the lower 48 states, less than half of what there were in 1600. Wetlands are lost when people drain and fill them in for farmland, dam them up to form ponds and lakes, or pave and build up surrounding areas.

◀ *Wetlands, Everglades National Park*

WATER WOES

Pollution Polluted water can't be used for drinking, swimming, or watering crops, or provide a habitat for plants and animals. Major sources of water pollutants are sewage, chemicals from factories, fertilizers and weed killers, and landfills that leak. In general, anything that anyone dumps on the ground finds its way into the water cycle. Each year, the United Nations promotes March 22 as **"World Water Day"** to remind people how important it is to protect precious freshwater.

Overuse Using water faster than nature can pass it through the hydrological cycle can create other problems. When more water is taken out of lakes and reservoirs (for drinking, bathing, and other uses) than is put back in, the water levels begin to drop. Combined with lower than normal rainfall, this can be devastating. In some cases, lakes become salty or dry up completely.

The Dreaded Dripping Faucet: Just one faucet, dripping very slowly (once a minute), can waste 38 gallons of water a year. Multiply that by several million houses and apartments, and you see a lot of water going down the drain!

WHERE GARBAGE GOES

Most of the things around you will be thrown away someday. Skates, clothes, the toaster, furniture—they can break or wear out, or you may get tired of them. Where will they go when they are thrown out? What kinds of waste will they create?

LOOK at WHAT Is NOW in U.S. LANDFILLS

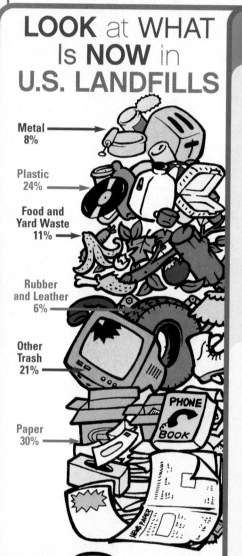

- Metal 8%
- Plastic 24%
- Food and Yard Waste 11%
- Rubber and Leather 6%
- Other Trash 21%
- Paper 30%

WHAT HAPPENS TO THINGS WE THROW AWAY?

Landfills

Most of our trash goes to places called landfills. A **landfill** (or dump) is a low area of land that is filled with garbage. Most modern landfills are lined with a layer of plastic or clay to try to keep dangerous liquids from seeping into the soil and ground water supply.

The Problem with Landfills

More than half of the states in this country are running out of places to dump their garbage. Because of the unhealthful materials many contain, landfills do not make good neighbors, and people don't want to live near them. But where can cities dispose of their waste? How can hazardous waste — material that can poison air, land, and water — be disposed of in a safe way?

Incinerators

One way to get rid of trash is to burn it. Trash is burned in a furnace-like device called an **incinerator**. Because incinerators can get rid of almost all of the bulk of the trash, some communities would rather use incinerators than landfills.

The Problem with Incinerators

Leftover ash and smoke from burning trash may contain harmful chemicals, called **pollutants**, and make it hard for some people to breathe. They can harm plants, animals, and people.

did you know?

That's a lot of paper! The U.S. recycled an all-time high of 50 million tons of paper, or about 300 pounds per person, in 2004. That's about half of the paper produced in the U.S. in a year. By the year 2012, the paper industry hopes to recycle 55% by the paper it produces. Germany and Finland currently reuse about 75% of the paper they produce. Back in 1990, the U.S. was recycling only about a third of its paper.

Reduce, Reuse, Recycle

You can help reduce waste by reusing containers, batteries, and paper. You can also recycle newspaper, glass, and plastics to provide materials for making other products. Below are some of the things you can do.

	TO REDUCE WASTE	TO RECYCLE
Paper	Use both sides of the paper. Use cloth towels instead of paper towels.	Recycle newspapers, magazines, comic books, and junk mail.
Plastic	Wash food containers and store leftovers in them. Reuse plastic bags.	Return soda bottles to the store. Recycle other plastics.
Glass	Keep bottles and jars to store other things.	Recycle glass bottles and jars.
Clothes	Give clothes to younger relatives or friends. Donate clothes to thrift shops.	Cut unwearable clothing into rags to use instead of paper towels.
Metal	Keep leftovers in storage containers instead of wrapping them in foil. Use glass or stainless steel pans instead of disposable pans.	Recycle aluminum cans and foil trays. Return wire hangers to the dry cleaner.
Food/ Yard Waste	Cut the amount of food you throw out. Try saving leftovers for snacks or meals later on.	Make a compost heap using food scraps, leaves, grass clippings, and the like.
Batteries	Use rechargeable batteries for toys and games, radios, tape players, and flashlights.	Find out about your town's rules for recycling or disposing of batteries.

What Is Made From RECYCLED MATERIALS?

▶ *From* RECYCLED PAPER we get newspapers, cereal boxes, wrapping paper, cardboard containers, and insulation.

▶ *From* RECYCLED PLASTIC we get soda bottles, tables, benches, bicycle racks, cameras, backpacks, carpeting, shoes, and clothes.

▶ *From* RECYCLED STEEL we get steel cans, cars, bicycles, nails, and refrigerators.

▶ *From* RECYCLED GLASS we get glass jars and tiles.

▶ *From* RECYCLED RUBBER we get bulletin boards, floor tiles, playground equipment, and speed bumps.

Fashion

What are waist overalls? page 83

What's in fashion now? Cargo pants? Tunic shirts? Flip-flops? Hip-hop hoodies might be popular in street-smart Manhattan, while Bermuda shorts set the scene in sunny California.

The idea of wearing fashionable clothes is fairly new. As late as the 1700s you couldn't just walk to the store and buy a new outfit—clothing took a long time to make and was often sewn at home. However, toward the end of the 18th century, engravings of fashionable clothes from Paris, France began to be shown around Europe. The first international fashion trends began.

In the 20th century, fashion really took off. Clothing could be made ready-to-wear, and bought cheaply from stores. Skirts were slim in the 1940s, and full in the 1950s. Then, in the 1960s, wild styles really took off. Young people set the trends, wearing dashikis, miniskirts, tie-dyed shirts, and bell-bottomed pants.

A couple in 18th-century fashions

Today, there are many different popular styles—hip-hop, surfer, punk, goth, and preppy, to name just a few. At schools, many students wear outfits that fit in with their particular group. Would the kids pictured at right fit in at your school? What do you think they should be wearing to look more fashionable?

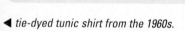

◀ *tie-dyed tunic shirt from the 1960s.*

did you know?

THE NAME GAME. *French designer Christian Dior was the first to have his name become known world-wide as a clothing brand. He introduced his "New Look" of clothing in 1947 in Paris. Since then, designers have put their names at the forefront of fashion—creating labels that announce who designed the clothing you wear. You've heard of Calvin Klein, Ralph Lauren, Sean Jean (a.k.a. P. Diddy, a.k.a. Sean Combs), Prada, and Jennifer Lopez. These are only a few designers whose names have become fashion statements.*

ALL ABOUT JEANS

Baggy or hip-hugger, straight-leg or boot-cut, jeans are one of the most fashionable garments in the world today. Their popularity and diversity would probably surprise Jacob Davis, the tailor who invented them in 1873. He simply wanted to make tough work pants for local miners in Reno, Nevada.

Davis used thick cloth, including denim. That was nothing new. His stroke of genius came with the addition of metal rivets, or fasteners, at stress points like the seams and pockets. Workers found that the rivets made the pants last much longer.

Davis went into business with Levi Strauss, a wealthy San Francisco merchant. Levi Strauss & Co. was soon cranking out thousands of "waist overalls"—as jeans were then called—for cowboys, lumberjacks, and anyone else who worked with their hands.

Levi Strauss changed its top product very little over the years. In 1922, the company added belt loops because men stopped using suspenders.

But the pace of change picked up in the 1960s. People began calling the pants "jeans" instead of "overalls." A T-shirt and jeans became the outfit of choice for casual baby boomers. Bell bottoms and boot-cut versions appeared in stores. In the 1970s, designer versions cemented jeans' place in popular culture. By the 1980s, hundreds of companies produced the pre-washed, pre-faded jeans so common today.

Threadbare Maze

Finish

See this pile of clothes? Does it remind you of the floor in your bedroom closet—or your whole room? Can you thread through this garment maze?

Start

ANSWERS ON PAGES 335-338. FOR MORE PUZZLES GO TO WWW.WORLDALMANACFORKIDS.COM

Games & Toys

How likely are you to roll a "7" with two dice?   page 86

Want to Play?

It's a safe bet that games and toys have been around as long as people have. The earliest toys were probably natural things kids found lying around: stones, clay, and sticks. Most of our clues about the earliest games come from things ancient peoples left behind. Baked clay marbles dating back to 3000 B.C. have been found in prehistoric caves.

Kids still play with simple things like blocks, clay, and sticks, but toys and games sure have come a long way in the age of machines and computers!

VIDEO GAME TIMELINE

1961—*Spacewar*, played on an early microcomputer, is the first fully interactive video game.

1974—Atari's *Pong*, one of the first home video games, has "paddles" to hit a white dot back and forth on-screen.

1980—*Pac-Man*, *Space Invaders*, and *Asteroids* (first to let high scorers enter initials) invade arcades.

1985—Nintendo Entertainment System comes to the U.S. *Super Mario Bros.* is a huge hit!

1987—*Legend of Zelda* game released.

1989—Nintendo's handheld video game system, Game Boy, debuts.

1996—Nintendo 64 is released.

2000—Sony's PlayStation 2 arrives.

2001—Microsoft's Xbox and Nintendo's GameCube hit the shelves.

2005—Sony's PSP, a new handheld video game system, goes on sale.

COOLEST KIDS' VIDEO GAMES

Are you interested in history? War? Football? Popular movies? Magic? Video games come in all styles—there's probably one that will capture your interest. Here are a few we think are the coolest.

- **Rome: Total War**—This is a strategic game where the player must figure out how wars can be won. The game also allows you to reenact real historical events.

- **Madden NFL 2005**—This is one of the most popular games in the world. You can play video-football alone or with friends, and even create a fan to cheer from the crowd.

- **Shrek 2**—Guide Shrek and his friends through an adventure both in familiar places from the movie and in all-new settings.

- **Tak 2: The Staff of Dreams**—Have you ever wanted to take a magical tour through a colorful world of nightmare creatures, juju gods, and spirit animals? *Tak 2* allows you to master ancient magic for an imaginary adventure.

TIMELESS TOYS

THE BOOMERANG is actually an ancient weapon invented by Australian Aborigines that is thought to be about 10,000 years old. Today, the returning boomerang is sold as a toy all over the world.

LINCOLN LOGS®, first sold in 1916, have been a popular toy for almost 90 years. This toy was invented by John Lloyd Wright, son of Frank Lloyd Wright, one of the most famous architects in U.S. history. John Lloyd Wright was inspired to built the toy after seeing the construction of the Imperial Hotel in Tokyo, which his father designed.

SILLY PUTTY® bounced into stores in 1949. It used to be called "Nutty Putty" and was designed by an engineer who mixed silicone oil with boric acid to create the rubbery substance.

MATCHBOX® CARS, invented in 1952, were first designed for a girl to play with! Jack Odell created a brass miniature of a Road Roller car and put it in a matchbox-size container so that his daughter could take it to school.

MR. POTATO HEAD, invented in 1952, was the first toy ever advertised on TV. This toy, with detachable nose, ears, and glasses, was designed to be used with a real potato.

BARBIE® DOLL, one of the most popular toys in history, was "born" in 1959. Created by Mattel, Inc. founders Ruth and Elliot Handler, the doll was named after their daughter Barbie. Ken, named after their son, came out in 1961.

ETCH A SKETCH® began entertainng "arty" kids in 1960. When you turn the knobs, a stylus scrapes aluminum powder off the inside of the screen to draw a line.

NERF® balls first floated onto the scene in 1969. This indoor/outdoor ball made of polyurethane foam sold 4 million in its first year. In 1972, the king of all Nerf toys—the Nerf football—was introduced.

Other Classic Toys

Teddy Bear	1902
Crayola® Crayons	1903
Erector Set®	1913
Tinkertoys	1914
Raggedy Ann Doll	1915
Yo-Yos	1929
Tonka® Trucks	1947
LEGO®	1949
Wiffle® Ball	1953
Play-Doh®	1956
Easy-Bake Oven	1963
G.I. JOE	1963
Twister®	1966
Battleship	1967
Hot Wheels	1968
Rubik's® Cube ➡	1979
Cabbage Patch Kids®	1983

A **Dice** Game **You** "Probably" **Know**

YAHTZEE is a popular dice game for two or more players. Players roll any or all dice up to three times per turn. Points are scored by rolling different combinations of dice (some combination names are borrowed from poker, like "straight," "full house," and "three of a kind"). Rolling the same number on all five dice is a "yahtzee." Scores are added in 13 categories, and the player with the highest point total wins.

According to Yahtzee's maker, Hasbro, the game was invented in 1956 by a wealthy Canadian couple who played a "yacht game" with friends on their yacht.

Homework Help

LUCKY 7:
UNDERSTANDING PROBABILITY

Probability can be a fun subject, and it may be a little more fun and easier to learn about if you think of it in terms of the dice you use to play games with.

A single die has six different faces, numbered 1 through 6. Each has an equal chance of coming up. So the chance, or **probability,** of rolling any one of the numbers with one die is one in six. We write this as the ratio or fraction: 1/6, because there are six possible **outcomes.**

What if you roll two dice? There are 36 possible outcomes, because each die can come out one of six ways; 6 x 6 = 36. The lowest possible outcome would be 2 (a 1 on each die). The highest possible outcome would be 12 (a 6 on each die).

With two dice, some totals are more likely to come up than others. Pretend that the dice are red and blue. The the only way to roll a total of 2 ("snake eyes") is for the red die to come up as a 1 and the blue die to come up as a 1. So the probability of shaking 2 is 1 in 36 (1/36). But there are two ways to shake a 3. The red die could have a 1 and the blue die could have a 2, or the red die could be a 2 and the blue die could be a 1. So the probability of shaking a 3 is 2 in 36 (2/36, which equals 1/18).

The total that has the most possible outcomes is 7. The red die can be any of the numbers from 1 to 6, and the blue die can be the number that makes seven when added to the number on the red die (1 and 6, 2 and 5, 3 and 4, 4 and 3, 5 and 2, 6 and 1). Since there are six possible combinations to total 7, the chances of rolling a 7 are 6 in 36 (6/36, which equals 1/6, or one out of six).

	Look below for your chances of shaking each total with two dice.
2	1 in 36
3	2 in 36
4	3 in 36
5	4 in 36
6	5 in 36
7	6 in 36
8	5 in 36
9	4 in 36
10	3 in 36
11	2 in 36
12	1 in 36

did you know?

Dice have been found in Egyptian tombs dating back to 2000 B.C..
Through history, dice have been made from the stones of fruit,
seeds, animal bones, horn, pebbles, pottery, walnut shells, and the teeth of beaver.

HOW TO PLAY SPADES

Spades is a popular four-player card game. Players sit across from each other and play as two two-player teams. All the cards are dealt out so that each player has 13. Before starting, each player must try to figure out how many "tricks" he or she can win during a hand. The partners can discuss how many tricks they think each can take, but they can't say what their cards are. The number they think they can win together is their "bid." The player to the left of the dealer puts down a card in the middle of the table. This is called "leading." Any card but a spade may be led to start the game. Each player, in turn, puts down one card of the same suit. A player who does not have any of the suit that has been led (cannot "follow suit") can play a spade. Spades are "trump" in this game, which means that spades beat cards of other suits.

Object: To be the first team to score 500 points by winning **tricks**.

WINNING TRICKS

Once the game begins, players can no longer communicate with their partners (including kicks under the table).

There are two ways to win a trick. The first way is to put down the highest card of the suit being played. The ace of diamonds, for example, would win any trick of all diamonds. The second way to win is by playing a trump. In this game, spades are a "trump" suit. The hand shown (above right) has no diamonds, so the player can put down a spade as a trump and win the trick (below right). That means that a spade beats a card of any other suit, even an ace. Once spades have been played in a round, or "broken," a spade can be led (played first). The player who wins a trick "leads" the next card. A hand is over when all 13 tricks have been won.

KEEPING SCORE

Suppose each partner thought four tricks could be won. Together, the partners' bid is eight. If they don't make their total bid, for example by getting only seven tricks, they lose 80 points—10 for each trick they bid. If they win 10 tricks, they get 82 points—10 points for each of the eight they bid and one point each for the two extra tricks (extra tricks are called "bags"). But, if a team keeps going over their bid during a game of Spades, they can lose points. Everytime a team has a total of 10 bags—a "sandbag"—they lose 100 points.

It is possible to bid "nil," or nothing. If a team makes it through a nil bid without winning a trick, they are rewarded with 100 points. If they win a trick, they lose 100 points.

The first team to reach 500 points wins. If both reach 500 on the same deal, the team with the higher score wins.

Toy Designer

Kate Lewis

Q: Is designing toys something you thought you might do for a living someday?

I knew that I wanted a career that was artistic and challenging. I wanted variety in my work. Also, I love children because they are so honest and funny. I wanted a job that would keep me close to kids.

Q: What got you interested in working as a designer?

I wanted to find a career in which I would use all sides of my brain. I considered architecture, graphic design, and Web design, but finally found product design most satisfying. Making products that all people could use seemed exciting. My love of kids led me to toy design. It is very satisfying, after working for many months, to hold the final product in your hand.

Q: What do you do on a typical day?

My job is different every day, but it is always fun. I might draw toy concepts with markers or on the computer, or I might review ideas with the people who will help sell the toys. At times, I work with engineers to fix mechanical problems with the products. On slower days we go to the toy store to see what else is out there or just surf the Internet for inspiration. A lot of time is spent simply playing with toys!

Q: What sort of skills or interests are needed for this kind of work?

It is most important that someone interested in being a toy designer likes to draw. We draw, draw, and draw every day. It is very important to be able to picture things in three dimensions in your head.

Kate designed the toy above, an activity table for infants. First, she brainstormed what parts the toy needed to work. Then, she started sketching ideas on paper. When she knew what she wanted the toy to look like, she drew the drawing at left with markers, to show how all of the parts work together. This drawing would help her company build the toy, because it shows how each part needs to look and fit together.

Geography

What is a compass rose?   page 92

Sizing up THE EARTH

The word "geography" comes from the Greek word *geographia*, meaning "writing about the earth." It was first used by the Greek scholar Eratosthenes, who was head of the great library of Alexandria in Egypt. Around 230 B.C., when many people believed the world was flat, he did a remarkable thing. He calculated the circumference of the Earth. His figure of about 25,000 miles was close to the modern measurement at 24,901 miles!

Actually, the Earth is not perfectly round. It's flatter at the poles and bulges out a little at the middle. This bulge around the equator is due to centrifugal force from the Earth's rotation. ("Centrifugal" means "moving away from the center." Think of how a merry-go-round pushes you to the outside as it spins.) The Earth's diameter is 7,926 miles at the equator, but only 7,900 miles from North Pole to South Pole. The total surface area of the Earth is 196,940,000 square miles.

Geography 1-2-3

LONGEST RIVERS	1. Nile (Egypt and Sudan)—4,160 miles 2. Amazon (Brazil and Peru)—4,000 miles 3. Chang (China)—3,940 miles (formerly called the Yangtze)
TALLEST MOUNTAINS	1. Mount Everest (Tibet and Nepal)—29,035 feet 2. K2 (Kashmir)—28,250 feet 3. Kanchenjunga (India and Nepal)—28,208 feet
BIGGEST ISLANDS	1. Greenland (Atlantic Ocean)—840,000 square miles 2. New Guinea (Pacific Ocean)—306,000 square miles 3. Borneo (Pacific Ocean)—280,100 square miles
BIGGEST DESERT REGIONS	1. Sahara Desert (North Africa)—3.5 million square miles 2. Australian Deserts—1.3 million square miles 3. Arabian Peninsula—1 million square miles
BIGGEST LAKES	1. Caspian Sea (Europe and Asia)—143,244 square miles 2. Superior (U.S. and Canada)—31,700 square miles 3. Victoria (Kenya, Tanzania, Uganda)—26,828 square miles
HIGHEST WATERFALLS	1. Angel Falls (Venezuela)—3,212 feet 2. Tugela Falls (South Africa)—2,800 feet 3. Monge Falls (Norway)—2,540 feet

THE **SEVEN CONTINENTS** AND **FOUR OCEANS**

ASIA
Area: 12,000,000 square miles
2005 population: 3,910,766,590
Highest pt.: Mt. Everest (Nepal/Tibet) 29,035 ft.
Lowest pt.: Dead Sea (Israel/Jordan) −1,348 ft.

OCEANIA (including Australia)
Area: 3,300,000 square miles
2005 population: 32,744,469
Highest pt.: Jaya, New Guinea 16,500
Lowest pt.: Lake Eyre, Australia −52 ft.

ARCTIC OCEAN
5,105,700 square miles
3,407 feet avg. depth

INDIAN OCEAN
28,350,500 square miles
12,598 feet avg. depth

EUROPE
Area: 8,800,000 square miles
2005 population: 729,441,727
Highest pt.: Mt. Elbrus (Russia) 18,510 ft.
Lowest pt.: Caspian Sea −92 ft.

ATLANTIC OCEAN
33,420,000 square miles
11,370 feet avg. depth

AFRICA
Area: 11,500,000 square miles
2005 population: 887,223,098
Highest pt.: Mt. Kilimanjaro (Tanzania) 19,340 ft.
Lowest pt.: Lake Assal (Djibouti) −512 ft.

NORTH AMERICA
Area: 8,300,000 square miles
2005 population: 541,684,479
Highest pt.: Mt. McKinley (AK) 20,320 ft.
Lowest pt.: Death Valley (CA) −282 ft.

PACIFIC OCEAN
64,186,300 square miles
12,925 feet avg. depth

SOUTH AMERICA
Area: 6,800,000 square miles
2005 population: 371,271,037
Highest pt.: Mt. Aconcagua (Arg.) 22,834 ft.
Lowest pt.: Valdes Peninsula (Arg.) −131 ft.

ANTARCTICA
Area: 5,400,000 square miles
2005 population: no permanent residents
Highest pt.: Vinson Massif 16,864 ft.
Lowest pt.: Bently Subglacial Trench −8,327 ft.

N E S W

LOOKING *at our* WORLD ★

THINKING **GLOBAL**

Shaped like a ball or sphere, a globe is a model of our planet. Like Earth, it's not perfectly round. It is an oblate spheroid (called a "geoid") that bulges a little in the middle.

In 1569, Gerardus Mercator found a way to project the Earth's curved surface onto a flat map. One problem with a Mercator map is that land closer to the poles appears bigger than it is. Australia looks smaller than Greenland on this type of map, but in reality it's not.

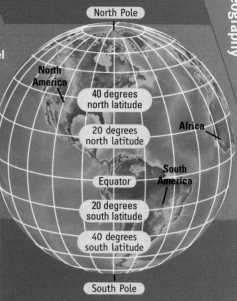

North Pole

North America

40 degrees north latitude

20 degrees north latitude

Africa

South America

Equator

20 degrees south latitude

40 degrees south latitude

South Pole

LATITUDE AND LONGITUDE

Imaginary lines that run east and west around Earth, parallel to the equator, are called **parallels**. They tell you the **latitude** of a place, or how far it is from the equator. The equator is at 0 degrees latitude. As you go farther north or south, the latitude increases. The North Pole is at 90 degrees **north latitude**. The South Pole is at 90 degrees **south latitude**.

Imaginary lines that run north and south around the globe, from one pole to the other, are called **meridians**. They tell you the degree of **longitude**, or how far east or west a place is from an imaginary line called the **Greenwich meridian** or **prime meridian** (0 degrees). That line runs through the city of Greenwich in England.

Which Hemispheres Do *You* Live In?

Draw an imaginary line around the middle of Earth. This is the **equator**. It splits Earth into two halves called **hemispheres**. The part north of the equator, including North America, is the **northern hemisphere**. The part south of the equator is the **southern hemisphere**.

You can also divide Earth into east and west. North and South America are in the **western hemisphere**. Africa, Asia, and most of Europe are in the **eastern hemisphere**.

THE **TROPICS** OF **CANCER** AND **CAPRICORN**

If you find the equator on a globe or map, you'll often see two dotted lines running parallel to it, one above and one below (see pages 153 and 162–163). The top one marks the Tropic of Cancer, an imaginary line marking the latitude (about 23.5° North) where the sun is directly overhead on June 21 or 22, the beginning of summer in the northern hemisphere.

Below the equator is the Tropic of Capricorn (about 23.5° South). This line marks the sun's path directly overhead at noon on December 21 or 22, the beginning of summer in the southern hemisphere. The area between these dotted lines is the tropics, where it is consistently hot because the sun's rays shine more directly than they do farther north or south.

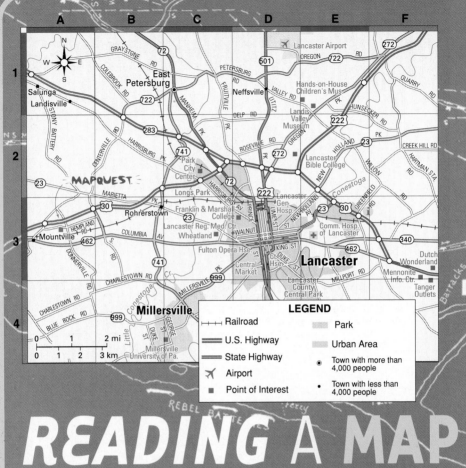

READING A MAP

DIRECTION Maps usually have a **compass rose** that shows you which way is north. On most maps, like this one, it's straight up. The compass rose on this map is in the upper left corner.

DISTANCE Of course the distances on a map are much shorter than the distances in the real world. The **scale** shows you how to estimate the real distance. This map's scale is in the lower left corner.

PICTURES Maps usually have little pictures or symbols to represent real things like roads, towns, airports, or other points of interest. The map **legend** (or **key**) tells what they mean.

FINDING PLACES Rather than use latitude and longitude to locate features, many maps, like this one, use a **grid system** with numbers on one side and letters on another. An **index**, listing place names in alphabetical order, gives a letter and a number for each. The letter and number tell you which square to look for a place on the map's **grid**. For example, Landisville can be found at A-1 on this map.

USING THE MAP People use maps to help them travel from one place to another. What if you lived in East Petersburg and wanted to go to the Hands-on-House Children's Museum? First, locate the two places on the map. East Petersburg is in C-1, and Hands-on-House is in E-1. Next, look at the roads that connect them and decide on the best route. (There could be several different ways to go.) One possibility is to head east on Route 722 until you get to Valley Road. Go southeast on Valley Road until you get to the museum.

VOLCANOES

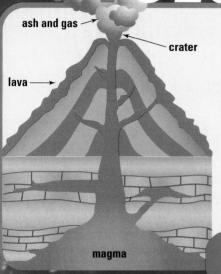

ash and gas
crater
lava
magma

A volcano is a mountain or hill (**cone**) with an opening on top known as a **crater**. Hot melted rock (**magma**), gases, and other material from inside the Earth mix together miles underground and rise up through cracks and weak spots. When enough pressure builds up, the magma may blast out, or erupt, through the crater. The magma is called **lava** when it reaches the air. This lava may be hotter than 2,000° Fahrenheit. The cone of this volcano is made of layers of lava and ash that have erupted, then cooled.

Some islands, like the Hawaiian islands, are really the tops of undersea volcanoes.

SOME FAMOUS VOLCANIC ERUPTIONS

Year	Volcano (place)	Deaths (approximate)
79	Mount Vesuvius (Italy)	16,000
1586	Kelut (Indonesia)	10,000
1792	Mount Unzen (Japan)	14,500
1815	Tambora (Indonesia)	10,000
1883	Krakatau or Krakatoa (Indonesia)	36,000
1902	Mount Pelée (Martinique)	28,000
1980	Mount St. Helens (U.S.)	57
1982	El Chichón (Mexico)	1,880
1985	Nevado del Ruiz (Colombia)	23,000
1986	Lake Nyos (Cameroon)	1,700
1991	Mt. Pinatubo (Philippines)	800

Where is the Ring of Fire?

The hundreds of active volcanoes found on the land near the edges of the Pacific Ocean make up what is called the **Ring of Fire**. They mark the boundary between the plates under the Pacific Ocean and the plates under the continents around the ocean. (The plates of the Earth are explained on page 94, with the help of a map.) The Ring of Fire runs all along the west coast of South and North America, from the southern tip of Chile to Alaska. The ring also runs down the east coast of Asia, starting in the far north in Kamchatka. It continues down past Australia.

Homework Help

There are three types of rock:

IGNEOUS rocks form from underground magma (melted rock) that cools and becomes solid. Granite is an igneous rock made from quartz, feldspar, and mica.

SEDIMENTARY rocks form on low-lying land or the bottom of seas. Layers of small particles harden into rock such as limestone or shale over millions of years.

METAMORPHIC rocks are igneous or sedimentary rocks that have been changed by chemistry, heat, or pressure (or all three). Marble is a metamorphic rock formed from limestone.

EARTHQUAKES

Earthquakes may be so weak that they are hardly felt, or strong enough to do great damage. There are thousands of earthquakes each year, but most are too small to be noticed. About 1 in 5 can be felt, and about 1 in 500 causes damage.

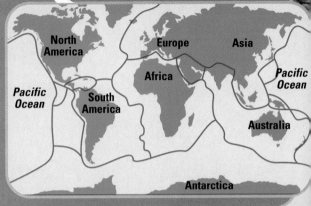

North America

Europe

Asia

Africa

Pacific Ocean

Pacific Ocean

South America

Australia

Antarctica

WHAT CAUSES EARTHQUAKES? To understand earthquakes, think of the Earth as a big round egg and imagine that the shell has been cracked. This cracked outer layer of the Earth (the eggshell) is called the **lithosphere,** and it is divided into huge pieces called **plates** (see map above). Underneath the lithosphere is a softer layer called the **asthenosphere.** The plates of the cracked lithosphere are constantly gliding over this softer layer, moving away from one another, toward one another, or past one another. These plates average about 60 miles thick. Earthquakes result when plates collide.

The cracks in the lithosphere that separate the plates are called **faults**. It is along these lines that many earthquakes occur as the plates smash into each other or grind alongside each other. Here are the different kinds of faults:

When the plates in Earth's outer layer slide against each other in a sideways motion, it's called a **strike-slip fault.**

When the plates move up and down, the fault is called a **dip-slip fault**. Dip-slip faults come in two varieties. When the higher plate ("hanging wall") moves down against the lower plate ("footwall") the result is called a **normal fault.**

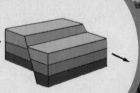

If the hanging wall moves up, it's called a **thrust fault** or a **reverse fault.** Thrust faults are the most common kind, and the largest earthquakes happen along thrust faults. One example was the big Northridge earthquake that struck near Los Angeles, California, in 1994, causing freeways and office buildings to collapse.

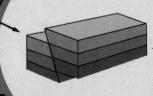

MAJOR EARTHQUAKES

The earthquakes listed here are among the largest and most destructive recorded in the past 100 years.

Year	Location	Magnitude	Deaths (approximate)
2005	near Indonesia	8.7	1,000+
2003	Iran (southeastern)	6.5	41,000+
2002	Afghanistan (northern)	6.1	1,000+
2001	India (western)	7.9	30,000+
1999	Turkey (western)	7.4	17,200+
1998	Afghanistan (northeastern)	6.9	4,700+
1995	Japan (Kobe)	6.9	5,502
1994	United States (Los Angeles area)	6.8	61
1990	Iran (western)	7.7	40,000+
1989	United States (San Francisco area)	7.1	62
1988	Soviet Armenia	7.0	55,000
1976	China (Tangshan)	8.0	255,000
1970	Peru (northern)	7.8	66,000
1960	near Chile	9.5	5,000
1939	Chile (Chillan)	8.3	28,000
1927	China (Nan-Shan)	8.3	200,000
1923	Japan (Yokohama)	8.3	143,000
1920	China (Gansu)	8.6	200,000
1906	Chile (Valparaiso)	8.6	20,000
	United States (San Francisco)	8.3	3,000+

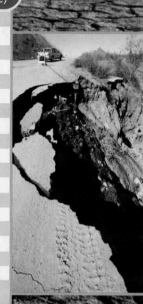

MEASURING EARTHQUAKES The Richter scale goes up to more than 9. These numbers indicate the strength of an earthquake. Each number means the quake releases about 30 times more energy than the number below it. An earthquake measuring 6 on the scale is about 30 times stronger than one measuring 5 and 900 times stronger than one measuring 4.

Earthquakes that are 4 or above are considered major. The damage and injuries caused by a quake also depend on other things, such as what the ground in the area is like, whether the area is heavily populated and built up, and how buildings are constructed.

TSUNAMI (pronounced *tsoo-NAH-mee*) comes from two Japanese words: "tsu" (harbor) and "nami" (wave). These huge waves are sometimes called tidal waves, but they have nothing to do with the tides.

The strongest tsunamis happen when a big part of the sea floor lifts along a fault (see page 94), pushing up a huge volume of water. The resulting waves are long and low, and might not even be noticed in deep water. They move at speeds of up to 500 miles per hour. As they near shore, they slow down and the great energy forces the water upward into big waves.

Many tsunamis are small, but sometimes they can reach heights of more than 90 feet. Tsunamis are most common in the Pacific Ocean because of the earthquake activity associated with the "Ring of Fire" (see page 93).

The **"Asian tsunami"** of Dec. 26, 2004, was triggered by a 9.0 magnitude earthquake off the coast of Indonesia in the Indian Ocean. As of late March 2005, estimates of the dead or missing were around 300,000 people in 12 countries. People were killed when the huge waves came unexpectedly on shore.

EARLY EXPLORATION

AROUND 1000 — **Leif Ericson**, from Iceland, explored "Vinland," which may have been the coasts of northeast Canada and New England.

1271-95 — **Marco Polo** (Italian) traveled through Central Asia, India, China, and Indonesia.

1488 — **Bartolomeu Dias** (Portuguese) explored the Cape of Good Hope in southern Africa.

1492-1504 — **Christopher Columbus** (Italian) sailed four times from Spain to America and started colonies there.

1497-98 — **Vasco da Gama** (Portuguese) sailed farther than Dias, around the Cape of Good Hope to East Africa and India.

1513 — **Juan Ponce de León** (Spanish) explored and named Florida.

1513 — **Vasco Núñez de Balboa** (Spanish) explored Panama and reached the Pacific Ocean.

1519-21 — **Ferdinand Magellan** (Portuguese) sailed from Spain around the tip of South America and across the Pacific Ocean to the Philippines, where he died. His expedition continued around the world.

1519-36 — **Hernando Cortés** (Spanish) conquered Mexico, traveling as far west as Baja California.

1527-42 — **Alvar Núñez Cabeza de Vaca** (Spanish) explored the southwestern United States, Brazil, and Paraguay.

1532-35 — **Francisco Pizarro** (Spanish) explored the west coast of South America and conquered Peru.

1534-36 — **Jacques Cartier** (French) sailed up the St. Lawrence River to the site of present-day Montreal.

1539-42 — **Hernando de Soto** (Spanish) explored the southeastern United States and the lower Mississippi Valley.

1603-13 — **Samuel de Champlain** (French) traced the course of the St. Lawrence River and explored the northeastern United States.

1609-10 — **Henry Hudson** (English), sailing from Holland, explored the Hudson River, Hudson Bay, and Hudson Strait.

1682 — **Robert Cavelier**, sieur de La Salle (French), traced the Mississippi River to its mouth in the Gulf of Mexico.

1768-78 — **James Cook** (English) charted the world's major bodies of water and explored Hawaii and Antarctica.

1804-06 — **Meriwether Lewis and William Clark** (American) traveled from St. Louis along the Missouri and Columbia rivers to the Pacific Ocean and back.

1849-59 — **David Livingstone** (Scottish) explored Southern Africa, including the Zambezi River and Victoria Falls.

ALL ABOUT... HERNANDO de SOTO

After helping conquer Peru in the 1530s, Hernando De Soto decided to conquer the unknown southern coast of what would become the United States. In May 1539, the wealthy Spanish explorer landed in what is now Tampa Bay, Florida, bringing along over 600 soldiers, nine ships, horses, pigs, attack dogs, and weapons. In 1540, De Soto marched across present-day Georgia, North and South Carolina, and Tennessee looking for riches. Along the way, his party abused many Indians living in nearby villages. Using Spain's cannons, muskets, and body armor, his men fought off Native Americans.

De Soto's men also carried fatal diseases from Europe, which killed thousands of Southeastern Indians, including people from the Cherokee, Seminole, and Choctaw tribes. After fighting their way north, DeSoto and his warriors turned backwards into present-day Alabama—searching unsuccessfully for gold, silver, and jewels. At the end of 1540, the explorer was wounded in a battle with Native Americans. De Soto stubbornly decided not to retreat to the Spanish ships waiting off the southern coast. During the winter, his soldiers set up camp in this area, which would become Mississippi, following King Charles V's order to "conquer, populate, and pacify" the area.

In the spring of 1541, the tired soldiers marched onwards. Even though the expedition was unprepared for another journey—supplies ran low and many soldiers had died—De Soto pushed north in a final attempt to conquer this vast country. Over the next few months, the group became the first Europeans to cross the Mississippi River. They followed the Arkansas River north, traveling all the way to present-day Oklahoma.

Once again, De Soto couldn't find any treasure, and his remaining troops limped back towards Florida empty-handed. Along the way, the Spanish conqueror fell ill with fever, and he died along the banks of the Mississippi River in May 1542. Fewer than half of De Soto's men survived the adventure. They struggled for another year without their leader. In 1543, they finally retreated to Spanish settlements in Mexico.

De Soto's expedition was a failure, but the survivors wrote vivid accounts of what they saw and experienced. These descriptions excited the imaginations of later adventurers. While De Soto thought only of riches, his expedition served to open up America for generations of explorers.

did you know?

Explorers Meriwether Lewis and William Clark brought food, clothing, and materials to build shelters on their expedition through the American West. They had almost two tons of supplies. However, there's one other important supply they brought—books! Their travel library included books on botany and history, a dictionary, a map, and, of course—an almanac!

What four basic qualities can your tongue taste? page 103

The New Food Pyramid

To stay healthy, it is important to eat the right foods and to exercise. In 2005, the U.S. government designed a new food pyramid to help people track what they should eat. The new pyramid shows that exercise is important to health, and comes with rules recommending different amounts of food depending on your age, gender, and activity level. The different widths of each part of the pyramid help you remember about how much you should be eating of each group.

GRAINS
Eat whole grain bread, cereal, crackers, rice, and pasta.

VEGETABLES
Try more dark green and orange vegetables.

FRUITS
Choose from fresh, frozen, canned or dried fruit.

OILS
Fish and nuts have oil. Vegetable oils are good, too. Butter and lard should be limited.

MILK
Low-fat or fat-free milk products are best.

MEAT & BEANS
Eat lean meats and poultry. Don't forget to try fish, beans, peas, and nuts.

MyPyramid.gov STEPS TO A HEALTHIER YOU

To figure out what you should be eating, based on your age, activity, and gender, use the calculator online: **WEB SITE** **www.mypyramid.gov**

For example, an active boy between ages 9 and 13 should eat about 2,600 calories daily, including:

Fruits	2 cups	Meat and Beans	6.5 ounces
Vegetables	3.5 cups	Milk	3 cups
Grains	9 ounces	Oils	8 teaspoons

We Are What We Eat

Have you ever noticed the labels on the packages of food you and your family buy? The labels provide information people need to make healthy choices about the foods they eat. Below are some terms you may see on labels.

NUTRIENTS ARE NEEDED

Nutrients are the parts of food the body can use for growth, for energy, and for repairing itself. Carbohydrates, fats, proteins, vitamins, minerals, and water are different kinds of nutrients found in food. **Carbohydrates** and **fats** provide energy. **Proteins** aid growth and help maintain and repair the body. **Vitamins** help the body use food, help eyesight and skin, and aid in fighting off infections. **Minerals** help build bones and teeth and aid in such functions as muscle contractions and blood clotting. **Water** helps with growth and repair of the body. It also helps the body digest food and get rid of wastes.

CALORIES COUNT

A **calorie** is a measure of how much energy we get from food. The government recommends the number of calories that should be taken in each day. Kids aged 7 to 12 and teenaged girls should eat about 2,200 calories daily. Teenaged boys need around 2,800. Active people—who play sports, for instance—may need more.

To maintain a **healthy weight,** it is important to balance the calories in the food you eat with the calories you use up. The more active you are, the more calories your body burns. If you eat more calories than your body uses, you will gain weight.

Junk food is a term for foods (such as candy, soda, and most desserts) that have lots of calories but not many nutrients.

Nutrition Facts

Serving Size 1/2 cup (1 oz.) = (30g)
Servings per container 14

Amount Per Serving	Cereal	Cereal w/ 1/2 cup Lowfat Milk
Calories	100	150
Calories from Fat	10	25

	% Daily Value**	
Total Fat 1g*	2%	4%
Saturated Fat 0g	0%	5%
Cholesterol 0mg	0%	3%
Sodium 50mg	2%	5%
Total Carbohydrates 20g	7%	9%
Dietary Fiber 2g	8%	8%
Sugars 5g		
Protein 4g		
Vitamin A	0%	6%
Vitamin C	0%	2%
Calcium	0%	15%
Iron	2%	4%

* Amount in Cereal. One half cup lowfat milk contributes an additional 50 calories, 1.5g total fat (1g saturated fat), 9 mg cholesterol, 60mg sodium, 6g total carbohydrates (6g sugars), and 3g protein.
** Percents (%) of a Daily Value are based on a 2,000 calorie diet. Your Daily Values may vary higher or lower depending on your calorie needs:

Nutrient	Calories	2,000	2,500
Total Fat	Less than	65g	80g
Sat Fat	Less than	20g	25g
Cholesterol	Less than	300mg	300mg
Sodium	Less than	2,400mg	2,400mg
Total Carbohydrates		300g	375g
Dietary Fiber		25g	30g

Calories per gram:
Fat 9 • Carbohydrate 4 • Protein

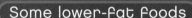

Some lower-fat foods

chicken burrito
baked chips
fruit salad
vegetable dumplings
oatmeal
frozen yogurt
green salad

Some fatty foods

beef burrito
fried chips
apple pie
pork dumplings
ham and egg sandwich
ice cream
potato salad

A Little Fat Goes a Long Way

Fat keeps your body warm. It gives the muscles energy. It helps keep skin soft and healthy. About 25% to 35% of your calories should come from fat, if you're over two years old. But many Americans have too much fat in their diets.

Cholesterol. Eating too much fat can make some people's bodies produce too much **cholesterol** (ka-**less**-ter-all). This waxy substance can build up over the years on the inside of arteries. Too much cholesterol keeps blood from flowing freely through the arteries and can cause serious health problems such as heart attacks.

Body Basics:

Your body is made up of many different parts that work together every minute of every day and night. It's more amazing than any machine or computer. Even though everyone's body looks different outside, people have the same parts inside. Each system of the body has its own job. Some of the systems also work together to keep you healthy and strong.

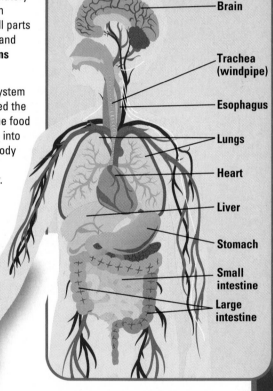

Brain

Trachea (windpipe)

Esophagus

Lungs

Heart

Liver

Stomach

Small intestine

Large intestine

CIRCULATORY SYSTEM In the circulatory system, the **heart** pumps **blood**, which then travels through tubes, called **arteries**, to all parts of the body. The blood carries the oxygen and food that the body needs to stay alive. **Veins** carry the blood back to the heart.

DIGESTIVE SYSTEM The digestive system moves food through parts of the body called the **esophagus**, **stomach**, and **intestines**. As the food passes through, some of it is broken down into tiny particles called **nutrients**, which the body needs. Nutrients enter the bloodstream, which carries them to all parts of the body. The digestive system then changes the remaining food into waste that is eliminated from the body.

ENDOCRINE SYSTEM

The endocrine system includes **glands** that are needed for some body functions. There are two kinds of glands. **Exocrine** glands produce liquids such as sweat and saliva. **Endocrine** glands produce chemicals called hormones. **Hormones** control body functions, such as growth.

NERVOUS SYSTEM The nervous system enables us to think, feel, move, hear, and see. It includes the **brain**, the **spinal cord**, and **nerves** in all parts of the body. Nerves in the spinal cord carry signals back and forth between the brain and the rest of the body. The brain tells us what to do and how to respond. It has three major parts. The **cerebrum** controls thinking, speech, and vision. The **cerebellum** is responsible for physical coordination. The **brain stem** controls the respiratory, circulatory, and digestive systems.

RESPIRATORY SYSTEM The respiratory system allows us to breathe. Air comes into the body through the nose and mouth. It goes through the **windpipe** (or **trachea**) to two tubes (called **bronchi**), which carry air to the **lungs**. Oxygen from the air is taken in by tiny blood vessels in the lungs. The blood then carries oxygen to the cells of the body.

What the Body's Systems Do

SKELETAL SYSTEM

SKELETAL SYSTEM The skeletal system is made up of the **bones** that hold your body upright. Some bones protect organs, such as the ribs that cover the lungs.

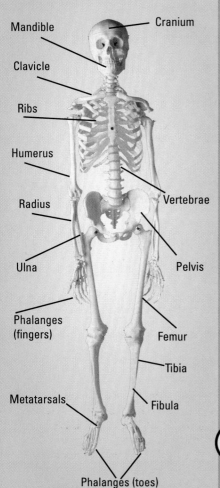

- Mandible
- Cranium
- Clavicle
- Ribs
- Humerus
- Radius
- Vertebrae
- Ulna
- Pelvis
- Phalanges (fingers)
- Femur
- Tibia
- Metatarsals
- Fibula
- Phalanges (toes)

MUSCULAR SYSTEM

MUSCULAR SYSTEM Muscles are made up of elastic fibers. There are three types of muscle: **skeletal, smooth,** and **cardiac.** The skeletal muscles help the body move—they are the large muscles we can see. Smooth muscles are found in our digestive system, blood vessels, and air passages. Cardiac muscle is found only in your heart. Smooth and cardiac muscles are **involuntary** muscles—they do their job without us having to think about them.

REPRODUCTIVE SYSTEM

REPRODUCTIVE SYSTEM Through the reproductive system, adult human beings are able to create new human beings. Reproduction begins when a **sperm** cell from a man fertilizes an **egg** cell from a woman.

URINARY SYSTEM

URINARY SYSTEM This system, which includes the **kidneys**, cleans waste from the blood and regulates the amount of water in the body.

IMMUNE SYSTEM

IMMUNE SYSTEM The immune system protects your body from diseases by fighting against certain substances that come from outside, or **antigens.** This happens in different ways. For example, white blood cells called **B lymphocytes** learn to fight certain viruses and bacteria by producing **antibodies,** which spread around the body to attack them. Sometimes, as with **allergies,** the immune system makes a mistake and creates antibodies to fight a substance that's really harmless.

BONY BABIES.
Humans are born with 350 bones, but by the time they reach adulthood, some of the bones have grown together, leaving a total of 206.

THE FIVE SENSES

Your senses gather information about the world around you. The five senses are **hearing**, **sight**, **smell**, **taste**, and **touch**. You need senses to find food, resist heat or cold, and avoid situations that might be harmful. Your ears, eyes, nose, tongue, and skin sense changes in the environment. Then, nerve receptors send signals to the brain, where the information is processed.

HEARING

1

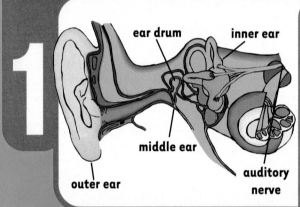

ear drum

inner ear

middle ear

auditory nerve

outer ear

The human ear is divided into three parts—the outer, middle, and inner. The **outer ear** is mainly the flap we can see from the outside. Its shape funnels sound waves into the **middle ear**, where the eardrum is located. The **eardrum** vibrates when the sound waves hit it, causing three tiny bones behind it to vibrate as well. These vibrations are picked up in the **inner ear** by tiny filaments of the **auditory nerve**. This nerve changes the vibrations into nerve impulses, and carries them to the brain.

SIGHT

2

The **lens** of the eye is the first stop for light waves, which tell you the shapes and colors of things around you. The lens focuses light waves onto the **retina**, located on the back wall of the eye. The retina has light-sensitive nerve cells. The cells translate the light waves into patterns of nerve impulses that travel along the **optic nerve** to your brain, where an image is produced. So in reality, all the eye does is collect light. It is the brain that actually forms the image.

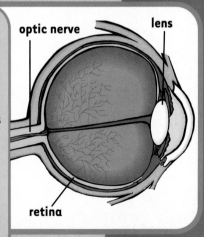

optic nerve

lens

retina

SMELL

3

In our noses we have nerve cells called **olfactory receptors**. Tiny mucus-covered hairs from these receptors detect chemicals in the air. These chemicals make what we call odor or scent. Once detected, this information travels along the **olfactory nerves** to the brain. An interesting thing about smell is that it is linked closely to memory. The nerves from the olfactory receptors are linked directly to the **limbic system**, the part of the brain that deals with emotions. This is why we tend to like or dislike a smell right away. The smell can leave a strong impression on our memory, and very often a smell triggers a particular memory. Sometimes, smelling a perfume might make you think of a particular person.

did you know?

Researchers at the Monell Chemical Senses Center in Philadelphia have been trying to create the most unpleasant smell to humans. They want to help build a non-lethal "stink bomb" for the U.S. military. So far, the most unpleasant odor is a combination of rotting garbage and human waste. Other terrible smells are burnt hair, vomit, body odor, and the rotten-egg smell of sulfur. Using chemicals, the Monell Center creats these smells in a lab.

TASTE

4

Taste buds are the primary receptors for taste. They are located on the surface and sides of the tongue, on the roof of the mouth, and at the back of the throat. These buds detect four qualities of a substance—**sweet** (like sugar), **sour** (like lemons), **salty** (like chips), and **bitter** (like tonic water). Scent and taste signals come together in the same part of your brain. That's why you need both taste and smell to get the full flavor of something. If you've ever had a stuffed up nose, you may have noticed that you can only taste the four things that a tongue can pick up, and nothing else.

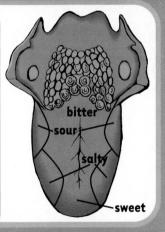

bitter
sour
salty
sweet

TOUCH

5

Your sense of touch allows you to feel heat, cold, pain, and pressure. These environmental factors are all sensed by nerve fibers located in the **epidermis** (outer layer of skin) and **dermis** (second layer of skin) in all parts of the body. Like with all the other senses, nerves send information to the brain through the nervous system.

Exercise *It's What You Do!*

If you watch TV in the afternoons after school or on Saturday mornings, you've probably seen the "VERB. It's What You Do" ads. They're part of a seven-year campaign sponsored by the government to encourage kids age 9–13 to get more exercise.

Why does the U.S. Department of Health and Human Services' Centers for Disease Control and Prevention (CDC) think exercise is important for kids? In 2002, the National Center for Health Statistics reported that an estimated 8.8 million U.S. kids age 6–19 were overweight. Being overweight increases a risk of developing high blood pressure, diabetes, and heart disease.

But daily exercise has other benefits, too: it makes you feel good. Exercise also helps you think better, sleep better, and feel more relaxed. Regular exercise will make you stronger and help you improve at physical activities. Breathing deeply during exercise gets more oxygen into your lungs with each breath. Your heart pumps more oxygen-filled blood all through your body with each beat. Muscles and joints get stronger and more flexible as you use them.

Organized sports are a good way to get a lot of exercise, but not the only way. You can shoot hoops, jog, ride a bike, or skate without being on a team. If you can't think of anything else, try walking in a safe place. Walk with friends or even try to get the adults in your life to join you. They could probably use the exercise, too!

Below are some activities, with a rough idea of how many calories a 100-pound person would burn per minute while doing them.

The CDC reports that the average kid spends 4.5 hours a day in front of some sort of screen (TV, video game, computer). That's 31.5 hours a week. In a year, that time adds up to 1,642.5 hours or 68.4 days!

ACTIVITY	CALORIES PER MINUTE
Jogging (6 miles per hour)	8
Jumping rope (easy pace)	7
Playing basketball	7
Playing soccer	6
Bicycling (9.4 miles per hour)	5
Skiing (downhill)	5
Raking the lawn	4
Rollerblading (easy pace)	4
Walking (4 miles per hour)	4
Bicycling (5.5 miles per hour)	3
Swimming (25 yards per minute)	3
Walking (3 miles per hour)	3

If you're interested in running, try **WEB SITE** www.kidsrunning.com/ There you'll find advice, activities, stories, poems, and more—all about running.

Holidays

When is National Ice Cream Day? page 107

CALENDAR BASICS

Holidays and calendars go hand in hand. Using a calendar, you can see what day of the week it is, and watch out for the next special day. Calendars divide time into days, weeks, months, and years. A year is the time it takes for one revolution of Earth around the Sun. Early calendars were lunar—based on the phases of the Moon. The ancient Egyptians were probably the first to develop a solar calendar, based on the movement of Earth around the Sun.

THE NAMES OF THE MONTHS

January	named for the Roman god Janus, guardian of gates (often shown with two faces, looking backward and forward)
February	named for Februalia, a Roman time of sacrifice
March	named for Mars, the Roman god of war (the end of winter meant fighting could begin again)
April	"aperire," Latin for "to open," as in flower buds
May	named for Maia, the goddess of plant growth
June	"Junius," the Latin word for the goddess Juno
July	named after the Roman ruler Julius Caesar
August	named for Augustus, the first Roman emperor
September	"septem," the Latin word for seven (the Roman year began in March)
October	"octo," the Latin word for eight
November	"novem," the Latin word for nine
December	"decem," the Latin word for ten

The Julian and Gregorian Calendars

In 46 B.C., the emperor Julius Caesar decided to use a calendar based on the movement of the Earth around the Sun. This calendar, called the **Julian calendar**, fixed the normal year at 365 days and added one day every fourth year (leap year), since each year really takes about 356$\frac{1}{4}$ days.

Pope Gregory XIII revised the Julian calendar in A.D. 1582 because the year was 11 minutes, 14 seconds too long. This added up to about 3 extra days every 400 years. To fix it, he made years ending in 00 leap years only if they can be divided by 400. Thus, 2000 was a leap year, but 2100 will not be. The **Gregorian calendar** is the one used today in most of the world.

Jewish, Islamic, and Chinese Calendars

The **Jewish calendar**, which began almost 6,000 years ago, is the official calendar of Israel. The year 2005 is the same as 5765-5766 on the Jewish calendar, which starts at Rosh Hashanah, usually in September. The **Islamic calendar** started in A.D. 622. The year 2005 is equivalent to 1425-1426 on the Islamic calendar, which begins with the month of Muharram, usually in February or March. The **Chinese calendar** has years named after animals. There are 12 of them: Rat, Ox, Tiger, Rabbit, Dragon, Snake, Horse, Sheep, Monkey, Rooster, Dog, and Pig. On February 9, 2005, the Year of the Rooster began. On January 29, 2006, the year of the Dog starts.

Holidays in the United States

There are no official holidays for the whole U.S. But most states celebrate the holidays listed below on the days shown. These are the federal holidays, when workers for the federal government get the day off. Many offices, and most banks and schools, in the 50 states are closed on these days.

NEW YEAR'S DAY The U.S. and most other countries celebrate the beginning of the new year on January 1.

MARTIN LUTHER KING JR. DAY Observed on the third Monday in January, this holiday marks the birth (January 15, 1929) of the African-American civil rights leader Rev. Martin Luther King Jr. In 2006, it will be celebrated on January 16.

PRESIDENTS' DAY On the third Monday in February (February 20, 2006), most states celebrate the births of both George Washington (born February 22, 1732) and Abraham Lincoln (born February 12, 1809).

MEMORIAL DAY OR DECORATION DAY Memorial Day, observed on the last Monday in May (May 29, 2006), is set aside to remember men and women who died serving in the military.

FOURTH OF JULY OR INDEPENDENCE DAY July 4 is the anniversary of the day in 1776 when the American colonies signed the Declaration of Independence. Kids and grownups celebrate with bands and parades, picnics, barbecues, and fireworks.

LABOR DAY Labor Day, the first Monday in September, honors the workers of America. It was first celebrated in 1882. It falls on September 5 in 2005 and September 4 in 2006.

COLUMBUS DAY Celebrated on the second Monday in October, Columbus Day is the anniversary of October 12, 1492, the day Christopher Columbus was traditionally thought to have arrived in the Americas (on the island of San Salvador). It falls on October 10 in 2005 and October 9 in 2006.

VETERANS DAY Veterans Day, November 11, honors veterans of wars. First called Armistice Day, it marked the armistice (agreement) that ended World War I. This was signed on the 11th hour of the 11th day of the 11th month of 1918.

THANKSGIVING Thanksgiving was first observed by the Pilgrims in 1621 as a harvest festival and a day for thanks and feasting. In 1863, Abraham Lincoln revived the tradition. It comes on the fourth Thursday in November— November 24 in 2005 and November 23 in 2006.

CHRISTMAS Christmas is both a religious holiday and a legal holiday. It is celebrated on December 25.

Election Day

Election Day, the first Tuesday after the first Monday in November (November 8 in 2005 and November 7 in 2006), is also a holiday in some states.

The Post Office in Valentine, Nebraska, is a very busy place around February 14. The local Chamber of Commerce runs a special program called "Cupid's Mailbox" so people can have their Valentine cards stamped in Valentine. About 15,000 pieces of mail come through the week before Valentine's Day, which is twice as many as normal.

Other **Special** Holidays

VALENTINE'S DAY February 14 is a day for sending cards or gifts to people you love.

MOTHER'S DAY AND FATHER'S DAY Mothers are honored on the second Sunday in May. Fathers are honored on the third Sunday in June.

GRANDPARENTS' DAY This day to honor grandparents comes every year on the first Sunday after Labor Day.

HALLOWEEN In ancient Britain, Druids wore grotesque costumes on October 31 to scare off evil spirits. Today, while "trick or treating," children ask for candy or money for UNICEF, the United Nations Children's Fund.

HANUKKAH (ALSO CHANUKAH) This eight-day Jewish festival of lights begins on the evening of December 25 in 2005 and December 15 in 2006.

KWANZAA This seven-day African-American festival begins on December 26. It celebrates seven virtues: unity, self-determination, collective work and responsibility, cooperative economics, purpose, creativity, and faith.

Odd Holidays

You can chase away the "back-to-school blues" by observing **Hobbit Day** or **Elephant Appreciation Day** on September 22. Here are a few other odd "days" you've probably never heard of:

July 2005
11: International Town Criers Day
17: National Ice Cream Day
28: National Drive-Thru Day

August 2005
6: National Fresh Breath Day
13: National Underwear Day
17: Sandcastle Day

September 2005
4: Newspaper Carrier Day
12: Video Games Day
19: Talk Like a Pirate Day

October 2005
1: Scare a Friend Day
26: Mule Day
31: National Knock-Knock Day

November 2005
6: Saxophone Day
21: World Hello Day
25: Buy Nothing Day

December 2005
4: National Dice Day
16: Underdog Day
31: Make Up Your Mind Day

January 2006
7: I'm Not Going to Take It Anymore Day
18: Pooh Day (A.A. Milne's Birthday)
21: Squirrel Appreciation Day

February 2006
14: Ferris Wheel Day
15: National Gum Drop Day

March 2006
1: National Pig Day
18: Awkward Moments Day
22: International Goof-Off Day
25: Pecan Day

April 2006
10: National Siblings Day
11: Barbershop Quartet Day
30: National Honesty Day

May 2006
1: Save the Rhino Day
12: Limerick Day
16: International Sea Monkey Day

June 2006
2: National Bubba Day
18: World Juggling Day
28: National Handshake Day

Special note: September 1-30 is Be Kind to Writers and Editors Month!

HOLIDAYS *Around the World*

CANADA DAY Canada's national holiday, July 1, commemorates the union of Canadian provinces in 1867.

CHILDREN'S DAY In Japan, May 5 is set aside to honor children.

CHINESE NEW YEAR China's biggest holiday starts the first month in the Chinese lunar calendar and falls on January 29 in 2006. Celebrations include parades, fireworks, and traditional meals.

CINCO DE MAYO Mexicans remember May 5, 1867, when Mexico defeated its French rulers and became independent.

DIWALI On November 1, 2005, Hindus across India and around the world decorate their homes with small oil lamps to celebrate this festival of lights.

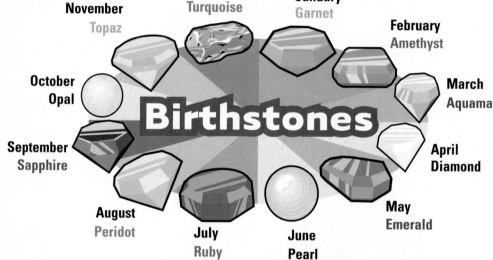

Birthstones

December Turquoise
January Garnet
November Topaz
February Amethyst
October Opal
March Aquamari
September Sapphire
April Diamond
August Peridot
May Emerald
July Ruby
June Pearl

Homework Help

Here's a useful way to keep your months straight:

30 days has September,
April, June, and November.
All the rest have 31,
Except the second month alone.
February has 28 days time,
Til leap year makes it 29.

did you know?

Friday the 13th is considered an unlucky day in much of America and Europe. In fact, there's a name for people who have a phobia about this day: paraskevidekatriaphobics. One study estimates that in the United States alone, $800 or $900 million is lost in business each Friday the 13th because some people will not travel or go to work.

Where can you find reference "books" online? **page 112**

If you need to study for an exam or write a research paper, there are helpful hints in this chapter.

In other chapters, you can find lots of information on topics you may write about or study in school. **Facts About Nations,** pages 147-188, and **Facts About U.S. States,** pages 260-309, are good places to look. For math tips and formulas, look up the chapter on **Numbers**. For good books to read, and write about, see the **Books** chapter. Plus, there are many other study and learning tips throughout the book. Look for the **"Homework Help" icon!** ▶

Those Tricky Tests

Getting Ready

Being prepared for a test can relieve some of your jitters and can make test taking a lot easier! Here are some tips to help you get ready.

▶ Take good notes in class and keep up with assignments, so you don't have to learn material at the last minute! Just writing down the notes helps you remember the information.

▶ Make a study schedule and stick to it! Don't watch TV or listen to distracting music while studying.

▶ Start reviewing early if you can—don't wait until the night before the test.

▶ Go over the headings, summaries, and questions in each chapter to review key points. Read your notes and highlight the most important topics.

▶ Take study breaks so you can concentrate and stay alert.

▶ Get a good night's sleep and eat a good breakfast before the test.

The Big Event

Follow these suggestions for smooth sailing during test time:

▶ Take a deep breath and relax! That will help calm your nerves.

▶ If you are allowed, skim through the entire exam so you know what to expect and how long it may take.

▶ As you start each part of the exam, read directions carefully.

▶ Read each question carefully before answering. For a multiple choice question, check every possible answer before you decide on one. The best answer could be the last one.

▶ Don't spend too much time on any one question. Skip hard questions and go back to them at the end.

▶ Keep track of time so you can pace yourself. Use any time left at the end to go back and review your answers. Make sure you've written the answer you meant to select.

How to write a research paper

Picking a Topic

Sometimes you not only have to research a topic and write about it—you have to pick the topic in the first place. Here are a few tips to keep in mind.

► **Start out by brainstorming.** Let your brain flow freely with ideas and write them down. Even if an idea seems doubtful, write it down anyway. You can be more picky later on.

► **Don't make the topic too big.** For example: "American Presidents" may be too big because it includes over 40 people; it would be better to narrow it down to just one.

► **Consider picking a subject you already like.** If you're already interested in something, like soccer or recycling or Sherlock Holmes, you'll enjoy writing about it and might well do a better job.

► **But don't rule out something unfamiliar or unusual.** Writing on a subject you don't know anything about is a great way to learn. And picking an unusual topic can add interest. For example, instead of writing about Abraham Lincoln, you could try James Buchanan, or Franklin Pierce!

Doing Research

Once you have a topic, the next step is to read all about it. Try to find information from a variety of good sources. If you can't come up with at least a few good sources, then the topic is too narrow. If you're overwhelmed with information about the topic, you need to go back and narrow the topic down.

► **Encyclopedias are a good place to start.** They can give you a good overview of the subject.

► **The electronic catalog** of your school or town library will probably be your main source for finding material about your subject. Keep in mind that books are not as current as magazines and newspapers, but they can still give you information you can use.

► **Check your library's indexes** for magazine or newspaper articles. *The Reader's Guide to Periodic Literature* can be a big help in finding articles; there's even an online version.

► You can also use **the Internet** as a research tool. For more details, see "Research on the Internet" (page 112).

► Don't be afraid to ask **the librarian** for help if you get stuck!

► As you read each source, **write down the facts and ideas** that you may need. You might try using 3 x 5 index cards.

► **Make sure** your cards show the title and author for each source and the page numbers for where you found the particular information.

Hint: Use quotation marks when you think you may want to use the same words as the author.

Writing It Down

The next step is to organize your facts. See which cards you still need and try to put them in the order you want to use. **Develop a rough outline** of your main ideas in the order in which they'll appear.

Now you're ready for the **first draft**. It can be a rough draft that gets your ideas down while they're fresh. You can worry about the exact wording, the spellings, and so forth later on.

Your paper should contain three main parts:

INTRODUCTION The introduction, or first paragraph, explains your topic and your point of view on it. It should draw readers into the paper and let them know what to expect.

BODY The body of the paper develops your ideas. Use specific facts, examples, and details to make your points clear and convincing. Use separate paragraphs for each new idea and use words and phrases that link one paragraph to the next so your ideas flow smoothly.

CONCLUSION Summarize your main points in the final paragraph, or conclusion.

Put your first draft aside for a few days, then go back and re-read it. You'll be able to make corrections more easily after seeing it with fresh eyes. After you're done making your **revisions,** read the paper (slowly!) to check for misspellings and mistakes in grammar or punctuation.

Showing Your Sources

▶ It is important in a paper to show what sources you used. This can be done with **footnotes** that go on the same page as the information itself and say where you got each key fact or quote.

▶ You may need to do a **bibliography** at the end. This is a list of all the sources you used to prepare the report—even some that you may not have actually ended up using in what you wrote.

▶ In the box below are samples of what you might put in your bibliography for a book, magazine article, or Internet source you used in your research. Your teacher will tell you exactly what format to use for showing your sources.

Hint: You usually will not have a reason to use the same wording as your source. If you do, refer to your source and use quotation marks.

FOR A BOOK: Author. *Title*. City Published: Publisher, Year.
   Kwek, Karen. *Welcome to Chile*. Milwaukee, Wisc.: Gareth Stevens, 2004.

FOR A MAGAZINE ARTICLE: Author. "Article Title." *Magazine Title*, Date of Issue, Pages.
   Silver, Michael. "Superbowl XXXIX: Three-Ring Circus." *Sports Illustrated*, February 14, 2005, 36-46.

FOR ONLINE (INTERNET): Author(s). Name of Page [online]. Date of Posting/Revision. [cited year day month]. <URL>.
   The World Almanac for Kids. Animals. [cited 2005 March 4]. <http://www.worldalmanacforkids.com/explore/animals.html>.

Research on the INTERNET

Using Library Resources Your school or public library is a great place to start. It probably has a list (catalog) of its books and periodicals (newspapers and magazines) available from computers at the library, or even from home over the Internet through your library's web site. You can search using **keywords** (words that describe your subject) in three basic ways: by **author**, by **title**, or by **subject**.

For example, doing a subject search for "Benjamin Franklin" will give you a list of books and articles about him, along with their locations in the library.

Your library may also subscribe to online reference databases that companies like The World Almanac create especially for research. These are accessible over the Internet and could contain almanacs, encyclopedias, other reference books, or collections of articles. You can access these databases from the library, and maybe even from home from your library's web site.

When you write your report, don't copy directly from books, articles, or the Internet—that's **plagiarism**, a form of cheating. Keep track of all your **sources**—the books, articles, and web sites you use—and list them in a **bibliography**. (See page 111 for some examples.)

Why shouldn't I just search the Internet?
The library's list may look just like other information on the Internet. But these sources usually have been checked by experts. This is not true of all the information on the Internet. It could come from almost anybody, and may not be trustworthy.

When can I use the Internet?
The Internet is still a great way to look things up. You can find addresses or recipes, listen to music, or find things to do. You can look up information on hobbies or musical instruments, or read a magazine or newspaper online.

If you search the internet on your own, make sure the web site you find is reliable. A U.S. government site or a site produced by a well-known organization or publication is usually your best bet.

Using a Search Engine
The best way to find web sites is to use a search engine. Here are some helpful ones:

Yahooligans (www.yahooligans.com)
Kidsclick (www.kidsclick.org)
Lycos Zone (lycoszone.lycos.com)
Ask Jeeves Kids (www.ajkids.com)

Start by typing one or two search terms—words that describe your topic. The search engine scans the Internet and gives you a list of sites that contain them. The results appear in a certain order, or **rank**. Search engines use different ways of measuring which web sites are likely to be the most helpful. One way is by counting how many times your search terms appear on each site. The site that's listed first may not have what you want. Explore as many of the sites as possible.

You might have to narrow your search by using more keywords. Or try using **directories** to help find what you need.

THE WORLD ALMANAC FOR KIDS has its own website at:
WEB SITE *www.worldalmanacforkids.com*

Genealogy Tracing Your Family Tree

Genealogy is the study of one's family, tracing back through generations of relatives. The first place to start in your family genealogy is with yourself. Write down the answers to the following questions:

● What is your full name (include middle name)?
● When and where were you born (town, city, state, country)?

Next, write down the name, birth date, and place of birth for each of your parents (ask them or the adult who takes care of you). Then, interview your grandparents and other relatives. Get their birthdates and places of birth as well. If any of these people have died, record their date of death. You might also ask about interesting events in their lives.

Now, you have the beginnings of a family tree.
Fill out as much of this chart as you can:

GRANDPARENT
Name:.....................................
Birth: ....
Death:....................................

PARENT
Name:.....................................
Birth: ....
Death:....................................

GRANDPARENT
Name:.....................................
Birth: ....
Death:....................................

ME
Your
Name:.....................................
Birth:.....................................

GRANDPARENT
Name:.....................................
Birth: ....
Death:....................................

PARENT
Name:.....................................
Birth: ....
Death:....................................

GRANDPARENT
Name:.....................................
Birth: ....
Death:....................................

When you find out more about a relative, you may get access to photographs and photocopies of important documents. Documents might include birth certificates, marriage licenses, or immigration papers.

To find out where you can get official copies of "vital records" such as birth, death, and marriage certificates for a particular state, check the website of the U.S. National Center for Health Statistics (www.cdc.gov/nchs). Baptism, marriage, and burial records can often be found at family churches. Also, many libraries have U.S. Census records for 1790-1930. Make sure to keep copies of the documents you find.

Additional Sources

The Church of Jesus Christ of Latter Day Saints (the Mormons) has Family History Centers throughout the world. There you can access their databases and programs, and possibly find members of your family.

A good book for children to read is *Climbing Your Family Tree: Online and Off-Line Genealogy for Kids*, by Ira Wolfman.
(*www.workman.com/familytree*)
Websites that can help you find out more information about your family and lead you further on your trail of discovery are
www.cyndislist.com/kids.htm, *www.ancestry.com*, and *www.familysearch.com*.

Old family photos are a great way to explore your family history.

113

Inventions

Which invention came first, Velcro or rollerblades? page 115

Many important inventions and discoveries came before history was written. These include the wheel, pottery, many tools, and the ability to make fire. More recent inventions help us to travel faster, communicate better, and live longer.

Invention TIME LINE

YEAR	INVENTION	INVENTOR (COUNTRY)
105	paper	Ts'ai Lun (China)
1250	magnifying glass	Roger Bacon (England)
1447	moveable type	Johann Gutenberg (Germany)
1590	2-lens microscope	Zacharias Janssen (Netherlands)
1608	telescope	Hans Lippershey (Netherlands)
1709	piano	Bartolomeo Cristofori (Italy)
1714	mercury thermometer	Gabriel D. Fahrenheit (Germany)
1752	lightning rod	Benjamin Franklin (U.S.)
1780	bifocal lenses for glasses	Benjamin Franklin (U.S.)
1785	parachute	Jean Pierre Blanchard (France)
1795	modern pencil	Nicolas Jacques Conté (France)
1800	electric battery	Alessandro Volta (Italy)
1807	steamboat (practical)	Robert Fulton (U.S.)
1815	safety lamp for miners	Sir Humphry Davy (England)
1819	stethoscope	René T.M.H. Laënnec (France)
1829	steam locomotive	George Stephenson (England)
1834	refrigeration	Jacob Perkins (England)
1837	telegraph	Samuel F.B. Morse (U.S.)
1842	anesthesia (ether)	Crawford W. Long (U.S.)
1845	rotary printing press	Richard M. Hoe (U.S.)
1846	sewing machine	Elias Howe (U.S.)
1851	cylinder (door) lock	Linus Yale (U.S.)
1852	elevator brake	Elisha G. Otis (U.S.)
1863	fire extinguisher	Alanson Crane (U.S.) ▶
1867	typewriter	Christopher Sholes, Carlos Glidden, & Samuel W. Soulé (U.S.)
1870s	*telephone ▶	Antonio Meucci (Italy), Alexander G. Bell (U.S.)
1877	phonograph	Thomas A. Edison (U.S.)
1877	microphone	Emile Berliner (U.S.)
1879	practical lightbulb	Thomas A. Edison (U.S.)
1885	bicycle (modern)	James Starley (England)
1885	motorcycle	Gottlieb Daimler (Germany)
1886	automobile (gasoline)	Karl Benz (Germany)
1886	dishwasher	Josephine Cochran (U.S.)
1888	ballpoint pen	John Loud (U.S.)
1888	portable camera	George Eastman (U.S.)
1891	escalator	Jesse W. Reno (U.S.)
1891	submarine (modern)	John Holland (U.S.)
1893	moving picture viewer	Thomas A. Edison (U.S.)

YEAR	INVENTION	INVENTOR (COUNTRY)
1894	motion picture projector	Charles F. Jenkins (U.S.)
1895	diesel engine	Rudolf Diesel (Germany)
1895	X ray	Wilhelm Roentgen (Germany) ▶
1899	tape recorder	Valdemar Poulsen (Denmark)
1901	washing machine	Langmuir Fisher (U.S.)
1903	propeller airplane	Orville & Wilbur Wright (U.S.)
1903	windshield wipers	Mary Anderson (U.S.)
1907	vacuum cleaner	J. Murray Spangler (U.S.)
1911	air conditioning	Willis H. Carrier (U.S.)
1913	modern radio receiver	Reginald A. Fessenden (U.S.)
1917	practical zipper	Gideon Sundback (Canada)
1922	insulin	Sir Frederick G. Banting (Canada)
1923	television**	Vladimir K. Zworykin** (U.S.)
1924	frozen packaged food	Clarence Birdseye (U.S.)
1926	rocket engine	Robert H. Goddard (U.S.)
1929	penicillin	Alexander Fleming (Scotland)
1930	cyclotron (atom smasher)	Ernest O. Lawrence (U.S.)
1937	xerography copies	Chester Carlson (U.S.)
1939	helicopter	Igor Sikorsky (U.S.)
1939	jet airplane	Hans van Ohain (Germany)
1942	electronic computer	John V. Atanasoff & Clifford Berry (U.S.)
1943	Aqua Lung	Jacques-Yves Cousteau & Emile Gagnan (France)
1947	transistor	William Shockley, Walter H. Brattain, & John Bardeen (U.S.)
1947	Tupperware®	Earl Silas Tupper (U.S.)
1948	Velcro®	Georges de Mestral (Switzerland)
1952	airbag	John Hetrick (U.S.)
1954	antibiotic for fungal diseases	R. F. Brown & E. L. Hazen (U.S.)
1955	fiber optics	Narinder S. Kapany (England)
1955	polio vaccine	Jonas E. Salk (U.S.)
1958	laser	A. L. Schawlow & C. H. Townes (U.S.)
1963	pop-top can	Ermal C. Fraze (U.S.)
1965	word processor	IBM (U.S.)
1968	computer mouse	Douglas Engelbart (U.S)
1969	cash machine (ATM)	Don Wetzel (U.S.)
1969	videotape cassette	Sony (Japan)
1969	battery operated smoke detector	Randolph Smith & Kenneth House (U.S.)
1971	food processor	Pierre Verdon (France)
1972	compact disc (CD)	RCA (U.S.)
1973	CAT scanner	Godfrey N. Hounsfield (England)
1973	Jet Ski®	Clayton Jacobsen II (U.S)
1977	space shuttle	NASA (U.S.)
1978	artificial heart	Robert K. Jarvik (U.S.)
1979	cellular telephone	Ericsson Company (Sweden)
1979	Walkman	Sony (Japan)
1980	rollerblades	Scott Olson (U.S.)
1980	Post-it®	3M Company (U.S.)
1987	laptop computer	Sir Clive Sinclair (England) ■
1987	meningitis vaccine	Connaught Lab (U.S.)
1994	digital camera	Apple Computer, Kodak (U.S.)
1995	DVD (digital video disk)	Matsushita (Japan)
2002	robot vacuum	iRobot Corp. (U.S.)
2004	thinking shoe	Adidas (U.S.)

X ray of human hand

*Meucci developed a version of the telephone (early 1870s); Bell received a patent for another version.
**Others who helped invent television include Philo T. Farnsworth (1926) and John Baird (1928).

KID INVENTORS

K-K GREGORY, Age 10, Inventor of Wristies

Kathryn (K-K) Gregory from Bedford, Massachusetts, became an inventor in 1994 at the age of 10. She began experimenting with different ways to play outside in the snow and keep the snow from finding its way up the sleeve of her coat. With some help from her mom, K-K sewed synthetic fleece into cylinders that would fit under her sleeve but over her gloves. However, in field tests, snow was still sneaking under the lower edge. Then K-K altered her design so that it could be worn under gloves. This time her invention did the job and became an instant hit with other kids in her Girl Scout troop.

When K-K knew she had a winning idea, she contacted a patent attorney, who found out that her idea was original. She named her invention Wristies, applied for a patent, and even started a company to market it. In 1997 K-K became the youngest person ever to promote a product on the QVC TV network, where in just 6 minutes the spot generated $22,000 in sales.

K-K went a long way, step by step, beginning with an original idea and sample design, going through field testing and revision, market testing, patent search and application, all the way to starting a company, selling the product, and making a profit!

RICHIE STACHOWSKI, Age 15, Inventor of Water Talkies

When Richie Stachowski went snorkeling on his vacation, he wished he could shout out to tell everybody how beautiful the fish were. But he couldn't because he was underwater. After returning home, he researched underwater acoustics on the Internet and then began to build sample designs of an underwater megaphone. Using $267 from his savings account, he was able to produce Water Talkies, a toy that lets kids talk underwater. The prototype was made from a plastic cone, a snorkel mouthpiece, and a blow valve with a plastic membrane to keep the water out.

Richie formed his own company and soon began selling his Water Talkies to major retailers.

2004 Craftsman/NSTA Young Inventors Award

Every year, the National Science Teachers Association (NSTA) and the Craftsman tool company hold a contest, judging the best new inventions created by kids. In 2004, these two students each won the top prize, a $10,000 U.S. savings bond.

Nicolette Mann, Christiansburg, Virginia, grade 4. Invention: *"Piano Peddles for Young Beginners."* This box has three 5-inch wooden poles placed on piano pedals so that children can reach them. Nicolette designed them with her little brother in mind.

Katelyn Eubank, Indianola, Iowa, grade 7. Invention: *"The Easy Door Assist."* This contraption puts four vertical rollers on the sides of a wheelchair. This helps older or disabled people get through doors more easily. Katelyn designed the invention to help her grandmother.

Any student in grades 2–8 is eligible to enter. Entries are usually due in March. For more information:  **WEB SITE** www.nsta.org/programs/craftsman/

Language

What language does "chocolate" come from?   page 118

TOP LANGUAGES

Would you have guessed that Mandarin, the principal language of China, is the most commonly spoken language in the world? Check out the list below, which shows languages spoken by at least 100 million people.*

LANGUAGE	WHERE SPOKEN	NATIVE SPEAKERS
Mandarin	China, Taiwan	873,000,000
Spanish	South American, Spain	322,000,000
English	U.S., Canada, Britain	309,000,000
Hindi	India	180,000,000
Portuguese	Portugal, Brazil	177,000,000
Bengali	India, Bangladesh	171,000,000
Russian	Russia	145,000,000
Japanese	Japan	125,000,000

*Estimates as of 2004.

¡Hola! (Spanish)

LANGUAGE USED AT HOME	SPEAKERS OVER 5 YEARS OLD
① Speak only English	215,423,557
② Spanish	28,101,052
③ Chinese	2,022,143
④ French	1,643,838
⑤ German	1,383,442
⑥ Tagalog (Philippines)	1,224,241
⑦ Vietnamese	1,009,627
⑧ Italian	1,008,370
⑨ Korean	894,063
⑩ Russian	706,242
⑪ Polish	667,414
⑫ Arabic	614,582
⑬ Portuguese	564,630
⑭ Japanese	477,997
⑮ French Creole	453,368
⑯ Greek	365,436
⑰ Hindi	317,057
⑱ Persian	312,085
⑲ Urdu	262,900
⑳ Gujarathi (from India & parts of Africa)	235,988

Which LANGUAGES Are SPOKEN in the UNITED STATES?

Most Americans speak English only. But since the beginning of American history, immigrants have come to the United States from all over the world. Many have brought other languages with them.

¡Hola! That's how more than 28 million Americans say "hi" at home.

The table at left lists the most frequently spoken languages in the U.S., as of the 2000 census.

Hello! (English)

Konnichi wa! (Japanese)

117

The English Language

Facts about English

► According to the Oxford English Dictionary, the English language contains between 250,000 and 750,000 words. (The number depends on whether you count different meanings of the same word as separate words and on how many obscure technical terms you count.)

► The most frequently used letters of the alphabet are E, T, A, and O, in that order.

► Here are the 30 most common English words: the, of, and, a, to, in, is, that, it, was, he, for, as, on, with, his, be, at, you, I, are, this, by, from, had, have, they, not, or, one.

► English has borrowed many words from different languages. For example, here are a few words from other languages:

from Arabic:	from Chinese:	from German:	from Spanish:
algebra, almanac, sherbet, spinach, sugar, sultan, syrup, tuna	gung-ho, kowtow, silk, tea, wok, wonton	finger, fish, hand, pretzel, sauerkraut, seltzer	alligator, chocolate, cocoa, hurricane, lasso, maize, tamale tomato, tortilla

New Words

English is always changing as new words are born and old ones die out. Many new words come from the field of electronics and computers, from the media, or from slang.

digital subscriber line (DSL): a high-speed communications connection used for getting onto the Internet and short-range transmissions over ordinary telephone lines. ("Before we got DSL at our house, it took five minutes to check my e-mail!")

egosurfing: looking up information about yourself on the internet. ("I got six hits for my name when I was egosurfing the web.")

megaplex: a very large movie theater typically housing 16 or more movie screens. ("My mom won't let me go with my friends to the new megaplex unless an adult is with us.")

peloton: the main group of riders in a bicycle race. ("When one of the riders in the crowded peloton fell, many others crashed into her.")

In Other Words: IDIOMS

Idioms are phrases that mean more than their words put together. Here are some "horsy" examples:

don't look a gift horse in the mouth–"accept gifts graciously." By checking how worn down a horse's teeth are you can get an idea of its age. Since the animal was a gift, checking its age is considered impolite. A more modern example might be looking for the label or the price tag on a gift.

closing the barn door after the horse has bolted–"doing something too late." Once the horse is gone, closing the door won't do any good.

put the cart before the horse–"do something in reverse order." If you brag to all your friends that you're going to the John Mayer concert before your parents have gotten tickets, you would be putting the cart before the horse.

GETTING TO THE ROOT

Many English words and parts of words can be traced back to Latin or Greek. If you know the meaning of a word's parts, you can probably guess what it means. A **root** (also called a stem) is the part of the word that gives its basic meaning, but can't be used by itself. Roots need other word parts to complete them: either a **prefix** at the beginning, or a **suffix** at the end, or sometimes both. The following tables give some examples of Greek and Latin roots, prefixes, and suffixes.

Latin

root	basic meaning	example
-gress-	walk	progress
-ject-	to throw	reject
-port-	to carry	transport
-scrib-/		
-script-	to write	prescription
-vert-	turn	invert

prefix	basic meaning	example
de-	away, off	defrost
inter-	between, among	international
non-	not	nontoxic
pre-	before	prevent
re-	again, back	rewrite
trans-	across, through	trans-Atlantic

suffix	basic meaning	example
-ation	(makes verbs into nouns)	invitation
-fy/-ify	make or cause to become	horrify
-ly	like, to the extent of	highly
-ment	(makes verbs into nouns)	government
-ty/-ity	state of	purity

Greek

root	basic meaning	example
-anthrop-	human	anthropology
-bio-	life	biology
-dem-	people	democracy
-phon-	sound	telephone
-photo-	light	telephoto
-scope-	to see	telescope

prefix	basic meaning	example
anti-/ant-	against	antisocial
auto-	self	autopilot
biblio-/		
bibl-	book	bibliography
micro-	small	microscope
tele-	far off	television

suffix	basic meaning	example
-graph	write, draw, describe, record	photograph
-ism	act, state, theory of	realism
-ist	one who believes in, practices	capitalist
-logue/		
-log	speech, to speak	dialogue
-scope	see	telescope

Homework Help

I before *E* except after *C*,

or when sounded like *A*, as in **neighbor** or **weigh**.

This is a pretty good rule and helpful in remembering how to spell lots of words. *Believe, receive,* and *sleigh* are just a few examples. But you do have to learn a few exceptions—cases where the rule doesn't work. The exceptions include *weird, either, neither, height,* and *leisure.*

Words About Words

An **acronym** is an abbreviation formed from the first letters or syllables of a group of words.

"Scuba" from "Self Contained Underwater Breathing Apparatus."

An **alliteration** is a repetition of the same beginning consonant sound for two or more words in a row.

Tiny Tim tripped two times today.

An **anagram** is a word or phrase made by rearranging the letters from another word or phrase, or perhaps from nonsense letters.

From "The best things in life are free" you can get "Nail biting refreshes the feet."

Antonyms are words that have opposite meanings.

fast and slow
early and late

A **cliché** is an expression used so often that it has lost its interest.

Don't beat around the bush.
She works like a dog.

An **eponym** is a word that comes from the name of a person or thing.

"Sideburns" comes from U.S. Civil War General Ambrose Everett Burnside, who set the style for wearing long side whiskers.

A **euphemism** is a pleasant word or phrase used to avoid a more direct word or phrase.

Instead of "died": passed away
Instead of "used car": pre-owned vehicle

Homophones are words that sound alike but have different meanings and spellings.

dear/deer
sight/site
fair/fare

A **palindrome** is a word, phrase, or sentence that has the same letters in the same order whether spelled backward or forward.

Madam, I'm Adam
reward drawer

A **pseudonym** is a name someone makes up and uses to hide his or her true identity.

Samuel Clemens, the author of *Huckleberry Finn*, used the pseudonym Mark Twain.

A **pun** is the use of a word with two different meanings, in a way that's humorous.

People tell worse puns when they get older. That's why you call them "groan–ups."

A **simile** is a comparison between two very different things using "like" or "as."

My heart was beating like a drum.

Synonyms are words that have the same or almost the same meanings.

quick and fast
tired and sleepy

Jokes and Riddles

When is the best time of day to go to the dentist?

A farmer had 12 cows. All but 9 died. How many cows did he have left?

Name the five days of the work week without using Monday, Tuesday, Wednesday, Thursday, or Friday.

In what way are the letter "A" and noon exactly the same?

Yo: I just got bit by a mosquito.

Bo: Man, I hate those arithmetic bugs!

Yo: Arithmetic bugs?

Bo: Sure. They add to misery, subtract from fun, divide your attention, and multiply quickly!

What newspaper did cave people read?

Zip: What's worse than finding a worm in your apple?

Zap: I don't know, that sounds pretty bad.

Zip: Not as bad as finding half of a worm!

What did the boyfriend melon say to the girlfriend melon?

Dad: Where are you going with my toolbox?

Son: It's for my math homework.

Dad: How can tools help you with math?

Son: The instructions said to find multi-pliers.

Why didn't the skeleton cross the road?

ANSWERS ON PAGES 335-338. FOR MORE PUZZLES GO TO WWW.WORLDALMANACFORKIDS.COM

I'm the beginning of eternity,
The end of space and time,
The middle of every buzzing bee,
And the end of every rhyme.

If 10 robins can catch 10 worms in 10 minutes, how long will it take one robin to catch a worm?

What starts with a P, ends with an E, and has thousands of letters in it?

Why did Cinderella's soccer team always lose?

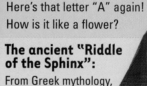

As I was walking to the mall, I met eight girls, all quite tall. Each tall girl carried a squirrel, except for the one whose hair was in curls. They also came with six young boys, who brought their mothers who carried their toys. How many were going to the mall?

What did the clock do when it was hungry?

What did the mover get when he dropped a computer on his toes?

Here's that letter "A" again! How is it like a flower?

The ancient "Riddle of the Sphinx":

From Greek mythology, this is the oldest known riddle. The heroic Oedipus knew the answer, do you?

What animal walks on four feet in the morning, two at noon, and three in the evening?

Language Express

Surprise your friends and family with words from other languages.

English	Spanish	French	German	Chinese
Monday	lunes	lundi	Montag	Xingqiyi
Tuesday	martes	mardi	Dienstag	Xingqier
Wednesday	miércoles	mercredi	Mittwoch	Xingqisan
Thursday	jueves	jeudi	Donnerstag	Xingqisi
Friday	viernes	vendredi	Freitag	Xingqiwu
Saturday	sábado	samedi	Samstag	Xingqiliu
Sunday	domingo	dimanche	Sonntag	Xingqitian
blue	azul	bleu	blau	lan
red	rojo	rouge	rot	hong
green	verde	vert	grün	lu
yellow	amarillo	jaune	gelb	huang
black	negro	noir	schwarz	hei
white	blanco	blanc	weiss	bai
happy birthday!	¡feliz cumpleaños!	joyeux anniversaire!	Glückwunsch zum Geburtstag!	sheng-ri kuai le!
hello!	¡hola!	bonjour!	hallo!	ni hao!
good-bye!	¡adios!	au revoir!	auf Wiedersehen!	zai-jian!
dog	perro	chien	Hund	gou
cat	gato	chat	Katze	mao
bear	oso	ours	Bär	xiong
one	uno	un	eins	yi
two	dos	deux	zwei	er
three	tres	trois	drei	san
four	cuatro	quatre	vier	si
five	cinco	cinq	fünf	wu
six	seis	six	sechs	liu
seven	siete	sept	sieben	qi
eight	ocho	huit	acht	ba
nine	nueve	neuf	neun	jiu
ten	diez	dix	zehn	shi

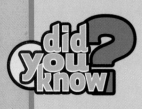

- *In many languages, the word for "mother" begins with the sound* ma *and the word for "father" begins with the sound* da. *But in the Georgian language,* deda *means "mother" and* mama *means "father."*
- *Navajo words can mean different things depending on whether they are pronounced in a high, low, rising, or falling tone. The word* tsin *can mean "log," "stick," "tree," or "bone," depending on the tone in which it is spoken.*
- *A mixture of Dutch, German, and other languages, Afrikaans is one of South Africa's two official languages, and is spoken by descendants of Dutch settlers. The other official language is English.*

Sign Language

Many people who are deaf or hearing-impaired use American Sign Language (ASL) to talk to each other. ASL is not just a form of English turned into gestures. It's a unique language with its own vocabulary, grammar, and punctuation. The position and movement of the hands and arms, facial expressions, and even moving your whole body is part of the language. To ask a question, for example, an ASL user might lean forward with raised eyebrows.

Below is the American Manual Alphabet, a system of "finger spelling" originally developed in France by Abbe Charles Michel De l'Epee in the late 1700s, the manual alphabet was later brought to the United States by Laurent Clerc (1785-1869), a Frenchman who taught people who were deaf.

▲ *American Manual Alphabet*

© National Association of the Deaf

INTERNATIONAL MORSE CODE

Today, many messages go through satellites and microwave radio links. But before the telephone was invented, the telegraph was the fastest way to communicate. Developed by Samuel F. B. Morse in 1837, the code uses a series of short ("dots") and long ("dashes") electrical pulses to represent letters and numbers. The code can also be used over radio waves and became very important to the military and shipping. Many amateur ham radio operators still use Morse code. Ships may also use it as a backup to satellite. Even the space shuttle has a small Morse key on its digital radio.

A	B	C	D	E	F	G	H	I	J	K	L	M
.-	-...	-.-.	-..	.	..-.	--.	....	..	.---	-.-	.-..	--

N	O	P	Q	R	S	T	U	V	W	X	Y	Z
-.	---	.--.	--.-	.-.	...	-	..-	...-	.--	-..-	-.--	--..

What do you get when you cross a parrot with a woodpecker? **Decode this message for the answer.**

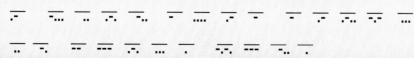

Military

What was the code name for D-Day?   page 126

Soldiers risk their lives to fight for their nation or cause, often to defend the lives and freedom of others. Since the beginning of the Revolutionary War, more than 2.6 million U.S. soldiers have been killed or wounded in wars (almost as many people as now live in Arkansas).

FAMOUS BATTLES IN HISTORY

Wars have been fought throughout human history. But only a few battles by themselves have changed the course of history. Here are some of those important battles. You may recognize some of their names.

THERMOPYLAE—Persia Vs. Greece (480 B.C.)

- **BACKGROUND:** A huge Persian army, led by King Xerxes I, invaded Greece in 480 B.C. The king planned to take a shortcut through Thermopylae, a narrow valley near the northern coast. The Greeks quickly gathered some soldiers, including 300 Spartan warriors, under King Leonidas of Sparta, to block the valley. (The city-state of Sparta had the finest soldiers in Greece.)
- **THE BATTLE:** The Greeks held back the Persian attack for two days. But a Greek traitor told the Persians of a secret goat path through the mountains. The invaders used the path to get behind, or "outflank," the Greeks the next day. Finally, the surrounded Spartans were the only Greeks still standing. The Persians were afraid to get within sword range of Leonidas's men. They shot arrows and threw spears to kill them all.
- **OUTCOME:** The battle at Thermopylae held the Persians long enough for the Greeks to form an army to drive them out. The 300 Spartans became a symbol of courage in the face of overwhelming odds.

 Before annihilating the Spartans, Xerxes offered them a chance to surrender. But the Spartans preferred death to captivity. "A Spartan leaves the field with his shield or on it," was the reply.

HASTINGS—Saxons Vs. Normans (October 14, 1066)

BACKGROUND: In the year 1066, two men claimed the English crown. One was the newly crowned King Harold (Harold Godwin, the former Earl of Wessex). The other was Duke William of Normandy (a region of France). Harold was an Anglo-Saxon, or an Englishman descended from Germans. William was a Norman, or a Frenchman descended from Scandinavians. Duke William, with an army of 6,000 men, invaded England to take the throne. King Harold, with an army of equal size, met William's force at Hastings, near the southeast English coast.

THE BATTLE: William's army was better trained and armed than Harold's. But King Harold's men were in a better defensive position, on a high rise called Senlac Hill. The battle raged from early morning into the afternoon. Then William came up with a very smart strategy. He had his soldiers pretend to retreat. Harold's eager men streamed down the hill in pursuit, and William's archers and cavalry slaughtered them. King Harold was mortally wounded in the fighting, and the English throne went to William.

OUTCOME: William became known in history as "William the Conqueror." He brought part of France under English rule. He also started the Norman line of English monarchs, who ruled the country until 1154.

William the Conqueror

did you know? King Harold was the only English monarch ever to die in battle.

TRAFALGAR—France Vs. Britain (October 21, 1805)

BACKGROUND: The Napoleonic Wars (1803-1814) made France the biggest military power in Europe, but only on land. Great Britain, France's enemy, blocked the French ports, disrupting France's overseas trade. In the fall of 1805, French warships escaped the blockade and joined with Spanish warships to form a fleet of 33 ships, commanded by Pierre de Villeneuve. The French-Spanish fleet fought a British fleet of 27 warships off the southwest coast of Spain, at the mouth of the Mediterranean Sea.

THE BATTLE: Admiral Horatio Nelson, a brilliant naval strategist, commanded the British fleet. He sent his ships, guns blazing, right into the center of the French-Spanish formation. The daring tactic surprised the enemy. The British sank or disabled 25 enemy ships without losing one of their own. But a French sniper mortally wounded Nelson during the battle.

OUTCOME: Trafalgar was Britain's greatest naval victory. It wrecked Napoleon's plan of invading England and left Britain in command of the seas for years to come.

Admiral Nelson is memorialized in a statue on top of Nelson's Column, in Trafalgar Square, in London.

did you know? At the start of the battle, Nelson signaled with flags to his fleet: "England expects that every man will do his duty."

GETTYSBURG—Union Vs. Confederacy (July 1-3, 1863)

- **BACKGROUND:** During the Civil War in the summer of 1863, the Army of Northern Virginia invaded Pennsylvania. The army's leader, General Robert E. Lee, was the South's finest general. Lee had 75,000 men. General George Gordon Meade, the Union commander, had 97,000 men. The two armies met in Gettysburg, Pennsylvania.

- **THE BATTLE:** When the Confederates arrived at Gettysburg July 1, they outnumbered the Union forces and nearly won the battle quickly. But more Union soldiers arrived early the next day, and the two armies took up positions on opposing ridges. The fighting on July 2 featured a heroic defense of the Union's left flank on a rocky hill called Little Round Top, by a small number of Northern troops from Maine and New York. On the third day, the Confederates launched "Pickett's Charge," a brave attack on the middle of the Union position. Some 15,000 Southerners crossed a mile of open ground directly into heavy Union fire. Only a few hundred made it as far as the Union lines. Lee's army was forced to retreat to Virginia.

- **OUTCOME:** Gettysburg was the largest and bloodiest battle ever fought on American soil. The North had an estimated 23,000 casualties and the South had about 25,000. After Gettysburg, Lee's force was on the defensive in Virginia until its surrender in April 1865.

 General Lee took full responsibility for the loss at Gettysburg. "It's all my fault," he said. "I thought my men were invincible."

D-DAY—Allies Vs. Germans (June 6, 1944)

- **BACKGROUND:** During World War II (1939-1945), Nazi German troops held most of Europe. The Allies came up with a secret plan to invade Normandy, the northern coast of occupied France, from England. The plan was code-named "Operation Overlord." The first day of the invasion was known as "D-Day."

- **THE BATTLE:** D-Day was the largest amphibious (land and sea) invasion in history. It involved more than 5,000 ships, and more than 150,000 troops, mainly from the U.S., Britain, and Canada. On June 6, the soldiers came ashore in landing craft at five beaches, code-named "Gold," "Sword," "Juno," "Utah," and "Omaha." The Germans were not expecting an attack there, and resistance at the first four beaches was fairly light. But there was horrific bloodshed at "Omaha," where the Germans put up a determined fight. The Allies suffered more than 9,500 casualties on D-Day. Most of those were among the soldiers of the U.S. 1st and 29th Infantry Divisions at "Omaha."

- **OUTCOME:** D-Day gave the Allies a toehold that they never gave up. From Normandy, they fought across occupied Europe and into Germany. Germany surrendered in May 1945.

U.S. soldiers storm the beach at Normandy

 The commander of Allied forces in Europe was U.S. General Dwight D. Eisenhower. "Ike" went on to become the 34th U.S. president.

Money

What does a tiny letter "D" mean on a penny? page 128

History of Money

Why Did People Start Using Money?

At first, people bartered, which means they traded goods they had for things they needed. A farmer who had cattle might want to have salt to preserve meat, or cloth to make clothing. He would barter his cattle to get what he needed. Valuable items that people used for trade became the earliest kinds of money.

What Objects Have Been Used as Money?

► cattle and clay tablets in Babylonia around 2500 B.C.

► wampum (beads) and beaver fur by Native Americans of the northeast around A.D. 1500

► tobacco by early American colonists around A.D. 1650

► whales' teeth by the Pacific peoples on the island of Fiji, until the early 1900s

▲ Wampum used by Native Americans

Coins, Gold, and Paper Money

The first government to make coins that looked alike and use them as money is thought to be the Greek city-state of Lydia in the 7th century B.C. These Lydian coins were actually bean-shaped lumps made from a mixture of gold and silver.

By the Middle Ages (about A.D. 800-1100), gold had become a popular medium for trade in Europe. But gold was heavy and difficult to carry, and the cities and the roads of Europe at that time were dangerous places to carry large amounts of gold. So merchants and goldsmiths began issuing notes promising to pay gold to the person carrying the note. These "promissory notes" were the beginning of paper money in Europe.

In the early 1700s, France's government became the first in Europe to issue paper money that looked alike. Paper money was probably also invented in China, where the explorer Marco Polo saw it around 1280.

TOTALLY NEW NICKEL. *In 2004 the U.S. Mint changed the nickel for the first time in 66 years, to commemorate the 200th anniversary of the Lousiana Purchase and the westward expansion of the U.S. In 2005, the Mint is changing both sides of the nickel. The front will have a radically new closeup of Thomas Jefferson. It will also have the word "Liberty" in a style similar to Jefferson's handwriting. On the back, there will be two designs: an American bison or a view of the Pacific Ocean.*

U.S. State Quarters

From 1999 to 2008, five new quarter designs are being minted each year. George Washington stays on the front, but a design honoring one of the 50 states appears on the back. The quarters for each state are coming out in the order in which the states joined the Union. In 2005, California, Minnesota, Oregon, Kansas, and West Virginia (pictured here) were put into circulation. Nevada, Nebraska, Colorado, North Dakota, and South Dakota quarters are due in 2006.

How Much Money Is In Circulation?

As of September 2004, the total amount of money in circulation in the United States came to **$738,359,165,630**. More than 33 billion dollars was in coins, the rest in paper money.

Paper Money

Coins

What Is the U.S. Mint?

The U.S. Mint, founded in 1792, is part of the Treasury Department. The Mint makes all U.S. coins and safeguards the nation's $100 million in gold and silver **bullion** (uncoined bars of metal). Reserves of these precious metals are held at West Point, New York, and Fort Knox, Kentucky. The Mint turns out coins at four production facilities (Denver, Philadelphia, San Francisco, and West Point). For more information, visit the U.S. Mint's website at

WEB SITE www.usmint.gov

What Coins Does the Mint Make?

Branches of the U.S. Mint in Denver and Philadelphia currently make coins for "circulation," or everyday use. In 2004, these two facilities made 13.2 billion coins, including 6.8 billion pennies, 1.4 billion nickels, 2.5 billion dimes, and 2.4 million quarters. A tiny "D" or "P" near the year, called a mint mark, tells you which one made the coin. A Lincoln cent or "penny" with no mint mark was probably made at the Philadelphia Mint, which has by tradition never marked pennies. The U.S. Mint also makes commemorative coins in honor of events, like the Olympics, or people, like Christopher Columbus.

Where is Paper Money Made?

The Bureau of Engraving and Printing (BEP), established in 1862, designs and prints all U.S. paper money. This agency, which is also part of the Treasury Department, also prints postage stamps and other official certificates. The BEP's production facilities in Washington, D.C., and Ft. Worth, Texas, made almost 9 billion bills in 2004. About 95% of them are used to replace worn out money. Even though bills are made of a special paper that is 75% cotton and 25% linen, they wear out pretty fast if they are used a lot. The $1 bill only lasts an average of 22 months, while the $50 bill lasts 5 years and $100 bill lasts 8.5 years. For more information visit the BEP's website:

WEB SITE www.moneyfactory.com

The U.S. $1 Bill: An Owner's Manual

Everybody knows that George Washington is on the U.S. one-dollar bill, but did you ever wonder what all that other stuff is? Here's a guide:

Plate position
Shows where on the 32-note plate this bill was printed.

The Treasury Department seal: The balancing scales represent justice. The pointed stripe across the middle has 13 stars for the original 13 colonies. The key represents authority.

Serial number
Each bill has its own.

Plate serial number
Shows which printing plate was used for the face of the bill.

Federal Reserve District Number
Shows which district issued the bill.

Secretary of the Treasury signature

Treasurer of the U.S. Signature

Series indicator (year note's design was first used)

(Since 1949, every Treasurer of the U.S. has been a woman.)

Federal Reserve District Seal
The name of the Federal Reserve Bank that issued the bill is printed in the seal. The letter tells you quickly where the bill is from. Here are the letter codes for the 12 Federal Reserve Districts:

A: Boston	**G:** Chicago
B: New York	**H:** St. Louis
C: Philadelphia	**I:** Minneapolis
D: Cleveland	**J:** Kansas City
E: Richmond	**K:** Dallas
F: Atlanta	**L:** San Francisco

Front of the Great Seal of the United States: The bald eagle is the national bird. The shield has 13 stripes for the 13 original colonies. The eagle holds 13 arrows (symbol of war) and an olive branch (symbol of peace). Above the eagle is the motto "E Pluribus Unum," Latin for "out of many, one," and a constellation of 13 stars.

Plate serial number
Shows which plate was used for the back.

Reverse of the Great Seal of the United States:
The pyramid symbolizes something that lasts for ages. It is unfinished because the U.S. is always growing. The eye, known as the "Eye of Providence," probably comes from an ancient Egyptian symbol. The pyramid has 13 levels; at its base are the Roman numerals for 1776, the year of American independence. "Annuit Coeptis" is Latin for "God has favored our undertaking." "Novus Ordo Seclorum" is Latin for "a new order of the ages." Both phrases are from the works of the Roman poet Virgil.

why BUDGETS are HELPFUL

A budget is a plan that estimates how much money a person, a business, or a government will receive during a period of time, how much money will be spent and what it will be spent on, and how much money will be left over (if any).

A Family Budget

Do you know what your family spends money on? Do you know where your family's income comes from? The chart below shows some sources of income and typical yearly expenses for a family's budget.

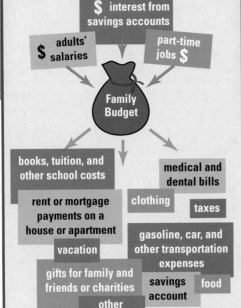

A BALANCED BUDGET

A budget is **balanced** when the amount of money you receive equals the amount of money you spend. A budget is **in deficit** when the amount of money you spend is greater than the amount of money you have.

Making Your Own Budget

Imagine that you have a weekly allowance of $10. With this money you have to pay for things like snacks and magazines and also try to save up for special things. Planning a budget will help you manage your money. Here are some items you might want to put in your budget:

Money Spent:

Snacks: ($.50 per day, 5 days)	$2.50
Magazine:	$3.00
Music Download:	$1.00
Other Spending:	$1.00
Total Spending:	**$7.50**

Savings:	**$2.50**

Now, list items you want to buy this week, and the cost of each item. Subtract those costs from your total weekly alowance to find out how much you can save.

Item	Cost
_____	____
_____	____
_____	____
_____	____
_____	____
_____	____
_____	____
_____	____
_____	____

Total Spending:

Savings:

MONEY MATCH UP

Do you know which famous face goes on which bill or coin? **Draw a line** matching each face to each coin or bill.

Abraham Lincoln

George Washington

Thomas Jefferson

Alexander Hamilton

50¢   **10¢**

25¢

5¢   **$1**

1¢

John F. Kennedy

$1

Ulysses S. Grant

$2   **$5**

$10   **$20**

$50   **$100**

Benjamin Franklin

Andrew Jackson

Sacagawea

Golden Dollar Obverse © 1999 United States Mint. All Rights Reserved. Used with permission.

Franklin D. Roosevelt

Bonus Money Questions

The portraits of three U.S. presidents appear on both a coin and a bill. Can you name them? Can you name the only three people who appear on money commonly in circulation today who were not U.S. presidents?

ANSWERS ON PAGES 335-338. FOR MORE PUZZLES GO TO WWW.WORLDALMANACFORKIDS.COM

131

Movie & TV
Facts

Nickelodeon storefront theater

- The news program *Meet the Press* is the longest running show on network television. It first appeared on NBC in 1947. Before that, *Meet the Press* was a radio show.

- Film credits: The "best boy" is the first assistant to the gaffer (head electrician) or the key grip (lighting and rigging technician).

- Nickelodeon is not just a TV channel. Around 1905-1915, nickelodeons were popular storefront theaters showing short films for a nickel.

- *The Simpsons* is the longest running situation comedy ever. The show started in 1989 and has been renewed for a 17th season. *The Adventures of Ozzie and Harriet*, which ran from 1952–1966 (14 seasons), held the record previously.

All-Time Top
Movies*

1. Titanic $600,779,824
2. Star Wars. $460,935,665
3. Shrek 2. . . . . $436,471,036
4. E.T. $434,949,459
5. Star Wars: Episode I—The Phantom Menace. . . . $431,065,444
6. Spider-Man $403,706,375
7. Lord of the Rings: The Return of the King . . $377,019,252
8. Spider-Man 2 . . . . $373,377,893
9. The Passion of the Christ $370,270,943
10. Jurassic Park $356,784,000

Source: Internet Movie Database
*As of April 7, 2005, based on U.S. ticket sales.

All-Time Top
Animated Movies*

1. Shrek 2 . . . . $436,471,036
2. Finding Nemo $339,714,367
3. The Lion King $328,423,001
4. Shrek $267,652,016
5. The Incredibles . . $261,970,615
6. Monsters, Inc. . . . $255,870,172
7. Toy Story 2 . . . . . . $245,823,397
8. Aladdin $217,350,219
9. Toy Story $191,773,049
10. Ice Age $176,387,405

Source: Internet Movie Database
*As of April 7, 2005, based on U.S. ticket sales.

Some Movie Hits of 2004

Garfield (PG)

Harry Potter and the Prisoner of Azkaban (PG)

The Incredibles (PG)

Lemony Snicket's A Series of Unfortunate Events (PG)

The Lord of the Rings: Return of the King (PG-13)

Mean Girls (PG-13)

National Treasure (PG)

Ocean's Twelve (PG-13)

The Polar Express (G)

Princess Diaries 2: The Royal Engagement (G)

Scooby-Doo 2: Monsters Unleashed (PG)

Shark Tale (PG)

Shrek 2 (PG) ▶

Spider-Man 2 (PG-13)

The SpongeBob SquarePants Movie (PG)

Top TV Shows in 2004-2005

AGES 6-11

1. American Idol
2. Survivor: Palau
3. Krypto the Super Dog
4. Zoey 101
5. Extreme Makeover: Home Edition
6. Drake and Josh
7. Ned's Declassified School Survival Guide
8. Survivor: Vanuatu
9. SpongeBob SquarePants
10. Unfabulous

AGES 12-17

1. Butt Ugly Martians
2. Powerpuff Girls
3. America's Next Top Model (3)
4. WWE Entertainment
5. .hack/Legend of the Twilight
6. Cyborg 009
7. Boy Meets World
8. Brandy & Mr. Wiskers
9. Recess
10. Fresh Prince of Bel-Air

American Idol's 2005 contestants

Top TV Shows in 1994-1995

AGES 6-11

1. Boy Meets World
2. Step by Step
3. Home Improvement
4. Hangin' with Mr. Cooper
5. Full House
6. Family Matters
7. Me and the Boys
8. Sister, Sister
9. On Our Own
10. Thunder Alley

AGES 12-17

1. Home Improvement
2. In the House
3. Blossom
4. Me and the Boys
5. Fresh Prince of Bel-Air
6. Grace Under Fire
7. Boy Meets World
8. Full House
9. Beverly Hills, 90210
10. Step by Step

The cast of Home Improvement

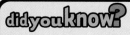 The Incredibles *took the Oscar for Best Animated Film (and Best Sound Editing) at the 2005 Academy Awards.*

133

10 years ago

Stars of 1995

The year 1995 was huge for **Tom Hanks**. He starred (center▶) in the still-popular astronaut drama *Apollo 13* and he was the voice of Woody in the smash-hit *Toy Story*, the first full-length film to be completely animated by computer. This ground-breaking CGI (computer-generated image) film also featured these celebrity voices: Tim Allen (Buzz Lightyear), Don Rickles (Mr. Potato Head), Jim Varney (Slinky Dog), Wallace Shawn (Rex), John Ratzenberger (Hamm), and Annie Potts (Bo Peep).

◀Superstar **Jim Carrey** has always been funny. But in 1994 and 1995 he really made a big splash with five films. In 1994, he starred in *The Mask*, *Dumb and Dumber* (with Jeff Daniels) and *Ace Ventura: Pet Detective*. Jim played the wild Riddler in *Batman Forever* in 1995 and also starred in the sequel *Ace Ventura: When Nature Calls*.

Box Office Hits of 1995

1. *Batman Forever*
2. *Apollo 13*
3. *Toy Story*
4. *Pocahontas*
5. *Ace Ventura: When Nature Calls*
6. *Casper*
7. *Die Hard With a Vengeance*
8. *Goldeneye*
9. *Crimson Tide*
10. *Waterworld*

1995 MOVIE QUIZ

1. What film, co-starring Kirsten Dunst (who later played Spider-Man's girlfriend, Mary Jane), took its name from a board game?
2. What film starred a little pig with a big heart?
3. What film about a tiny Native American was based on a book by Lynne Reid Banks?
4. Buzz Lightyear was a character in *Toy Story*. What is a light-year?
5. What film, based on a 1970s TV show, featured a blended family with a "bunch" of six kids?
6. What film featured yellow, black, red, white, pink, and blue characters?

Answers on Pages 335—338. For more puzzles go to
WWW.WORLDALMANACFORKIDS.COM

MOVIES TO LOOK FOR IN 2005

Batman Begins—The story of how the young Bruce Wayne becomes the "caped crusader" (July).

Charlie and the Chocolate Factory—Johnny Depp stars as Willy Wonka in this remake of a 1971 classic film about a magical candy factory, based on the book by Roald Dahl (July).

Chicken Little—This Disney animated film picks up at the end of the classic fable, telling "the rest of the story" of Chicken Little (July).

The Chronicles of Narnia: The Lion, The Witch, and The Wardrobe—The second book of the classic fantasy series was filmed in New Zealand (December).

Curse of the Were-Rabbit Starring Wallace & Gromit—From the British stop-action animators who made *Chicken Run*—and the wonderful "Wallace & Gromit" short films (October).

Fantastic Four—Comic book heroes The Thing, Mr. Fantastic, Invisible Girl, and The Human Torch come to life on the big screen (July).

Harry Potter and the Goblet of Fire—The world's favorite wizard continues his magical education (November).

Herbie: Fully Loaded—Disney's legendary VW Lovebug, Herbie, co-stars with Lindsay Lohan (June).

Madagascar—From Dreamworks, the makers of the *Shrek* movies. Ben Stiller, Chris Rock, Jada Pinkett-Smith, and David Schwimmer provide voices for this animated animal adventure (May).

The cast of The Sisterhood of the Traveling Pants.

The Sisterhood of the Traveling Pants—Based on Ann Brashares' novel, stars Amber Tamblyn (*Joan of Arcadia*) and Alexis Bledel (*Gilmore Girls*) (June).

Star Wars: Episode III—Revenge of the Sith—The greatest series of science fiction adventure films concludes (May). ▼

Keisha Castle-Hughes as Queen Apailana

Looking Waaay Ahead to 2006

Cars—From Pixar, makers of *The Incredibles*, *Finding Nemo* and the *Toy Story* movies.

Iron Man—The Marvel Comic super hero Tony Stark in his first feature film.

Superman Returns—Superman will be played by 25-year-old Brandon Routh. He will also play Clark Kent.

Pirates of the Caribbean 2: Dead Man's Chest—Johnny Depp, Captain Jack Sparrow, will be back, along with Orlando Bloom and Keira Knightley.

X3: X-Men 3—Your favorite mutant superhero team back in action.

And lastly, look for *Spider-Man 3* sometime in 2007!

People to Watch

Emily Browning

Born: December 7, 1988, in Melbourne, Victoria, Australia

Known for: Starring as Violet Baudelaire to Jim Carrey's Count Olaf in the 2004 hit film *Lemony Snicket's A Series of Unfortunate Events*.

did you know? Emily, who has two years of high school left, still lives in Australia.

Devon Werkheiser

Born: March 8, 1991, in Atlanta, Georgia.

Known for: Starring as Ned Bigby on the Nickelodeon TV show *Ned's Declassified School Survival Guide*.

did you know? Devon first got into acting by reciting lines from *Ace Ventura Pet Detective*.

All About...
Pixar Animation Studios

In 1984 a man named John Lasseter left Disney to work for director George Lucas's computer special-effects group. Two years after that, in 1986, Steve Jobs (the head of Apple computers) bought the computer graphics group and named it "Pixar." There were about 44 people working at the company then. That same year, Pixar released its first short film, *Luxo Jr.*, about a baby desk lamp and his father. The film was nominated for an Academy Award for Best Short Film. (It didn't win, but two years later, Pixar's *Tin Toy* did.)

For the next nine years, Pixar made award-winning short films and commercials. The company pioneered many new techniques in computer graphics for film and designed its own software. But most people had probably never heard of Pixar. That all changed in 1995, with the release of *Toy Story*—the first full-length film to be animated entirely by computer. Lasseter got a special achievement award at the 1995 Academy Awards for his inspired leadership of the Pixar *Toy Story* team.

Next came *A Bug's Life* (1998), *Toy Story 2* (1999), *Monsters, Inc.* (2001), *Finding Nemo* (2003), and *The Incredibles* (2004). *Shrek* (Dreamworks) may have won the first-ever Oscar for Best Animated Feature Film in 2001, but Pixar is on a roll, winning the award in 2003 (*Finding Nemo*) and 2004 (*The Incredibles*).

The animators at Pixar are hard at work on *Cars*, a new film set for a summer 2006 release. It's about a hotshot racecar named Lightning McQueen.

The company's logo includes a picture of a desk lamp, honoring the first film Pixar ever made.

Museums

When will the U.S. National Slavery Museum open? page 138

The Smithsonian Institution

The word *museum* comes from a Greek word that means "temple of the Muses." The Muses were the Greek goddesses of art and science.

The oldest museum in the U.S. is The Charleston Museum, founded in South Carolina in 1773. The U.S. now has about 16,000 museums. Some are described here. For others, look in the Index under "Museums." You can also check out the Association of Children's Museums on the Internet at

WEB SITE www.childrensmuseums.org

In 1835, the people of the United States received a unique gift from an English scientist. In his will, James Smithson left $508,318 to the U.S. to set up an institution for the "increase and diffusion of knowledge." Today, the Smithsonian is the biggest museum complex in the world, with museums devoted to aviation and space exploration, American history, the arts, natural history, postal history, cultural history, and other fields. In addition to its 18 museums and 9 research centers, the Smithsonian also includes the National Zoo. Admission is free for all Smithsonian museums in Washington, D.C.

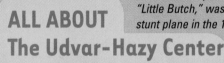

This Monocoupe 110 Special, "Little Butch," was used as a stunt plane in the 1940s.

ALL ABOUT The Udvar-Hazy Center

The Udvar-Hazy Center's Hanger

The most popular museum in Washington, D.C., is the Smithsonian Institution's National Air and Space Museum, which recently which opened a new facility, the Steven F. Udvar-Hazy Center, at Washington Dulles International Airport in Chantilly, Virginia. Although the museum in downtown Washington exhibits some pretty big items, the new branch can display the really big stuff.

The Udvar-Hazy Center includes a hangar for aviation exhibits and another for space exhibits, as well as a 164-foot tower for observing planes flying in and out of Dulles Airport. Among the centers exhibits are the Space Shuttle *Enterprise*, the B-29 Superfortress *Enola Gay* that dropped an atomic bomb on Hiroshima, Japan during World War II, the de Havilland Chipmunk aerobatic plane, and the Concorde supersonic jetliner. One popular feature is SpaceWalk 2004 3D, which takes you on a virtual trip around the International Space Station. Even more popular is the "At the Controls" flight simulator, which lets you select from dozens of aircraft to pilot in a simulated flight.

The Underground Railroad

The new **National Underground Railroad Freedom Center** opened in August 2004 in Cincinnati. That city on the Ohio River was an important crossroads in the Underground Railroad that helped escaped slaves journey north to freedom. The river was the legal boundary between slave-owning states and free states. A restored two-story slave pen is a featured exhibit of the center. There is also a specially designed exhibit called "Escape!" that helps kids learn what life was like on the Underground Railroad from 1830 to 1861.

didyouknow?

In 2007, the United States National Slavery Museum will open in Fredericksburg, Virginia (near Washington, D.C.). The 100,000-square-foot building will house exhibits that trace African-Americans' journeys from Africa on slave ships through the Civil War and the continuing struggle for equality.

WEB SITE www.usnationalslaverymuseum.org

Children's Museums

10th ANNIVERSARY

Here is a list of children's musems from the first-ever *World Almanac for Kids 1996*. They are still around. One thing that was missing from that list, which we've included here, are websites! Back in 1996, very few people were using the Internet.

Children's Museum, Boston, Massachusetts. Has a full-size wigwam and contemporary American Indian house; a 28-foot-long, 800-gallon water tank for model boats; and climbing walls. **WEB SITE** *www.bostonkids.org*

Children's Museum of Indianapolis, ▶
Indianapolis, Indiana. Enter the "Dinosphere" one of the country's biggest displays of juvenile and family dinosaur fossils. There is also a functioning Paleo Lab, a hands-on dig, and a great collection of dinosaur art.
WEB SITE *www.childrensmuseum.org*

Children's Musuem of Manhattan, New York, New York. Go exploring with Dora or take a hands-on trip into the upsidedown world of Dr. Seuss.
WEB SITE *www.cmom.org*

Portland Children's Museum, Portland, Oregon. Across the street from the Oregon Zoo, this museum has exhibits that let you build, create, and learn to do things you've never done before.
WEB SITE *www.portlandcm2.org*

Children's Museum of Los Angeles, Los Angeles, California. This hands-on museum will be moving to a new building in 2007. The environmentally friendly building will practically be an exhibit all by itself. **WEB SITE** *www.childrensmuseumla.org*

These are just a few well-known children's museums. To find another one near you, go to the "Locate a U.S. Children's Museum" page on the Association of Children's Museums Web site:
WEB SITE *www.childrensmuseums.org/full-us.htm*

MUSEUMS OF ALL KINDS

The American Celebration on Parade, near New Market, Virginia, is the place for you if you've ever wondered where floats go after the parade is over. The 40,000-square-foot museum holds floats from the Rose Parade, presidential inaugurals, and many other events.

WEB SITE *www.americancelebrationonparade.com*

The American Sanitary Plumbing Museum in Worcester, Massachusetts is not glamorous; exhibits on the history of toilets, sinks, and pipes do show how indoor plumbing has made our lives healthier and happier.

The International UFO Museum and Research Center in Roswell, New Mexico, is dedicated to research into UFOs, or "unidentified flying objects" from outer space. Some say that a UFO crashed in the nearby desert back in 1947.

WEB SITE *www.iufomrc.org*

The Mütter Museum in Philadelphia, Pennsylvania, is filled with strange medical wonders. The fascinating but gross items on display include buttons, safety pins, and children's toys removed from people's stomachs, as well as preserved brains, tumors, and other body parts.

WEB SITE *www.collphyphil.org/muttvisi.htm*

National Automobile Museum, Reno, Nevada. Many of its more than 200 cars were collected by casino owner Bill Harrah. Opened in 1989, the building has rounded walls painted in the 1950s car color "Heather Fire Mist," complete with chrome trim. Inside is one of the world's biggest collections of "horseless carriages," from 1892 to the present. The collection is known for its one-of-a-kind experimental cars. **WEB SITE** *www.automuseum.org*

A 1938 Packard

National Museum of Health and Medicine, Washington, D.C. Founded during the Civil War as the Army Medical Museum, it holds specimens for research in military medicine and surgery. One of the most popular exhibits has artifacts from President Lincoln's assassination, including the bullet. There is an exibit on battlefield surgery and the world's largest collection of microscopes. **WEB SITE** *nmhm.washingtondc.museum*

Dr. Samuel D. Harris National Museum of Dentistry, Baltimore, Maryland. This museum is located on the campus of the University of Maryland Baltimore, near the world's oldest dental college (founded in 1840). The "tooth jukebox" is a popular exhibit. And don't miss the new exhibit on "Saliva: a Remarkable Fluid." It's supposed to be "spit-tacular."

WEB SITE *www.dentalmuseum.umaryland.edu*

Music & Dance

At what age did Mozart write his first symphony?   page 142

Musical Instruments

There are many kinds of musical instruments. Instruments in an orchestra are divided into four groups, or sections: string, woodwind, brass, and percussion.

PERCUSSION INSTRUMENTS

Percussion instruments make sounds when they are struck. The most common percussion instrument is the drum. Others include cymbals, triangles, gongs, bells, and xylophone. Keyboard instruments, like the piano, are sometimes included in percussion instruments.

BRASSES

Brass instruments are hollow inside. They make sounds when air is blown into a mouthpiece shaped like a cup or a funnel. The trumpet, French horn, trombone, and tuba are brasses.

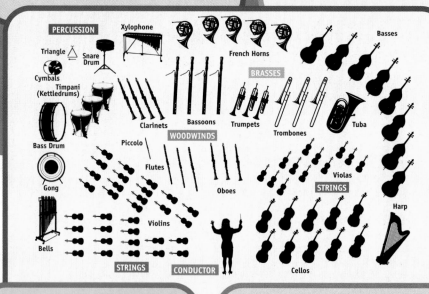

PERCUSSION
Xylophone
Triangle
Snare Drum
Cymbals
Timpani (Kettledrums)
Bass Drum
Piccolo
Clarinets
Bassoons
WOODWINDS
Flutes
Gong
Oboes
Violins
Bells
STRINGS
CONDUCTOR
French Horns
BRASSES
Trumpets
Trombones
Tuba
Basses
Violas
STRINGS
Harp
Cellos

WOODWINDS

Woodwind instruments are long and cylindrical and hollow inside. They make sounds when air is blown into them through a mouth hole or a reed. The clarinet, flute, oboe, bassoon, and piccolo are woodwinds.

STRINGS

Stringed instruments make sounds when the strings are either stroked with a bow or plucked with the fingers. The violin, viola, cello, bass, and harp are used in an orchestra. The guitar, banjo, and mandolin are other stringed instruments.

Chart-Topping Albums—Then and Now

Ten years ago, when the first *World Almanac for Kids* was published, hardly anyone had ever heard of Britney Spears or Christina Aguilera. In 1993-94, they were on Disney's "The Mickey Mouse Club" TV show with Justin Timberlake and JC Chasez. Justin and JC went on to join *NSYNC, which debuted in 1995.

Check out the chart-topping albums of today, below. Then, take a look at what was popular back in 1994. Do you recognize any of the singers or albums?

TOP ALBUMS of 2004

1. *Confessions*, Usher
2. *Speakerboxx/The Love Below*, OutKast*
3. *Closer*, Josh Groban
4. *The Diary of Alicia Keys*, Alicia Keys
5. *Feels Like Home*, Norah Jones
6. *Fallen*, Evanescence
7. *Shock'n Y'all*, Toby Keith
8. *In the Zone*, Britney Spears
9. *The Very Best of Sheryl Crow*, Sheryl Crow
10. *When the Sun Goes Down*, Kenny Chesney

*These albums contain explicit lyrics. Edited versions suitable for kids are widely available.

▲ Chart-topping singer Usher shares a performance with fellow star Alicia Keys.

TOP ALBUMS of 1994

1. *The Sign*, Ace of Base
2. *Music Box*, Mariah Carey ▶
3. *Doggie Style*, Snoop Doggy Dogg*
4. *The Lion King*, Soundtrack
5. *August and Everything After*, Counting Crows
6. *Vs.*, Pearl Jam
7. *Toni Braxton*, Toni Braxton
8. *Janet*, Janet Jackson
9. *Bat Out of Hell II: Back Into Hell*, Meat Loaf
10. *The One Thing*, Michael Bolton

*This album contains explicit lyrics.

ALL ABOUT . . .
MOZART, CHILD PRODIGY

Have you ever wished you were a genius? Have you ever imagined what it would be like to be able to do something amazing that no one else could do? That's what it must have been like for Wolfgang Amadeus Mozart. Born in 1756 in the city of Salzburg in the Austrian Alps, Mozart showed his musical genius at an early age. Encouraged by his father, an accomplished violinist and composer, Mozart began to play the harpsichord at the age of three! At age four he could compose piano music and play the violin. He began composing minuets at age five and symphonies at age nine.

Mozart could compose a long piece of music in his head by imagining what he wanted it to sound like, and then play it perfectly, often without writing it down. And when he did write it down it was flawless. When Mozart was 12, he and his father visited St. Peter's Cathedral in Rome, where they heard a famous piece of music called a *Miserere*.

This music was so beautiful that the Church did not allow it to be copied or performed elsewhere. But Mozart loved the piece so much that he wrote it down from memory so he could play it himself.

During his lifetime, Mozart produced over 600 musical works, including operas, symphonies, chamber music, and church music. His best-known operas are *The Marriage of Figaro, Don Giovanni,* and *The Magic Flute.*

When Mozart was a child prodigy, people were astounded at his musical genius. But as he got older, he was no longer the amazing boy wonder people wanted to see. Much of his musical career was spent as a paid servant to the royal court or to wealthy patrons, who hired him to compose a specific piece of music. Mozart didn't like being a "composer for hire." "I get paid too much for what I do," he said, "and far too little for what I could do."

Mozart died poor in 1791 at the early age of 35, probably from typhoid fever. Although he was buried in an unmarked grave, he is remembered as perhaps the most brilliant composer who ever lived, and his joyous music is performed throughout the world today.

EXTRA CREDIT: What was the title of the 1984 hit movie about Mozart?

Answer: *Amadeus*

Musical Theater

"The sun will come out tomorrow." We bet your bottom dollar that you know that song. It's "Tomorrow" from the musical *Annie*, about a poor red-haired orphan girl who ends up with a happy future. American musical theater uses singing, dancing, music, and dialogue to tell meaningful stories in exciting ways. People come from all over the world to see musicals on Broadway, New York City's theater district. Musicals are also staged in theaters big and small around the world.

Some current musicals, like *Hairspray* (2002) and *Wicked* (2003), have been especially popular with kids. Many classic musicals, including *Annie*, have been made into movies that you could watch at home. Do you recognize any of the songs below?

Show	Year Opened	Great Song
Annie Get Your Gun	1946	"There's No Business Like Show Business"
The King and I	1951	"Getting to Know You"
My Fair Lady	1956	"Wouldn't It Be Loverly?"
The Music Man	1957	"Seventy-Six Trombones"
The Sound of Music	1959	"My Favorite Things"
Fiddler on the Roof	1964	"If I Were a Rich Man"
Grease	1972	"Summer Nights"

ALL ABOUT... YOUTH THEATER

Musicals about adults can be fun, but what about musicals about kids? In some musicals, you'll find songs about bullies, after-school jobs, monsters, and sleepovers.

At Tada!, a youth theater in New York City, kids 8 to 18 sing and dance their way through original musicals in which kids play the roles of . . . kids! Each year dozens of kids in Tada!'s "great big, happy hard-working family" get the chance to perform for thousands of theater-goers!

Kids work long hours to learn their lines, songs, and choreography (dances). But as 16-year-old Tada! actor Phoebe Duncan says, "There's something amazing about opening night. You've worked for so many weeks on a show, you feel like it'll never be good, everyone is panicking ... and then, somehow, it all comes together. It's an incredible feeling."

Youth theaters aren't just in New York. You can find them in Flint, MI; Mason City, IA; San Jose, CA., and lots of other towns and cities. To find one in your area visit

WEB SITE dir.yahoo.com/arts/performing_arts/theatre/youth_theatre/theater_companies/

Mythology

Which day is named for the Norse thunder god? page 146

MYTHS of the GREEKS

As the ancient Greeks went about their daily lives, they believed that a big family of gods and goddesses were watching over them from Mount Olympus. Farmers planting crops, sailors crossing the sea, and poets writing verses thought that these powerful beings could help or harm them. Stories of the gods and goddesses are called myths. Some of the oldest myths came from the *Iliad* and *Odyssey*, long poems in Greek composed around 700 B.C.

After the Romans conquered Greece in 146 B.C., they adopted Greek myths but gave Roman names to the main gods and goddesses. Today, the other planets in our solar system are named after Roman gods.

GREEK & ROMAN GODS

The family of Greek and Roman gods and goddesses was large. Their family tree would have more than 50 figures on it. Here are some major gods. Those with * are children of Zeus (Jupiter).

Greek Name	Roman Name	Description
Aphrodite	Venus	Goddess of beauty and of love.
*Apollo	Phoebus	God of prophecy, music, and medicine.
*Ares	Mars	God of war; protector of the city.
*Artemis	Diana	Goddess of the Moon; a great huntress.
*Athena	Minerva	Goddess of wisdom and of war.
Cronus	Saturn	Father of Jupiter (Zeus), Neptune (Poseidon), Pluto (Hades), Juno (Hera), and Ceres (Demeter)
Demeter	Ceres	Goddess of crops and harvest, sister of Zeus (Jupiter).
*Dionysus	Bacchus	God of wine, dancing, and theater.
Hades	Pluto	Ruler of the underworld, brother of Zeus (Jupiter).
Hephaestus	Vulcan	God of fire.
Hera	Juno	Queen of the gods, wife of Zeus (Jupiter), goddess of marriage.
*Hermes	Mercury	Messenger god, had winged helmet and sandals.
Poseidon	Neptune	God of the sea and of earthquakes, brother of Zeus (Jupiter).
Zeus	Jupiter	Sky god, ruler of gods and mortals.

MAKING SENSE of the WORLD

Unlike folklore or fables, myths were once thought to be true. The Greeks and Romans explained many of the things in nature by referring to the gods. (So did other ancient peoples, such as the Egyptians and the Norse). To the Greeks a rough sea meant that POSEIDON was angry. Lightning was the work of ZEUS, ruler of the universe. The sun went across the sky because APOLLO was driving the chariot of the sun.

One of the most famous nature stories is about PERSEPHONE, or Proserpina, the daughter of Zeus and DEMETER. HADES, who fell in love with her, kidnapped her and carried her off to the underworld (where people went after death). The gods asked Hades to bring her back, but while in the underworld Persephone had eaten part of a pomegranate (the food of the dead), which meant she could not return. Eventually the gods worked out a deal. She could spend half of every year on earth and half in the underworld. When Persephone is on earth, flowers bloom and crops grow, but when she is with Hades, plants wither and die. This is how the Greeks explained the seasons.

A famous place in ancient Greece was the TEMPLE OF APOLLO AT DELPHI. Inside it was a sacred stone that the Greeks believed to be the center of the world. The most important thing about Delphi, however, was its oracle. This was a priestess through whom, it was believed, Apollo spoke.

Statue of Poseidon

Greek and Roman Heroes

Besides the gods, Greek and Roman mythology has many stories about "heroes" who had superhuman qualities. They were somewhere between ordinary humans and full-blown gods. Often, a hero became famous for destroying some kind of monster:

- THESEUS went into the great maze known as the Labyrinth and killed the **Minotaur**, a man-eating creature with the head of a bull and the body of a man.

- PERSEUS cut off the head of **Medusa**, a terrifying woman who had snakes for hair and whose stare turned people to stone.

- BELLEROPHON, with the help of the famous winged horse **Pegasus**, killed the fire-breathing **Chimaera**.

But the most popular hero was Herakles, or **Hercules**. The most famous of his deeds were his twelve labors. They included killing the **Hydra**, a many-headed monster, and capturing the horrible three-headed dog **Cerberus**, who guarded the gates of the underworld. Hercules was so great a hero that the gods granted him immortality. When his body lay on his funeral pyre, Athena came and carried him off to Mount Olympus in her chariot.

Norse Mythology

You may never had heard of the gods and goddesses from Norse mythology, but you use their names all the time, in a way. Tuesday is named after the Norse god Tyr (later known as Tiw), Wednesday after Wodan (usually spelled Odin), Thursday after Thor, and Friday after Frigg and Freya. (Saturday is another story—you can look up the Roman god it was named after.)

Norse mythology was developed by peoples in far Northern Europe (Scandinavia). They sailed far from their homelands and carried their legends to Iceland, England, Germany, and the Netherlands.

The Norse myths tell us that the gods and goddesses live in the heavens in a place called **Asgard**, which is reached by a rainbow bridge. Other beings, such as giants, elves, and humans, have their own homes. The goddess Hel rules over **Niflheim**, the underworld or home of the dead. Humans live in **Midgard**, or Middle Earth. The end of the world, the myths say, will come in a great battle called **Ragnarök** (doomsday). In Asgard there is a great hall with a roof of shields, called **Valhalla**, where warriors killed in battle go. There they wait for the time when they will fight with Odin against the giants at the end of the world.

Major Norse Gods

Name	Description
Odin	One-eyed king of the gods. God of war, death, poetry, wisdom, and magic.
Thor	Son of Odin. God of thunder, lightning, and rain.
Frigg	Wife of Odin. Goddess of marriage, motherhood, and the home.
Freya	Goddess of birth and of crops.
Tyr	Sky god and god of war and justice. His hand was bitten off by the wolf Fenrir.
Baldur	Son of Odin. God of light, purity, and beauty. Best loved of the gods.
Loki	Son of giants and father of Hel. Clever trickster who sometimes helped Thor and Odin and was sometimes their enemy.
Hel	Goddess of death. Daughter of Loki.
Heimdall	Son of nine giantesses. Watchman of the rainbow bridge. Known for his keen eyes and ears, he could hear grass growing.

Nations

Which country is the least crowded? page 149

GOVERNMENTS around the WORLD

Among the world's 193 independent nations there are various kinds of governments.

WHAT IS TOTALITARIANISM?

In **totalitarian** countries the rulers have strong power and the people have little freedom. Germany under Adolf Hitler and Iraq under Saddam Hussein had one all-powerful ruler or dictator. Today, North Korea has a totalitarian government. Dictators usually try to put down anyone opposing them. If they hold elections, they may be the only candidate allowed to campaign freely, or the only candidate on the ballot!

WHAT IS A MONARCHY?

A country with a king or queen can be called a **monarchy**. Monarchies are almost always hereditary, meaning the throne is passed down in one family. In the United Kingdom and most other nations that still have kings or queens, royal figures have charitable and ceremonial duties but hold little real power—elected officials head the government. These countries are constitutional monarchies. But some countries still are traditional monarchies, governed by their royal families; Saudi Arabia is an example.

WHAT IS A DEMOCRACY?

The word **democracy** comes from the Greek words **demos** ("people") and **kratia** ("rule"). In a democracy, the people rule. Since there are too many people to agree on everyday decisions themselves, democracies nowadays are **representative** democracies; this means the people make decisions through the leaders they choose. In the U.S., these include the president and members of Congress. Mexico and some other countries also have a "presidential" system, where voters elect the head of the government. But many democracies use a "parliamentary system." In these countries—the United Kingdom, Canada, and Japan, for example—voters elect members of a parliament, or legislature, and then the members of parliament pick a cabinet to head the government. The leader of the cabinet is called the prime minister.

In a democracy people can complain about the government and vote it out of office, which they often do. Winston Churchill, one of Britain's greatest prime ministers, probably had this in mind when he said, "Democracy is the worst form of government except for all those others that have been tried."

Winston Churchill

Homework Help

A *Head of State* is the person with the highest rank or office, such as the queen of the United Kingdom or the president of Italy. That person may often have little or no political power. The *Head of Government*, on the other hand, is the political leader in charge of the government. In many countries, such as Canada or Italy, that would be the prime minister. In the U.S. and some other countries the president is both Head of State and Head of Government.

WHERE DO PEOPLE LIVE?

In 1959, there were three billion people in the world. In 1999, the number hit six billion. According to the latest estimates by the UN, the world population will have reached 6.4 billion by mid-2005, and will grow to almost nine billion by 2050. This is a lot of people, but not as many as predicted a few years ago. The UN lowered its estimates of how many people will be born and increased its estimates of deaths from the deadly AIDS epidemic.

POPULATIONS

Smallest (2005)

	Country	Population
1.	Vatican City	921
2.	Tuvalu	11,636
3.	Nauru	13,048
4.	Palau	20,303
5.	San Marino	28,880
6.	Monaco	32,409
7.	Liechtenstein	33,717
8.	Saint Kitts and Nevis	38,958
9.	Marshall Islands	59,071
10.	Antigua and Barbuda	68,722

Largest (2005)

	Country	Population
1.	China*	1,306,313,812
2.	India	1,080,264,388
3.	United States	295,734,134
4.	Indonesia	241,973,879
5.	Brazil	186,112,794
6.	Pakistan	162,419,946
7.	Bangladesh	144,319,628
8.	Russia	143,420,309
9.	Nigeria	128,771,988
10.	Japan	127,417,244

* Excluding Taiwan, pop. 22,894,384; Hong Kong, pop. 6,898,686, and Macao, pop. 449,19

Source: U.S. Census Bureau, *CIA World Factbook*

Largest Ten Cities in the World

Here are the ten cities that had the most people, according to UN estimates for 2003. Numbers include people from the built-up area around each city (metropolitan area), not just the city. (See page 200 for the ten biggest U.S. cities.)

City, Country	Population	City, Country	Population
1. Tokyo, Japan	34,997,300	6. Delhi, India	14,146,000
2. Mexico City, Mexico	18,660,200	7. Calcutta, India	13,805,700
3. New York area, U.S.	18,252,300	8. Buenos Aires, Argentina	13,047,000
4. São Paulo, Brazil	17,857,000	9. Shanghai, China	12,759,000
5. Mumbai (Bombay), India	17,431,300	10. Jakarta, Indonesia	12,296,000

Biggest, Smallest, Most Crowded

It's a big world out there! Our planet has about 196,940,000 square miles of surface area. However, over 70 percent of that area is water. The total land area, 57,506,000 square miles, is about 16 times the area of the United States.

So, which nation is the biggest? Russia is on top with over 6.5 million square miles of land area. China comes in a distant second with 3.6 million square miles, while the U.S. and Canada are close behind.

The smallest countries are Vatican City, Monaco, and Nauru. These countries are also among the most crowded (densely populated).

Land areas for countries below do not include inland water. Rankings by total area, including inland water, will differ from these.

Largest (2005)

	Country	sq mi
1.	Russia	6,562,112
2.	China	3,600,946
3.	United States	3,537,437
4.	Canada	3,511,021
5.	Brazil	3,265,075
6.	Australia	2,941,298
7.	India	1,147,955
8.	Argentina	1,056,641
9.	Kazakhstan	1,030,815
10.	Algeria	919,595

Smallest (2005)

	Country	sq mi
1.	Vatican City	0.17
2.	Monaco	0.75
3.	Nauru	8
4.	Tuvalu	10
5.	San Marino	24
6.	Liechtenstein	62
7.	Marshall Islands	70
8.	Saint Kitts and Nevis	101
9.	Maldives	116
10.	Malta	122

Source: U.S. Census Bureau, *CIA World Factbook*

Most Densely Populated

	Country	Persons per sq mi*
1.	Monaco	43,045
2.	Singapore	16,790
3.	Vatican City	5,418
4.	Malta	3,266
5.	Maldives	3,014
6.	Bangladesh	2,791
7.	Bahrain	2,681
8.	Taiwan	1,838
9.	Nauru	1,609
10.	Mauritius	1,570

* For comparison, New Jersey is the most densely populated state, with 1,164 people per square mile.

To get the population density, divide the population by the area. Density is calculated here according to land area, based on 2005 population.

Most Sparsely Populated

	Country	Persons per sq mi
1.	Mongolia	4.7
2.	Namibia	6.4
3.	Australia	6.8
4.	Suriname	7.0
5.	Botswana	7.3
6.	Iceland	7.7
7.	Mauritania	7.8
8.	Libya	8.5
9.	Canada	9.3
10.	Guyana	10.1

KIDS
AROUND THE W🌐RLD

INDONESIA

Indonesia is made up of more than 13,000 islands. It has people from many different ethnic groups. They speak over 250 languages. Most of Indonesia's 230 million people are Muslims, like these kids. Families in rural areas often live in small houses on platforms, with a ladder to get in and out. Relatives usually live near each other and do lots of things together. Indonesian kids like video games, cartoons, and Harry Potter. Their favorite sports include soccer, badminton, and a kind of volleyball called *sepak takraw*.

JAPAN

Japan is made up of four large islands and lots of smaller ones. Most of the people live in big cities such as Tokyo and Osaka. Japanese is the official language, but many people speak English when conducting business. Most people are Buddhist and also practice the Japanese religion Shinto. The Japanese love to read and are proud of their 100% literacy rate. The main part of their diet is rice and fish, but fast food like McDonald's is very popular among young people. Japanese kids also love baseball and Western music, and like to dress in jeans and T-shirts. Children have 240 school days every year, (compared to about 180 a year in the U.S.).

NIGERIA

Nigeria has more people than any other country in Africa. Nigerians have big families, and they value family life and education. Christianity and Islam are the major religions. Western culture has influenced many areas of their life, from business to music to food. The children like to watch American shows on satellite TV. But they still like dressing in their colorful native clothes. Nigerians love soccer and other competitive sports, and they enjoy meeting friends and shopping in the markets. These markets are busy and crowded. Besides fruits and vegetables, they sell live chickens, goats, and cows!

PERU

The kids shown here live in the Andes Mountains. In all, four out of five people in Peru are native or part native in ancestry. Many speak Quechua, the language of the ancient Incas. Most Peruvians are Catholics, and seven out of ten live in urban areas. Peruvians often live in extended families, with aunts, uncles, cousins, and grandparents. Soccer and volleyball are popular sports. In some villages where electricity is scarce, there is a TV in the town plaza which everybody can watch.

RUSSIA

Russia is almost twice as big as the U.S. and extends over two continents (Europe and Asia), but has fewer people. Most Russians live in the western part and three out of four live in cities, often in apartment buildings. Russia was part of the former Soviet Union, a Communist country, and the government controlled many aspects of life. Now it is a democracy, but the economy is not doing well and times are hard. All over Russia, "Day of Knowledge" celebrations are held for students on September 1, the traditional start of the school year. Politicians—even the president—give speeches at schools around the country. If the first falls on a day off, kids still go to their schools for concerts, games, sports, and other activities. Chess, gymnastics, ice hockey, soccer, skiing, and skating are some of the most popular activities for kids in Russia.

Maps showing Nations of the World

Maps showing the continents and nations of the world appear on pages 152-163. Flags of the nations appear on pages 164-187. A map of the United States appears on pages 288-289.

AUSTRALIA

⊛ National Capital

★ State Capital

• Other City

1:40,886,000

0   250   500 mi
0   250   500 km

Two-Point Equidistant Projection

©MAPQUEST.COM

PACIFIC ISLANDS

⊛ National Capital

★ Territorial Capital

• Other City

1:84,569,000

0   500   1,000 mi

0   500   1,000 km

Miller Projection

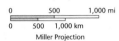

Sala y Gomez (Chile)

Isla de Pascua (Easter I.) (Chile)

Tropic of Capricorn

Pitcairn (Brit.)

Equator

Tropic of Cancer

Marquesas Islands

FRENCH POLYNESIA (Fr.)

Tuamotu Archipelago

Society Islands ★ Papeete Tahiti

PACIFIC OCEAN

Line Islands

Hawaiian Islands (U.S.)

Kauai Oahu Maui Hawaii
Honolulu

Palmyra Atoll (U.S.)

Howland I. (U.S.) Jarvis I. (U.S.)
Baker I. (U.S.)

KIRIBATI

AMERICAN SAMOA

COOK ISLANDS (N.Z.)

★ Avarua

TOKELAU (N.Z.)

SAMOA AND AMERICAN SAMOA
Apia Pago Pago (U.S.)

NIUE (N.Z.)

Wake I. (U.S.)

MARSHALL ISLANDS

Tarawa (Bairiki)
Banaba

Majuro

TUVALU
Funafuti

WALLIS AND FUTUNA (Fr.)

Suva

FIJI

TONGA
Nukualofa

Kermadec I. (N.Z.)

NORTHERN MARIANA ISLANDS
Saipan Tinian Guam (U.S.)

Truk Is.

Caroline Islands

MICRONESIA

Palikir

Yaren
NAURU

SOLOMON ISLANDS
Honiara

VANUATU

Port-Vila

NEW CALEDONIA (Fr.)
★ Nouméa

Norfolk I. (Australia)

North Island

Auckland
Tauranga Gisborne
Hamilton Napier
New Plymouth Nelson
Wellington ⊛

Christchurch Chatham Is. (N.Z.)
Dunedin
Invercargill

South Island

NEW ZEALAND

Tasman Sea

PALAU
Koror

Yap Is.

PAPUA NEW GUINEA
Madang Lae
Port Moresby ⊛ Rabaul Bougainville
Guadalcanal

New Guinea

Coral Sea

Cape York

INDONESIA

Arafura Sea

Melville I.

Brisbane

Sydney
Canberra ⊛
Melbourne

AUSTRALIA

TASMANIA

Bass Strait

Adelaide

Bass Strait

©MAPQUEST.COM

SWEDEN
NORWAY
GREAT BRITAIN
ICELAND

Greenland Sea
Denmark Strait
Cape Farewell

Tasiilaq

Nuuk (Godthaab)

Labrador Sea

NEWFOUNDLAND
St. Anthony
Island of Newfoundland
St. John's
Corner Brook
St. Pierre & Miquelon Is. (Fr.)
Happy Valley
Goose Bay
Anticosti
Hebron
Sept-Îles
Schefferville
Labrador City
QUÉBEC
SHIELD

GREENLAND (KALAALLIT NUNAAT) (Den.)

Davis Strait

Arctic Circle

Spitsbergen

Nord

Knud Rasmussen Land
Qaanaaq (Thule)
Gibe Fiord
Ellesmere I.
Alert

Cape Morris Jessup

North Pole

Arctic Ocean

Baffin Bay
Arctic Bay
Pond Inlet
Pangnirtung
Iqaluit
Baffin Island

Hudson Strait
Ungava Peninsula
Povungnituk

Belcher Is.
James Bay
Mooseonee

Repulse Bay

Southampton I.

CANADIAN

Churchill
York Factory

Hudson Bay

MANITOBA
Thompson
Flin Flon
La Ronge
Uranium City

NUNAVUT

Queen Elizabeth Islands
Resolute

Cambridge Bay
Victoria I.
Holman

Banks I.

Sachs Harbour

Beaufort Sea

Point Barrow
Barrow

Kugluktuk

Great Bear L.
Déline

Inuvik
Fort McPherson
Mackenzie

NORTHWEST TERRITORIES
Ft. Simpson
Yellowknife
Fort Smith
Hay River
Great Slave L.

SASK.
La Loche
Ft. McMurray
Athabasca
Prince Albert
Saskatoon
Saskatchewan

ALBERTA
Peace River
Edmonton
Calgary
GREAT

ROCKY

BRITISH COLUMBIA
Watson Lake
Prince George
Jasper
Williams Lake
Fraser
Columbia

RUSSIA

Bering Strait
Point Hope
Kotzebue
Nome
Bethel

Kobuk
BROOKS RANGE
Fort Yukon
Fairbanks
Yukon

ALASKA
RANGE
Mt. McKinley 6,194 m (20,320 ft.)

ALASKA

Kodiak
Kenai
Seward
Valdez
Anchorage

Gulf of Alaska

Bering Sea

Dawson
Mayo
YUKON
Carmacks
Whitehorse

COAST MOUNTAINS
Skagway
Juneau
Sitka
Yakutat
Mt. Logan 5,959 m (19,551 ft.)

Ketchikan
Kitimat
Prince Rupert
Queen Charlotte Is.

Vancouver I.
Vancouver

Arctic Circle

ATLANTIC OCEAN

PACIFIC OCEAN

Caribbean Sea

Gulf of Mexico

UNITED STATES

MEXICO

VENEZUELA

COLOMBIA

BRAZIL

CUBA

HAITI

DOMINICAN REPUBLIC

JAMAICA

NICARAGUA

COSTA RICA

PANAMA

GUATEMALA

HONDURAS

EL SALVADOR

BELIZE

Bermuda (Brit.)

THE BAHAMAS

Mt. Whitney 4,418 m. (14,494 ft.)

Orizaba Pk. (18,405 ft) 5,610 m.

NORTH AMERICA

- ⊛ National Capital
- ★ Territorial Capital
- • Other City

1:39,978,000

0   350   700 mi

0   350   700 km

Azimuthal Equal Area Projection

©MAPQUEST.COM

155

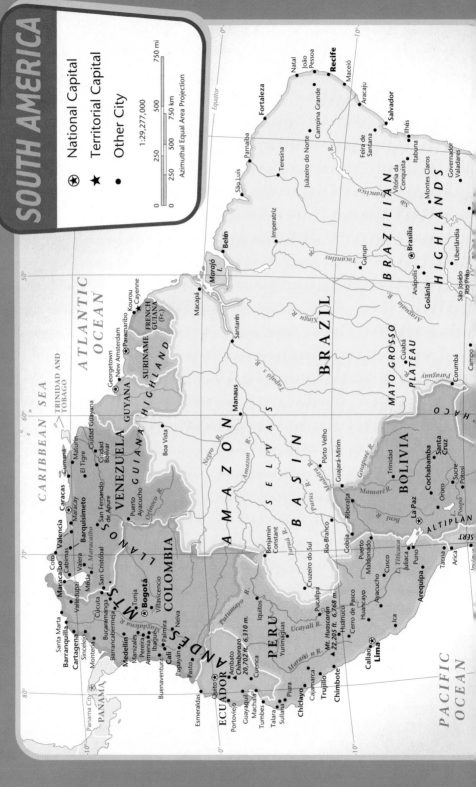

SOUTH AMERICA

- ⊛ National Capital
- ★ Territorial Capital
- • Other City

1:29,277,000

0   250   500   750 km
0   250   500   750 mi

Azimuthal Equal Area Projection

CARIBBEAN SEA

TRINIDAD AND TOBAGO

ATLANTIC OCEAN

Santa Marta
Barranquilla
Cartagena
Sincelejo
Montería
Barrancabermeja
Cúcuta
Bucaramanga
Cota
Valencia
Maracaibo
Cabimas
Valledupar
Mérida
L. Maracaibo
Valera
San Cristóbal
Caracas
Maracay
Barquisimeto
Cumaná
Maturín
El Tigre
Ciudad Guayana
Ciudad Bolívar

Georgetown
New Amsterdam
Paramaribo
Cayenne
Kourou

GUYANA
SURINAME
FRENCH GUIANA (Fr.)

San Fernando de Apure
Puerto Ayacucho

VENEZUELA

GUIANA HIGHLAND

Boa Vista

Macapá
Marajó I.

Belén

Santarém

Manaus

COLOMBIA

Bogotá
Tunja
Villavicencio
Medellín
Manizales
Pereira
Armenia
Ibagué
Palmira
Cali
Buenaventura
Neiva
Popayán
Pasto

ANDES MTS.

Quito
Esmeraldas
Portoviejo
Ambato
Chimborazo 20,702 ft. 6,310 m.
Guayaquil
Machala
Cuenca

ECUADOR

Tumbes
Talara
Sullana
Piura
Cajamarca
Chiclayo
Trujillo
Chimbote
Mt. Huascarán 22,205 ft. 6,768 m.

PERU

Iquitos
Yurimaguas
Pucallpa
Huánuco
Cerro de Pasco
Callao
Lima
Huancayo
Ayacucho
Ica
Cusco
Puerto Maldonado
Juliaca
Puno
Arequipa
Tacna
Arica

AMAZON BASIN

SELVAS

Benjamin Constant
Cruzeiro do Sul
Rio Branco
Pôrto Velho
Guajará-Mirim
Riberalta
Cobija
Puerto Maldonado

BRAZIL

Cuiabá
Corumbá
Campo

MATO GROSSO PLATEAU

Trinidad
Cochabamba
Santa Cruz
La Paz
Oruro
Sucre
Potosí

BOLIVIA

L. Titicaca
L. Poopó

ALTIPLAN

CHACO

DESERT

BRAZILIAN HIGHLANDS

Fortaleza
Natal
João Pessoa
Recife
Maceió
Aracaju
Salvador
Ilhéus
Itabuna
Feira de Santana
Vitória da Conquista
Montes Claros
Governador Valadares
Uberlândia
Brasília
Anápolis
Goiânia
São José do Rio Preto

São Luís
Parnaíba
Teresina
Juazeiro do Norte
Campina Grande
Imperatriz
Gurupi

São Francisco R.
Tocantins R.
Araguaia R.
Paraguay R.
Xingu R.
Tapajós R.
Amazon R.
Negro R.
Madeira R.
Purús R.
Juruá R.
Ucayali R.
Marañón R.
Putumayo R.
Magdalena R.
Orinoco R.
Guaporé R.
Mamoré R.
Beni R.

Equator

0°
10°
50°
60°
70°
80°

PACIFIC OCEAN

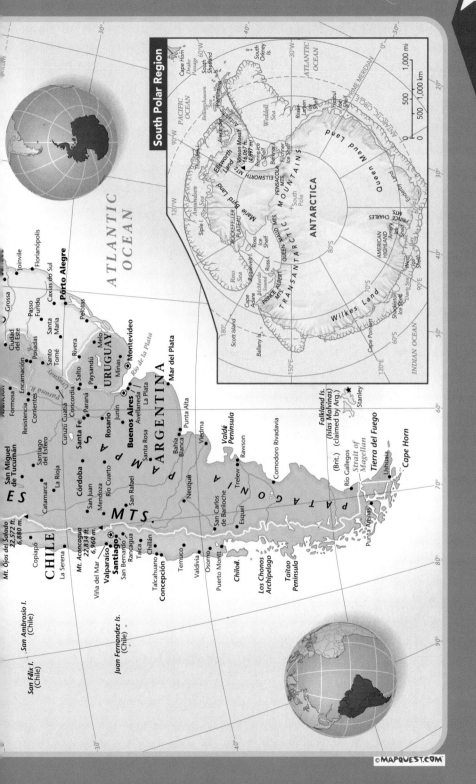

South Polar Region

Cape Horn
Drake Passage
South Orkney Is.
South Shetland Is.
ATLANTIC OCEAN
PACIFIC OCEAN
Bellingshausen Sea
Antarctic Peninsula
Alexander I.
Weddell Sea
Ronne Ice Shelf
Riiser-Larsen Ice Shelf
Fimbul Ice Shelf
PRIME MERIDIAN
ANTARCTIC CIRCLE
Thurston I.
Ellsworth Land
Berkner I.
Filchner Ice Shelf
Queen Maud Land
Amundsen Sea
Vinson Massif 16,067 ft. (4,897 m.)
ELLSWORTH MTS.
PENSACOLA MTS.
Ekström Ice Shelf
Peter I I.
Marie Byrd Land
ROCKEFELLER PLATEAU
QUEEN MAUD MTS.
South Pole
ANTARCTICA
TRANSANTARCTIC MOUNTAINS
PRINCE CHARLES MTS.
Siple I.
Ross Ice Shelf
Roosevelt I.
Ross Sea
PRINCE ALBERT MTS.
AMERICAN HIGHLAND
West Ice Shelf
Cape Adare
McMurdo
Wilkes Land
Amery Ice Shelf
Scott Island
Ross Sea
Shackleton Ice Shelf
Cape Poinsett
INDIAN OCEAN
Balleny Is.
Davis Sea

1,000 mi
1,000 km
500
500
0

ATLANTIC OCEAN

Joinville
Florianópolis
Grossa
Passo Fundo
Caxias do Sul
Porto Alegre
Pelotas
Santa Maria
Rivera
Melo
Santo Tomé
Posadas
Encarnación
Santa Fe
Corrientes
Resistencia
Formosa
Paraná R.
Curuzú Cuatiá
Concordia
Salto
Paysandú
URUGUAY
Minas
Montevideo
Río de la Plata
Mar del Plata
La Plata
Buenos Aires
Avellaneda
Rosario
Junín
Santa Fe
Santiago del Estero
San Miguel de Tucumán
Catamarca
La Rioja
Córdoba
San Juan
Río Cuarto
Santa Rosa
Punta Alta
Bahía Blanca
Viedma
Valdé Peninsula
Rawson
ARGENTINA
A N D E S
M T S.
Mt. Ojos del Salado 22,572 ft. 6,880 m.
Copiapó
La Serena
CHILE
Mt. Aconcagua 22,834 ft. 6,960 m.
San Rafael
Mendoza
Viña del Mar
Valparaíso
Santiago
San Bernardo
Rancagua
Talca
Chillán
Concepción
Talcahuano
Temuco
Valdivia
Osorno
Puerto Montt
Chiloé I.
Los Chonos Archipelago
Taitao Peninsula
Neuquén
San Carlos de Bariloche
Esquel
Trelew
P A T A G O N I A
Comodoro Rivadavia
Río Gallegos
Puerto Natales
Strait of Magellan
Tierra del Fuego
Ushuaia
Cape Horn
Falkland Is. (Islas Malvinas) (claimed by Arg.) (Brit.)
Stanley

San Félix I. (Chile)
San Ambrosio I. (Chile)
Juan Fernández Is. (Chile)

©MAPQUEST.COM

157

EUROPE

★ National Capital
● Other City

1:22,107,000

0 — 250 — 500 mi
0 — 250 — 500 km
Azimuthal Equal Area Projection

ATLANTIC OCEAN

ICELAND
Reykjavik · Akureyri

Norwegian Sea

Faroe Is. (Den.)

Shetland Is. (Brit.)

Trondheim

NORWAY
Bergen
Oslo
Stavanger

SWEDEN
Uppsala
Stockholm
Linköping
Göteborg

Bodø

Sundsvall

Orkney Is.
Aberdeen

Glasgow · Edinburgh
Belfast
GREAT BRITAIN
Newcastle
(UNITED KINGDOM)
IRELAND Dublin · Liverpool · Leeds
Cork · Manchester · Sheffield
Birmingham
Cardiff · Bristol
Land's End · Portsmouth · **London**
Channel Is. (Brit.)
Brest

Irish Sea

North Sea

Skagerrak
Kattegat
Jutland
DENMARK Copenhagen ★ Helsingborg
Århus Odense Malmö

NETHERLANDS
Amsterdam · Bremen Hamburg ★**Berlin** Szczecin
Rotterdam Hannover
Antwerp **GERMANY** Poznań
Brussels Essen
BELGIUM Lille Cologne Leipzig Dresden
Bonn
LUXEMBOURG Liège Frankfurt Prague Kato
Le Havre ★ Luxembourg Mannheim **CZECH REP.** Brno Os
Rouen Strasbourg Stuttgart
Paris ★ Nantes Dijon Munich Linz Vienna Bra
Loire Bern Zürich **LIECHTENSTEIN** **SLC**
FRANCE Geneva **SWITZERLAND** **AUSTRIA** Graz
Mt. Blanc **ALPS** Bu
4807 m Lyon **SLOVENIA** HU
(15,771 ft) Milan Ljubljana
Bay of Biscay Bordeaux Turin Verona Venice **CROATIA**
Cape Finisterre Genoa Bologna **DINAR** Zagr
Vigo Gijón Marseille Nice Po **APENNINES** BOSN
Porto Bilbao Toulouse Toulon **MONACO** Florence **SAN** HERZEC
Valladolid *Ligurian Sea* **MARINO** Sarajevo
PYRENEES Nantes Split
Pico de Aneto Corsica Elba
PORTUGAL **IBERIAN** 3404 m (Fr.) VATICAN ★**Rome** Dubrovn
Lisbon ★ (11,168 ft) **ANDORRA** CITY **ITALY** Po
Badajoz Zaragoza **Barcelona** Bari
Tagus **PENINSULA** Valencia *Balearic Sea*
Madrid ★ Majorca Naples Salerno
Córdoba **SPAIN** Minorca
Cape St. Vincent Sevilla · Alicante Palma *Tyrrhenian Sea*
Cádiz Granada *Balearic Is. (Sp.)* Sardinia
Málaga (It.) Palermo
Strait of Gibraltar **GIBRALTAR (Brit.)** Cagliari Catania **Sicily** Mt. Etna
3323 m
★Rabat ★Algiers *Mediterranean* Valletta (10,902 ft)
Casablanca Tunis **MALTA**
MOROCCO **ATLAS MOUNTAINS** **ALGERIA** **TUNISIA** *Sea*

Ebro
Rhône
Elbe
Oder
Danube
Rhine
Adriatic Sea

60°
40°
30°
20°
10°
0°
10°
70°
40°
30°

Hebrides
English Channel

North Cape
merfest
Barents Sea
LAND
Murmansk
KOLA PENINSULA
Apatity
Nar'yan-Mar
Pechora
Ob
Irtysh
White Sea
Arkhangel'sk
Ukhta
Arctic Circle
Pechora
R U S S I A
Serov
Petropavl
Oulu
Belomorsk
Dvina
Syktyvkar
Berezniki
Yekaterinburg
INLAND
Lake Onega
Kotlas
Perm'
Chelyabinsk
ampere
Lahti
Petrozavodsk
PLAIN
Kirov
Izhevsk
Ufa
Qostanay
Helsinki
Lake Ladoga
Vologda
Naberezhnyye Chelny
Magnitogorsk
St. Petersburg
Cherepovets
Kazan
Tallinn
Velikiy Novgorod
Yaroslavl'
Nizhniy Novgorod
STONIA
Tartu
Ivanovo
Ul'yanovsk
Tol'yatti
Orenburg
Orsk
LATVIA
Pskov
EUROPEAN
Tver'
Samara
Aktobe
Daugavpils
Moscow
Ryazan'
Saransk
Oral
KAZAKHSTAN
UANIA
Vitsyebsk
Penza
Vilnius
Smolensk
Tula
Ural
Aral Sea
N
Hrodna
Mahilyow
Bryansk
Tambov
Saratov
UZBEKISTAN
Minsk
Lipetsk
BELARUS
Homyel
Kursk
Voronezh
Atyraū
Brest
Volgograd
Aktaū
Kiev
Kharkiv
Luhans'k
Astrakhan
UKRAINE
Dnieper
Donets'k
Don
L'viv
Dnipropetrovs'k
Rostov na Donu
Caspian
Dniester
Chernivtsi
Zaporizhzhia
Mariupol'
TURKMENISTAN
MOLDOVA
Kryvyy Rih
Mykolaiv
Sea of Azov
Stavropol'
Makhachkala
Sea
recen
Iaşi
Chişinău
Odesa
Krasnodar
Grozny
Türkmenbashy
ROMANIA
CRIMEA
Simferopol'
CAUCASUS
oara
Ploieşti
Sevastopol'
GEORGIA
Baku
Bucharest
Constanţa
Black Sea
T'bilisi
AZERBAIJAN
le
Danube
ARMENIA
BULGARIA
Varna
Yerevan
O
Sofia
Burgas
Trabzon
HIAN
MTS.
opje
Plovdiv
Tabriz
Tehran
NIA
Istanbul
Izmir
Ankara
TURKEY
IRAN
Thessaloniki
Larisa
Adana
CE
Athens
Aegean Sea
Adana
IRAQ
NNESE
Cyclades
Baghdad
Rhodes
Nicosia
SYRIA
Sea of Crete
LEBANON
Euphrates
Crete
Iraklion
CYPRUS
Beirut
Damascus
Persian G

© MAPQUEST.COM

ATLANTIC OCEAN

IRELAND

GREAT BRITAIN

PORTUGAL

SPAIN

MOROCCO

FRANCE

BEL. NETH. DEN.

SWITZ.

GERMANY

NORWAY

SWEDEN

FINLAND

Barents Sea

Murmansk

ALGERIA

ITALY

AUS.

CZECH REP.

POLAND

LITH. LAT.

ESTONIA

St. Petersburg

Arkhangel'sk

E U R O P E

TUNISIA

HUNG.

BELARUS

Moscow

R U S S

SERB. & MONT.

ALB.

ROM.

MOL.

UKRAINE

GREECE

BUL.

URAL MOUNTAINS

Yekaterinburg

Chelyabinsk

Irtysh

Mediterranean Sea

LIBYA

Izmir

Istanbul

Ankara

Black Sea

Volgograd

Volga

Magnitogorsk

Omsk

Novosit

TURKEY

GEORGIA

T'bilisi

Astrakhan'

Caspian Sea

KAZAKHSTAN

Astana

Pav

CYPRUS

Nicosia

ARMENIA

Aral Sea

Karaganda

Semey

LEBANON

Beirut

Yerevan

AZERBAIJAN

(Semipalatinsk)

Tel Aviv

SYRIA

Baku

Lake Balkhash

CHAD

Jerusalem

Damascus

Tabriz

TURKMENISTAN

UZBEKISTAN

Almaty

ISRAEL

Amman

Tehran

Ashgabat

Bishkek

KYRGYZSTAN

EGYPT

JORDAN

IRAQ

Tehran

Tashkent

Dushanbe

Kashi

Sinai

20°

Baghdad

Mashhad

TAJIKISTAN

Takla De

SAUDI

Al Basrah

Esfahan

IRAN

AFGHANISTAN

Islamabad

XIZ (TI

ARABIA

Kuwait City

Kabul

Srinagar

HIMA

KUWAIT

Shiraz

Qandahar

Amritsar

Jeddah

Manama

Kerman

Lahore

Delhi

Mecca

Riyadh

BAHRAIN

Doha

PAKISTAN

NEPAL

Sanaa

QATAR

Abu Dhabi

Sukkur

New Delhi

Kathma

UNITED ARAB EMIRATES

Muscat

Karachi

Hyderabad

Jaipur

Luck

Kanpur

AFRICA

SUDAN

Red Sea

Nile

ERITREA

OMAN

Gulf of Oman

Ahmadabad

INDIA

YEMEN

Aden

Gulf of Aden

Nagpur

ETHIOPIA

DJI.

Socotra (Yemen)

Arabian Sea

Mumbai

Hyderabad

SOMALIA

ASIA

dishu

Lakshadweep (India)

Bangalore

Madras (Chenn

Kochi

Madurai

SRI LAN

Colombo

⊛ National Capital

★ Territorial Capital

• Other City

1:51,084,000

Male

MALDIVES

INDIAN

OCE

0   500   1,000 mi

0   500   1,000 km

Two-Point Equidistant Projection

160

th Pole
Chukchi Sea
80°
70°
60°
180°
160°
140°
120°

TIC
EAN
Laptev Sea

East Siberian Sea

Anadyr
Bering Sea
50°
40°
A L A S K A
170°

KAMCHATKA PENINSULA
Magadan

Petropavlovsk-Kamchatskiy

Yakutsk

Sea of Okhotsk
180°

170°

30°

S I B E R I A

Sakhalin
Kuril Islands (Russia)

arsk
tsk
Bratsk
Lake Baikal
Chita
Irkutsk
Ulan-Ude
Ulaanbaatar

Komsomolsk na Amure
Blagoveshchensk
Khabarovsk

Sapporo

Harbin

JAPAN

Sendai
160°

MONGOLIA
GOBI DESERT
NG

Changchun
Shenyang

Vladivostok
Sea of Japan (East Sea)
Tokyo
Yokohama

PACIFIC OCEAN

Hohhot
Beijing
Huang
Tianjin
Dalian
Pyongyang
N. KOREA
Seoul
S. KOREA
Kyoto
Kobe
Osaka
Hiroshima

20°

Lanzhou
Taiyuan
Jinan
Qingdao
Yellow Sea
Nagasaki

Zhengzhou
HINA
Xi'an
Nanjing
Shanghai
East China Sea

Ryukyu Islands
Okinawa (Japan)

150°

Chengdu
Chongqing
Chang
Changsha
Wuhan
Wenzhou
Fuzhou

Lhasa
TAN
u
ta)
ADESH
ka
ta)
Kunming
Xiamen
Taipei
TAIWAN
10°

Guangzhou
Nanning
Hong Kong (Xianggang)
Macao

Philippine Sea

Mandalay
Hanoi
Gulf of Tonkin
LUZON

MYANMAR (BURMA)
LAOS
Da Nang
Manila
PHILIPPINES

Yangon angoon)
THAILAND
Vientiane
VIETNAM
South China Sea
Cebu
MINDANAO

Bangkok
CAMBODIA
Sulu Sea
Davao

Andaman Sea
Phnom Penh
Ho Chi Minh City
Gulf of Thailand
Kota Kinabalu
Celebes Sea
Manado

NEW GUINEA
PAPUA

Bandar Seri Begawan
BRUNEI
Kuching
BORNEO

ar ds a)
Medan
Kuala Lumpur
MALAYSIA
SINGAPORE
Singapore

Banda Sea
Arafura Sea

Padang
SUMATRA
I N D O N E S I A
Banjarmasin
Makassar
Java Sea
Dili
Timor Sea
TIMOR-LESTE

Palembang
Jakarta
Surabaya
Bandung
JAVA
Kupang
AUSTRALIA

100°
110°
120°
130°
140°

Mekong

©MAPQUEST.COM

161

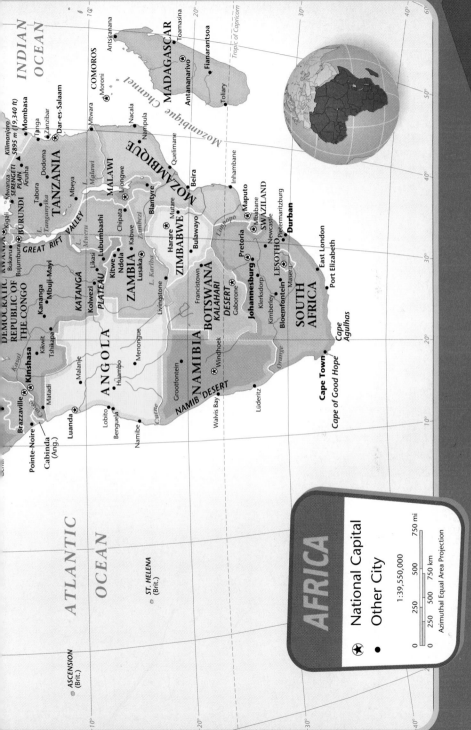

INDIAN OCEAN

COMOROS
Moroni

MADAGASCAR
Antsirahana
Toamasina
Antananarivo
Fianarantsoa
Toliary

Tropic of Capricorn

Mombasa
Tanga
Zanzibar
Dar-es-Salaam
Mtwara
Nacala
Nampula

Kilimanjaro
5895 m (19,340 ft)
Serengeti Plain
Arusha
Dodoma
Mbeya

Mozambique Channel

MOZAMBIQUE
Quelimane
Beira
Inhambane
Maputo

TANZANIA
Tabora
BURUNDI
Bujumbura
Kigali
Bukavu
L. Tanganyika
GREAT RIFT VALLEY

MALAWI
Malawi
Lilongwe
Blantyre
Mutare
Harare
Bulawayo

ZIMBABWE
Francistown

SWAZILAND
Mbabane
Newcastle
Pietermaritzburg
Durban

DEMOCRATIC REPUBLIC OF THE CONGO
Kananga
Mbuji-Mayi
KATANGA
Kolwezi
Likasi
Lubumbashi
Kitwe
Ndola
Kabwe
PLATEAU
ZAMBIA
Lusaka
L. Kariba
Livingstone

Pretoria
Johannesburg
Klerksdorp
Kimberley
Bloemfontein
LESOTHO
Maseru
East London
Port Elizabeth

SOUTH AFRICA

Kinshasa
Brazzaville
Matadi
Pointe-Noire
Cabinda (Ang.)
Luanda
Lobito
Benguela
Namibe

ANGOLA
Malanje
Huambo
Menongue
Grootfontein
NAMIBIA
NAMIB DESERT
Windhoek
Walvis Bay
Lüderitz

BOTSWANA
KALAHARI DESERT
Gaborone

Cape Town
Cape of Good Hope
Cape Agulhas

ATLANTIC OCEAN

ST. HELENA (Brit.)

ASCENSION (Brit.)

©MAPQUEST.COM

AFRICA

⊛ National Capital
• Other City

1:39,550,000

0   250   500   750 mi
0   250   500   750 km

Azimuthal Equal Area Projection

FACTS ABOUT NATIONS

Here are basic facts about each of the 193 independent nations in the world. The color of the heading for each country tells you what continent it belongs in. The population is an estimate for mid-2005. The currency entry shows how much one U.S. dollar was worth in each country's currency as of early 2005. The language entry gives official languages and other common languages.

COLOR KEY

- Africa
- Asia
- Australia
- Europe
- North America
- Pacific Islands
- South America

Afghanistan

- **Capital:** Kabul
- **Population:** 29,928,987
- **Area:** 250,000 sq. mi. (647,500 sq. km.)
- **Currency:** $1 = 42.79 afghanis
- **Language:** Afghan Persian (Dari), Pashtu
- **Did You Know:** Hamid Karzai won Afghanistan's first presidential election, on October 9, 2004.

Albania

- **Capital:** Tiranë
- **Population:** 3,563,112
- **Area:** 11,100 sq. mi. (28,748 sq. km.)
- **Currency:** $1 = 97.16 leke
- **Language:** Albanian, Greek
- **Did You Know:** Ancient people called Illyrians lived in Albania around A.D. 1000.

Algeria

- **Capital:** Algiers
- **Population:** 32,531,853
- **Area:** 919,590 sq. mi. (2,381,740 sq. km.)
- **Currency:** $1 = 71.64 dinars
- **Language:** Arabic, French, Berber dialects
- **Did You Know:** Algeria was a colony of France from 1834 to 1963.

Andorra

- **Capital:** Andorra la Vella
- **Population:** 70,549
- **Area:** 181 sq. mi. (468 sq. km.)
- **Currency:** $1 = .77 euros
- **Language:** Catalan, French, Castilian
- **Did You Know:** The main sources of income for this tiny mountain nation, located between France and Spain, are tourism and ski resorts.

Angola

- **Capital:** Luanda
- **Population:** 11,190,786
- **Area:** 481,350 sq. mi. (1,246,700 sq. km.)
- **Currency:** $1 = 86.24 kwanza
- **Language:** Portuguese, African dialects
- **Did You Know:** Decades of civil war, now ended, left Angola with millions of land mines.

Antigua & Barbuda

- **Capital:** St. John's
- **Population:** 68,722
- **Area:** 171 sq. mi. (443 sq. km.)
- **Currency:** $1 = 2.67 East Carribean dollars
- **Language:** English
- **Did You Know:** Admiral Horatio Nelson made these islands a base for the British Navy in 1784.

ARCTIC OCEAN

ASIA

EUROPE

NORTH AMERICA

ATLANTIC OCEAN

AFRICA

PACIFIC OCEAN

SOUTH AMERICA

INDIAN OCEAN

PACIFIC OCEAN

AUSTRALIA

ANTARCTICA

Argentina

- **Capital:** Buenos Aires
- **Population:** 39,537,943
- **Area:** 1,068,302 sq. mi. (2,766,890 sq. km.)
- **Currency:** $1 = 2.94 pesos
- **Language:** Spanish, English, Italian
- **Did You Know:** Argentina's central grasslands, called "the Pampas," are one of the world's largest cattle-producing areas.

Armenia

- **Capital:** Yerevan
- **Population:** 2,982,904
- **Area:** 11,506 sq. mi. (29,800 sq. km.)
- **Currency:** $1 = 495 drams
- **Language:** Armenian
- **Did You Know:** This nation between the Black and Caspian Seas has an average altitude of 5,900 feet, more than a mile above sea level.

Australia

- **Capital:** Canberra
- **Population:** 20,090,437
- **Area:** 2,967,908 sq. mi. (7,686,850 sq. km.)
- **Currency:** $1 = 1.3 Australian dollars
- **Language:** English, Aboriginal languages
- **Did You Know:** The Great Barrier Reef, running about 1,250 miles along Australia's coast, is the world's biggest coral reef.

Austria

- **Capital:** Vienna
- **Population:** 8,184,691
- **Area:** 32,382 sq. mi. (83,870 sq. km.)
- **Currency:** $1 = .77 euros
- **Language:** German
- **Did You Know:** The composers Mozart, Strauss, Beethoven, Haydn, and Schubert all came to Vienna, which remains a center for classical music today.

Azerbaijan

- **Capital:** Baku
- **Population:** 7,911,974
- **Area:** 33,436 sq. mi. (86,600 sq. km.)
- **Currency:** $1 = 4,894 manats
- **Language:** Azeri, Russian, Armenian
- **Did You Know:** Azerbaijan borders the Caspian Sea, the world's largest inland body of water.

The Bahamas

- **Capital:** Nassau
- **Population:** 301,790
- **Area:** 5,382 sq. mi. (13,940 sq. km.)
- **Currency:** $1 = Bahamian Dollar
- **Language:** English, Creole
- **Did You Know:** Christopher Columbus first landed in the New World on San Salvador, an island in the Bahamas.

Bahrain

- **Capital:** Manama
- **Population:** 688,345
- **Area:** 257 sq. mi. (665 sq. km.)
- **Currency:** $1 = .38 dinars
- **Language:** Arabic, English, Farsi, Urdu
- **Did You Know:** Only 1% of this island nation's land can be used for farming.

Bangladesh

- **Capital:** Dhaka
- **Population:** 144,319,628
- **Area:** 55,599 sq. mi. (144,000 sq. km.)
- **Currency:** $1 = 59.95 takas
- **Language:** Bangla, English
- **Did You Know:** Bangladesh is the sixth most densely populated country in the world, with 2,791 people per square mile.

Barbados

- **Capital:** Bridgetown
- **Population:** 279,254
- **Area:** 166 sq. mi. (431 sq. km.)
- **Currency:** $1 = 2.04 Barbados dollars
- **Language:** English
- **Did You Know:** Barbados is named after the island's bearded fig trees (barbados means "bearded ones" in Spanish).

Belarus

- **Capital:** Minsk
- **Population:** 10,300,483
- **Area:** 80,155 sq. mi. (207,600 sq. km.)
- **Currency:** $1 = 2,191 rubli
- **Language:** Byelorussian, Russian
- **Did You Know:** Belarus became independent when the Soviet Union broke up in late 1991.

Belgium

- **Capital:** Brussels
- **Population:** 10,364,388
- **Area:** 11,787 sq. mi. (30,528 sq. km.)
- **Currency:** $1 = .77 euros
- **Language:** Flemish (Dutch), French, German
- **Did You Know:** Belgium's second largest city, Antwerp, has been a world-famous center for diamond-cutting since the 16th century.

Belize

- **Capital:** Belmopan
- **Population:** 279,457
- **Area:** 8,867 sq. mi. (22,966 sq. km.)
- **Currency:** $1 = 1.97 Belize dollars
- **Language:** English, Spanish, Mayan, Garifuna
- **Did You Know:** A new capital was built 50 miles inland after the coastal Belize City was damaged by hurricanes in 1961.

Benin

- **Capital:** Porto–Novo (constit.) Contonou (admin.)
- **Population:** 7,460,025
- **Area:** 43,483 sq. mi. (112,620 sq. km.)
- **Currency:** $1 = 506 CFA francs
- **Language:** French, Fon, Yonuba
- **Did You Know:** The port city of Ouidah was a major center for the slave trade in the early 1700s.

Bhutan

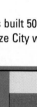

- **Capital:** Thimphu
- **Population:** 2,232,291
- **Area:** 18,147 sq. mi. (47,000 sq. km.)
- **Currency:** $1 = 43.68 ngultrums
- **Language:** Dzongkha, Tibetan
- **Did You Know:** The Bhutanese name for their nation is Druk Yulm, which translates as "Kingdom of the Thunder Dragon."

Bolivia

- **Capital:** La Paz
- **Population:** 8,857,870
- **Area:** 424,164 sq. mi. (1,098,580 sq. km.)
- **Currency:** $1 = 8.06 bolivianos
- **Language:** Spanish, Quechua, Aymara
- **Did You Know:** Bolivia and Paraguay are the only South American countries with no coastline.

Bosnia and Herzegovina

- **Capital:** Sarajevo
- **Population:** 4,025,476
- **Area:** 19,741 sq. mi. (51,129 sq. km.)
- **Currency:** $1 = 1.51 convertible marks
- **Language:** Serbo-Croatian
- **Did You Know:** The 1914 assassination of an archduke in Sarajevo triggered the start of World War I.

Botswana

- **Capital:** Gaborone
- **Population:** 1,640,115
- **Area:** 231,804 sq. mi. (600,370 sq. km.)
- **Currency:** $1 = 4.46 pulas
- **Language:** English, Setswana
- **Did You Know:** The Kalahari Desert, a land of bush and grasslands, covers 84% of this country.

Brazil

- **Capital:** Brasília
- **Population:** 186,112,794
- **Area:** 3,286,487 sq. mi. (8,511,965 sq. km.)
- **Currency:** $1 = 2.68 reais
- **Language:** Portuguese, Spanish, English
- **Did You Know:** Brazil is bigger than the 48 contiguous, or "touching," U.S. states.

Brunei

- **Capital:** Bandar Seri Begawan
- **Population:** 372,361
- **Area:** 2,228 sq. mi. (5,770 sq. km.)
- **Currency:** $1 = 1.64 Brunei dollars
- **Language:** Malay, English, Chinese
- **Did You Know:** This leading oil producer is located in the Pacific, not in the Middle East.

Bulgaria

- **Capital:** Sophia
- **Population:** 7,450,349
- **Area:** 42,823 sq. mi. (110,910 sq. km.)
- **Currency:** $1 = 1.5 Leva
- **Language:** Bulgarian
- **Did You Know:** In 1989, more than 300,000 Turks fled Bulgaria to escape persecution.

Burkina Faso

- **Capital:** Ouagadougou
- **Population:** 13,925,313
- **Area:** 105,869 sq. mi. (274,200 sq. km.)
- **Currency:** $1 = 506 CFA francs
- **Language:** French, indigenous languages
- **Did You Know:** Since the government made them a protected species in the 1980s, the number of elephants in Burkina Faso has grown from 350 to as many as 5,000.

Burundi

- **Capital:** Bujumbura
- **Population:** 6,370,609
- **Area:** 10,745 sq. mi. (27,830 sq. km.)
- **Currency:** $1 = 1,060 francs
- **Language:** Kirundi, French, Swahili
- **Did You Know:** Tutsi-Hutu ethnic violence killed 200,000 Burundians in the 1990s.

COLOR KEY

- Europe
- Africa
- North America
- Asia
- Pacific Islands
- Australia
- South America

FACTS ABOUT NATIONS

Cambodia

- **Capital:** Phnom Penh
- **Population:** 13,607,069
- **Area:** 69,900 sq. mi. (181,040 sq. km.)
- **Currency:** $1 = 3,849 riels
- **Language:** Khmer, French
- **Did You Know:** A lake called the Tonle Sap expands from 1,200 to 3,000 square miles in area every year during the wet season.

Cameroon

- **Capital:** Yaoundé
- **Population:** 16,380,005
- **Area:** 183,568 sq. mi. (475,440 sq. km.)
- **Currency:** $1 = 506 CFA francs
- **Language:** English, French
- **Did You Know:** Cameroon was a German colony from the 1880s until 1919.

Canada

- **Capital:** Ottawa
- **Population:** 32,805,041
- **Area:** 3,855,101 sq. mi. (9,984,670 sq. km.)
- **Currency:** $1 = 1.23 Canada dollars
- **Language:** English, French
- **Did You Know:** In the War of 1812, U.S. forces tried unsuccessfully to invade Canada.

Cape Verde (not on map)

- **Capital:** Praia
- **Population:** 418,224
- **Area:** 1,557 sq. mi. (4,033 sq. km.)
- **Currency:** $1 = 85.27 escudos
- **Language:** Portuguese, Crioulo
- **Did You Know:** These islands were uninhabited when the Portuguese arrived around 1460.

Central African Republic

- **Capital:** Bangui
- **Population:** 3,799,897
- **Area:** 240,535 sq. mi. (622,984 sq. km.)
- **Currency:** $1 = 506 CFA francs
- **Language:** French, Sangho, Arabic, Hunsa, Swahili
- **Did You Know:** Diamonds are the leading export of this developing nation.

Chad

- **Capital:** N'Djamena
- **Population:** 9,826,419
- **Area:** 495,755 sq. mi. (1,284,000 sq. km.)
- **Currency:** $1 = 506 CFA francs
- **Language:** French, Arabic, Sara, Sango
- **Did You Know:** In 2004, thousands of refugees fled from the fighting in Sudan to refugee camps in Chad.

Chile

- **Capital:** Santiago
- **Population:** 15,980,912
- **Area:** 292,260 sq. mi. (756,950 sq. km.)
- **Currency:** $1 = 581.25 pesos
- **Language:** Spanish
- **Did You Know:** Easter Island, which lies nearly 3,000 miles off Chile's coast, was annexed by Chile in 1888.

China

- **Capital:** Beijing
- **Population:** 1,306,313,812
- **Area:** 3,705,405 sq. mi. (9,596,960 sq. km.)
- **Currency:** $1 = 8.28 Yuan Renminbi
- **Language:** Mandarin, Yue Cantonese
- **Did You Know:** The Great Wall of China once extended some 1,500 miles.

Colombia

- **Capital:** Bogotá
- **Population:** 42,954,279
- **Area:** 439,735 sq. mi. (1,138,910 sq. km.)
- **Currency:** $1 = 2,374 pesos
- **Language:** Spanish
- **Did You Know:** This nation is the world's biggest source of emeralds.

Comoros

- **Capital:** Moroni
- **Population:** 671,247
- **Area:** 838 sq. mi. (2,170 sq. km.)
- **Currency:** $1 = 379.57 francs
- **Language:** Spanish
- **Did You Know:** Comoros is made up of mountainous islands of volcanic origin.

Congo, Democratic Republic of the

- **Capital:** Kinshasa
- **Population:** 60,085,004
- **Area:** 905,567 sq. mi. (2,345,410 sq. km.)
- **Currency:** $1 = 433.5 francs
- **Language:** Arabic, French, Comorian
- **Did You Know:** This country, the former "Belgian" Congo, lies east of the smaller Republic of the Congo.

Congo, Republic of the

- **Capital:** Brazzaville
- **Population:** 3,039,126
- **Area:** 132,047 sq. mi. (342,000 sq. km.)
- **Currency:** $1 = 506 CFA francs
- **Language:** French
- **Did You Know:** Most people in the Republic of the Congo live in cities or towns; the rain forests there are largely uninhabited.

Costa Rica

- **Capital:** San José
- **Population:** 4,016,173
- **Area:** 19,730 sq. mi. (51,100 sq. km.)
- **Currency:** $1 = 461.63 colones
- **Language:** Spanish
- **Did You Know:** An early Spanish explorer gave Costa Rica its current name, which means "rich coast" in English.

Côte d'Ivoire (Ivory Coast)

- **Capital:** Yamoussoukro
- **Population:** 17,298,040
- **Area:** 124,502 sq. mi. (322,460 sq. km.)
- **Currency:** $1 = 506 CFA francs
- **Language:** French, Dioula
- **Did You Know:** This nation is the world's leading producer of cocoa beans.

Croatia

- **Capital:** Zagreb
- **Population:** 4,495,904
- **Area:** 21,831 sq. mi. (56,542 sq. km.)
- **Currency:** $1 = 5.8 kune
- **Language:** Serbo-Croatian
- **Did You Know:** Croatia was part of Yugoslavia until declaring independence in 1991.

Cuba

- **Capital:** Spanish
- **Population:** 11,346,670
- **Area:** 42,803 sq. mi. (110,860 sq. km.)
- **Currency:** $1 = 21 pesos
- **Language:** Spanish
- **Did You Know:** Cuba was one of the places Christopher Columbus visited in 1492.

COLOR KEY
- Africa
- Asia
- Australia
- Europe
- North America
- Pacific Islands
- South America

FACTS ABOUT NATIONS

Cyprus

- **Capital:** Nicosia
- **Population:** 780,133
- **Area:** 3,571 sq. mi. (9,250 sq. km.)
- **Currency:** $1 = 0.45 pounds
- **Language:** Greek, Turkish, English
- **Did You Know:** Cyprus is divided into Greek and Turkish areas.

Czech Republic

- **Capital:** Prague
- **Population:** 10,241,138
- **Area:** 30,450 sq. mi. (78,866 sq. km.)
- **Currency:** $1 = 23.1 koruna
- **Language:** Czech, Slovak
- **Did You Know:** Except for adding more words, the Czech language has changed very little since the 16th century.

Denmark

- **Capital:** Copenhagen
- **Population:** 5,432,335
- **Area:** 16,639 sq. mi. (43,094 sq. km.)
- **Currency:** $1 = 5.71 kroner
- **Language:** Danish, Faroese
- **Did You Know:** Denmark is located on a peninsula but it also includes more than 400 islands.

Djibouti

- **Capital:** Djibouti
- **Population:** 476,703
- **Area:** 8,880 sq. mi. (23,000 sq. km.)
- **Currency:** $1 = 175.80 Djibouti francs
- **Language:** French, Arabic, Afar, Somali
- **Did You Know:** French colonizers started building Djibouti City, now the capital, in 1888.

Dominica

- **Capital:** Roseau
- **Population:** 69,029
- **Area:** 291 sq. mi. (754 sq. km.)
- **Currency:** 2.67 East Carribean dollars
- **Language:** English, French patois
- **Did You Know:** Banana plantations are vital to Dominica's economy.

Dominican Republic

- **Capital:** Santo Domingo
- **Population:** 8,950,034
- **Area:** 18,815 sq. mi. (48,730 sq. km.)
- **Currency:** $1 = 27 Dominican pesos
- **Language:** Spanish
- **Did You Know:** U.S. Marines occupied this nation from 1916 to 1924, and intervened there again in 1965.

Ecuador

- **Capital:** Quito
- **Population:** 13,363,593
- **Area:** 109,483 sq. mi. (283,560 sq. km.)
- **Currency:** $1 = Ecuador sucre
- **Language:** Spanish, Quechua
- **Did You Know:** The equator passes through this small country whose name in English is "the Republic of the Equator."

Egypt

- **Capital:** Cairo
- **Population:** 77,505,756
- **Area:** 386,662 sq. mi. (1,001,450 sq. km.)
- **Currency:** $1 = 5.85 pounds
- **Language:** Arabic, English, French
- **Did You Know:** The 4,500-year-old Great Pyramid of Giza near Cairo is all that is left of the "Seven Wonders of the Ancient World."

COLOR KEY

- Africa
- Asia
- Australia
- Europe
- North America
- Pacific Islands
- South America

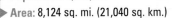

El Salvador

- Capital: San Salvador
- Population: 6,704,932
- Area: 8,124 sq. mi. (21,040 sq. km.)
- Currency: $1 = 8.75 colones
- Language: Spanish
- Did You Know: This smallest of Central American countries is the only one without a Caribbean coastline.

Equatorial Guinea

- Capital: Malabo
- Population: 535,881
- Area: 10,831 sq. mi. (28,051 sq. km.)
- Currency: $1 = 506 CFA francs
- Language: Spanish, French, Fang, Bubi
- Did You Know: Equatorial Guinea won independence from Spain in 1968.

Eritrea

- Capital: Asmara
- Population: 4,561,599
- Area: 46,842 sq. mi. (121,320 sq. km.)
- Currency: $1 = 13.5 nakfa
- Language: Tigrinya, Tigre, Kunama, Afar
- Did You Know: Once an Italian colony, Eritrea was occupied by Britain during World War II.

Estonia

- Capital: Tallinn
- Population: 1,332,893
- Area: 17,462 sq. mi. (45,226 sq. km.)
- Currency: $1 = 12.1 krooni
- Language: Estonian, Russian
- Did You Know: Estonians especially like to eat smoked fish and sausages.

Ethiopia

- Capital: Addis Ababa
- Population: 73,053,286
- Area: 435,186 sq. mi. (1,127,127 sq. km.)
- Currency: $1 = 8.7 birr
- Language: Amharic, Tigrinya, Orominga
- Did You Know: The 3.7-million-year-old skeleton of "Lucy," one of the earliest ancestors of modern humans, is in the Ethiopian National Museum.

Fiji

- Capital: Suva
- Population: 893,354
- Area: 7,054 sq. mi. (18,270 sq. km.)
- Currency: $1 = 1.66 Fiji dollars
- Language: English, Fijian, Hindustan
- Did You Know: Wearing a hat is a sign of disrespect in Fijian culture.

Finland

- Capital: Helsinki
- Population: 5,223,442
- Area: 130,127 sq. mi. (337,030 sq. km.)
- Currency: $1 = .77 euros
- Language: Finnish, Swedish
- Did You Know: Lapland in the North is home to the Saami (Lapps), traditionally a hunting, fishing, and reindeer-herding people.

France

- Capital: Paris
- Population: 60,656,178
- Area: 211,209 sq. mi. (547,030 sq. km.)
- Currency: $1 = .77 euros
- Language: French
- Did You Know: About one-fifth of the French people live in Paris or its suburbs.

FACTS
ABOUT
NATIONS

Gabon

▶ **Capital:** Libreville
▶ **Population:** 1,389,201
▶ **Area:** 103,347 sq. mi. (267,667 sq. km.)
▶ **Currency:** $1 = 506 CFA francs
▶ **Language:** French, Bantu dialects
▶ **Did You Know:** Gabon's climate is hot and humid. Nearly 75% of the land is covered by dense rainforest.

The Gambia

▶ **Capital:** Banjul
▶ **Population:** 1,593,256
▶ **Area:** 4,363 sq. mi. (11,300 sq. km.)
▶ **Currency:** $1 = 29.13 dalasi
▶ **Language:** English, Mandinka, Wolof
▶ **Did You Know:** This narrow nation lies along both banks of the lower Gambia River.

Georgia

▶ **Capital:** Tbilisi
▶ **Population:** 4,677,401
▶ **Area:** 26,911 sq. mi. (69,700 sq. km.)
▶ **Currency:** $1 = 1.78 laris
▶ **Language:** Georgian, Russian
▶ **Did You Know:** In 2004, the Georgian parliament adopted a new national flag.

Germany

▶ **Capital:** Berlin
▶ **Population:** 82,431,390
▶ **Area:** 137,847 sq. mi. (357,021 sq. km.)
▶ **Currency:** $1 = .77 euros
▶ **Language:** German
▶ **Did You Know:** The next World Cup soccer championships will be held in 12 German cities, in June and July 2006.

Ghana

▶ **Capital:** Accra
▶ **Population:** 21,029,853
▶ **Area:** 92,456 sq. mi. (239,460 sq. km.)
▶ **Currency:** $1 = 9,002 cedis
▶ **Language:** English, Akan, Ewe, Moshi-Dagomba, Ga
▶ **Did You Know:** Led by Kwame Nkrumah, Ghana won independence from Great Britain in 1957.

Greece

▶ **Capital:** Athens
▶ **Population:** 10,668,354
▶ **Area:** 50,942 sq. mi. (131,940 sq. km.)
▶ **Currency:** $1 = .77 euros
▶ **Language:** Greek, English, French
▶ **Did You Know:** Ancient Greeks believed Mount Olympus (9,570 feet), the highest point in Greece, was the home of the gods.

Grenada

▶ **Capital:** Saint George's
▶ **Population:** 89,502
▶ **Area:** 133 sq. mi. (344 sq. km.)
▶ **Currency:** $1 = 2.67 East Carribean dollars
▶ **Language:** Spanish, Mayan languages
▶ **Did You Know:** Grenada is the world's second-largest producer of nutmeg, after Indonesia.

Guatemala

▶ **Capital:** Guatemala City
▶ **Population:** 14,655,189
▶ **Area:** 42,043 sq. mi. (108,890 sq. km.)
▶ **Currency:** $1 = 7.78 quetzals
▶ **Language:** Spanish, Mayan languages
▶ **Did You Know:** There are 23 Amerindian dialects spoken in Guatemala.

Guinea
- **Capital:** Conakry
- **Population:** 9,467,866
- **Area:** 94,926 sq. mi. (245,857 sq. km.)
- **Currency:** $1 = 2,835 francs
- **Language:** French, tribal languages
- **Did You Know:** About 85% of Guinea's population is Muslim. Bauxite (used in making aluminum) is its main export.

Guinea-Bissau
- **Capital:** Bissau
- **Population:** 1,416,027
- **Area:** 13,946 sq. mi. (36,120 sq. km.)
- **Currency:** $1 = 506 CFA francs
- **Language:** Portuguese, Crioulo
- **Did You Know:** At carnival time people here wear masks of sharks, hippos, and bulls.

Guyana
- **Capital:** Georgetown
- **Population:** 765,283
- **Area:** 83,000 sq. mi. (214,970 sq. km.)
- **Currency:** $1 = 178.5 Guyana dollars
- **Language:** English, Amerindian dialects
- **Did You Know:** Kaieteur Falls (740 feet) is one of the highest single-drop waterfalls in the world.

Haiti
- **Capital:** Port-au-Prince
- **Population:** 8,121,622
- **Area:** 10,714 sq. mi. (27,750 sq. km.)
- **Currency:** $1 = 36.26 gourdes
- **Language:** Haitian Creole, French
- **Did You Know:** In December 1492, Christopher Columbus left 39 of his men in Haiti to look for gold; they didn't survive.

Honduras
- **Capital:** Tegucigalpa
- **Population:** 6,975,204
- **Area:** 43,278 sq. mi. (112,090 sq. km.)
- **Currency:** $1 = 18.68 lempiras
- **Language:** Spanish
- **Did You Know:** Copán, a center for the Mayan empire, is an important archaeological site in Honduras.

Hungary
- **Capital:** Budapest
- **Population:** 10,006,835
- **Area:** 35,919 sq. mi. (93,030 sq. km.)
- **Currency:** $1 = 188.23 forint
- **Language:** Hungarian (Magyar)
- **Did You Know:** Hungary is a little smaller than the state of Indiana.

Iceland
- **Capital:** Reykjavik
- **Population:** 296,737
- **Area:** 39,769 sq. mi. (103,000 sq. km.)
- **Currency:** $1 = 62.41 kronur
- **Language:** Icelandic (Islenska)
- **Did You Know:** The "Land of Fire and Ice" has more than 100 volcanoes and 120 glaciers.

India
- **Capital:** New Delhi
- **Population:** 1,080,264,388
- **Area:** 741,100 sq. mi. (3,287,590 sq. km.)
- **Currency:** $1 = 43.68 rupees
- **Language:** Hindi, English
- **Did You Know:** India has more people than the U.S., Indonesia, Brazil, Pakistan, and Bangladesh combined.

COLOR KEY
- Africa
- Asia
- Australia
- Europe
- North America
- Pacific Islands
- South America

FACTS ABOUT NATIONS

Indonesia

- Capital: Jakarta
- Population: 241,973,879
- Area: 741,100 sq. mi. (1,919,440 sq. km.)
- Currency: $1 = 9,142 rupiahs
- Language: Bahasa Indonesian, English, Dutch
- Did You Know: This nation of 17,000 islands (6,000 inhabited) is home to the world's largest Muslim population.

Iran

- Capital: Tehran
- Population: 68,017,860
- Area: 636,296 sq. mi. (1,648,000 sq. km.)
- Currency: $1 = 8,853 rials
- Language: Persian (Farsi), Turkic, Luri
- Did You Know: Tehran is believed to have been a suburb of Rayy, an ancient city destroyed by Mongol invaders in A.D. 1220.

Iraq

- Capital: Baghdad
- Population: 26,074,906
- Area: 168,754 sq. mi. (437,072 sq. km.)
- Currency: $1 = 1,462 dinars
- Language: Arabic, Kurdish
- Did You Know: The ancient land of Mesopotamia was located between the Tigris and Euphrates rivers in what is now Iraq.

Ireland

- Capital: Dublin
- Population: 4,015,676
- Area: 27,135 sq. mi. (70,280 sq. km.)
- Currency: $1 = .77 euros
- Language: English, Gaelic
- Did You Know: The first known settlers at Dublin were Norsemen, or Vikings, who landed in the ninth century.

Israel

- Capital: Jerusalem
- Population: 6,276,883
- Area: 8,019 sq. mi. (20,770 sq. km.)
- Currency: $1 = 4.39 new shekels
- Language: Hebrew, Arabic, English
- Did You Know: Israel signed a peace treaty with Egypt in 1979, its first with an Arab nation.

Italy

- Capital: Rome
- Population: 58,103,033
- Area: 116,306 sq. mi. (301,230 sq. km.)
- Currency: $1 = .77 euros
- Language: Italian, German, French, Slovene
- Did You Know: The Renaissance, the 15th– and 16th–century revival of learning, began in Italy.

Jamaica

- Capital: Kingston
- Population: 2,731,832
- Area: 4,244 sq. mi. (10,991 sq. km.)
- Currency: $1 = 61.63 Jamaica dollars
- Language: English, Jamaican, Creole
- Did You Know: Jamaica is the third-largest island in the Caribbean Sea, after Cuba and Hispaniola.

Japan

- Capital: Tokyo
- Population: 127,417,244
- Area: 145,883 sq. mi. (377,835 sq. km.)
- Currency: $1 = 102.7 yen
- Language: Japanese
- Did You Know: The islands of Japan are very narrow. No part of Japan is more than 100 miles from the sea.

Jordan

- **Capital:** Amman
- **Population:** 5,759,732
- **Area:** 35,637 sq. mi. (92,300 sq. km.)
- **Currency:** $1 = .71 dinars
- **Language:** Arabic, English
- **Did You Know:** The Dead Sea, on the Israel-Jordan border, is six times saltier than the ocean.

Kazakhstan

- **Capital:** Astana
- **Population:** 15,185,844
- **Area:** 1,049,155 sq. mi. (2,717,300 sq. km.)
- **Currency:** $1 = 130.4 tenge
- **Language:** Kazakh, Russian
- **Did You Know:** Kazakhstan is the world's ninth-largest country in land area.

Kenya

- **Capital:** Nairobi
- **Population:** 33,829,590
- **Area:** 224,962 sq. mi. (582,650 sq. km.)
- **Currency:** $1 = 77.19 shillings
- **Language:** Swahili, English
- **Did You Know:** The coast of this east African nation has seen the influence of traders from Persia, China, the Malay peninsula, Portugal, and England.

Kiribati

- **Capital:** Tarawa
- **Population:** 103,092
- **Area:** 313 sq. mi. (811 sq. km.)
- **Currency:** $1 = 1.3 Australian dollars
- **Language:** English, Gilbertese
- **Did You Know:** The island of Tarawa was the scene of fierce fighting in World War II.

Korea, North

- **Capital:** Pyongyang
- **Population:** 22,912,177
- **Area:** 46,541 sq. mi. (120,540 sq. km.)
- **Currency:** $1 = 2.2 won
- **Language:** Korean
- **Did You Know:** This Communist country shares an 880-mile border with China and a 12-mile border with Russia.

Korea, South

- **Capital:** Seoul
- **Population:** 48,422,644
- **Area:** 38,023 sq. mi. (98,480 sq. km.)
- **Currency:** $1 = 1,033 won
- **Language:** Korean
- **Did You Know:** This country on the southern half of the Korean peninsula shares a 148-mile border with North Korea, established in 1953.

Kuwait

- **Capital:** Kuwait City
- **Population:** 2,335,648
- **Area:** 6,880 sq. mi. (17,820 sq. km.)
- **Currency:** $1 = .29 dinars
- **Language:** Arabic, English
- **Did You Know:** The 1991 Gulf War freed Kuwait from Iraqi forces that had invaded in 1990.

Kyrgyzstan

- **Capital:** Bishkek
- **Population:** 5,146,281
- **Area:** 76,641 sq. mi. (198,500 sq. km.)
- **Currency:** $1 = 41.2 soms
- **Language:** Kyrgyz, Russian
- **Did You Know:** This Central Asian country is almost entirely mountainous.

COLOR KEY
- Africa
- Asia
- Australia
- Europe
- North America
- Pacific Islands
- South America

FACTS ABOUT NATIONS

Laos

- **Capital:** Vientiane
- **Population:** 6,217,141
- **Area:** 91,429 sq. mi. (236,800 sq. km.)
- **Currency:** $1 = 10,570 kips
- **Language:** Lao, French, English
- **Did You Know:** During the Vietnam War (1957-1975), fighting also took place in neighboring Laos and Cambodia.

Latvia

- **Capital:** Riga
- **Population:** 2,290,237
- **Area:** 24,938 sq. mi. (64,589 sq. km.)
- **Currency:** $1 = .54 lat
- **Language:** Lettish, Lithuanian
- **Did You Know:** For over 300 years, this area on the Baltic Sea was part of the domain of the Teutonic Knights.

Lebanon

- **Capital:** Beirut
- **Population:** 3,826,018
- **Area:** 4,015 sq. mi. (10,400 sq. km.)
- **Currency:** $1 = 1,515 pounds
- **Language:** Arabic, French, English, Armenian
- **Did You Know:** The Ottoman Turks ruled Lebanon for 400 years, until World War I.

Lesotho

- **Capital:** Maweru
- **Population:** 1,867,035
- **Area:** 11,720 sq. mi. (30,355 sq. km.)
- **Currency:** $1 = 5.95 maloti
- **Language:** English, Sesotho
- **Did You Know:** The average life expectancy in Lesotho is less than 37 years.

Liberia

- **Capital:** Monrovia
- **Population:** 3,482,211
- **Area:** 43,000 sq. mi. (111,370 sq. km.)
- **Currency:** $1 = 55 Liberian dollars
- **Language:** English, tribal language
- **Did You Know:** Established in 1847, Liberia is the oldest republic in Africa, and in 1945 it became one of the original member states of the UN.

Libya

- **Capital:** Tripoli
- **Population:** 5,765,563
- **Area:** 679,362 sq. mi. (1,759,540 sq. km.)
- **Currency:** $1 = 1.27 dinars
- **Language:** Arabic, Italian, English
- **Did You Know:** In late 2003, Libya agreed to abandon efforts to make atomic weapons.

Liechtenstein

- **Capital:** Vaduz
- **Population:** 33,717
- **Area:** 62 sq. mi. (160 sq. km.)
- **Currency:** $1 = 1.19 Swiss francs
- **Language:** German, Alemanic dialect
- **Did You Know:** Surrounded by Switzerland and Austria, which themselves also have no access to the sea, Liechtenstein is said to be "doubly landlocked."

Lithuania

- **Capital:** Vilnius
- **Population:** 3,596,617
- **Area:** 25,174 sq. mi. (65,200 sq. km.)
- **Currency:** $1 = 2.66 litas
- **Language:** Lithuanian, Polish, Russian
- **Did You Know:** Russians are Lithuania's largest ethnic minority.

Luxembourg

- **Capital:** Luxembourg
- **Population:** 468,571
- **Area:** 998 sq. mi. (2,586 sq. km.)
- **Currency:** $1 = 77 euros
- **Language:** French, German
- **Did You Know:** This country takes its name from a Roman castle on the Alzette River whose name, *Lucilinburhuc*, meant "Little Fortress."

Macedonia

- **Capital:** Skopje
- **Population:** 2,045,262
- **Area:** 9,781 sq. mi. (25,333 sq. km.)
- **Currency:** $1 = 46.46 denars
- **Language:** Macedonian, Albanian
- **Did You Know:** Alexander the Great set out to conquer a vast empire after becoming King of Macedonia in 336 B.C.

Madagascar

- **Capital:** Antananarivo
- **Population:** 18,040,341
- **Area:** 226,657 sq. mi. (587,040 sq. km.)
- **Currency:** $1 = 1,760 ariary
- **Language:** Malagasy, French
- **Did You Know:** Madagascar, the world's fourth largest island, is home to about 90% of the known species of lemurs, and half the world's chameleons.

Malawi

- **Capital:** Lilongwe
- **Population:** 12,158,924
- **Area:** 45,745 sq. mi. (118,480 sq. km.)
- **Currency:** $1 = 108 kwacha
- **Language:** English, Chichewa
- **Did You Know:** Malawi is one of Africa's most densely populated countries.

Malaysia

- **Capital:** Kuala-Lumpur
- **Population:** 23,953,136
- **Area:** 127,317 sq. mi. (329,750 sq. km.)
- **Currency:** $1 = 3.8 ringgits
- **Language:** Malay, English, Chinese dialects
- **Did You Know:** Malaysia's animal life includes elephants, tigers, and orangutans.

Maldives

- **Capital:** Male
- **Population:** 349,106
- **Area:** 116 sq. mi. (300 sq. km.)
- **Currency:** $1 = 11.77 rufiyaa
- **Language:** Maldivian, Divehi, English
- **Did You Know:** The inhabitants of these islands were converted to Islam in A.D. 1153.

Mali

- **Capital:** Bamako
- **Population:** 12,291,529
- **Area:** 478,766 sq. mi. (1,240,000 sq. km.)
- **Currency:** $1 = 506 CFA francs
- **Language:** French, Bambara
- **Did You Know:** Timbuktu was a great learning center in the 15th and 16th centuries.

Malta

- **Capital:** Valletta
- **Population:** 398,534
- **Area:** 122 sq. mi. (316 sq. km.)
- **Currency:** $1 = .33 liri
- **Language:** Maltese, English
- **Did You Know:** Valletta is a 16th-century fortress-city built by the Knights of St. John.

COLOR KEY

- Africa
- Asia
- Australia
- Europe
- North America
- Pacific Islands
- South America

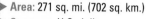

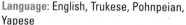
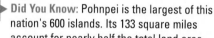

FACTS ABOUT NATIONS

Marshall Islands

- **Capital:** Majuro
- **Population:** 59,071
- **Area:** 70 sq. mi. (181 sq. km.)
- **Currency:** U.S. dollar
- **Language:** English, Marshallese
- **Did You Know:** Bikini Atoll, where the first hydrogen bomb was tested, is located here.

Mauritania

- **Capital:** Nouakchott
- **Population:** 3,086,859
- **Area:** 397,955 sq. mi. (1,030,700 sq. km.)
- **Currency:** $1 = 258.1 ouguiyas
- **Language:** Hasaniya Arabic, Wolof, Pular
- **Did You Know:** About 40% of Mauritania's land area is covered by sand.

Mauritius

- **Capital:** Port Louis
- **Population:** 1,230,602
- **Area:** 788 sq. mi. (2,040 sq. km.)
- **Currency:** $1 = 28.57 Mauritian rupees
- **Language:** English, French, Creole, Hindi
- **Did You Know:** The dodo became extinct here by 1681, 83 years after the Dutch arrived.

Mexico

- **Capital:** Mexico City
- **Population:** 106,202,903
- **Area:** 761,606 sq. mi. (1,972,550 sq. km.)
- **Currency:** $1 = 11.24 pesos
- **Language:** Spanish, Mayan dialects
- **Did You Know:** The Aztec capital of Tenochtitlan was destroyed by the Spanish in 1521.

Micronesia

- **Capital:** Palikir
- **Population:** 108,105
- **Area:** 271 sq. mi. (702 sq. km.)
- **Currency:** U.S. dollar
- **Language:** English, Trukese, Pohnpeian, Yapese
- **Did You Know:** Pohnpei is the largest of this nation's 600 islands. Its 133 square miles account for nearly half the total land area.

Moldova

- **Capital:** Chisinau
- **Population:** 4,455,421
- **Area:** 13,067 sq. mi. (33,843 sq. km.)
- **Currency:** $1 = 12.52 lei
- **Language:** Moldovan, Russian
- **Did You Know:** Grapes are a major crop, in Moldova, and winemaking is a major industry.

Monaco

- **Capital:** Monaco
- **Population:** 32,409
- **Area:** 1 sq. mi. (1.95 sq. km.)
- **Currency:** $1 = .77 euros
- **Language:** French, English, Italian
- **Did You Know:** Monaco is the most densely populated country in the world.

Mongolia

- **Capital:** Ulaanbaatar
- **Population:** 2,791,272
- **Area:** 604,250 sq. mi. (1,565,000 sq. km.)
- **Currency:** $1 = 1,212 tugriks
- **Language:** Khalkha Mongolian
- **Did You Know:** Mongolia is the most thinly populated country in the world.

Morocco

- **Capital:** Rabat
- **Population:** 32,725,847
- **Area:** 172,414 sq. mi. (446,550 sq. km.)
- **Currency:** $1 = 8.54 dirhams
- **Language:** Arabic, Berber dialects
- **Did You Know:** Casablanca is Morocco's largest city and main seaport.

Mozambique

- **Capital:** Maputo
- **Population:** 19,406,703
- **Area:** 309,496 sq. mi. (801,590 sq. km.)
- **Currency:** $1 = 18,685 meticals
- **Language:** Portuguese, native dialects
- **Did You Know:** Decades of civil war have left over a million land mines buried here.

Myanmar (Burma)

- **Capital:** Yangon (Rangoon)
- **Population:** 42,909,464
- **Area:** 261,970 sq. mi. (678,500 sq. km.)
- **Currency:** $1 = 5.6 kyats
- **Language:** Burmese
- **Did You Know:** More than 100 native languages are spoken in Myanmar.

Namibia

- **Capital:** Windhoek
- **Population:** 2,030,692
- **Area:** 318,696 sq. mi. (825,418 sq. km.)
- **Currency:** $1 = 5.95 Namibian dollars
- **Language:** Afrikaans, English, German
- **Did You Know:** Namibia included protection of the environment as a goal in its constitution.

Nauru

- **Capital:** Yaren district
- **Population:** 13,048
- **Area:** 8 sq. mi. (21 sq. km.)
- **Currency:** $1 = 1.30 Australian dollars
- **Language:** Nauruan, English
- **Did You Know:** Phosphates created from millions of years of bird droppings are nearly used up.

Nepal

- **Capital:** Kathmandu
- **Population:** 27,676,547
- **Area:** 54,363 sq. mi. (140,800 sq. km.)
- **Currency:** $1 = 70.95 rupees
- **Language:** Nepali, many dialects
- **Did You Know:** Mt. Everest, the world's highest mountain, is partly in Nepal.

Netherlands

- **Capital:** Amsterdam
- **Population:** 16,407,491
- **Area:** 16,033 sq. mi. (41,526 sq. km.)
- **Currency:** $1 = .77 euros
- **Language:** Dutch
- **Did You Know:** Nowadays in the Netherlands, wooden shoes are worn mostly by farmers.

New Zealand

- **Capital:** Wellington
- **Population:** 4,035,461
- **Area:** 103,738 sq. mi. (268,680 sq. km.)
- **Currency:** $1 = 1.4 New Zealand dollars
- **Language:** English, Maori
- **Did You Know:** New Zealand was the first country to grant women full voting rights (in 1893).

Nicaragua

- **Capital:** Managua
- **Population:** 5,465,100
- **Area:** 49,998 sq. mi. (129,494 sq. km.)
- **Currency:** $1 = 16.18 gold córdobas
- **Language:** Spanish
- **Did You Know:** The eastern shore is called Costa de Mosquitos (Mosquito Coast).

COLOR KEY
- Africa
- Asia
- Australia
- Europe
- North America
- Pacific Islands
- South America

FACTS ABOUT NATIONS

Niger

- **Capital:** Niamey
- **Population:** 11,665,937
- **Area:** 489,191 sq. mi. (1,267,000 sq. km.)
- **Currency:** $1 = 506 CFA francs
- **Language:** French, Hausa, Djerma
- **Did You Know:** Temperatures can exceed 122° F in the hot season, which lasts from March to June.

Nigeria

- **Capital:** Abuja
- **Population:** 128,771,988
- **Area:** 356,669 sq. mi. (923,768 sq. km.)
- **Currency:** $1 = 132.64 nairas
- **Language:** English, Hausa, Yoruba, Ibo
- **Did You Know:** Nigeria is the biggest oil-producing country in Africa.

Norway

- **Capital:** Oslo
- **Population:** 4,593,041
- **Area:** 125,182 sq. mi. (324,220 sq. km.)
- **Currency:** $1 = 6.29 kroner
- **Language:** Norwegian
- **Did You Know:** The UN ranks Norway as the world's top country in "quality of life."

Oman

- **Capital:** Muscat
- **Population:** 3,001,583
- **Area:** 82,031 sq. mi. (212,460 sq. km.)
- **Currency:** $1 = 0.38 rials
- **Language:** Arabic
- **Did You Know:** Oman has about 13 males for every 10 females.

Pakistan

- **Capital:** Islamabad
- **Population:** 162,419,946
- **Area:** 310,403 sq. mi. (803,940 sq. km.)
- **Currency:** $1 = 59.29 rupees
- **Language:** Urdu, English, Punjabi, Sindhi
- **Did You Know:** Pakistan is mostly (97%) Muslim; its neighbor India is mostly Hindu (82%).

Palau

- **Capital:** Koror
- **Population:** 20,303
- **Area:** 177 sq. mi. (458 sq. km.)
- **Currency:** same as U.S. dollar
- **Language:** English, Palauan
- **Did You Know:** The islands of Palau are old coral reefs that have risen above the sea.

Panama

- **Capital:** Panama CIty
- **Population:** 3,039,150
- **Area:** 30,193 sq. mi. (78,200 sq. km.)
- **Currency:** $1 = 1 balboa
- **Language:** Spanish, English
- **Did You Know:** It takes 8 to 10 hours for a ship to travel through the 50-mile Panama Canal from the Caribbean Sea to the Pacific Ocean.

Papua New Guinea

- **Capital:** Port Moresby
- **Population:** 5,545,268
- **Area:** 178,703 sq. mi. (462,840 sq. km.)
- **Currency:** $1 = 3.08 kinas
- **Language:** English, Motu
- **Did You Know:** Papua New Guinea takes up the eastern half of New Guinea, the world's second largest island after Greenland.

Paraguay

- **Capital:** Asuncíon
- **Population:** 6,347,884
- **Area:** 157,047 sq. mi. (406,750 sq. km.)
- **Currency:** $1 = 6,301 guarani
- **Language:** Spanish, Guarani
- **Did You Know:** The capital of this landlocked South American nation is a port with access to the Atlantic Ocean through a system of rivers.

Peru

- **Capital:** Lima
- **Population:** 27,925,628
- **Area:** 496,226 sq. mi. (1,285,220 sq. km.)
- **Currency:** $1 = 3.27 new soles
- **Language:** Spanish, Quechua, Aymara
- **Did You Know:** Spanish conquistadors came in 1532 with horses and gunpowder— and conquered the Inca civilization within 40 years.

Philippines

- **Capital:** Manila
- **Population:** 87,857,473
- **Area:** 115,831 sq. mi. (300,000 sq. km.)
- **Currency:** $1 = 55.4 pesos
- **Language:** Pilipino, English
- **Did You Know:** The Philippines consist of about 7,100 Islands, but most of the people live on 1 of the 11 largest islands.

Poland

- **Capital:** Warsaw
- **Population:** 38,635,144
- **Area:** 120,728 sq. mi. (312,685 sq. km.)
- **Currency:** $1 = 3.11 zlotych
- **Language:** Polish
- **Did You Know:** Germany invaded Poland on September 1, 1939, the start of World War II.

Portugal

- **Capital:** Lisbon
- **Population:** 10,566,212
- **Area:** 35,672 sq. mi. (92,391 sq. km.)
- **Currency:** $1 = .77 euros
- **Language:** Portuguese
- **Did You Know:** In 1497, a Portuguese captain, Vasco da Gama, became the first to sail around the tip of Africa and into the Indian Ocean.

Qatar

- **Capital:** Doha
- **Population:** 863,051
- **Area:** 4,416 sq. mi. (11,437 sq. km.)
- **Currency:** $1 = 3.64 riyals
- **Language:** Arabic, English
- **Did You Know:** Workers from South Asia and other Arab states outnumber the citizens of Qatar by more than three to one.

Romania

- **Capital:** Bucharest
- **Population:** 22,329,977
- **Area:** 91,699 sq. mi. (237,500 sq. km.)
- **Currency:** $1 = 29,362 lei
- **Language:** Romanian, Hungarian
- **Did You Know:** The coastal city of Varna, Romania's third largest, was founded by the Greeks in the sixth century.

Russia

- **Capital:** Moscow
- **Population:** 143,420,309
- **Area:** 6,592,769 sq. mi. (17,075,200 sq. km.)
- **Currency:** $1 = 28 rubles
- **Language:** Russian, many others
- **Did You Know:** Record lows of −90° F have been recorded in the region of Siberia.

COLOR KEY
- Africa
- Asia
- Australia
- Europe
- North America
- Pacific Islands
- South America

Rwanda

- **Capital:** Kigali
- **Population:** 8,440,820
- **Area:** 10,169 sq. mi. (26,338 sq. km.)
- **Currency:** $1 = 555.70 francs
- **Language:** French, English, Kinyarwanda
- **Did You Know:** The source of the Nile River has been located in Rwanda.

Saint Kitts and Nevis

- **Capital:** Basseterre
- **Population:** 38,958
- **Area:** 101 sq. mi. (261 sq. km.)
- **Currency:** $1 = 2.67 East Carribean dollars
- **Language:** English
- **Did You Know:** St. Kitts was the first island in the West Indies settled by the British, in 1623.

Saint Lucia

- **Capital:** Castries
- **Population:** 166,312
- **Area:** 238 sq. mi. (616 sq. km.)
- **Currency:** $1 = 2.67 East Carribean dollars
- **Language:** English, French patois
- **Did You Know:** The island has switched hands between the British and French 14 times.

Saint Vincent and the Grenadines

- **Capital:** Kingston
- **Population:** 117,534
- **Area:** 150 sq. mi. (389 sq. km.)
- **Currency:** $1 = 2.67 East Carribean dollars
- **Language:** English, French patois
- **Did You Know:** Black Caribs living here are descended from slaves and native Indians.

Samoa (formerly Western Samoa)

- **Capital:** Apia
- **Population:** 177,287
- **Area:** 1,137 sq. mi. (2,944 sq. km.)
- **Currency:** $1 = 2.67 tala
- **Language:** English, Samoan
- **Did You Know:** Most Samoans live in small seashore villages of 100 to 500 people.

San Marino

- **Capital:** San Marino
- **Population:** 28,880
- **Area:** 24 sq. mi. (61 sq. km.)
- **Currency:** $1 = .77 euros • **Language:** Italian
- **Did You Know:** San Marino claims to be Europe's oldest country, founded in A.D. 301.

São Tomé and Príncipe

- **Capital:** São Tomé
- **Population:** 187,410
- **Area:** 386 sq. mi. (1,001 sq. km.)
- **Currency:** $1 = 9,043 dobras
- **Language:** Portuguese
- **Did You Know:** Portugal ruled these islands for nearly 300 years, leaving in 1975.

Saudi Arabia

- **Capital:** Riyadh
- **Population:** 26,417,599
- **Area:** 756,985 sq. mi. (1,960,582 sq. km.)
- **Currency:** $1 = 3.75 riyals • **Language:** Arabic
- **Did You Know:** Mecca, the birthplace of Muhammad, is the holiest city of Islam.

Senegal

- **Capital:** Dakar
- **Population:** 11,126,832
- **Area:** 75,749 sq. mi. (196,190 sq. km.)
- **Currency:** $1 = 506 CFA francs
- **Language:** French, Wolof
- **Did You Know:** Senegal is among the world's largest producers of peanuts.

Serbia and Montenegro

- **Capital:** Belgrade, Podgorica
- **Population:** 10,829,175
- **Area:** 39,518 sq. mi. (102,350 sq. km.)
- **Currency:** $1 = 61.38 new dinars
- **Language:** Serbo-Croatian, Albanian
- **Did You Know:** Ruins of the Roman town of Singidunum can still be seen in Belgrade.

Seychelles (not on map)

- **Capital:** Victoria
- **Population:** 81,188
- **Area:** 176 sq. mi. (455 sq. km.)
- **Currency:** $1 = 5.43 rupees
- **Language:** English, French, Creole
- **Did You Know:** These islands were uninhabited when ships sailing for the British East India Company landed there in 1609.

Sierra Leone

- **Capital:** Freetown
- **Population:** 6,017,643
- **Area:** 27,699 sq. mi. (71,740 sq. km.)
- **Currency:** $1 = 2,356 leones
- **Language:** English, Mende, Temne, Krio
- **Did You Know:** Portuguese explorer Pedro da Cintra called the area Serra Layoa, "Lion Mountains," in 1460.

Singapore

- **Capital:** Singapore
- **Population:** 4,425,720
- **Area:** 267 sq. mi. (693 sq. km.)
- **Currency:** $1 = 1.63 Singapore dollars
- **Language:** Chinese, Malay, Tamil, English
- **Did You Know:** Singapore is the world's second most densely populated country after Monaco.

Slovakia

- **Capital:** Bratislava
- **Population:** 5,431,363
- **Area:** 18,859 sq. mi. (48,845 sq. km.)
- **Currency:** $1 = 29.54 koruny
- **Language:** Slovak, Hungarian
- **Did You Know:** This nation became independent when Czechoslovakia split into the Czech Republic and Slovakia in 1993.

Slovenia

- **Capital:** Ljubljana
- **Population:** 2,011,070
- **Area:** 7,827 sq. mi. (20,273 sq. km.)
- **Currency:** $1 = 184.72 tolars
- **Language:** Slovenian, Serbo-Croatian
- **Did You Know:** Slovenia escaped the violence that affected Yugoslavia in the 1990s.

Solomon Islands

- **Capital:** Honiara
- **Population:** 538,032
- **Area:** 10,985 sq. mi. (28,450 sq. km.)
- **Currency:** $1 = 7.12 Solomon Islands dollars
- **Language:** English, Melanesian
- **Did You Know:** Guadalcanal, one of the Solomon Islands, was the site of a key World War II battle.

Somalia

- **Capital:** Mogadishu
- **Population:** 8,591,629
- **Area:** 246,201 sq. mi. (637,657 sq. km.)
- **Currency:** $1 = 3,088 shillings
- **Language:** Somali, Arabic, Italian, English
- **Did You Know:** Thirty U.S. soldiers were killed here during UN peacekeeping work (1992-1994).

COLOR KEY
- Africa
- Asia
- Australia
- Europe
- North America
- Pacific Islands
- South America

FACTS ABOUT NATIONS

South Africa

- **Capital:** Pretoria (admin.)
  Cape Town (legisl.)
- **Population:** 44,344,136
- **Area:** 471,010 sq. mi. (1,219,912 sq. km.)
- **Currency:** $1 = 5.94 rand
- **Language:** Afrikaans, English, Ndebele, Sotho
- **Did You Know:** South Africa has 11 official languages; 9 of them are native.

Spain

- **Capital:** Madrid
- **Population:** 40,341,462
- **Area:** 194,897 sq. mi. (504,782 sq. km.)
- **Currency:** $1 = .77 euros
- **Language:** Castilian Spanish, Catalan, Galician
- **Did You Know:** Spanish rulers grew rich in the 1500s from New World gold and silver.

Sri Lanka

- **Capital:** Colombo
- **Population:** 20,064,776
- **Area:** 25,332 sq. mi. (65,610 sq. km.)
- **Currency:** $1 = 98.65 rupees
- **Language:** Sinhala, Tamil, English
- **Did You Know:** In 1960, Sri Lanka chose the world's first elected female prime minister.

Sudan

- **Capital:** Khartoum
- **Population:** 40,187,486
- **Area:** 967,498 sq. mi. (2,505,810 sq. km.)
- **Currency:** $1 = 256.11 dinars
- **Language:** Arabic, Nubian, Ta Bedawie
- **Did You Know:** Sudan is the largest country in Africa in total area, while Algeria is the largest in land area.

Suriname

- **Capital:** Paramaribo
- **Population:** 438,144
- **Area:** 63,039 sq. mi. (163,270 sq. km.)
- **Currency:** $1 = 2.8 Suriname dollars
- **Language:** Dutch, Sranang Tongo
- **Did You Know:** In 1677, Britain "traded" Suriname to the Dutch for New York City.

Swaziland

- **Capital:** Mbabane
- **Population:** 1,173,900
- **Area:** 6,704 sq. mi. (17,363 sq. km.)
- **Currency:** $1 = 5.96 emalangeni
- **Language:** English, siSwati
- **Did You Know:** 4 out of 10 adults in Swaziland have the AIDS virus.

Sweden

- **Capital:** Stockholm
- **Population:** 9,001,774
- **Area:** 173,732 sq. mi. (449,964 sq. km.)
- **Currency:** $1 = 6.95 kronor
- **Language:** Swedish
- **Did You Know:** In 1910, Sweden created Europe's first national park. In all, some 7,700 square miles of land is now preserved.

Switzerland

- **Capital:** Bern (admin.)
  Lausanne (judicial)
- **Population:** 7,489,370
- **Area:** 15,942 sq. mi. (41,290 sq. km.)
- **Currency:** $1 = 1.19 Swiss francs
- **Language:** German, French, Italian, Romansch
- **Did You Know:** Though it is home to the European headquarters of the United Nations, Switzerland did not join the UN until 2002.

COLOR KEY

- Africa
- Asia
- Australia
- Europe
- North America
- Pacific Islands
- South America

Syria

- **Capital:** Damascus
- **Population:** 18,448,752
- **Area:** 71,498 sq. mi. (185,180 sq. km.)
- **Currency:** $1 = 51.96 pounds
- **Language:** Arabic, Kurdish, Armenian
- **Did You Know:** Damascus may be the world's oldest continuously occupied city.

Taiwan

- **Capital:** Taipei
- **Population:** 22,894,384
- **Area:** 13,892 sq. mi. (35,980 sq. km.)
- **Currency:** $1 = 31.67 Taiwan new dollars
- **Language:** Mandarin Chinese, Taiwanese
- **Did You Know:** Anti-Communists founded this "Republic of China" in 1949.

Tajikistan

- **Capital:** Dushanbe
- **Population:** 7,163,506
- **Area:** 55,251 sq. mi. (143,100 sq. km.)
- **Currency:** $1 = 2.79 somoni
- **Language:** Tajik, Russia
- **Did You Know:** Dust can take up to 10 days to settle after a strong dust storm here.

Tanzania

- **Capital:** Dar-es-Salaam
- **Population:** 36,766,356
- **Area:** 364,900 sq. mi. (945,087 sq. km.)
- **Currency:** $1 = 1,129 shillings
- **Language:** Swahili, English
- **Did You Know:** Tanganyika and Zanzibar joined to form Tanzania in 1964.

Thailand

- **Capital:** Bangkok
- **Population:** 65,444,371
- **Area:** 198,456 sq. mi. (514,000 sq. km.)
- **Currency:** $1 = 38.44 baht
- **Language:** Thai, English
- **Did You Know:** Thailand is one of the world's largest tin producers, and a major source of gems and jewelry, especially rubies and sapphires.

Timor-Leste (East Timor)

- **Capital:** Dili
- **Population:** 1,040,880
- **Area:** 5,794 sq. mi. (15,007 sq. km.)
- **Currency:** U.S. Dollar
- **Language:** Tetum, Portuguese, Indonesian, English
- **Did You Know:** During Indonesia's 25-year occupation, 25% of the population may have died.

Togo

- **Capital:** Lomé
- **Population:** 5,681,519
- **Area:** 21,925 sq. mi. (56,785 sq. km.)
- **Currency:** $1 = 506 CFA francs
- **Language:** French, Ewe, Kabye
- **Did You Know:** About 70% of Togolese people practice traditional African religions.

Tonga

- **Capital:** Nuku'alofa
- **Population:** 112,422
- **Area:** 289 sq. mi. (748 sq. km.)
- **Currency:** $1 = 1.92 pa'angas
- **Language:** Tongan, English
- **Did You Know:** The Polynesian people of these islands trace heritage along their mothers' line, and newlyweds live near the bride's relatives.

Trinidad and Tobago

- **Capital:** Port-of-Spain
- **Population:** 1,088,644
- **Area:** 1,980 sq. mi. (5,128 sq. km.)
- **Currency:** $1 = 6.19 Trinidad and Tobago dollars
- **Language:** English, Hindi, French, Spanish
- **Did You Know:** East Indians, who came here in 1800s, make up 40% of the population.

FACTS ABOUT NATIONS

Tunisia

- **Capital:** Tunis
- **Population:** 10,074,951
- **Area:** 63,170 sq. mi. (163,610 sq. km.)
- **Currency:** $1 = 1.24 dinars
- **Language:** Arabic, French
- **Did You Know:** With more than 800 miles of coastline on the Mediterranean Sea, Tunisia is a popular vacation spot for European tourists.

Turkey
- **Capital:** Ankara
- **Population:** 69,660,559
- **Area:** 301,383 sq. mi. (780,580 sq. km.)
- **Currency:** $1 = 1.34 new lira
- **Language:** Turkish, Kurdish, Arabic
- **Did You Know:** More than 20 of Turkey's mountains are higher than 10,000 feet.

Turkmenistan

- **Capital:** Ashgabat
- **Population:** 4,952,081
- **Area:** 188,456 sq. mi. (488,100 sq. km.)
- **Currency:** $1 = 5,200 manats
- **Language:** Turkmen, Russian, Uzbek
- **Did You Know:** Turkmen are famed for the beautiful carpets they weave from sheep wool.

Tuvalu

- **Capital:** Funafuti-Atoll
- **Population:** 11,636
- **Area:** 10 sq. mi. (26 sq. km.)
- **Currency:** $1 = 1.31 Tuvalu dollars
- **Language:** Tuvaluan, English
- **Did You Know:** These low-lying islands are threatened by rising sea levels.

Uganda

- **Capital:** Kampala
- **Population:** 27,269,482
- **Area:** 91,136 sq. mi. (236,040 sq. km.)
- **Currency:** $1 = 1,712 shillings
- **Language:** English, Luganda, Swahili
- **Did You Know:** Bwindi Impenetrable National Park is a home to endangered mountain gorillas.

Ukraine

- **Capital:** Kiev
- **Population:** 47,425,336
- **Area:** 233,090 sq. mi. (603,700 sq. km.)
- **Currency:** $1 = 5.31 hryvnia
- **Language:** Ukrainian, Russian
- **Did You Know:** In the 1840s, Russian rulers banned the Ukrainian language from schools here.

United Arab Emirates

- **Capital:** Abu-Dhabi
- **Population:** 2,563,212
- **Area:** 32,000 sq. mi. (82,880 sq. km.)
- **Currency:** $1 = 3.67 dirhams
- **Language:** Arabic, Persian, English, Hindi
- **Did You Know:** Abu Dhabi is the largest of these seven states, occupying about 90% of the country's land area.

United Kingdom (Great Britain)

- **Capital:** London
- **Population:** 60,441,457
- **Area:** 94,525 sq. mi. (244,820 sq. km.)
- **Currency:** $1 = .54 pounds
- **Language:** English
- **Did You Know:** England, Northern Ireland, Scotland, and Wales make up the United Kingdom.

United States

- **Capital:** Washington, D.C.
- **Population:** 295,734,134
- **Area:** 3,718,710 sq. mi. (9,631,418 sq. km.)
- **Currency:** U.S. dollar
- **Language:** English, Spanish
- **Did You Know:** The population center of the U.S. is near Edgar Springs, MO.

Uruguay

- **Capital:** Montevideo
- **Population:** 3,415,920
- **Area:** 68,039 sq. mi. (176,220 sq. km.)
- **Currency:** $1 = 25.33 pesos
- **Language:** Spanish
- **Did You Know:** Uruguay hosted, and won, soccer's first World Cup (in 1930).

Uzbekistan

- **Capital:** Tashkent
- **Population:** 26,851,195
- **Area:** 172,742 sq. mi. (447,400 sq. km.)
- **Currency:** $1 = 1,070 sumy
- **Language:** Uzbek, Russian
- **Did You Know:** Alexander the Great and Genghis Khan both conquered this region.

Vanuatu

- **Capital:** Port-Vila
- **Population:** 205,754
- **Area:** 4,710 sq. mi. (12,200 sq. km.)
- **Currency:** $1 = 107.6 vatus
- **Language:** French, English, Bislama
- **Did You Know:** Before independence in 1980, Britain and France jointly ruled these islands.

Vatican City

- **Population:** 921
- **Area:** .17 sq. mi. (.44 sq. km.)
- **Currency:** $1 = .77 euros
- **Language:** Italian, Latin
- **Did You Know:** The world's smallest country is less than 0.2 square miles in area and is surrounded by the city of Rome.

Venezuela

- **Capital:** Caracas
- **Population:** 25,375,281
- **Area:** 352,144 sq. mi. (912,050 sq. km.)
- **Currency:** $1 = 1,915 boliviares
- **Language:** Spanish
- **Did You Know:** Angel Falls, the world's highest waterfall, drops 3,212 feet.

Vietnam

- **Capital:** Hanoi
- **Population:** 83,535,576
- **Area:** 127,244 sq. mi. (329,560 sq. km.)
- **Currency:** $1 = 15,782 dong
- **Language:** Vietnamese, French, Chinese
- **Did You Know:** France took over Vietnam in 1854, and ruled there until 1954.

Yemen

- **Capital:** Sanaa
- **Population:** 20,727,063
- **Area:** 203,850 sq. mi. (527,970 sq. km.)
- **Currency:** $1 = 181.82 rials
- **Language:** Arabic
- **Did You Know:** "Mocha" coffee takes its name from a Yemeni seaport.

Zambia

- **Capital:** Lusaka
- **Population:** 11,261,795
- **Area:** 290,586 sq. mi. (752,614 sq. km.)
- **Currency:** $1 = 4,627 kwacha
- **Language:** English, native languages
- **Did You Know:** Fossils show that humans inhabited Zambia 100,000 years ago.

Zimbabwe

- **Capital:** Harare
- **Population:** 12,746,990
- **Area:** 150,804 sq. mi. (390,580 sq. km.)
- **Currency:** $1 = 5,605 Zimbabwe dollars
- **Language:** English, Shona, Sindebele
- **Did You Know:** The lake behind Kariba Dam is the world's largest-capacity reservoir.

A COMMUNITY OF NATIONS

UNITED NATIONS

The United Nations (UN) was started in 1945 after World War II. The first members were 50 nations that met in San Francisco, California. They signed an agreement known as the UN Charter. The UN now has 191 members—including Timor-Leste—and Switzerland, which joined in 2002. Only two independent nations—Taiwan and Vatican City—are not members.

HOW THE UN IS ORGANIZED

GENERAL ASSEMBLY **What It Does:** discusses world problems, admits new members, appoints the secretary-general, decides the UN budget **Members:** All UN members belong to it; each country has one vote.

SECURITY COUNCIL **What It Does:** handles questions of peace and security **Members:** Five permanent members (China, France, Great Britain, Russia, U.S.), each of whom can veto any proposed action; ten elected by the General Assembly for two-year terms. In early 2004 the ten were Angola, Chile, Germany, Pakistan, and Spain (ending 2004) and Algeria, Benin, Brazil, the Philippines, and Romaina (ending 2005).

ECONOMIC AND SOCIAL COUNCIL **What It Does:** deals with issues related to trade, economic development, industry, population, children, food, education, health, and human rights **Members:** Fifty-four member countries elected for three-year terms.

INTERNATIONAL COURT OF JUSTICE (WORLD COURT) located at The Hague, Netherlands **What It Does:** highest court for disputes between countries **Members:** Fifteen judges, each from a different country, elected to nine-year terms.

SECRETARIAT **What It Does:** carries out day-to-day operations of the UN **Members:** UN staff, headed by the secretary-general.

UN PEACEKEEPERS

The Security Council sets up UN peacekeeping missions to try to stop people from fighting while the countries or groups try to work out their differences. There were 16 peacekeeping missions operating around the globe in January 2005. UN peacekeepers usually wear blue helmets or berets with white UN letters.

For more information about the UN, you can write to:
Public Inquiries Unit, United Nations, Room GA-57, New York, NY 10017
Website: www.un.org

Native Americans

What "Mankiller" received the Presidential Medal of Freedom? page 192

When European explorers first sailed to North America, they thought they had arrived in the East Indies, near the continent of Asia. That's why the explorers called the people they found "Indians."

Scientists now believe that these "American Indians," commonly known today as Native Americans, arrived in the Americas about 18,000 years ago, most likely from Northeast Asia. Native Americans are not one people, but many different peoples with their own distinct cultures and traditions. Many probably came from Siberia by a "land bridge" that existed when sea levels were lower.

ole from the : Northwest

There were at least 8 million Native Americans living in the Americas when Columbus arrived. During the 17th, 18th, and 19th centuries, diseases (including many brought by Europeans) and wars with European settlers and soldiers caused the deaths of millions of American Indians. The Indian Removal Act of 1830 allowed the government to force all Indians east of the Mississippi to move to Indian Territory (part of what is now Oklahoma). In 1838 and 1839, in what came to be known as the "Trail of Tears," 16,000 Cherokee Indians in Alabama, Georgia, North Carolina, and Tennessee traveled by foot and horse cart from their homelands to Indian Territory. Nearly a quarter of them died on the way, of hunger, disease, or cold.

By 1910, there were only about 220,000 Native Americans left in the U.S. In 1924, Congress granted native peoples citizenship. Since then, the American Indian population has increased dramatically, to more than 2.7 million in 2002 (not counting people who also reported belonging to other ethnic groups.)

WHO AM I?

I was a Native American of Sac and Fox ancestry born in 1888, and many have called me America's greatest athlete. I was All-American in football and a stand-out player in track and field, baseball, lacrosse, basketball, hockey, swimming, boxing, tennis, and archery. In the 1912 Olympic Games, I won the decathlon (10 events) and pentathlon (five events).

Answer: Jim Thorpe

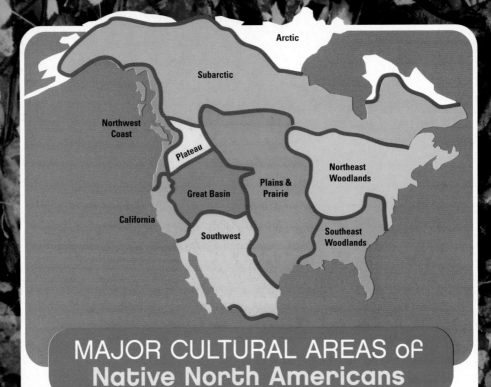

Arctic

Subarctic

Northwest Coast

Plateau

Great Basin

Plains & Prairie

Northeast Woodlands

California

Southwest

Southeast Woodlands

MAJOR CULTURAL AREAS of Native North Americans

Climate and geography influenced the culture of the people who lived in these regions. On the plains, for example, people depended on the great herds of buffalo for food. For Aleuts and Eskimos in the far North, seals and whales were an important food source. There are more than 560 tribes officially recognized by the U.S. government today and more than 56 million acres of tribal lands. Below are just a few well-known tribal groups that have lived in these areas.

NORTHEAST WOODLANDS
The Illinois, Iroquois (Mohawk, Onondaga, Cayuga, Oneida, Seneca, and Tuscarora), Lenape, Menominee, Micmac, Narragansett, Potawatomi, Shawnee.

SOUTHEAST WOODLANDS
The Cherokee, Chickasaw, Choctaw, Creek, Seminole.

PLAINS & PRAIRIE The Arapaho, Blackfoot, Cheyenne, Comanche, Hidatsa, Mandan, Sioux.

SOUTHWEST The Navajo, Apache, Havasupai, Mojave, Pima, Pueblo (Hopi, Isleta, Laguna, Zuñi).

GREAT BASIN The Paiute, Shoshoni, Ute.

CALIFORNIA The Klamath, Maidu, Miwok, Modoc, Patwin, Pomo, Wintun, Yurok.

PLATEAU The Cayuse, Nez Percé, Okanagon, Salish, Spokan, Umatilla, Walla Walla, Yakima.

NORTHWEST COAST The Chinook, Haida, Kwakiutl, Makah, Nootka, Salish, Tlinigit, Tsimshian, Tillamook.

SUBARCTIC The Beaver, Cree, Chipewyan, Chippewa, Ingalik, Kaska, Kutchin, Montagnais, Naskapi, Tanana.

ARCTIC The Eskimo (Inuit and Yipuk), Aleut.

uit girls with sled dogs

Largest U.S. Tribal Groupings*

1. Cherokee, 281,069	6. Choctaw, 87,349
2. Navajo, 269,202	7. Pueblo, 59,533
3. Sioux, 108,272	8. Apache, 57,060
4. Chippewa, 105,907	9. Eskimo, 45,919
5. Latin American Indian, 104,354	10. Iroquois, 45,212

*According to the U.S. Census 2000. Figures are for people reporting only one tribal grouping.

Native American Populations by State*

Alabama	22,840	Maine	7,291	Oregon	48,341
Alaska	100,494	Maryland	17,379	Pennsylvania	20,900
Arizona	286,680	Massachusetts	18,354	Rhode Island	6,105
Arkansas	18,477	Michigan	60,105	South Carolina	15,069
California	410,501	Minnesota	57,340	South Dakota	63,390
Colorado	51,182	Mississippi	12,431	Tennessee	16,576
Connecticut	11,275	Missouri	25,953	Texas	145,954
Delaware	3,087	Montana	58,048	Utah	32,886
Florida	66,138	Nebraska	16,280	Vermont	2,492
Georgia	25,991	Nevada	31,281	Virginia	23,778
Hawaii	3,863	New Hampshire	3,213	Washington	99,446
Idaho	19,268	New Jersey	25,741	West Virginia	3,686
Illinois	38,815	New Mexico	183,972	Wisconsin	50,042
Indiana	17,249	New York	103,337	Wyoming	11,641
Iowa	10,058	North Carolina	106,454	Wash., D.C.	2,062
Kansas	26,085	North Dakota	31,104	**U.S. total**	**2,752,158**
Kentucky	9,437	Ohio	25,870		
Louisiana	26,073	Oklahoma	278,124		

*2002 U.S. Census estimates. Figures do not include people who reported belonging to other ethnic groups in addition to Native American.

NATIONAL MUSEUM OF THE AMERICAN INDIAN

In September 2004, 20,000 Native Americans in traditional dress gathered for the opening of the new National Museum of the American Indian (NMAI) in Washington, D.C. The NMAI is dedicated to the life, culture, and traditions of Native Americans throughout North, South, and Central America. Some 4 million people a year are expected to visit the new museum.

The NMAI is a learning center and showcase for the Smithsonian's collection of more than 800,000 Native objects, including items of artistic, religious, and historical importance, as well as everyday things. The NMAI, the 16th Smithsonian museum on the National Mall, was designed by American Indian architects and engineers and is meant to reflect the beliefs and principles of many different Native American groups.

Famous Native Americans

Here are a few famous Native Americans who are admired for their bravery, leadership, and contributions to American history.

SEQUOYAH ▶ (1766?-1843), a Cherokee silversmith and trader, created a written form of his native language that included 85 characters. Soon, parts of the Bible were translated into Cherokee, and a Cherokee newspaper was founded. In his travels, he taught thousands of Cherokee to read and write. His efforts helped to make the Cherokee one of the most prominent Native American tribes. The sequoia, the giant evergreen tree of California, was named after him.

SACAGAWEA (1787?-1812), of the Shoshone tribe, served as an interpreter and guide for Meriwether Lewis and William Clark, who explored the American Northwest from 1804 to 1806. It's doubtful that the expedition could have succeeded without her. She showed the explorers what plants to use for food and medicine, guided them along trails, saved their supplies from a capsized boat, and persuaded the Native Americans they met that their intentions were peaceful.

GERONIMO (1829-1909) was a leader of the Chiricahua Apache tribe, and became a medicine man in his early years. When Mexican bandits killed his wife, children, and mother, he became a leader of Native American resisters, fighting off Mexicans and U.S. troops. He was considered one of the last Native American leaders to resist the U.S. government settlement of Native American lands. Later in life, he wrote an autobiography that explained much about Apache culture and tradition as well as his own early life, battles, and hopes for the future.

SITTING BULL (1834-1890), also known as Tatanka-Iyotanka, was a Lakota tribal leader during the mid-19th century expansion of white settlers into the American West. Sitting Bull fought against U.S. efforts to put his people on a reservation. His most famous victory against the U.S. Army was at the Battle of Little Bighorn, where, along with Crazy Horse of the Oglala Lakota (1849?-1877), he crushed the outnumbered troops of Lt. Col. George Armstrong Custer. This battle, known as "Custer's Last Stand" prompted the U.S. government to send thousands of troops to chase Sitting Bull and other Lakota chiefs, and jail or kill them. Sitting Bull escaped to Canada for four years, but then decided to return to his native land in South Dakota so that he could continue to help lead his people. He died in a shootout between his fellow Lakota and U.S. soldiers who were trying to arrest him.

WILMA MANKILLER (1945-) was the first woman elected Cherokee principal chief in 1987. She created health care programs and fought for the rights of children. Under her leadership, membership in the tribe had increased to 156,000 from 55,000. She served as chief until 1995. She received the Presidential Medal of Freedom in 1996.

Numbers

What's another name for a pyramid? page 196

NUMERALS *in Ancient Civilization*

People have been counting since the earliest of times. This is what some numerals looked like in different cultures.

Modern	1	2	3	4	5	6	7	8	9	10	20	50	100
Egyptian	I	II	III	IIII	III/II	III/III	IIII/III	IIII/IIII	IIIII/IIII	∩	∩∩	∩∩∩∩∩	৭
Babylonian	𒁹	𒈫	𒐈	𒐉	𒐊	𒐋	𒐌	𒐍	𒐎	𒌋	𒌋𒌋	𒌍	𒐏
Greek	A	B	Γ	Δ	E	F	Z	H	θ	I	K	N	P
Mayan	•	••	•••	••••	—	•⎯	••⎯	•••⎯	••••⎯	═	⊙	⊜	⊚
Chinese	一	二	三	四	五	六	七	八	九	十	二十	五十	百
Hindu	۱	۲	۳	٤	٥	٦	٧	٨	٩	۱۰	۲۰	٤۰	۱۰۰
Arabic	١	٢	٣	٤	٥	٦	٧	٨	٩	١٠	٢٠	٥٠	١٠٠

ROMAN *NUMERALS*

Roman numerals are still used today. They are built up from different letters: I (1), V (5), X (10), L (50), C (100), D (500), and M (1,000). If one Roman numeral is followed by a bigger one, the first is subtracted from the second. For example, IX means 10 − 1 = 9. Think of it as "one less than ten." On the other hand, if a Roman numeral is followed by one or more others that are equal or smaller, add them together. Thus, LXI means 50 + 10 + 1 = 61.

What year is it now? Can you put that in Roman numerals?

The Colosseum in Rome probably fit about 50,000 people. Can you put that number in Roman numerals? (This will give you a clue as to why Roman numerals lost popularity.)

1	I	14	XIV	90	XC
2	II	15	XV	100	C
3	III	16	XVI	200	CC
4	IV	17	XVII	300	CCC
5	V	18	XVIII	400	CD
6	VI	19	XIX	500	D
7	VII	20	XX	600	DC
8	VIII	30	XXX	700	DCC
9	IX	40	XL	800	DCCC
10	X	50	L	900	CM
11	XI	60	LX	1,000	M
12	XII	70	LXX	2,000	MM
13	XIII	80	LXXX	3,000	MMM

▼ *The Colosseum*

ANSWERS ON PAGES 335-338. FOR MORE PUZZLES GO TO WWW.WORLDALMANACFORKIDS.COM

FRACTIONS, PERCENTS, AND DECIMALS

FRACTIONS What's a fraction? It's a part of a whole. It helps to think of a fraction as a slice of a circle, the circle being the whole (represented by the number 1). Check out these common fractions below.

$^1/_2$
$^2/_3$
$^3/_4$
$^3/_5$
$^7/_8$

$^1/_2$ is missing $^1/_3$ is missing $^1/_4$ is missing $^2/_5$ is missing $^1/_8$ is missing

To reduce a fraction to its lowest terms, divide both the numerator (top number) and the denominator (bottom number) by the largest number by which both can be divided evenly. For example, to reduce $^8/_{16}$ to lowest terms, divide 8 by 8 on top and 16 by 8 on bottom. You end up with $^1/_2$.

PERCENTS Percents also represent a part of a whole. A percent means "per hundred." So, a percent is like a fraction with a denominator of 100. You see percents every day. If you got a score of 80% on a test at school, you got most of the problems right—80 points out of 100. If a video game is marked "20% off," you may have a bargain.

Changing percents to fractions is not hard. Here are a few examples:

80% = $^{80}/_{100}$; reduced to its lowest terms it becomes $^4/_5$.

20% = $^{20}/_{100}$; reduced to its lowest terms it becomes $^1/_5$.

47% = $^{47}/_{100}$, which cannot be reduced.

DECIMALS Decimals are also part of a whole. They are represented with numbers placed to the right of a decimal point.

To convert a decimal to a percentage or a fraction, you have to pay attention to the placement of the numbers after the decimal point. 0.2 means 2 tenths, or $^2/_{10}$, which can be reduced to $^1/_5$. 0.25 means 25 hundredths or $^{25}/_{100}$, which can be reduced to $^1/_4$. To convert a decimal to a percent, just move the decimal point to the right of the hundredths place:

.25 = 25%

Can you change these decimals to fractions that are reduced to lowest terms?

.3   **.4**   **.5**   **.6**

ANSWERS ON PAGES 335–338.

6.25

$^1/_{100}$'s (hundredths) place

$^1/_{10}$'s (tenths) place

1's place

Multiplication Table

x	0	1	2	3	4	5	6	7	8	9	10	11	12
0	0	0	0	0	0	0	0	0	0	0	0	0	0
1	0	1	2	3	4	5	6	7	8	9	10	11	12
2	0	2	4	6	8	10	12	14	16	18	20	22	24
3	0	3	6	9	12	15	18	21	24	27	30	33	36
4	0	4	8	12	16	20	24	28	32	36	40	44	48
5	0	5	10	15	20	25	30	35	40	45	50	55	60
6	0	6	12	18	24	30	36	42	48	54	60	66	72
7	0	7	14	21	28	35	42	49	56	63	70	77	84
8	0	8	16	24	32	40	48	56	64	72	80	88	96
9	0	9	18	27	36	45	54	63	72	81	90	99	108
10	0	10	20	30	40	50	60	70	80	90	100	110	120
11	0	11	22	33	44	55	66	77	88	99	110	121	132
12	0	12	24	36	48	60	72	84	96	108	120	132	144

Here's a finger trick that only works for multiplying by 9. Spread your fingers out in front of you. Your left pinky is 1, your left ring finger is 2, and so on. Your right pinky is 10. To find the answer to 9 x 4, fold down your 4th finger (left index finger). Look to the left of the folded finger. You have 3 still sticking out. To the right of the folded finger, you have 6 fingers out (your left thumb, plus the 5 on your right hand). The answer is 36.

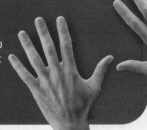

Homework Help

Can you learn all the number facts in the table above? It's not as hard as it sounds. Here are a few hints:

► First, you can skip half the numbers! If you know that 4 x 2 = 8, you also know that 2 x 4 = 8. Changing the order of the numbers being multiplied doesn't change the result—that's what's called the commutative property.

► You don't have to memorize the row for zero or one. Any time you multiply a number by zero, the answer is zero: 2 x 0 = 0. Multiplying a number by 1 doesn't change its value: 12 x 1 = 12. That's called the identity property.

► Now you have only 66 calculations to memorize. You can find them in the triangle in the chart above. And some of them are easy to learn.

► Multiplying by 5 and 10 is like *counting* by 5 or 10. Start with 25, for example: 5 x 5 = 25. To multiply 5 by 6, simply add 5 to get 30. Then 35, 40, and so on. All multiplication is really a series of additions: 3 x 5 is the same as 5 + 5 + 5 = 15. To multiply any number by 10, just add a 0 to it: 12 x 10 = 120.

How Many SIDES and FACES Do They Have?

When a figure is flat (two-dimensional), it is a **plane** figure. When a figure takes up space (three-dimensional), it is a **solid** figure. The flat surface of a solid figure is called a **face**. Plane and solid figures come in many different shapes.

TWO-DIMENSIONAL
 square   circle   triangle

THREE-DIMENSIONAL
cube   sphere   tetrahedron (pyramid)

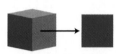

The flat surface of a cube is a square.

What Are POLYGONS?

A polygon is a two-dimensional figure with three or more straight sides (called line segments). A square is a polygon. Polygons have different numbers of sides—and each has a different name. If the sides are all the same length and all the angles between the sides are equal, the polygon is called regular. If the sides are of different lengths or the angles are not equal, the polygon is called irregular. At right are some regular and irregular polygons.

NAME & NUMBER OF SIDES	REGULAR	IRREGULAR
triangle — 3		
quadrilateral or tetragon — 4		
pentagon — 5		
hexagon — 6		
heptagon — 7		
octagon — 8		
nonagon — 9		
decagon — 10		

What Are Polyhedrons?

A polyhedron is a three-dimensional figure with four or more faces. Each face on a polyhedron is a polygon. Below are some polyhedrons with many faces.

tetrahedron 4 faces	hexahedron 6 faces	octahedron 8 faces	dodecahedron 12 faces	icosahedron 20 faces

 Great Pyramid of Khefren (a tetrahedron)

Homework Help

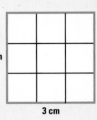

F inding areas can be easy, if you know the not-so-secret formula.

AREA OF A SQUARE:

A plane figure with four sides is called a **quadrilateral.** A square is a quadrilateral with four right angles and four equal sides, like the figure you see here. To find the area for a square, use this formula: side x side (side x side can also be written as s^2, pronounced "side squared"). **3 cm**

The sides of this square are each 3 centimeters long. So the area is 3 x 3, or 9. These are no longer centimeters but **square centimeters**.

3 cm

AREA OF A RECTANGLE:

Rectangles are another type of quadrilateral. They have four right angles, but unlike a square, the sides are not all equal.
To find the area of a rectangle, multiply BASE x HEIGHT (width x length).

This rectangle has a base of 2 centimeters and a height of 4 centimeters. Its area is 8 square centimeters.

4 cm

2 cm

AREA OF A PARALLELOGRAM:

Parallelograms are quadrilaterals that have parallel opposite sides, but no right angles. The formula for the area of parallelogram is the same as for a rectangle—BASE X HEIGHT.

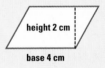

height 2 cm

base 4 cm

AREA OF A TRIANGLE:

A triangle is a three-sided plane figure. The prefix "tri" means three, which refers to the three points where the sides of a triangle meet.

To find the area for a triangle use 1/2 x (BASE x HEIGHT) (first multiply the base by the height, then multiply that number by 1/2).

This triangle has a base of 2 centimeters and a height of 3 centimeters. So the area will be 3 square centimeters.

3 cm

2 cm

AREA OF A CIRCLE:

The distance around a circle is called its **circumference.** All the points on the circumference are an equal distance from the center. That distance is the **radius.** A **diameter** is any straight line that has both ends on the circle and passes through its center. The diameter is twice the radius.
To find the circle's area you need to use a number called **pi** (π) that equals about 3.14. The formula for area is:
π x RADIUS x RADIUS (or π x RADIUS SQUARED).
For instance, this circle has a radius of 3 centimeters, so its area = π x 3 x 3, or π x 3^2; that is, about 3.14 x 9. This comes to 28.26 square centimeters.

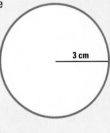

3 cm

What is Pi? The Greek letter pi (π) stands for the number you get when you divide the circumference of a circle by its diameter. It is always the same, no matter how big the circle is! The Babylonians discovered this in 2000 B.C. Actually, no one can say exactly what the value of π is. When you divide the circumference by the diameter it does not come out even, and you can keep going as many places as you want: 3.14159265…it goes on forever. Using a computer, Yasumasa Kanada of The University of Tokyo so far has calculated the value of pi to 1,241,100,000,000 places.

197

TRICKY TRIANGLE

Can you place the numbers 1-6 in the circles so that the numbers on each side of the triangle add up to the same total?

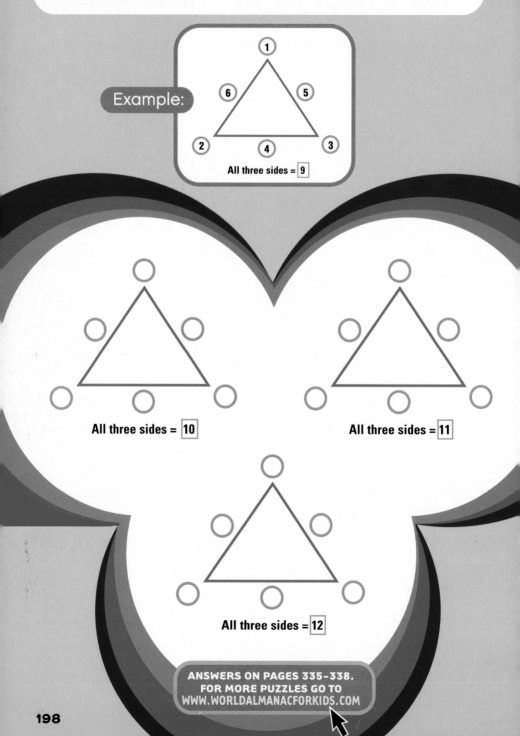

Example:

All three sides = 9

All three sides = 10

All three sides = 11

All three sides = 12

ANSWERS ON PAGES 335-338.
FOR MORE PUZZLES GO TO
WWW.WORLDALMANACFORKIDS.COM

Population

What's the smallest state in population? page 200

Taking the Census: Everyone Counts

Were you counted during Census 2000?

The United States takes a census every 10 years to try to count all the people and learn some basic things about the population. Census takers try to track down and count people who did not send back forms, so that the census will be as accurate as possible. Census officials believe the 2000 census was one of the most accurate ever, but that it still missed about 1 out of 100 people. As of July 1, 2004, the total U.S. population was estimated to be 293,655,404, according to the Census Bureau.

Why is the census needed?

► The census provides a picture of the people. Where do they live? How old are they? What do they do? How much do they earn? How many kids do they have? What is their background?

► Census information helps the federal government in Washington, D.C. decide which public services must be provided and where.

► The population of a state determines how many representatives it has in the U.S. House and how many electoral votes it gets for presidential elections.

When was the first U.S. census taken?

It was in 1790 just after the American Revolution. That year census takers counted 3,929,214 people living in what was then the United States. Most lived on farms or in small towns. (Today, three out of four Americans live in or near cities.)

The Growing U.S. Population

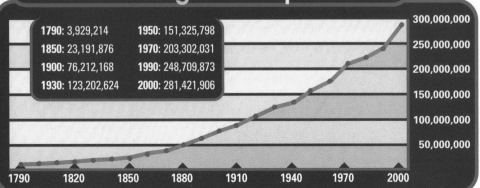

1790: 3,929,214	**1950:** 151,325,798
1850: 23,191,876	**1970:** 203,302,031
1900: 76,212,168	**1990:** 248,709,873
1930: 123,202,624	**2000:** 281,421,906

Population of the UNITED STATES, 2004

Estimated U.S. Population on July 1, 2004: 293,655,404.

Rank & State Name	Population	Rank & State Name	Population
1 California	35,893,799	26 Kentucky	4,145,922
2 Texas	22,490,022	27 Oregon	3,594,586
3 New York	19,227,088	28 Oklahoma	3,523,553
4 Florida	17,397,161	29 Connecticut	3,503,604
5 Illinois	12,713,634	30 Iowa	2,954,451
6 Pennsylvania	12,406,292	31 Mississippi	2,902,966
7 Ohio	11,459,011	32 Arkansas	2,752,629
8 Michigan	10,112,620	33 Kansas	2,735,502
9 Georgia	8,829,383	34 Utah	2,389,039
10 New Jersey	8,698,879	35 Nevada	2,334,771
11 North Carolina	8,541,221	36 New Mexico	1,903,289
12 Virginia	7,459,827	37 West Virginia	1,815,354
13 Massachusetts	6,416,505	38 Nebraska	1,747,214
14 Indiana	6,237,569	39 Idaho	1,393,262
15 Washington	6,203,788	40 Maine	1,317,253
16 Tennessee	5,900,962	41 New Hampshire	1,299,500
17 Missouri	5,754,618	42 Hawaii	1,262,840
18 Arizona	5,743,834	43 Rhode Island	1,080,632
19 Maryland	5,558,058	44 Montana	926,865
20 Wisconsin	5,509,026	45 Delaware	830,364
21 Minnesota	5,100,958	46 South Dakota	770,883
22 Colorado	4,601,403	47 Alaska	655,435
23 Alabama	4,530,182	48 North Dakota	634,366
24 Louisiana	4,515,770	49 Vermont	621,394
25 South Carolina	4,198,068	50 District of Columbia	553,523
		51 Wyoming	506,529

Largest Cities in the United States

Cities grow and shrink in population. At right is a list of the largest cities in the United States in 2003 compared with their populations in 1950. Which seven cities increased in population? Which three decreased?

Rank & City	2003	1950
1 New York, NY	8,085,742	7,891,957
2 Los Angeles, CA	3,819,951	1,970,358
3 Chicago, IL	2,869,121	3,620,962
4 Houston, TX	2,009,690	596,163
5 Philadelphia, PA	1,479,339	2,071,605
6 Phoenix, AZ	1,388,416	106,818
7 San Diego, CA	1,266,753	334,387
8 San Antonio, TX	1,214,725	408,442
9 Dallas, TX	1,208,318	434,462
10 Detroit, MI	911,402	1,849,568

did you know?

In 2003, the number of legal immigrants entering the U.S. was 703,542, down significantly from 1,063,732 in 2002.

The Many Faces of America:
IMMIGRATION

▼ *Immigrants entering the U.S. at Ellis Island, early 1900s*

The number of people in the U.S. who were born in another country (foreign-born) reached 33.5 million in 2003, or 11.7 percent of the population. This percent has been rising since 1970, when it was down to 4.7 percent, and is the highest since 1930. In the early 1900s, most immigrants came from Europe; in 2003, 53% of the foreign-born population were from Latin America, and 25% were born in Asia.

Immigrants come for various reasons, such as to live in freedom, to escape poverty or oppression, and to make better lives for themselves and their children. The figures below, from U.S. Citizenship and Immigration Services, part of the Department of Homeland Security, cover legal immigrants only. In addition, the U.S. government estimates that in the 1990s about 350,000 people each year came across the border illegally or overstayed their temporary visa. There were an estimated 7 million unauthorized immigrants in the U.S. in 2000; about 70% of these were from Mexico.

What Countries Do Immigrants Come From?

Below are some of the countries immigrants came from in 2003. Immigration from all countries to the U.S. totaled 705,827 in 2003.

	Number	Percent of total
Mexico	115,864	16.4
India	50,372	7.1
Philippines	45,397	6.4
China	40,659	5.8
El Salvador	28,296	4.0
Dominican Republic	26,205	3.7
Vietnam	22,133	3.1
Colombia	14,777	2.1
Guatemala	14,415	2.0
Russia	13,951	2.0
Jamaica	13,384	1.9
Korea	12,512	1.8
Haiti	12,314	1.7
Ukraine	11,666	1.7
Canada	11,446	1.6

Where Do Immigrants Settle?

In 2003, about 63% of all immigrants to the U.S. moved to the states below. California received almost 44% of the immigrants from Mexico, 40% of those from the Philippines and Vietnam, and about one-third of those from China and Korea. Florida received 68% of the immigrants from Cuba, 44% of those from Haiti, and about one-third of those from Colombia. Half of the immigrants from the Dominican Republic chose New York.

California
176,375

New York
89,661

Texas
53,592

Florida
52,969

New Jersey
40,818

Illinois
32,488

This bar chart shows the states that received the highest number of immigrants in 2003.

Prizes & Contests

What family won the Best Animated Film Oscar in 2005? page 204

NOBEL PRIZES

The Nobel Prizes are named after Alfred B. Nobel (1833–1896), a Swedish scientist who invented dynamite, and left money for these prizes. They are given every year for promoting peace, as well as for physics, chemistry, medicine-physiology, literature, and economics.

In 2004, Wangari Maathai of Kenya won the Nobel Peace Prize. Her Green Belt Movement has planted more than 30 million trees since 1977. The movement also promotes education, family planning, nutrition, and the fight against corruption. She is the first African woman to win the prize.

PAST WINNERS OF THE NOBEL PEACE PRIZE INCLUDE:

◄ **2003: SHIRIN EBADI,** Iranian activist for democracy and human rights

2002 JIMMY CARTER, former U.S. president and peace negotiator

2001 UNITED NATIONS (UN); KOFI ANNAN, UN secretary-general

1999 MÉDECINS SANS FRONTIÈRES (DOCTORS WITHOUT BORDERS), an organization that gives medical help to disaster and war victims

1997 JODY WILLIAMS and the **INTERNATIONAL CAMPAIGN TO BAN LANDMINES**

1994 YASIR ARAFAT, Palestinian leader; **SHIMON PERES,** foreign minister of Israel; **YITZHAK RABIN,** prime minister of Israel

1993 NELSON MANDELA, leader of South African blacks; **F. W. DE KLERK,** president of South Africa

1990 MIKHAIL GORBACHEV, President of the Soviet Union, helped to bring the Cold War to an end

1989 DALAI LAMA, Tibetan Buddhist leader, forced into exile in 1959

1987 OSCAR ARIAS SÁNCHEZ, President of Costa Rica, initiator of peace negotiations in Central America

1986 ELIE WIESEL, Holocaust survivor and author

1979 MOTHER TERESA, leader of the order of the Missionaries of Charity, who care for the sick and dying in India

1965 UNICEF (UN Children's Fund)

1964 MARTIN LUTHER KING JR., civil rights leader

1919 WOODROW WILSON, U.S. president who played the key role in founding the League of Nations

1906 THEODORE ► ROOSEVELT, U.S. president who helped settle the Russo-Japanese War

Bee Involved

If you have a knack for spelling or an interest in world geography, then these two national contests may be for you.

NATIONAL SPELLING BEE

The **National Spelling Bee** was started in Louisville, Kentucky, by the *Courier-Journal* in 1925. Newspapers across the U.S. run spelling bees for kids 15 and under. Winners may qualify for the Scripps Howard National Spelling Bee held in Washington, D.C., in late May or early June. If interested, ask your school principal to contact your local newspaper. (For a behind-the-scenes look at the National Spelling Bee, try the 2002 film *Spellbound*.)

DAVID SCOTT TIDMARSH, 14-year-old from South Bend, Indiana, is the 77th Annual Scripps National Spelling Bee Champion. He defeated 264 other contestants in the national finals held in Washington, DC, on June 3, 2004. David won the title in the 15th round after correctly spelling *autochthonous*, which means "native, indigenous, especially of floras and faunas." This was the second National Spelling Bee in which David competed. He tied for 16th place in the 2003 finals.

Finishing second in the competition was **AKSHAY BUDDIGA** from Colorado Springs, Colorado, whose brother Pratyush was the 2002 national champion.

WEB SITE www.spellingbee.com

Here are the words David spelled on his way to the top. Some of them are just a little bit difficult!

phalanx	balancelle	sophrosyne
kiwi	ecdysis	arete
ombrophilous	politeia	gaminerie
succenturiate	serpiginous	autochthonous
foudroyant	sumpsimus	

National Geographic BEE

After 10+ rounds, the winner is . . .

ANDREW WOJTANIK, a 14-year-old from Overland Park, Kansas, is the 2004 National Geographic Bee Champion. After 10 rounds of regular questions and a lightning elimination set, Andrew advanced to the championship round. He won first place by correctly answering these three questions in a row, in a two-person round against 13-year-old Matthew Wells from Bozeman, Montana.

1. In March 2004 seven Eastern European countries joined NATO (North Atlantic Treaty Organization). Of these new members, name the one that borders the Russian oblast of Kaliningrad. (Answer: *Lithuania*)

2. Khark Island is an important oil export terminal in the Persian Gulf. This island belongs to what country? (Answer: *Iran*)

3. Peshawar, a city in the North-West Frontier Province of Pakistan, has had strategic importance because of its location near what historic pass? (Answer: *Khyber Pass*)

WOW! For taking top honors, Andrew won a $25,000 scholarship from *National Geographic*, a lifetime National Geographic membership, and a trip to Busch Gardens/Sea World Adventure Camp.

How did Andrew learn so much? He prepared for the contest by compiling a study book with information on all 193 countries. The book is 432 pages and weighs 5 pounds!

To enter, you must be in grades 4 through 8. School-level bees are followed by state-level bees and then the nationals. For more information: **WEB SITE** www.nationalgeographic.com

ENTERTAINMENT Awards

The Oscar ceremonies are watched on TV by tens of millions of people around the world. Among other entertainment awards are the Grammys and the MTV Video Music Awards.

Academy Awards

The winners of the 77th Annual Academy Awards were announced on February 27, 2005. Some of the Oscar winners for 2004 are listed here:

Best Picture:	*Million Dollar Baby*
Best Actor:	Jamie Foxx, *Ray*
Best Actress:	Hilary Swank, *Million Dollar Baby*
Best Supporting Actor:	Morgan Freeman, *Million Dollar Baby*
Best Supporting Actress:	Cate Blanchett, *The Aviator*
Best Director:	Clint Eastwood, *Million Dollar Baby*
Best Original Screenplay:	*Eternal Sunshine of the Spotless Mind* by Charlie Kaufman, Michael Gondry, and Pierre Bismuth
Best Animated Feature Film:	*The Incredibles*
Best Visual Effects:	*Spider-Man 2*
Achievement in Makeup:	*Lemony Snicket's A Series of Unfortunate Events*

Grammy Awards

The Grammy Awards were presented on February 13, 2005. Winners included:

Record of the Year (single): "Here We Go Again," Ray Charles and Norah Jones

Album of the Year: *Genius Loves Company*, Ray Charles and Various Artists

Song of the Year: "Daughters," (John Mayer); John Mayer, songwriter

New Artist: Maroon 5

Rock Song: "Vertigo," Bono, Adam Clayton, The Edge, and Larry Mullen (U2), songwriters

R&B Song: "You Don't Know My Name," ▶ (Alicia Keys); Alicia Keys, Harold Lilly, and Kanye West, songwriters

Rap Song: "Jesus Walks," (Kanye West); C. Smith and Kanye West, songwriters

Country Song: "Live Like You Were Dying," (Tim McGraw); Tim Nichols and Craig Wiseman, songwriters

MTV Video Music Awards

MTV Video Music Awards for 2004 were presented in Miami, Florida, on August 29, 2004. Winners included:

Best Video of the Year: Outkast, "Hey Ya!"

Best New Artist: Maroon 5, "This Love"

Best Male Video: Usher featuring Lil'John and Ludacris, "Yeah"

Best Female Video: Beyoncé Knowles,"Naughty Girl"

Contests, Contests EVERYWHERE!

It just seems to be part of human nature to find out who is the best at something, no matter what it is! There are state, national, and international competitions in a wild variety of events. Here are some contests that are a strain on your brain, some that are just fun—and some that are both. Contests like these may take place near you.

ROTTEN SNEAKER CONTEST

Held annually in Montpelier, Vermont, the Odor-Eaters Rotten Sneaker Contest was won in 2004 by local 10-year-old Daegan Goodman. Daegan beat competitors from all over the country. And he did it with just his normal sweating and playing sports. For his win, Daegan received a $500 savings bond, $100 for new sneakers, the Golden Sneaker trophy, and a year's supply of Odor-Eaters products. His sneakers are now enshrined in the Odor-Eaters Hall of Fumes. The contest is held in mid-March each year. For more information, visit the Odor-Eaters web site: **www.odoreaters.com**

GO FLY A KITE!

Children of all ages are invited to enter their own handmade kites into the Smithsonian Kite Festival, which is held every year in Washington, D.C., at cherry blossom time (late March to early April) on the National Mall. There are first, second, and third place prizes offered in six categories for kids 11-and-under and 12-15.

The event was founded by aviation pioneer Paul E. Garber and is sponsored by The Smithsonian Associates and the National Air and Space Museum. Kite fliers from across the U.S. and all over the world participate. The sky is filled with all types from bowed to box/cellular to fighter and delta kites. There are also exhibitions by kite-flying masters and kite-making demonstrations.

For more information, visit the festival's web site: **www.kitefestival.org**

MIXED-UP MOVIE MARQUEE

This marquee has three award-winning movie titles on it. To find out what the titles are, you have to find the right starting place. Then "skip" along the marquee counter-clockwise to find the answers.

Hint: All three movies are listed in "Some Movie Hits of 2004" on page 133.

205

Religion

When is Christmas clebrated in Russia? see page 208

How did the universe begin? Why are we here on Earth? What happens to us after we die? For most people, religion is a way of answering questions like these. Believing in a God or gods, or in a higher power, is one way of making sense of the world around us. Religions can also help guide people's lives. About six billion people all over the world are religious believers.

Different religions have different beliefs. For example, Christians, Jews, and Muslims all believe in one God, while Hindus believe in many gods. On this page and the next are some facts about the world's major religions.

Christianity

WHO STARTED CHRISTIANITY? Christianity is based on the teachings of Jesus Christ. He was born in Bethlehem between 8 B.C. and 4 B.C. and died about A.D. 29.

WHAT WRITINGS ARE THERE? The **Bible**, including the Old Testament and New Testament, is the main religious writing of Christianity.

WHAT DO CHRISTIANS BELIEVE? That there is one God. That Jesus Christ is the Son of God, who came on Earth, died to save humankind, and rose from the dead.

HOW MANY ARE THERE? Christianity is the world's biggest religion. In 2005, there were more than 2.1 billion Christians, in nearly all parts of the world. More than one billion of the Christians were **Roman Catholics**, who follow the leadership of the pope in Rome. Other groups of Christians include **Orthodox Christians**, who accept most of the same teachings as Roman Catholics but follow different leadership, and **Protestants**, who often disagree with Catholic teachings. Protestants rely especially on the Bible itself. They belong to many different groups or "denominations."

Buddhism

WHO STARTED BUDDHISM? Gautama Siddhartha (the Buddha), around 525 B.C.

WHAT WRITINGS ARE THERE? The three main collections of Buddhist writings are called the **Tripitaka**, or "Three Baskets." Many of these writings are called **sutras** or "teachings."

WHAT DO BUDDHISTS BELIEVE? Buddha taught that life is filled with suffering. In order to be free of that suffering, believers have to give up worldly possessions and worldly goals and try to achieve a state of perfect peace known as *nirvana*.

HOW MANY ARE THERE? In 2005, there were nearly 375 million Buddhists in the world, 98% of them in Asia.

WHAT KINDS ARE THERE? There are two main kinds of Buddhists. **Theravada** ("Path of the Elders") **Buddhism**, the older kind, is more common in the southern part of Asia. **Mahayana** ("Great Vessel") **Buddhism** is more common in northern Asia.

Hinduism

WHO STARTED HINDUISM? Aryan beliefs spread into India, around 1500 B.C. These beliefs were mixed with the beliefs of the people who already lived there.

WHAT WRITINGS ARE THERE? The **Vedas** are the most important writings in Hinduism. They include ancient hymns and rules for religious ceremonies. Other writings include the teachings of the **Upanishads** and a long poem about war, the **Mahabharata**.

WHAT DO HINDUS BELIEVE? Hindus believe there are many gods and many ways of worshipping and that people die and are reborn many times as other living things. They also believe there is a universal soul, known as *Brahman*. The goal of life is to escape the cycle of birth and death and become part of the *Brahman*. This is done by leading a good life.

HOW MANY ARE THERE? In 2005, there were about 851 million Hindus, mainly in India and places where people from India have gone to live.

WHAT KINDS ARE THERE? There are many kinds of Hindus, who worship different gods or goddesses.

Islam

WHO STARTED ISLAM? Muhammad, the Prophet, in A.D. 610.

WHAT WRITINGS ARE THERE? The **Koran** (al-Qur'an in Arabic) sets out the main beliefs and practices of Islam, the religion of Muslims.

WHAT DO MUSLIMS BELIEVE? People who believe in Islam are known as Muslims. The word **"Islam"** means submission to God. Muslims believe that there is no other god than the one God; that Muhammad is the prophet and lawgiver of his community; that they should pray five times a day, fast during the month of **Ramadan**, give to the poor, and once during their life make a pilgrimage to Mecca in Saudi Arabia *(hajj)* if they can afford it.

HOW MANY ARE THERE? In 2005, there were more than 1.3 billion Muslims, mostly in parts of Africa and Asia. The two main branches are: **Sunni Muslims**, who make up 83% of all Muslims today, and **Shiite Muslims**, who broke away in a dispute over leadership after Muhammad died in 632.

Judaism

WHO STARTED JUDAISM? Abraham is considered to be the founder of Judaism. He lived around 1300 B.C.

WHAT WRITINGS ARE THERE? The most important is the **Torah**, the first five books of the Old Testament of the Bible.

WHAT DO JEWS BELIEVE? Jews believe that there is one God who created the universe and rules over it, and that they should be faithful to God and carry out God's commandments.

HOW MANY ARE THERE? In 2005, there were about 15 million Jews living around the world. Many live in Israel and the United States.

WHAT KINDS ARE THERE? In the United States and Europe there are three main forms: **Orthodox**, **Conservative**, and **Reform**. Orthodox Jews are the most traditional. They follow strict laws about how they dress, what they can eat, and how they conduct their lives. Conservative Jews follow many of the traditions. Reform Jews are the least traditional.

Major Holy Days for

CHRISTIAN HOLY DAYS

	2005	2006	2007
Ash Wednesday	February 9	March 1	February 21
Good Friday	March 25	April 14	April 6
Easter Sunday	March 27	April 16	April 8
Easter for Orthodox Churches	May 1	April 23	April 8
Christmas	December 25	December 25	December 25

*Russian, Greek, and other Orthodox churches celebrate Christmas in January.

JEWISH HOLY DAYS

The Jewish holy days begin at sundown the night before the first full day of the observance. The dates of first full days are listed below.

	2005-6 (5766)	2006-7 (5767)	2007-8 (5768)
Rosh Hashanah (New Year)	October 4	September 23	September 13
Yom Kippur (Day of Atonement)	October 13	October 2	September 22
Hanukkah (Festival of Lights)	December 26	December 16	December 5
Passover	April 13	April 3	April 20

ISLAMIC (MUSLIM) HOLY DAYS

The Islamic holy days begin at sundown the night before the first full day of the observance. The dates of first full days are listed below.

	2005-6 (1426)	2006 (1427)	2007 (1428)
Muharram 1 (New Year)	February 10	January 30	January 20
Mawlid (Birthday of Muhammad)	April 21	April 10	March 31
Ramadan 1	October 4	September 23	September 21
Eid al-Fitr (Shawwal 1)	November 3	October 23	October 12
Eid al-Adha (Dhûl-Hijjah 10)	January 10	December 30	December 20

BUDDHIST HOLY DAYS

Not all Buddhists use the same calendar to determine holidays and festivals. Here are some well known Buddhist observances and the months in which they may fall:

The Dalai Lama

Nirvana Day, mid-February: marks the death of Siddhartha Gautama (the Buddha).

Vesak or Visakah Puja (Buddha Day), April/May: the most important holiday. Celebrates the birth, enlightenment, and death of the Buddha.

Asalha Puja (Dharma Day), July: commemorates the Buddha's first teaching, in which he revealed the Four Noble Truths.

Magha Puja or Sangha Day, February: commemorates the day when 1,250 of Buddha's disciples (sangha) visited him without being called.

Vassa (Rains Retreat), July-October: a 3-month period during Asia's rainy season, when monks stay inside and study. Other people try to live simply and give up bad habits. Sometimes called "Buddhist Lent."

HINDU HOLY DAYS

Different Hindu groups use different calendars. Here are a few of the many Hindu festivals and the months in which they may fall:

Maha Shivaratri, February/March: festival dedicated to Shiva, creator and destroyer.

Holi, March/April: festival of spring.

Ramanavami, March/April: anniversary of the birth of Rama, who is Vishnu in human form.

Diwali, October/November: Hindu New Year, the "Festival of Lights."

RELIGIOUS MEMBERSHIP in the UNITED STATES

The two largest religious groups in the U.S. are Protestants followed by Roman Catholics. The pie chart below shows about how many people belong to these and other religious groups. These numbers are only estimates; no one knows exactly how many people belong to each group.

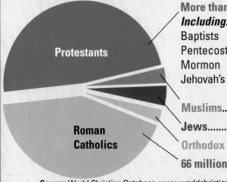

Protestants

Roman Catholics

More than 72 million
Including:

Baptists	24 million	Methodists	10 million
Pentecostals	6 million	Lutherans	8 million
Mormon	6 million	Presbyterians	4 million
Jehovah's Witnesses*	2 million	Episcopalians	2 million

Muslims.........................5 million
Jews.............................6 million
Orthodox Christians.....4 million
66 million

There were also an estimated 2.7 million Buddhists and 1 million Hindus.

HOLY PLACES

Here are a few of the most famous holy sites around the globe.

TEMPLE OF THE RECLINING BUDDHA, Bangkok, Thailand

Built in the 16th century, this temple, known as Wat Pho, is the oldest and largest Buddhist wat (temple) in Bangkok, Thailand. Wat Pho has the country's largest collection of Buddha images, including a reclining Buddha (right) covered in gold leaf, about 150 feet long and 49 feet high.

GANGES RIVER, India

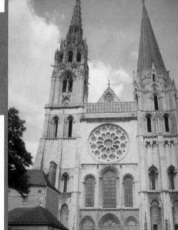

Hindus believe that the Ganges River can wash away sin, and many Hindus visit its banks to bathe and meditate. In addition, Hindus believe that having their ashes scattered in the river will improve their next life.

CHARTRES CATHEDRAL, Chartres, France

French Christians of the Middle Ages built Chartres Cathedral, one of the finest examples of Gothic architecture, starting in 1145. The cathedral has two spires, an ancient crypt, 152 stained glass windows from the 13th century, and a labyrinth over 850 feet long.

KAABA: Mecca, Saudi Arabia

When Muslims pray, they face the Kaaba (Arabic for "cube"), in Mecca, Saudi Arabia. They believe this stone structure was first built by Adam. Every year, about two million Muslims travel there during the ritual of *hajj*, a pilgrimage.

Science

Aurum is Latin for which precious metal? page 214

THE WORLD OF Science

The Latin root of the word "science" is *scire*, meaning "to know." There are many kinds of knowledge, but when people use the word *science* they usually mean a kind of knowledge that can be discovered and backed up by observation or experiments.

The branches of scientific study can be loosely grouped into the four main areas shown below. Each branch of science has more specific areas of study within it than can be listed here. For example **zoology** includes *entomology* (study of insects), which in turn includes *lepidopterology*, the study of butterflies and moths!

In answering questions about our lives, our world, and our universe, scientists must often draw from more than one discipline. **Biochemists**, for example, deal with the chemistry that happens inside living things. **Paleontologists** study fossil remains of ancient plants and animals. **Astrophysicists** study matter and energy in outer space. And mathematics, considered by many to be an art and a science by itself, is used by all scientists.

Physical Science

ASTRONOMY—stars, planets, outer space
CHEMISTRY—properties and behavior of substances
PHYSICS—matter and energy

Life Science (Biology)

ANATOMY—structure of the human body
BOTANY—plants
ECOLOGY—living things in relation to their environment
GENETICS—heredity
PATHOLOGY—diseases and their effects on the human body
PHYSIOLOGY—the body's biological processes
ZOOLOGY—animals

Earth Science

GEOGRAPHY—Earth's surface and its relationship to humans
GEOLOGY—Earth's structure
  MINERALOGY—minerals
  PETROLOGY—rocks
  SEISMOLOGY—earthquakes
  VOLCANOLOGY—volcanoes
HYDROLOGY—water
METEOROLOGY—Earth's atmosphere and weather
  OCEANOGRAPHY—the sea, including currents and tides

Social Science

ANTHROPOLOGY—human cultures and physical characteristics
ECONOMICS—production and distribution of goods and services
POLITICAL SCIENCE—governments
PSYCHOLOGY—mental processes and behavior
SOCIOLOGY—human society and community life

ENERGY

The term energy comes from energeia, the Greek word for "work." Energy is defined as the capacity to do work.

Energy cannot be created or destroyed, but it can change form. Heat, light, and electricity are forms of energy. Other forms include **mechanical, chemical,** and **nuclear** energy. You can feel heat and see light, but most energy, like electricity, is invisible. We only see the result—like the lighting of a bulb.

All of the forms of energy we use come from the energy stored in natural resources. Sunlight, water, wind, petroleum, coal, and natural gas are natural resources. From these resources, we get heat, electricity, and mechanical power to run machines.

It STARTS with the SUN

Most of our energy traces its source to the Sun. Inside the Sun, hydrogen atoms join together and become helium. This process releases energy that radiates into space in the form of waves. These waves give us heat and light.

Energy from the Sun is stored in plants and animals that we eat. Long before humans existed, these ancient plants absorbed the Sun's energy, and animals ate the plants as well as smaller animals. After the plants and animals died, they got buried deeper and deeper underground. After millions of years, they turned into coal and petroleum—what we call fossil fuels—that we are so dependent on today.

Plants absorb energy from the Sun (solar energy) and convert it to chemical energy for storage.

Animals eat plants and gain the stored chemical energy.

Food gives the body energy.

People eat plants and meat.

Homework Help

The different forms of energy fall into two main categories. It helps to try and picture each one:

Kinetic Energy is the energy of objects in motion. Water in a river, electricity in a wire, and a sled going down a hill are good examples.

Potential Energy is the energy of objects that are not moving—but could move. If you stretch a rubber band and hold it, it has potential energy. Let it go and its potential energy changes to kinetic energy with a snap! Natural gas, coal, and food are other examples of potential energy.

WHAT EVERYTHING *IS* MADE OF

Everything we see and use is made up of basic ingredients called elements. There are more than 100 elements. Most have been found in nature. Some are created by scientists in labs.

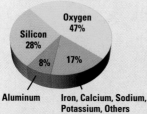

Elements in Earth's Crust
(percent by weight)

Oxygen 47%
Silicon 28%
8%
17%
Aluminum
Iron, Calcium, Sodium, Potassium, Others

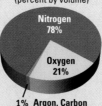

Elements in the Atmosphere
(percent by volume)

Nitrogen 78%
Oxygen 21%
1% Argon, Carbon Dioxide, Others

How Elements Are Named
How many of these elements have you heard of?

Elements are named after places, scientists, figures in mythology, or properties of the element. But no element gets a name until the International Union of Pure and Applied Chemistry (IUPAC) accepts it. In November 2004, the 111th element was approved and named. Roentgenium, with symbol Rg, was discovered by German scientists in 1995.

NAME	SYMBOL	WHAT IT IS	WHEN FOUND	NAMED FOR
Aluminum	Al	metal	1825	*alumen,* Latin word for "alum"
Helium	He	gas	1868	the Greek work *helios,* meaning sun
Iodine	I	nonmetallic solid	1811	the Greek word *iodes,* meaning violet
Iridium	Ir	transitional metal	1804	the Latin word *iridis,* meaning rainbow
Krypton	Kr	gas	1898	the Greek word *kryptos,* meaning hidden
Mercury	Hg	transitional metal	1500 B.C.	the Roman god Mercury
Neon	Ne	gas	1898	the Greek word *neon,* meaning new
Polonium	Po	metal	1898	Poland, native land of chemist Marie Curie; she and her husband discovered it.
Uranium	U	radioactive metal	1789	the planet Uranus

All About...
Compounds

Carbon, hydrogen, nitrogen, and oxygen are the most common chemical elements in the human body. Many other elements may be found in small amounts. These include calcium, iron, phosphorus, potassium, and sodium.

When elements join together, they form compounds. Water is a compound made up of hydrogen and oxygen. Salt is a compound made up of sodium and chlorine.

COMMON NAME	CONTAINS THE COMPOUND	CONTAINS THE ELEMENTS
Baking soda	sodium bicarbonate	sodium, hydrogen, carbon, oxygen
Chalk	calcium carbonate	calcium, carbon, oxygen
Hydrogen peroxide	hydrogen peroxide	hydrogen, oxygen
Rust	iron oxide	iron, oxygen
Sugar	sucrose	carbon, hydrogen, oxygen
Toothpaste	sodium fluoride	sodium, fluorine
Vinegar	acetic acid	carbon, hydrogen, oxygen

CHEMICAL SYMBOLS ARE SCIENTIFIC SHORTHAND

When scientists write the names of elements, they often use a symbol instead of spelling out the full name. The symbol for each element is one or two letters. Scientists write O for oxygen and He for helium. The symbols usually come from the English name for the element (C for carbon). The symbols for some of the elements come from the element's Latin name. For example, the symbol for gold is Au, which is short for *aurum*, the Latin word for gold.

Homework Help

It All Starts With an Atom

The smallest possible piece of an element that has all the properties of the original element is called an **atom**. Each tiny atom is made up of even smaller particles called **protons**, **neutrons**, and **electrons**. These are made up of even smaller particles called **quarks**.

To tell one element from another, scientists count the number of protons in an atom. The total number of protons is called the element's **atomic number**. All of the atoms of an element have the same number of protons and electrons, but some atoms have a different number of neutrons. For example, carbon-12 has six protons and six neutrons, and carbon-13 has six protons and seven neutrons.

We call the amount of matter in an atom its **atomic mass**. Carbon-13 has a greater atomic mass than carbon-12. The average atomic mass of all of the different atoms of the same element is called the element's **atomic weight**. Every element has a different atomic number and a different atomic weight.

All About... Cells

Cells are sometimes called the "building blocks" of all living things. Complex life forms have many cells. There are trillions of them in the human body.

There are two main kinds of cells: **eukaryotic** and **prokaryotic**. All the cells in your body—along with the cells of other animals, plants, and fungi—are eukaryotic. These contain several different structures, called **organelles**. Like tools in a toolbox, each kind of organelle has its own function. The **nucleus**, for example, contains most of the cell's DNA, while the **mitochondria** provide energy for the body. The **ribosomes** are involved in making proteins.

Though both plant and animal cells are eukaryotic, they are different in a few ways. Animal cells rely only on mitochondria for energy, but plant cells also make use of another kind of organelle called a **chloroplast**. Chloroplasts contain chlorophyll, a green chemical plants use to make oxygen and energy from sunlight and water. This process is called **photosynthesis**. And unlike animal cells, plant cells are surrounded by a nonliving, rigid cell wall made of **cellulose**.

Prokaryotes (organisms with prokaryotic instead of eukaryotic cells) are all around you—and even inside of you—but they're difficult to spot. That's because most prokaryotes, such as bacteria, are single-celled. They don't have the variety of organelles that eukaryotic cells do.

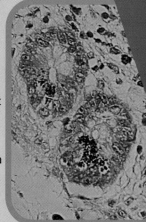
▲ Plant cell

WHAT IS DNA?

Every cell in every living thing (or organism) has **DNA**, a molecule that holds all the information about that organism. The structure of DNA was discovered in 1953 by the British scientist Francis Crick and the American scientist James Watson. James Watson was a *World Almanac* reader as a kid.

Lengths of connected DNA molecules, called **genes**, are tiny pieces of code. They determine what each organism is like. Almost all the DNA and genes come packaged in thread-like structures called **chromosomes**—humans have 46. There are 22 almost identical pairs, plus the X and Y chromosomes, which determine whether a human is male (one X chromosome and one Y chromosome) or female (two X chromosomes).

Genes are passed on from parents to children, and no two organisms (except clones or identical twins) have the same DNA.

Many things—the color of our eyes or hair, whether we're tall or short, our chances of getting certain diseases—depend on our genes.

The Human Genome

In 2000, the U.S. Human Genome Project and the company Celera Genomics identified the 3.1 billion separate codes in human DNA. In 2003, researchers succeeded in mapping out all the human chromosomes.

The human genome contains 20,000 to 25,000 genes. That's fewer than the 50,000-plus genes of a rice plant! But unlike many other genes, human genes can produce more than one kind of protein. Proteins perform most life functions and make up a large part of cellular structures.

By studying human genes, scientists can learn more about hereditary diseases and get a better idea of how humans evolved.

215

SCIENCE q&a

WHY DO PLANTS NEED SUNLIGHT? Sunlight—along with water and carbon dioxide, a gas found in the air—is necessary for **photosynthesis**. That's the process by which plants make their food. In fact, the word *photosynthesis* means putting together (*synthesis*) with light (*photo*). Leaves are the food factories in plants, where photosynthesis takes place. Chlorophyll, a chemical that gives leaves their green color, plays a key role in the process. Photosynthesis also releases oxygen into the atmosphere—a good thing, since that's what people breathe! In winter when there is less sunlight, photosynthesis slows down and then stops, and plants live off the food they have stored. When the green chlorophyll goes out of the leaves, they take on the color of other chemicals in them—that's how trees get their beautiful autumn leaves.

HOW DOES A CELL PHONE WORK? In its simplest form, a cell phone is a radio that connects to other telephones through a radio tower, or base station. Radios transmit sound on a specific frequency. (For example, each radio station you listen to has a different frequency.) The tricky part is that only one person can transmit over a frequency at one time. With 150 million cell phones in use today in the U.S. there wouldn't be enough frequencies for everyone to talk. The problem was solved by dividing cities into small "cells," or areas. Each cell has its own base station that receives and sends low-power radio signals that don't spread into other cells. This allows the same frequencies to be re-used in cells that aren't right next to each other.

WHY IS OCEAN WATER SALTY? When it rains, fresh water falls to Earth. This water doesn't taste salty if you drink it. The water then seeps through the ground into streams. Along the way, it erodes rocks and soil, and picks up minerals or "salts." Then the water flows into the ocean. When the water evaporates into the air and becomes rain water again, the salt stays in the ocean because it doesn't evaporate.

HOW DO FISH BREATHE? Like humans and other animals, fish need to take in oxygen. But they get it in a different way—through their *gills*, which are located on either side of the body, just behind the mouth. When fish open their mouths, water comes in; when they close their mouths the water is pumped over the gills. (This is how it works for most fish; sharks and some other species don't have as good a pumping system and so they need to keep swimming to force water over the gills.) The gills have surfaces with many tiny blood vessels—capillaries—and when the water passes over these surfaces, the oxygen in the water passes into the blood of the fish (as it does in people's lungs). The gills are delicate structures, held up by the water. When a fish is taken out of water, the gills collapse and the fish suffocates.

WHY DOES HELIUM MAKE YOUR VOICE SOUND FUNNY? If you suck a little helium from a balloon, your voice will sound high and squeaky. That's because helium is lighter than air. (That's also why helium balloons float.) When we speak, air comes out of the lungs and is pushed through the vocal cords, creating vibrations that become sound. Because helium is lighter, sound can travel faster in a helium environment. (Sound travels at about 1,100 feet per second through air. But it travels at 3,300 feet per second in helium.) The faster speed increases the frequency of vibrations in your throat, making your voice sound higher pitched. That's why if you inhale a little helium and talk, your voice sounds squeaky. But remember, we all need oxygen to survive, so you should **never try this without an adult nearby.**

WHY DOES MY STOMACH GROWL? It's because there's air in your stomach. When you eat, the stomach tightens up to mix and break up food. When you don't eat, the stomach is mostly filled with air, and there is nothing to muffle the sound of the movement. Think of a bottle of water—if you shake it when it's full, it barely makes noise. But if the bottle is half-empty, the shaking makes a sloshing sound. The Greeks called these stomach noises *borborygmi*, because that's what the rumbling stomach sounded like to them.

WHAT IS AN ECHO? An *echo* is a reflection of a sound. Sound travels in waves, which can bounce off another surface. The speed of sound is slow enough so that you can hear a repeat of the sound after a slight delay when the sound waves bounce back to you. When sound waves bounce off many surfaces, such as in a cave or a canyon, you might hear several echoes.

CAN A BASEBALL PITCHER REALLY MAKE A BALL CURVE? Pitchers can make a ball curve as much as $17\frac{1}{2}$ inches from its path. A snap of the wrist puts extra *spin* on the ball. As it spins, the stitches on one side move with the airflow around it. The stitches on the other side move against the airflow. When stitches and air move together, the flow is faster. The increased speed reduces the air pressure on that side. On the opposite side, the air pressure is increased. The ball moves—curves—toward the side of the ball with the lower pressure.

WHAT CAUSES RAINBOWS? The light we usually see (visible light) is made up of different frequencies, or colors, in a certain range, called the *spectrum.* The colors of the visible spectrum are red, orange, yellow, green, blue, indigo, and violet. White light is a mixture of all these colors. A *prism* can separate the frequencies mixed in a beam of white light. When you see a rainbow, the tiny water droplets in the air act as many tiny prisms, separating the Sun's white light into the colors of the spectrum.

Homework Help

Here's a useful way to remember the order of the colors of the spectrum. Remember the name ROY G. BIV

R = red, O = orange, Y = yellow, G = green, B = blue, I = indigo, V = violet

Some **FAMOUS** Scientists

ARCHIMEDES (about 287 B.C.–212 B.C.), Greek mathematician and inventor who discovered that heavy objects could be moved using pulleys and levers. He was one of the first to test his ideas with experiments. He also is said to have shouted "Eureka!" ("I have found it!").

NICOLAUS COPERNICUS (1473–1543), Polish scientist who is known as the founder of modern astronomy. He came up with the theory that Earth and other planets revolve around the Sun. But most thinkers continued to believe that Earth was the center of the universe.

SIR ISAAC NEWTON (1642–1727), British scientist who worked out the basic laws of motion and gravity. He also showed that sunlight is made up of all the colors of the rainbow. He invented the branch of mathematics called calculus about the same time as the German scientist **Gottfried von Leibniz** (1646–1716), who was the first to make it widely known.

CHARLES DARWIN (1809–1882), British scientist who is best known for his theory of evolution by natural selection. According to this theory, living creatures, by gradually changing so as to have the best chances of survival, slowly developed over millions of years into the forms they have today.

GEORGE WASHINGTON CARVER (1864–1943), born in Missouri of slave parents, became world-famous for his agricultural research. He found many nutritious uses for peanuts and sweet potatoes, and taught farmers in the South to rotate their crops to increase their yield.

ALBERT EINSTEIN (1879–1955), German-American physicist who developed revolutionary theories about the relationships between time, space, matter, and energy. He won a Nobel Prize in 1921.

RACHEL CARSON (1907–1964), U.S. biologist and leading environmentalist whose 1962 book *Silent Spring* warned that chemicals used to kill pests were killing harmless wildlife. Eventually DDT and certain other pesticides were banned in the U.S.

JANE GOODALL (1934-), British scientist who is a leading authority on chimpanzee behavior. Goodall discovered that chimpanzees use tools, such as twigs to "fish" for ants. She also found that chimpanzees have complex family structures and personalities. Today, Goodall writes books, creates movies, and speaks publicly as an advocate for the preservation of wild habitats.

STEPHEN HAWKING (1942-), British physicist and leading authority on black holes—dense objects in space whose gravity is so strong that not even light can escape them. Hawking has also written best-selling books, including *A Brief History of Time* (1988) and *The Universe in a Nutshell* (2001).

LINDA SPILKER (1955-), space scientist who is deputy project scientist for the current *Cassini* mission to Saturn. The *Cassini* orbiter is expected to orbit Saturn for several years, measuring and recording data on Saturn, its rings, and its 34 known moons. "Saturn's rings have always fascinated me," Spilker says. "Now I can bring some of the new ring data back to earth."

PAUL SERENO (1957-), American paleontologist who has traveled over much of the world to discover and study early dinosaur fossils. His research has helped explain dinosaur evolution and behavior.

HOW DO SCIENTISTS MAKE DISCOVERIES? THE SCIENTIFIC METHOD

The scientific method was developed over many centuries, and today it is a logical and well-defined system. You can think of the method as having five steps:

1. Ask a question.
2. Gather information through observation.
3. Based on that information, make an educated guess—or **hypothesis**—about the answer to your question.
4. Design an experiment to test that hypothesis.
5. Evaluate the results.

If the experiment shows that your hypothesis is wrong, make up a new hypothesis. If the experiment supports your hypothesis, then your hypothesis may be correct! However, it is usually necessary to test a hypothesis with many different experiments before it can be accepted as a scientific law—something that is universally accepted as true.

You can apply the scientific method to problems in everyday life. For example, suppose you plant some seeds and they fail to sprout. You would probably ask yourself, "Why didn't they sprout?"—and that would be step one of the scientific method. The next step would be to make observations; for example, you might take note of how deep the seeds were planted, how often they were watered, and what kind of soil was used. Then, you would make an educated guess about what went wrong—for example, you might hypothesize that the seeds didn't sprout because you didn't water them enough. After that, you would test your hypothesis—perhaps by trying to grow the seeds again, under the exact same conditions as before, except that this time you would water them more frequently.

Finally, you would wait and evaluate the results of your experiment. If the seeds sprouted, then you could conclude that your hypothesis may be correct. If they don't sprout, you'd continue to use the method to find a scientific answer to your original question.

FIBONACCI PUZZLE

In 1202 an Italian mathematician called Leonardo Fibonacci, "Leonardo of Pisa," published the first European work on the Indian and Arabic system of numbers. Also in the book is what has become known as the "Fibonacci sequence." This sequence of numbers describes the growth of many things in nature, like spiral seashells, flowers, leaves, pinecones, and pineapples. Can you figure out which numbers come next?

0 1 1 2 3 5 8 13 ? ? ?

ANSWERS ON PAGES 335-338. FOR MORE PUZZLES GO TO WWW.WORLDALMANACFORKIDS.COM

Fizz Rocket

Did you ever see a rocket taking off? It climbs into the sky on a pillar of fire. But how exactly does it work? You can get an idea by building your own rocket and launching it. (For safety reasons, be sure to have an adult with you when you're doing this.)

WHAT YOU NEED:

► A 35-mm film canister with a cap that fits *inside* the rim—a photography store may have extra ones they'll give you if you explain it's for a science project.

► A fizzing antacid tablet, the kind sold to cure upset stomachs.

► Paper—a few sheets of normal printer paper are fine.

► Scissors and tape.

► A cup of water.

► Goggles or sunglasses to wear as eye protection.

WHAT TO DO:

❶ Make the body of the rocket—a cylinder—by cutting a strip of paper, then taping it to the film canister. *Make sure the cap end is at the bottom!*

❷ Make a nose cone for the rocket by cutting a circle out of the paper, then cutting a wedge out of the circle.

❸ When you tape together the edges of the wedge, you'll get a cone.

❹ Have fun with your rocket design—you can add fins if you want. Try short or tall rockets, and make the nose cone more or less pointed.

❺ Take your rocket outside and put on your eye protection.

❻ With the rocket pointing down, fill the canister about one-third full of water.

❼ Drop half the antacid tablet in the canister. Then quickly put the cap back on, turn the rocket right side up, and put it on the ground for blasting off.

❽ Stand back and see how high it goes!

WHAT HAPPENED?

Rockets—yours and the ones NASA sends into space—work because of Newton's Third Law of Motion: for every action there is an equal and opposite reaction. In the fizz rocket, the antacid tablet dissolves in the water and releases bubbles of gas. In a balloon, which is elastic, the gas would blow up the balloon. But the film canister in the rocket isn't elastic; the bubbles build up pressure until finally they pop out the cap. The cap and water rush out in a downward direction, and the rocket blasts off in the opposite direction—toward the sky. Real rockets, of course, use a different fuel, but the same basic principle.

Space

Who first noticed Saturn's rings? page 222

The SOLAR SYSTEM

Earth and the planets travel around the Sun. Together with the Sun, they are part of the solar system..

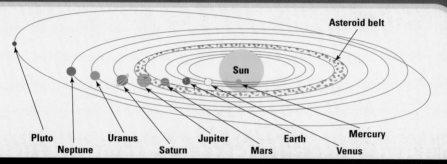

Asteroid belt

Sun

Pluto
Neptune
Uranus
Saturn
Jupiter
Mars
Earth
Venus
Mercury

The SUN is a STAR

Did you know that the Sun is a star, like the other stars you see at night? It is a typical, medium-size star. But because the Sun is much closer to our planet than any other star, we can study it in great detail. The diameter of the Sun is 865,000 miles—more than 100 times Earth's diameter. The gravity of the Sun is nearly 28 times the gravity of Earth.

How Hot Is the Sun? The surface temperature of the sun is close to 10,000° F, and it is believed that the Sun's inner core may reach temperatures around 30 million degrees! The Sun provides enough light and heat energy to support all forms of life on our planet.

The Planets are in Motion

The planets move around the Sun along elliptical paths called **orbits**. One complete path around the Sun is called a **revolution**. Earth takes one year, or 365 1/4 days, to make one revolution around the Sun. Planets that are farther away from the Sun take longer. Some planets have one or more **moons**. A moon orbits a planet in much the same way that the planets orbit the Sun. Each planet also spins (or rotates) on its **axis**. An axis is an imaginary line running through the center of a planet. The time it takes Earth to rotate on its axis equals one day.

Homework Help

Here's a useful way to remember the names of planets in order of their usual distance from the Sun. Think of this sentence: **M**y **V**ery **E**xcellent **M**other **J**ust **S**ent **U**s **N**ine **P**izzas.

M = Mercury, **V** = Venus, **E** = Earth, **M** = Mars, **J** = Jupiter, **S** = Saturn, **U** = Uranus, **N** = Neptune, **P** = Pluto.

THE PLANETS

1 MERCURY

Average distance from the Sun: 36 million miles
Diameter: 3,032 miles
Average temp.: 333° F
Surface: silicate rock
Time to revolve around the Sun: 88 days
Day (synodic—midday to midday): 175.94 days
Number of moons: 0

did you know? *Mercury is the closest planet to the Sun, but it gets very cold there. Since Mercury has almost no atmosphere, most of its heat escapes at night, and temperatures can fall to –300°.*

2 VENUS

Average distance from the Sun: 67 million miles
Diameter: 7,521 miles
Average temp.: 867° F
Surface: silicate rock
Time to revolve around the Sun: 224.7 days
Day (synodic—midday to midday): 116.75 days
Number of moons: 0

did you know? *Venus rotates in the opposite direction from all the other planets. Unlike on Earth, on Venus the sun rises in the west and sets in the east.*

3 EARTH

Average distance from the Sun: 93 million miles
Diameter: 7,926 miles
Average temp.: 59° F
Surface: water, basalt and granite rock
Time to revolve around the Sun: 365 ¼ days
Day (synodic—midday to midday): 24h
Number of moons: 1

did you know? *The Earth travels around the Sun at a speed of more than 66,000 miles per hour.*

4 MARS

Average distance from the Sun: 142 million miles
Diameter: 4,213 miles
Average temp.: –81° F
Surface: iron-rich basaltic rock
Time to revolve around the Sun: 687 days
Day (synodic—midday to midday): 24h 39m 35s
Number of moons: 2

did you know? *In 1877, astronomer Giovanni Schiaparelli thought he saw lines on Mars, which he called "channels," or "canali" in Italian. This was mistranslated into English as "canals," making people think there were canal-building Martians.*

5 JUPITER

Average distance from the Sun: 484 million miles
Diameter: 88,732 miles
Average temp.: –162° F
Surface: liquid hydrogen
Time to revolve around the Sun: 11.9 years
Time to rotate on its axis: 9h, 55m, 30s
Number of moons: 63

did you know? *The 4 largest moons were discovered by Galileo in 1610; 21 others were not found until 2003.*

6 SATURN

Average distance from the Sun: 887 million miles
Diameter: 74,975 miles
Average temp.: –218° F
Surface: liquid hydrogen
Time to revolve around the Sun: 29.5 years
Day (synodic—midday to midday): 10h 39m 23s
Number of moons: 34

did you know? *Using a simple early telescope, Galileo discovered what turned out to be rings around Saturn.*

7 URANUS

Average distance from the Sun: 1.8 billion miles
Diameter: 31,763 miles
Average temp.: −323° F
Surface: liquid hydrogen and helium
Time to revolve around the Sun: 84 years
Day (synodic—midday to midday): 17h 14m 23s
Number of moons: 27

didyouknow? *Because Uranus is tipped 98 degrees on its axis, its seasons are far more extreme than those of Earth: the north pole is dark for 42 years at a time.*

8 NEPTUNE

Average distance from the Sun: 2.8 billion miles
Diameter: 30,603 miles
Average temp.: −330° F
Surface: liquid hydrogen and helium
Time to revolve around the Sun: 164.8 years
Day (synodic—midday to midday): 16d 6h 37m
Number of moons: 13

didyouknow? *Neptune was discovered in 1846, after British astronomer John Adams and French mathematician Urbain Le Verrier independently predicted where it would be, based on its effect on Uranus's orbit.*

9 PLUTO

Average distance from the Sun: 3.6 billion miles
Diameter: 1,485 miles
Average temp.: −369° F
Surface: rock and frozen gases
Time to revolve around the Sun: 247.7 years
Day (synodic—midday to midday): 6d 9h 17m
Number of moons: 1

didyouknow? *Pluto is the smallest planet. Some scientists do not consider it a planet, just one of many large objects orbiting the Sun outside Neptune's orbit.*

In *December 2004* the *Huygens* probe detached from its "mother ship" *Cassini*, and the following month it landed on Titan, one of Saturn's many moons. The first probe to land on a moon other than the Earth's, *Huygens* sent back images of Titan. The images showed what might be oceans and rivers on the surface. However, these oceans wouldn't be filled with water, but probably with methane. On Earth methane is a gas. However, Titan has extremely low temperatures (about 290 degrees below zero Fahrenheit), which turns methane into a liquid.

More Planet Facts

Largest planet: JUPITER (88,732 miles diameter)

Smallest planet: PLUTO (1,485 miles diameter)

Coldest planet: PLUTO (-369° F)

Fastest orbiting planet: MERCURY (88 days)

Shortest day: JUPITER (9 hours, 55 minutes, 30 seconds)

Slowest orbiting planet: PLUTO (247.7 years)

Longest day: MERCURY (175.94 days)

Tallest mountain: MARS (Mount Olympus, 15 miles high)

No moons: MERCURY, VENUS

Hottest planet: VENUS (867° F)

Most moons: JUPITER (63 known satellites)

What's Out There?

What else is out in space besides planets?

Comet Wild 2 is millions of miles away from Earth.

A **GALAXY** is a group of billions of stars held together by gravity. Galaxies also contain interstellar gas and dust. The universe may have about as many as 100 billion galaxies! The one we live in is called the **Milky Way**. Our Sun and planets are a small part of it. Scientists think it may have 200 billion or more stars.

NEBULA is the name astronomers give to any fuzzy patch in the sky, even galaxies and star clusters. **Planetary nebulas** come from the late stages of some stars, while star clusters and galaxies are star groupings. **Emission nebulas**, reflection nebulas, and dark dust clouds are regions of interstellar gas and dust that may be hundreds of light years wide and are often birthplaces of stars. Emission nebulas often give off a reddish glow, caused when their hydrogen gas is heated by newly formed, hot stars in the vicinity. Dust particles in some areas reflect hot blue starlight and appear as reflection nebulas. Dark dust clouds, though still mainly gas, contain enough dust to absorb starlight and appear as **dark nebulas**.

BLACK HOLE is the name given to a region in space with gravity so strong that nothing can get out—not even light. Many black holes are probably formed when giant stars at least 20 times as massive as our Sun burn up their fuel and collapse, creating very dense cores. Scientists also think bigger, "supermassive" black holes may form from the collapse of many stars in the centers of galaxies. Astronomers can't see black holes, since they do not give off light. They watch for signs, such as effects on the orbits of nearby stars, or X-ray bursts from matter being sucked into the black hole.

SATELLITES are objects that move in an orbit around a planet. Moons are natural satellites. Artificial satellites, launched into orbit by humans, are used as space stations and observatories. They are also used to take pictures of Earth's surface and to transmit communications signals.

ASTEROIDS (or minor planets) are solid chunks of rock or metal that range in size from small boulders to hundreds of miles across. Ceres, the largest, is about 600 miles in diameter. Hundreds of thousands of asteroids orbit the Sun between Mars and Jupiter in the asteroid belt.

COMETS are moving chunks of ice, dust, and rock that form huge gaseous heads and tails as they move nearer to the Sun. One of the most well-known is Halley's Comet. It can be seen about every 76 years and will appear next again in the year 2061.

Comet Hale-Bopp, discovered in 1995.

METEOROIDS are small pieces of stone or metal traveling in space. Most meteoroids are fragments from comets or asteroids that broke off from crashes in space with other objects. A few are actually chunks that blew off the Moon or Mars after an asteroid hit. When a meteoroid enters the Earth's atmosphere, it usually burns up completely. This streak of light is called a meteor, or "shooting star." If a piece of a meteoroid survives its trip through our atmosphere and lands on Earth, it is called a meteorite.

The MOON

The moon is about 238,900 miles from Earth. It is 2,160 miles in diameter and has no atmosphere. The dusty surface is covered with deep craters. It takes the same time for the moon to rotate on its axis as it does to orbit Earth (27 days, 7 hours, 43 minutes). This is why one side of the moon is always facing Earth. The moon has no light of its own, but reflects light from the Sun. The lighted part of the moon that we see changes in a regular cycle. It takes the moon about 29½ days to go through all the "phases" in this cycle. This is called a **lunar month.**

PHASES of the MOON

New Moon	Crescent Moon	First Quarter	Full Moon	Last Quarter	Crescent Moon	New Moon

What is an ECLIPSE?

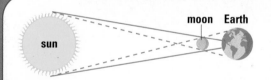

moon   Earth

sun

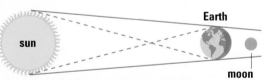

Earth

sun

moon

During a **solar eclipse,** the moon casts a shadow on Earth. A total solar eclipse is when the Sun is completely blocked out. When this happens, the halo of gas around the Sun called the **corona** can be seen.

Sometimes Earth casts a shadow on the moon. During a total **lunar eclipse,** the moon remains visible, but it looks dark, often with a reddish tinge (from sunlight bent through Earth's atmosphere).

Upcoming Total Solar Eclipses

TOTAL SOLAR ECLIPSES
March 29, 2006
Will be seen across the Atlantic Ocean, Africa, and part of Asia.
August 1, 2008
Will be seen in northern Canada, Greenland, and Asia.
July 22, 2009
Will be seen in eastern Asia and the central Pacific Ocean.

Upcoming Total Lunar Eclipses

TOTAL LUNAR ECLIPSES
March 3-4, 2007
Will be seen in Africa, Europe, and most of Asia.
August 28, 2007
Will be seen in eastern Asia, Australia, the Pacific Ocean, and the Americas.
Feb. 21, 2008
Will be seen in Americas, Europe, Africa, and the Pacific.

225

EXPLORING SPACE

American space exploration began in 1958, when the *Explorer I* satellite was launched into orbit and NASA (the National Aeronautics and Space Administration) was formed.

SEARCHING for LIFE

For years scientists have tried to discover whether there is life on other planets in our solar system or elsewhere. They look for signs of what is needed for life on Earth—basics like water and proper temperature.

NASA and the European Space Agency are searching for signs of life on Mars. This is carried out by spacecraft that fly around Mars taking pictures as well as by probes that land on the planet to study soil and rocks and look for living things. Scientists have already found evidence that there was considerable water on Mars in the past.

NASA is planning a new telescope mission called the Terrestrial Planet Finder. It will look for planets similar to Earth in other solar systems through two giant, space-based observatories, scheduled to be launched around 2014 and 2020.

Outside of NASA, another program is looking for life on other worlds. It is called SETI (Search for Extraterrestrial Intelligence). Most often it uses powerful radio telescopes to detect signs of life. Recently, however, astronomers began searching for light signals as signs of extraterrestrial life.

SOME UNMANNED MISSIONS in the Solar System

LAUNCH DATE

- **1962** **Mariner 2** First successful flyby of Venus.
- **1964** **Mariner 4** First probe to reach Mars, 1965.
- **1972** **Pioneer 10** First probe to reach Jupiter, 1973.
- **1973** **Mariner 10** Only U.S. probe to reach Mercury, 1974.
- **1975** **Viking 1 and 2** Landed on Mars in 1976.
- **1977** **Voyager 1** Reached Jupiter in 1979 and Saturn in 1980.
- **1977** **Voyager 2** Reached Jupiter in 1979, Saturn in 1981, Uranus in 1986, Neptune in 1989.
- **1989** **Magellan** Orbited Venus and mapped its surface.
- **1989** **Galileo** Reached Jupiter, 1995.
- **1996** **Mars Global Surveyor** Began mapping surface in 1999.
- **1996** **Mars Pathfinder** Landed on Mars, sent a roving vehicle (Sojourner) to explore the surface in 1997.
- **1996** **Near Shoemaker** First to land on an asteroid (Eros), early 2001.
- **1997** **Cassini** Reached Saturn in June 2004.
- **2001** **Mars Odyssey** Began mapping and studying Mars in early 2002.
- **2003** **Mars Rovers Spirit and Opportunity** Landed on Mars in early 2004.
- **2004** **Rosetta** Expected to land on a faraway comet in 2014.
- **2005** **Deep Impact** Launched in January, should reach a nearer comet by July 2005.

First Astronauts in SPACE

The start of the U.S. space program in 1958 was a response to the Soviet Union's launching of its satellite *Sputnik I* into orbit on October 4, 1957. In 1961, three years after NASA was formed, President John F. Kennedy promised Americans that the United States would land a person on the moon by the end of the 1960s. NASA landed men on the moon in July 1969. Since then, more than 400 astronauts have made trips into outer space. This time line shows some of their early flights.

1961 — On April 12, Soviet cosmonaut Yuri Gagarin, in *Vostok 1,* became the **first human to orbit Earth**. On May 5, U.S. astronaut Alan B. Shepard Jr. of the *Mercury 3* mission became the first American in space.

1962 — On February 20, U.S. astronaut John H. Glenn Jr. of *Mercury 6* became the **first American to orbit Earth**.

1963 — From June 16 to 19, the Soviet spacecraft *Vostok 6* carried the **first woman in space**, Valentina V. Tereshkova.

1965 — On March 18, Soviet cosmonaut Aleksei A. Leonov became the **first person to walk in space**. He spent 10 minutes outside the spaceship. On December 15, *U.S. Gemini 6A* and *7* (with astronauts) became the **first vehicles to rendezvous** (approach and see each other) **in space**.

1966 — On March 16, *U.S. Gemini 8* became the **first craft to dock with** (become attached to) **another vehicle** (an unmanned *Agena* rocket).

1967 — On January 27, a fire in a U.S. *Apollo* spacecraft on the ground killed astronauts Virgil I. Grissom, Edward H. White, and Roger B. Chaffee. On April 24, *Soyuz 1* crashed on Earth, killing Soviet cosmonaut Vladimir Komarov.

1969 — On July 20, after successful flights of *Apollo 8, 9,* and *10,* U.S. *Apollo 11*'s lunar module *Eagle* landed on the moon's surface in the area known as the Sea of Tranquility. Neil Armstrong became the **first person ever to walk on the moon**.

1970 — In April, *Apollo 13* astronauts returned safely to Earth after an explosion damaged their spacecraft and prevented them from landing on the moon.

1971 — In July and August, U.S. *Apollo 15* astronauts tested the **Lunar Rover** on the moon.

1972 — In December, *Apollo 17* was the sixth and **final U.S. space mission to land successfully on the moon**.

1973 — On May 14, the U.S. put its **first space station, *Skylab*,** into orbit. The last *Skylab* crew left in January 1974.

1975 — On July 15, the U.S. launched an *Apollo* spacecraft and the U.S.S.R. launched a *Soyuz* spacecraft. Two days later, the **American and Soviet crafts docked**, and for several days their crews worked and spent time together in space. This was NASA's last space mission with astronauts until the space shuttle.

Shuttles and Space Stations

In the 1970s, NASA developed the space shuttle program. Earlier space capsules could not be used again after returning to Earth. In 1986, the Soviet Union launched its *Mir* space station. By the mid-1990s, the U.S. and Russia were sharing projects in space.

1977 — The first shuttle, ***Enterprise***, took off from the back of a 747 jet airliner.

1981 — ***Columbia*** was launched and became the first shuttle to reach Earth's orbit.

1983 — In April, NASA began using a third shuttle, ***Challenger***.

1984 — In August, the shuttle ***Discovery*** was launched for the first time.

1985 — In October, the shuttle ***Atlantis*** was launched for the first time.

1986 — On January 28, after 24 successful missions, ***Challenger*** exploded 73 seconds after takeoff. All seven astronauts, including teacher Christa McAuliffe, died. In February, the Soviet space station ***Mir*** was launched into orbit.

1988 — In September new safety procedures led to a successful launch of ***Discovery***.

1990 — On April 24, the ***Hubble Space Telescope*** was launched from ***Discovery***.

1992 — In May, NASA launched a new shuttle, ***Endeavour***.

1995 — In June, ***Atlantis*** docked with ***Mir*** for the first time.

1998 — In December, ***Endeavour*** was launched with ***Unity***, a U.S.-built part of the International Space Station (ISS). The crew attached it to the Russian-built ***Zarya*** control module.

2000 — The first crew arrived at the ISS in November.

2001 — In February, ***Atlantis*** carried the lab module ***Destiny*** to the ISS. ***Mir*** parts splashed down in the Pacific in March, ending the 15-year Russian program.

2002 — In March, ***Columbia*** astronauts carried out the fourth repair/upgrade of the ***Hubble Space Telescope***.

2003 — On February 1, 2003, after a 16-day scientific mission, space shuttle ***Columbia*** disintegrated during its reentry into the Earth's atmosphere, killing the seven-member crew.

The ***International Space Station*** (ISS) is being built by 16 countries, including the U.S. and Russia. When it's finished, the ISS will weigh over 1 million pounds. It will be about a hundred yards square (356 feet wide and 290 feet long). That's four times bigger than the Russian ***Mir*** space station. There will be almost an acre of solar panels to supply electricity to the 52 computers and six scientific laboratories on board. The ISS is orbiting the Earth at an average altitude of 240 miles.

After the February 2003 ***Columbia*** disaster, U.S. space shuttles were grounded. The space shuttles' return-to-flight mission was scheduled for launch mid-2005. The crew planned to deliver supplies to the *ISS* and conduct spacewalks. Since the space shuttles are the only vehicles that can carry the big parts needed to finish the ISS, the date for completing work on the space station has been pushed back several years.

From Sea to Space

Astronauts take to the ocean to practice medicine in space.

Astronauts are diving into a new kind of mission. Their special voyage is taking them more than 60 feet beneath the ocean's surface.

The astronauts—called "aquanauts"—are training for space missions in an underwater laboratory called Aquarius. The lab rests on the ocean floor off the coast of Florida.

Space Mission: "Aquanauts" train for space in Aquarius, an underwater steel lab.

DIVE TO FLY

A recent ocean mission began October 11, 2004, when three astronauts and a doctor from Canada took the plunge. The crew's job includes testing medical equipment that may be used to treat astronauts when they get sick in space.

The journey marked the seventh mission the U.S. space agency, NASA, has made to Aquarius. The 10-day mission is referred to as NEEMO 7 (NASA Extreme Environment Mission Operations).

UNDERWATER HOSPITAL

Astronauts are using the underwater lab to learn what it may be like to live and work in space. They are preparing for extreme environments, such as the moon and the planet Mars. The conditions underwater are similar to those in space.

The goal of this latest voyage, or expedition, was to learn how to treat patients in space from a distance. Part of the underwater mission involved performing robotic surgery on a fake patient. Doctors on land guided the astronauts through the procedure.

Why is exploring this technology important? "Astronauts navigating between planets won't be able to turn around and come home when someone gets sick," said NEEMO's project manager, Bill Todd, "and this undersea mission will help us respond to medical emergencies in space."

FISH-EYE VIEW: Astronauts peer through the lab's windows.

Aquarius is located off the coast of Key Largo, Florida.

Undersea Home

Aquarius is the only underwater training center and research laboratory of its kind. The astronauts live, sleep, and work there. The lab, which is 45 feet long, has some of the comforts of home. Aquarius is equipped with bunks, a shower, computers, and even a refrigerator and microwave. Plus it has an ocean view!

SPACE NEWS

Mars Rovers Anniversary

January 2005 marked the first anniversary NASA's Mars Rover mission. Rovers *Spirit* and *Opportunity* were expected to last only about 92 days in the Martian environment. But they've beaten expectations and in early 2005 were still making new discoveries while taking amazing pictures of the red planet's surface. They have sent back a lot of information about Martian geology and climate, and have provided scientists with evidence that water may have once flowed on Mars.

Opportunity's rover's rock abrasion tool after it ground into a rock at Meridiani Planum, Mars. ▶

SpaceShipOne Captures the X Prize

On Oct. 4, 2004, the *SpaceShipOne* team won the $10 million Ansari X Prize for developing the first privately funded piloted spacecraft to make two trips into space within two weeks. The competition was put in place to encourage private companies to develop piloted spacecraft. All other U.S. piloted spacecraft were developed by NASA.

First flown into space (a height of at least 60 miles) by Mike Melvill on June 21, 2004, *SpaceShipOne* won the X Prize with two flights in the fall, reaching an altitude of about 69.6 mi. and then 68.2 mi.. The craft looks like a small stubby airplane. Unlike the space shuttles or capsules, *SpaceShipOne* is not launched from a rocket. Instead it is hooked to the bottom of a special plane, called the *White Knight*, which carries it to an altitude of 46,000 feet. *SpaceShipOne* then detaches from the plane, and under its own power rockets into the sky. Its special wings help to slow the craft on re-entry, and it then glides toward the ground and lands like a regular airplane.

SpaceShipOne was built by a company called Scaled Composites.

Cassini/Huygens Reach Saturn

The *Cassini* orbiter, with the *Huygens* probe piggy backed onto it, entered Saturn's orbit on June 30, 2004. It sent back unbelievable photos of the planet, which included stunning, up-close views of the planet's rings. *Cassini* also found two previously unknown moons, raising the total for Saturn to 34. The *Huygens* probe detached from *Cassini* and later landed on Titan, one of Saturn's moons, on Jan. 14, 2005. Titan is of particular interest to scientists because they believe its atmosphere resembles that of Earth's, millions of years ago. Photos sent back show a landscape totally alien to ours, where it is icy and rains liquid methane. From photos taken during *Huygens'* descent, NASA scientists think they may have seen what look like coastlines, meaning Titan may have oceans of liquid methane.

Cassini's view of Saturn as it sped from the planet on its orbit.

CONSTELLATIONS ★

Ancient cultures used myths to explain how constellations came to be. The constellation of Cassiopeia looks like the letter "W" in the sky. In Greek mythology, Cassiopeia was an Ethiopian queen. She was the wife of Cepheus and the mother of Andromeda. According to tradition, when she died she was changed into the constellation that is named after her. Today there are 88 officially recognized constellations.

Andromeda

Cassiopeia

Cepheus

POLARIS
(North Star)

Ursa Minor
(Little Dipper)

Big Dipper

Ursa Major

The ZODIAC

The **zodiac** is an imaginary belt that goes around the sky. The orbits of the Sun, the moon, and planets known to ancient peoples are within it. The zodiac is divided into 12 sections, which are called **signs of the zodiac**. The ancient Babylonians named each of the sections for a constellation that could be seen within its limits during ancient times. Astrologers believe that your personality and fortune are influenced by the sign under which you were born. But this belief has no scientific basis.

ARIES (Ram)
March 21–April 19

TAURUS (Bull)
April 20–May 20

GEMINI (Twins)
May 21–June 21

CANCER (Crab)
June 22–July 22

LEO (Lion)
July 23–August 22

VIRGO (Maiden)
August 23–Sept. 22

LIBRA (Balance)
Sept. 23–Oct. 23

SCORPIO (Scorpion)
Oct. 24–Nov. 21

SAGITTARIUS
(Archer)
Nov. 22–Dec. 21

CAPRICORN (Goat)
Dec. 22–Jan. 19

AQUARIUS
(Water Bearer)
Jan. 20–Feb. 18

PISCES (Fishes)
Feb. 19–March 20

ASTEROID HOPPING

You've got your suit on and you're ready for a space walk. You are free to hop from one asteroid to another—up, down, diagonally and back again if you need to. See if you can spell out the names of all nine planets and the star they revolve around.

**ANSWERS ON PAGES 335-338.
FOR MORE PUZZLES GO TO
WWW.WORLDALMANACFORKIDS.COM**

232

Sports

Who is "Automatic Adam"? page 239

BASEBALL

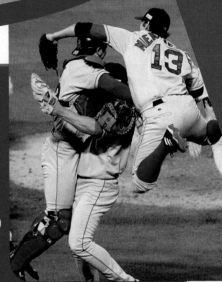

In the 2004 World Series, the Boston Red Sox snapped one of baseball's most famous losing streaks, sweeping the St. Louis Cardinals in four games. It was the first time a Red Sox team had won in a World Series since 1918. At first it looked as though Boston might not even reach the Fall Classic. In the American League Championship Series, the rival New York Yankees defeated the Red Sox in the first three games. But the Red Sox rebounded, winning the next four games and the AL pennant. In the World Series itself, the Red Sox dominated St. Louis and became the first team since 1989 to never trail in any game. Pitcher Derek Lowe capped the series in Game 4 by allowing just three hits over seven innings in a 3-0 victory on October 27, 2004.

2004 MAJOR LEAGUE STANDOUTS

MVP AWARD
NL: Barry Bonds, San Francisco
AL: Vladimir Guerrero, Anaheim Angels

CY YOUNG AWARD (top pitcher)
NL: Roger Clemens, Houston
AL: Johan Santana, Minnesota

ROOKIE OF THE YEAR
NL: Jason Bay, Pittsburgh
AL: Bobby Crosby, Oakland

BATTING CHAMPS
NL: Barry Bonds, San Francisco, .362
AL: Ichiro Suzuki, Seattle, .372

HOME RUN LEADERS
NL: Adrian Beltre, Los Angeles Dodgers, 48
AL: Manny Ramirez, Boston, 43

EARNED RUN AVERAGE LEADERS
NL: Jake Peavy, San Diego, 2.27
AL: Johan Santana, Minnesota, 2.61

COOL FEATS, FACTS, & FIRSTS

▶ In the 2004 American League Championship Series, the Boston Red Sox became the first team in playoff history to be down 0-3 in a seven-game series and still win the series. The Red Sox took the last four games of the ALCS against the New York Yankees and then the first four of the World Series. That made Boston the only team to win eight consecutive games in one postseason.

▶ In 2004, Ichiro Suzuki of the Seattle Mariners broke the record for most hits in a single season, with 262 hits. The previous record was 257 hits, set in 1920 by George Sisler.

▶ In 2005, the Montreal Expos moved to Washington, D.C., to become the Washington Nationals. The Nationals are the first Major League Baseball team to represent D.C. since 1971, when the Washington Senators left for Texas to become the Rangers.

Some Major League Records*

BATTERS

Most home runs
Career: 755, Hank Aaron (1954-76)
Season: 73, **Barry Bonds** (2001)
Game: 4, by 15 different players

Most hits
Career: 4,256, Pete Rose (1963-86)
Season: 262, **Ichiro Suzuki** (2004)
Game: 7, Rennie Stennett (1975)

Most stolen bases
Career: 1,406, Rickey Henderson (1979-2003)
Season: 130, Rickey Henderson (1982)
Game: 6, Eddie Collins (1912)

PITCHERS

Most strikeouts
Career: 5,714, Nolan Ryan (1966-93)
Season: 383, Nolan Ryan (1973)
Game: 20, **Roger Clemens** (1986, 1996);
Kerry Wood (1998)

Most wins
Career: 511, Cy Young (1890-1911)
Season: 41, Jack Chesbro (1904)

Most saves
Career: 478, Lee Smith (1980-97)
Season: 57, Bobby Thigpen (1990)

*Through the 2004 season. Players in bold played in 2004. Game stats are for nine-inning games only.

The Curse of the Bambino

In 1918, the Boston Red Sox seemed to own the World Series. They had won it five times—more than any other team up to that point.

Boston's star player back then was pitcher/outfielder George Herman "Babe" Ruth. But in 1920, Red Sox owner Harry Frazee sold Ruth to the New York Yankees. Ruth then led the Yankees to four World Series victories and set Major League home run records (since broken). New Yorkers affectionately nicknamed Ruth "the Bambino."

Meanwhile, once-mighty Boston wallowed in defeat. Discouraged fans called their bad luck "the curse of the Bambino." The Red Sox did not return to the World Series again until 1946. They lost that series—barely—as well as three more during the next five decades.

The Red Sox's fortunes finally changed in 2004. Boston beat the Yankees to win the American League championship and then swept the St. Louis Cardinals in the World Series. The "Curse of the Bambino" had finally been lifted.

BASEBALL HALL of FAME

The National Baseball Hall of Fame and Museum opened in 1939, in Cooperstown, New York. To be eligible for membership, players must be retired from baseball for five years. In 2005, Wade Boggs and Ryan Sandberg were elected to "The Hall."

WEB SITE www.baseballhalloffame.org

LITTLE LEAGUE

Little League Baseball is the largest youth sports program in the world. It began in 1939 in Williamsport, Pennsylvania, with 45 boys playing on three teams. Now millions of boys and girls ages 5 to 18 play on over 200,000 Little League teams in more than 100 countries.

WEB SITE www.littleleague.org

Basketball began in 1891 in Springfield, Massachusetts, when Dr. James Naismith invented it, using peach baskets as hoops. At first, each team had nine players instead of five. Big-time pro basketball started in 1949, when the National Basketball Association (NBA) was formed. The Women's National Basketball Association (WNBA) began play in 1997.

HIGHLIGHTS OF THE 2004–2005 NBA SEASON

SCORING LEADER:
Allen Iverson,
Philadelphia 76ers

Games: 75
Points: 2,302
Average: 30.7

REBOUNDING LEADER:
Kevin Garnett,
Minnesota Timberwolves

Games: 82
Rebounds: 1,108
Average: 13.5

BLOCKED SHOTS LEADER:
Andrei Kirilenko,
Utah Jazz

Games: 41
Blocks: 136
Average: 3.32

STEALS LEADER:
Larry Hughes,
Washington
Wizards

Games: 61
Steals: 176
Average: 2.89

ASSISTS LEADER:
Steve Nash,
Phoenix Suns

Games: 75
Assists: 861
Average: 11.5

Hall of Fame

The Naismith Memorial Hall of Fame in Springfield, Massachusetts, was founded to honor great basketball players, coaches, referees, and others important to the history of the game. The newest class, heading for the hall in September 2005, includes college coaching legends Jim Calhoun and Jim Boeheim, NBA coach and broadcaster Hubie Brown, and women's coach Sue Gunter. International star Hortencia de Fatima Marcari of Brazil, who led her country to a World Championship in 1994, will also be enshrined.

WEB SITE www.hoophall.com

Prior to the 2004-2005 season, the Chicago Bulls had not made the NBA playoffs since Michael Jordan led them to a sixth championship in the 1997-1998 season. In that span, the Bulls lost 341 games. This year they started the season 0-9, but clinched a playoff spot before the season ended.

235

Some All-Time NBA Records*

POINTS

Career: 38,387, Kareem Abdul Jabbar (1969-89)

Season: 4,029, Wilt Chamberlain (1961-62)

Game: 100, Wilt Chamberlain (1962)

ASSISTS

Career: 15,806, John Stockton (1984-2003)

Season: 1,164 John Stockton (1990-91)

Game: 30, Scott Skiles (1990)

REBOUNDS

Career: 23,924, Wilt Chamberlain (1959-73)

Season: 2,149, Wilt Chamberlain (1960-61)

Game: 55, Wilt Chamberlain (1960)

3-POINTERS

Career: 2,560, **Reggie Miller** (1987-)

Season: 267, Dennis Scott (1996-97)

Game: 12, **Kobe Bryant** (2003)

Through the 2004-2005 season. Players in bold were active in the 2004-2005 season.

HIGHLIGHTS
of the
2004 WNBA SEASON

The Seattle Storm defeated the Connecticut Sun, 74-60, in Seattle, WA, on Oct. 12, 2004, to take the third and deciding game of the WNBA finals. Seattle's Betty Lennox averaged 22.3 points per game in the finals and was named most valuable player of the series. Led by two-time WNBA scoring leader Lauren Jackson and guard Sue Bird, the Storm defeated the Minnesota Lynx and the Sacramento Monarchs on their way to the title. The WNBA took a month off for the Summer Olympics in Athens. The all-WNBA U.S. team won the gold medal.

WNBA STATISTICAL LEADERS AND AWARDS IN 2004

Most Valuable Player: Lisa Leslie, Los Angeles

Defensive Player of the Year: Lisa Leslie, Los Angeles

Coach of the Year: Suzie McConnell Serio, Minnesota

Most Improved Player of the Year: (tie) Wendy Palmer, Connecticut and Kelly Miller, Indiana

◄ **Rookie of the Year:** Diana Taurasi, Phoenix

Scoring Leader: Lauren Jackson, Seattle
Games: 31   Points: 634   Average: 20.5

Rebounding Leader: Lisa Leslie, Los Angeles
Games: 34   Rebounds: 336   Average: 9.9

Assists Leader: Nikki Teasley, Los Angeles
Games: 34   Assists: 207   Average: 6.1

College Basketball

The men's National Collegiate Athletic Association (NCAA) Tournament began in 1939. Today, it is a spectacular 65-team extravaganza. The Final Four weekend, when the semi-finals and finals are played, is one of the most-watched sports competitions in the U.S. The Women's NCAA Tournament began in 1982. Since then, the popularity of the women's game has grown by leaps and (re)bounds.

THE 2005 NCAA TOURNAMENT RESULTS

MEN'S FINAL FOUR	WOMEN'S FINAL FOUR
SEMI-FINALS:	**SEMI-FINALS:**
Illinois 72, Louisville 57	Baylor 68, LSU 57
North Carolina 87, Michigan St. 71	Michigan State 68, Tennessee 64
FINALS:	**FINALS:**
North Carolina 75, Illinois 70	Baylor 84, Michigan St. 62
MOST OUTSTANDING PLAYER:	**MOST OUTSTANDING PLAYER:**
Sean May, North Carolina	Sophia Young, Baylor

THE JOHN R. WOODEN AWARD	THE WADE TROPHY
Awarded to the nation's outstanding male college basketball player by the Los Angeles Athletic Club.	Awarded to the nation's outstanding female college basketball player by the National Association for Girls and Women in Sport.
2005 winner: Andrew Bogut, Utah	**2005 winner:** Seimone Augustus, LSU

CYCLING

The "modern" bicycle, with two wheels the same size, pedals, and a chain drive, appeared at the end of the 1800s. The name "bicycle" itself was first used in 1869. Before that, the various two-wheeled inventions were known as "velocipedes." Clubs were formed and races held, but cycling was mostly a sport for the upper classes; bicycles were too expensive for most people. The world's best-known cycling race, the Tour de France, was first held in 1903.

Tour De Lance!

In July of 2004, American Lance Armstrong became the only cyclist to ever win the grueling Tour de France six times. He finished the three-week, 2,110-mile race with an overall time of 83 hours, 36 minutes, and 2 seconds. The 32-year-old Texan averaged about 25 miles per hour and beat his nearest rival by 6 minutes and 19 seconds.

Lance's first win, in 1999, was very special. In 1996, he had been diagnosed with cancer. He had two operations and went through chemotherapy. This didn't stop him. In May 1998, he came back and signed with the U.S. Postal Service Team, setting his sights on the Tour de France. In 2003, Lance tied the previous record of five Tour de France wins. Only four other cyclists—Jacques Anquetil, Bernard Hinault, Miguel Indurain, and Eddy Merckx—had ever achieved that feat.

Lance was born September 18, 1971, and raised by his mother in Plano, Texas. When he was 13, he won the first Iron Kids Triathlon (1985), beating lots of bigger kids. The cycling part was his favorite. By 1991, he was the U.S. national amateur champion.

FOOTBALL

American football began as a college sport. The first game that was like today's football took place between Yale and Harvard in New Haven, Connecticut, on November 13, 1875. The National Football League started in 1922. The rival American Football League began in 1960. The two leagues played the first Super Bowl in 1967. In 1970, the leagues merged as the NFL with an American Football Conference (AFC) and a National Football Conference (AFC).

Pats Top Eagles

At Super Bowl XXXIX in Jacksonville, Florida, the AFC's New England Patriots beat the NFC Philadelphia Eagles, 24-21. It was New England's second straight Super Bowl victory and the third in four years. Only the Dallas Cowboys have won that many championships in such a short span.

Patriot quarterback Tom Brady recorded 23 complete passes for 236 yards and no interceptions. But the game's Most Valuable Player award went to receiver Deion Branch, who grabbed a record-tying 11 catches for 133 yards. Perhaps his most crucial play was a leaping 19-yard reception over the middle early in the fourth quarter. That set up kicker Adam Vinatieri's game-winning 22-yard field goal.

2004 NFL LEADERS & AWARDS

RUSHING YARDS: Curtis Martin, New York Jets, 1,697
RUSHING TDS: LaDainian Tomlinson, San Diego Chargers, 17
RECEPTIONS: Tony Gonzalez, Kansas City, 102
RECEIVING YARDS: Muhsin Muhammad, Carolina Panthers, 1,405
RECEIVING TDS: Muhsin Muhammad, Carolina Panthers, 16
PASSING YARDS: Daunte Culpepper, Minnesota Vikings, 4,717
PASSER RATING: Peyton Manning, Indianapolis Colts, 121.1
PASSING TDS: Peyton Manning, Indianapolis Colts, 49*
INTERCEPTIONS: Ed Reed, Baltimore Ravens, 9
SACKS: Dwight Freeny, Indianapolis Colts, 16

2004 ASSOCIATED PRESS AWARDS

Most Valuable Player: Peyton Manning, Indianapolis Colts
Offensive Player of the Year: Peyton Manning, Indianapolis Colts
Defensive Player of the Year: Ed Reed, Baltimore Ravens
Coach of the Year: Marty Schottenheimer, San Diego Chargers
Offensive Rookie of the Year: Ben Roethlisberger, Pittsburgh Steelers

Defensive Rookie of the Year: Jonathan Vilma, New York Jets
Comeback Player of the Year: Drew Brees, San Diego Chargers

Peyton Manning

FAMOUS NFL GAMES

Alan Ameche scores.

"THE GREATEST GAME EVER PLAYED" December 28, 1958, NFL Championship, New York City (Yankee Stadium): Baltimore Colts 23, New York Giants 17.

With a 14-3 lead in the 3rd quarter, the Colts had the ball on the Giants' 1-yard line and seemed to be on their way to an easy win. But the Giants made a determined goal-line stand, got the ball on their own 5-yard line, and drove downfield for a TD. In the 4th quarter, Frank Gifford caught a TD pass to give the Giants a 17-14 lead. But the Colts' star quarterback, Johnny Unitas, passed his team down the field, completing 3 to Ray Berry for 62 yards. With 7 seconds left, the Colts kicked a field goal to force the first post season overtime. In the extra period, the Giants punted and Unitas went to work. He took the Colts 80 yards before fullback Alan "The Horse" Ameche bulled into the end zone from the 1-yard line, to end what many still call "the greatest game ever played."

"WIDE RIGHT" January 27, 1991, Super Bowl XXV, Tampa Bay, Florida: New York Giants 20, Buffalo Bills 19.

The Bills were heavily favored, and fans were shocked to see them down 20-19 as the game neared its close. With only a few seconds left in the 4th quarter, Buffalo drove into Giant territory to set up a 47-yard field goal attempt for kicker Scott Norwood. Norwood's kick had the distance but, in words that would echo in Buffalo for years after, the ball sailed "wide right." The Giants won. It was one of the most intense, exciting, and heartbreaking moments in NFL history.

"AUTOMATIC ADAM" February 3, 2002, Super Bowl XXXVI, New Orleans, Louisiana: New England Patriots 20, St. Louis Rams 17.

The Patriots went into Super Bowl XXVI as heavy underdogs against the Rams' offense, widely known as the "Greatest Show on Turf." During the game, the Rams outgained the Patriots in total offensive yards, but the Patriots were able to force three turnovers, keeping the score close. With the game tied late in the 4th quarter, young quarterback Tom Brady led New England downfield to set up a 48-yard field goal attempt with only 7 seconds remaining. On the game's last play, kicker "Automatic" Adam Vinatieri sent the ball sailing through the uprights to give the Patriots their very first Super Bowl victory.

NFL All-Time Record Holders*

RUSHING YARDS
Career: 18,355, **Emmitt Smith** (1990-2004)
Season: 2,105, Eric Dickerson (1984)
Game: 295, **Jamal Lewis** (2003)

RECEIVING YARDS
Career: 22,466, **Jerry Rice** (1985-)
Season: 1,848, **Jerry Rice** (1995)
Game: 336, Willie Anderson (1985)

PASSING YARDS
Career: 61,361, Dan Marino (1983-99)
Season: 5,084, Dan Marino (1984)
Game: 554, Norm Van Brocklin (1951)

POINTS SCORED
Career: 2,434, **Gary Anderson** (1982-)
Season: 176, Paul Hornung (1960)
Game: 40, Ernie Nevers (1929)

*Through the 2004 season. Players in bold played in 2004. Game stats don't include overtime games.

Pro Football HALL of FAME

Football's Hall of Fame in Canton, Ohio, was founded in 1963 by the National Football League to honor outstanding players, coaches, and contributors.

Four people—quarterback Benny Friedman, quarterback Dan Marino, back and coach Fritz Pollard, and quarterback Steve Young—were to be inducted into the hall in August 2005.

WEB SITE www.profootballhof.com

College Football

College football is one of America's most colorful and exciting sports. The National Collegiate Athletic Association (NCAA), founded in 1906, oversees the sport today.

On January 4, 2005, the University of Southern California (USC) won its second straight national championship by beating Oklahoma in the Orange Bowl, 55-19. The previous year, USC shared the national title with Louisiana State University (LSU).

Unlike college basketball, there is no playoff in college football to determine a single champion. So the best team is determined by polls of sports writers and coaches. In 2004, USC topped one major poll while LSU led in the other. In 2005, both polls named USC as No. 1 (see box).

2004 *TOP 5* COLLEGE TEAMS

Chosen by the Associated Press Poll and the USA Today/ESPN Poll

Rank	AP	USA Today/ESPN
❶	USC	USC
❷	Auburn	Auburn
❸	Oklahoma	Oklahoma
❹	Utah	Texas
❺	Texas	Utah

HEISMAN TROPHY

Quarterback Matt Leinart of the University of Southern California (USC) was the 2004 winner. The 21-year-old junior passed for an average 255.5 yards per game for 33 touchdowns while yielding only six interceptions. He also led the Trojans to their 11th national title. Since Leinart became starting quarterback as a sophomore, the team has gone 25-1 and won 22 straight games. Leinart planned to return to USC for the 2005 season.

ALL-TIME DIVISION I NCAA LEADERS

RUSHING YARDS
1. 6,397, Ron Dayne, Wisconsin
2. 6,297, Ricky Williams, Texas
3. 6,082, Tony Dorsett, Pittsburgh
4. 5,598, Charles White, USC
5. 5,596, Travis Prentice, Miami (OH)

PASSING YARDS
1. 17,072, Timmy Chang, Hawaii
2. 15,031, Ty Detmer, Brigham Young
3. 12,746, Tim Rattay, Louisiana Tech
4. 12,541, Chris Redman, Louisville
5. 12,429, Kliff Kingsbury, Texas Tech

Great Moment in College Football

JANUARY 1, 1970, COTTON BOWL, TEXAS 21, NOTRE DAME 17. The top-ranked Texas Longhorns entered the game as 7-point favorites against the Notre Dame Fighting Irish, making their first bowl appearance in 44 years. But the No. 9 Fighting Irish put 10 points on the board quickly and seemed ready to snap Texas's 19-game winning streak. Two tough Longhorn drives led by quarterback James Street made it 14-10 early in the second half. Irish quarterback Joe Theismann bounced back with his own 80-yard march capped by a 24-yard TD pass. With less than 7 minutes to play, Street began an epic 17-play drive from the Texas 24. The 'Horns converted two fourth-and-two situations and broke through a gutsy Irish goal-line stand to score a touchdown and win the national championship.

GOLF

Golf began in Scotland as early as the 1400s. The first golf course in the U.S. opened in 1888 in Yonkers, NY. The sport has grown to include both men's and women's professional tours. And millions play golf just for fun.

The men's tour in the U.S. is run by the Professional Golf Association (PGA). The four major championships (with the year first played) are:

British Open (1860)
United States Open (1895)
PGA Championship (1916)
Masters Tournament (1934)

The women's tour in the U.S. is guided by the Ladies Professional Golf Association (LPGA). The four major championships are:

United States Women's Open (1946)
McDonalds LPGA Championship (1955)
Nabisco Championship (1972)
Women's British Open (1976)

The All-Time "Major" Players

Here is a list of the pro golfers who've won the most major championships.

MEN
1. Jack Nicklaus, 18
2. Walter Hagan, 11
3. Ben Hogan, 9
   Gary Player, 9
   Tiger Woods, 9
6. Tom Watson, 8

WOMEN
1. Patty Berg, 15
2. Mickey Wright, 13
3. Louise Suggs, 11
4. Babe Didrikson Zaharias, 10
5. Betsy Rawls, 8
   Annika Sorenstam, 8

did you know?

In April 2005, Annika Sorenstam ▶ won her 8th Ladies Professional Golf Association major title, tying her for fifth on the all-time list. The victory for the Swedish-born golfer also tied the LPGA record of five straight tournament victories. In 2001 she set an LPGA record with a one-round score of 59. Annika even played in a men's PGA tournament, the Colonial, in 2003.

GYMNASTICS

It takes strength, coordination, and grace to become a top gymnast. Although the sport goes back to ancient Egypt, modern-day gymnastics began in Europe in the early 1800s. The sport has been part of the Olympics since 1896. The first World Gymnastic Championships were held in Antwerp, Belgium, in 1903.

Men today compete in the All-Around, High Bar, Parallel Bars, Rings, Vault, Pommel Horse, Floor Exercises, and Team Combined. The women's events are the All-Around, Uneven Parallel Bars, Balance Beam, Floor Exercises, and Team Combined. In rhythmic gymnastics, women compete in All-Around, Rope, Hoop, Ball, Clubs, and Ribbon.

The U.S. excelled in both men's and women's gymnastics at the 2004 Athens Olympics. Women won six medals and the men won three, the most since U.S. gymnasts won 14 medals at the 1984 Olympic Games. Carly Patterson led the women by taking three medals, including a gold in the all-around. The women also won the team silver medal. Paul Hamm won two silvers for the men and a disputed gold in the all-around.

ICE HOCKEY

Ice hockey began in Canada in the mid-1800s. The National Hockey League (NHL) was formed in 1916. In 2003, the NHL had 30 teams—24 in the U.S. and 6 in Canada.

HIGHLIGHTS

In 2004, the Tampa Bay Lightning won its first ever Stanley Cup, defeating the Calgary Flames, four games to three. Lightning center Brad Richards was the playoffs' high scorer with 26 points and winner of the Conn Smythe Trophy as playoff MVP. The Stanley Cup, North America's oldest professional championship, went to one of the NHL's youngest teams. The Lightning joined the league in 1992 and had won just one playoff game before 2004.

SEASON	WINNER	RUNNER-UP
1990-91	Pittsburgh Penguins	Minnesota North Stars
1991-92	Pittsburgh Penguins	Chicago Black Hawks
1992-93	Montreal Canadiens	Los Angeles Kings
1993-94	New York Rangers	Vancouver Canucks
1994-95	New Jersey Devils	Detroit Red Wings
1995-96	Colorado Avalanche	Florida Panthers
1996-97	Detroit Red Wings	Philadelphia Flyers
1997-98	Detroit Red WIngs	Washington Capitals
1998-99	Dallas Stars	Buffalo Sabres
1999-2000	New Jersey Devils	Dallas Stars
2000-2001	Colorado Avalanche	New Jersey Devils
2001-2002	Detroit Red Wings	Carolina Hurricanes
2002-2003	New Jersey Devils	Anaheim Mighty Ducks
2003-2004	Tampa Bay Lightning	Calgary Flames

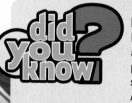

did you know?

NHL LOCKOUT Sadly for hockey fans, the 2004-05 NHL season never reached the ice. Team owners and players could not agree on salary caps for players. The standoff caused the entire season to be scrapped. It was the first time a major sport in North America lost an entire season due to a labor dispute. Hockey was already less popular than football, baseball, and basketball in the U.S. The lost season raised big questions about the NHL's future.

Some All-time NHL Records*

GOALS SCORED
Career: 894, Wayne Gretzky (1979-99)
Season: 92, Wayne Gretzky (1981-82)
Game: 7, Joe Malone (1920)

POINTS
Career: 2,857, Wayne Gretzky (1979-99)
Season: 215, Wayne Gretzky (1985-86)
Game: 10, Darryl Sittler (1976)

GOALIE WINS
Career: 551, Patrick Roy (1984-2003)
Season: 47, Bernie Parent (1973-74)

GOALIE SHUTOUTS
Career: 103, Terry Sawchuk (1949-70)
Season: 22, George Hainsworth (1928-29)

HOCKEY HALL of FAME

The Hockey Hall of Fame in Toronto, Ontario, Canada, was founded in 1943 to honor hockey greats. **WEB SITE** www.hhof.com

WORLD CUP HOCKEY

Canada captured the 2004 World Cup of Hockey with a 3-2 win over Finland. The Canadians became the first team in World Cup history to go 6-0 in the tournament. Vincent Lecavalier won the tournament's Most Valuable Player award after leading Team Canada with seven points.

The OLYMPIC GAMES

The first Olympics were held in Greece more than 2,500 years ago. In 776 B.C. they featured just one event—a footrace. Boxing, wrestling, chariot racing, and the pentathlon (which consisted of five different events) came later. The Olympic Games were held every four years for more than 1,000 years, until A.D. 393, Roman emperor Theodosius stopped them.

2006 WINTER OLYMPICS: *TURIN, ITALY*

NEVE   GLIZ

Turin, Italy, will host 2,500 athletes and over 1.5 million spectators in 2006 at the 20th Winter Games, February10-26. The Olympics began in ancient Greece, and the first modern Games were held in Athens in 1896. The Winter Olympics began in 1924.

The athletes in Turin will represent 85 countries and compete for 84 gold medals in the sports listed below. The 2006 mascots will be Neve and Gliz, which represent snow and ice. The emblem of the Turin Winter Olympics shows an ice crystal silhouette of the Mole Antonelliana, a domed building that symbolizes Turin.

Originally, the winter and summer games were both held every four years. But starting in 1994, the schedule changed. Now the winter and summer games alternate every two years. The next Summer Games will be held in Beijing in 2008, and the next Winter Games will be held in Vancouver, Canada, in 2010.

2006 *WINTER* OLYMPIC SPORTS

Alpine Skiing
Biathlon
Bobsled (bobsleigh)
Cross-country skiing
Curling
Freestyle (skiing)
Figure Skating
Ice Hockey
Luge
Nordic combined
Short track Speed Skating
Ski Jumping
Skeleton
Snowboard
Speed Skating (long track)

SOME **MODERN** OLYMPIC FIRSTS

1896 — **The first modern Olympic Games were held in Athens, Greece.** A total of 312 athletes from 13 nations participated in nine sports.

1900 — **Women competed in the Olympic Games for the first time.**

1908 — **For the first time, medals were awarded to the first three people to finish each event**—a gold for first, a silver for second, and a bronze for third.

1920 — **The Olympic flag was raised for the first time, and the Olympic oath was introduced.** The five interlaced rings of the flag represent: Africa, America, Europe, Asia, and Australia.

1924 — **The first Winter Olympics, featuring skiing and skating events, were held.**

The Olympic flame was introduced at the Olympic Games. A relay of runners carries a torch with the flame from Olympia, Greece, to the site of each Olympics.

1994 — **Starting with the 1994 Winter Olympics, the winter and summer Games have alternated every two years,** instead of being held in the same year, every fourth year.

SPEED SKATING

Speed skating was one of the events at the first ever Winter Olympic Games, held in 1924. It features athletes racing around a frozen track. Sometimes skaters compete against each other, but other times they race against a clock. Skates have existed for a long time. In Sweden, skates from 1000 B.C. have been found. Since then, the invention of metal skates has allowed competitors to practically fly across the ice.

Famous U.S Olympic Speed Skaters

Dan Jansen was the favorite in the 500-meters race in 1988. But during the event, he fell while rounding a turn. In 1994, he made a huge comeback by setting world record time in the 1000 meters race.

Bonnie Blair skated in three Olympic Games. She won five gold medals and holds the record for the most gold medals won by an American woman. She's also the United States's most decorated Winter Olympian.

Chris Witty won two speed skating medals at the Olympics in 2002. She had already been to the Olympics in 2000—for cycling. She's one of only nine people to compete in the summer and winter Olympic Games.

Apolo Anton Ohno didn't begin skating until 1994, when he was 11 years old. By 1997, he was the U.S short track champion. In 2002, he won Olympic gold in the 1500 meters and silver in the 1000 meters. He is expected to skate again at the 2006 games in Turin. (See page 16.)

WHO AM I?

I was named the greatest woman athlete of the first half of the 20th century by an Associated Press poll. That's because I excelled in baseball, basketball, swimming, track and field, and especially golf. I competed in the 1932 Olympics, and not only won but set records for the javelin throw and the 80-meter hurdles.

Answer: "Babe" Didrikson Zaharias

Soccer, also called football outside the U.S., is the number one sport worldwide, played by the most people, and in almost every country. More than 240 million people play organized soccer, according to a 2000 survey done by FIFA (Fédération Internationale de Football Association), the sport's international governing body. That's one out of every 25 people on the planet. The survey also found that more than 20 million women play soccer. The United States was the country with the highest number of regular adult soccer players, with about 18 million, followed by Indonesia (10 million), Mexico (7.4 million), China (7.2 million), Brazil (7 million), and Germany (6.3 million).

THE WORLD CUP

Germany will become the focus of the sporting world June 9 with the kick off of the 2006 Men's World Cup. The month-long tournament is held every four years and remains the world's biggest soccer event. Twelve German cities will host teams from all over the globe. The championship game will be played in Berlin on July 9.

The U.S. team has played in the last four World Cup tournaments, but before 1990, suffered a 40-year drought when it came to qualifying for the World Cup. To win one of the 32 spots in the tournament, the U.S. has to play a series of matches against other Caribbean, North American and Central American teams. The three teams with the best records automatically play in the World Cup. The fourth-place team must square off against an Asian team to win a final spot.

Eddie Johnson

About 3.2 million tickets will be sold for the 2006 matches, and more than 1 billion people are expected to watch matches on television. Scoring sensation Eddie Johnson, 21, hopes to lead the U.S. team to the finals. The Women's World Cup is also held every four years. The next one is scheduled for 2007 in China.

MLS MAJOR LEAGUE SOCCER

D.C. United won its fourth MLS Cup Championship November 14, 2004, with a 3-2 victory over the Kansas City Wizards at the Home Depot Center in Carson, California. It was D.C.'s first title since 1999. Alecko Eskandarian earned the MLS Cup Most Valuable Player award by scoring two of United's three goals within seven minutes. **WEB SITE** *www.mlsnet.com*

did you know?

Sixteen-year-old Freddy Adu (born June 2, 1989) has given a big boost to U.S. soccer and the MLS. The star American player was born in Ghana and signed with the D.C. United team in 2004. D.C.'s win of the MLS Cup that year made him, at 15, the youngest person ever to win a championship on a major U.S. professional team. Freddy played in all 30 regular-season games and helped D.C. United draw an average of 23,686 fans per game. That is more than 8,000 above average attendance for league match-ups.

SPECIAL OLYMPICS

The Special Olympics is the world's largest program of sports training and athletic competition for children and adults with intellectual disabilities. Founded in 1968, Special Olympics has offices in all 50 U.S. states and Washington, D.C., and throughout the world. The organization offers training and competition to nearly 2 million athletes in 150 countries. The Special Olympics holds World Games every two years. These alternate between summer and winter sports. In winter 2005, Nagano, Japan hosted 1,829 athletes from 80 countries in the 8th Special Olympic World Winter Games. The next World Summer Games are scheduled for October 10-19, 2007, in Shanghai, China. In 2006, the U.S. will hold nationwide games for the first time. The Special Olympics USA National Games will take place July 3-8 in Ames, Iowa.

SPECIAL OLYMPICS **OFFICIAL SPORTS**

▶ **Winter:** alpine and cross-country skiing, figure and speed skating, floor hockey, snowshoeing, snowboarding

▶ **Summer:** aquatics (swimming and diving), athletics (track and field), badminton, basketball, bocce, bowling, cycling, equestrian, golf, gymnastics, powerlifting, roller skating, sailing, soccer, softball, tennis, volleyball

WEB SITE www.specialolympics.org

Tennis

Modern tennis began in 1873. It was based on court tennis. In 1877 the first championships were held in Wimbledon, near London. In 1881 the first official U.S. men's championships were held at Newport, Rhode Island. Six years later, the first U.S. women's championships took place, in Philadelphia. The four most important ("grand slam") tournaments today are the Australian Open, the French Open, the All-England (Wimbledon) Championships, and the U.S. Open.

Grand Slam Tournaments

ALL-TIME **GRAND SLAM** SINGLES WINNERS

MEN	Australian	French	Wimbledon	U.S.	Total
Pete Sampras (b. 1971)	2	0	7	5	14
Roy Emerson (b. 1936)	6	2	2	2	12
Bjorn Borg (b. 1956)	0	6	5	0	11
Rod Laver (b. 1938)	3	2	4	2	11
Bill Tilden (1893-1953)	*	0	3	7	10
WOMEN					
Margaret Smith-Court (b. 1942)	11	5	3	5	24
Steffi Graf (b. 1969)	4	6	7	5	22
Helen Wills Moody (1905-1998)	*	4	8	7	19
Chris Evert (b. 1954)	2	7	3	6	18
Martina Navratilova (b. 1956)	3	2	9	4	18

*Never played in tournament.

XGAMES

The X Games, founded by ESPN television executive Ron Semiao, were first held in June 1995 in Newport, Rhode Island. They originally featured skateboarding and BMX biking events. Considered the Olympics of action sports, the X Games include both summer and winter competitions, each held annually in the United States. Star athletes include skateboarder Paul Rodriguez Jr, super motocross champion Jeremy McGrath, and BMX (bicycle) freestyler Dave Mirra.

2004 WINTER X GAMES
About 230 athletes from all over the world competed in the ninth annual Winter X Games, held January 29 to February 1 at Aspen and Snowmass in Colorado. Events included Snowboarding, Skiing, Snowmobiling, and the Moto X (off-road motorcycling). Among the highlights: Blair Morgan dominated the men's Snocross racing to win his fourth gold medal; nineteen-year-old Sanna Tindstrom became the game's youngest gold medalist by winning the women's Skier X speed skiing.

SUMMER X GAMES
The Summer X Games, held every year since 1995, feature competitions in such events as In-line Skating, Bike Stunt, Downhill BMX, Moto X (off-road motorcycling), Skateboard, Surfing, and Wakeboard. The 11th X Games were set to be held in August 2005 in Los Angeles, California. **WEB SITE** *http://expn.go.com*

X GAMES GLOBAL CHAMPIONSHIP
The first-ever Global X Games were held in May 2003. This team event featured six world regions competing against each other in both summer and winter action sports. The summer sports were contested in San Antonio, Texas. The winter events were held in Whistler Blackcomb, British Columbia, Canada. In all, six sports and 11 events were featured, with a total of 126 athletes competing (21 per team). Team USA took home the gold with a total of 196 points, beating Team Europe (167 points) and Team Australia (142).

Paul Rodriguez Jr. got his first skateboard when he was six years old. Thirteen years later, in August 2004, he claimed his first skateboarding gold medal in the Summer X Games. "P Rod," as he's called, is also the son of comedian and actor Paul Rodriguez Sr.

did you know?

X-Fact-ors

- ◄ X BMX rider Dave Mirra holds the record for the most X Games medals, with 18.

- X Brian Deegan set a Winter X Games record by winning Moto X Best Trick for the second time in 2005 (he also won in 2003) with a mid-blizzard no-footed flip. It's his 10th career medal.

- X At the 2004 Summer X Games, Elissa Streamer became the first woman to win a gold medal in Skateboard Street—the first street event women were invited to attend.

- X Jeremy McGrath became the new champion of Moto X Step Up at the 2004 Summer X Games. He beat defending champ Matt Buyten, but only after Matt dislocated his shoulder and popped it back in himself—twice—during the competition.

Sportswriter

Chip Towers, sportswriter for the *Atlanta Journal Constitution*

Q: **Did you think you would be a sportswriter when you grew up?**
I grew up thinking I was going to be a professional football player. It wasn't until late in high school, when I was 5-feet, 7 inches tall, weighed about 140 pounds, and was about to be cut from the varsity football team, that I realized a professional sports career probably wasn't going to work out. My high school English teacher, Mrs. Zimmerman, suggested that I consider a career in writing. I don't think it really occurred to me before then.

Q: **What got you interested in working for a newspaper?**
First of all, I always enjoyed reading the newspaper, especially the sports section. I was a big Atlanta Braves fan growing up and always looked forward to reading articles about them. I particularly enjoyed reading the columnists, such as Lewis Grizzard and Dave Kindred.

After I started college, I decided write for the school newspaper. That's when I really got excited about the business. As we newspaper enthusiasts say, "The ink gets in your blood."

Q: **What do you do on a typical day?**
A newspaper comes out *every day*. So you always have to plan for the next story you need to work on. Most reporters are assigned "beats" that we cover. My current "beat" is the University of Georgia Bulldogs. I have to make sure I know everything there is to know about the Bulldogs. So I go to practices, talk to players and coaches, and do interviews almost every day.

Q: **What kind of special training did you need for your job?**
Being able to read and write well is important, but there is no better preparation for this job than doing it. Working at my college newspaper, *The Red and Black*, taught me the realities of having to write a story quickly and the importance of meeting a deadline.

Q: **What do you like best about your job?**
I enjoy covering the games more than anything. There is nothing like going to work where there are 90,000 spectators, television cameras, and two teams, all awaiting a much-anticipated and unknown outcome. Meeting stars is another enjoyable aspect of the job. Even though you must maintain a professional attitude, it is still exciting interviewing Michael Vick or Tiger Woods or Barry Bonds.

Sports Word Search

```
F A H A J L N W C A N A A S U P E R B O W L A E A A Q
C O G C Z C J C V C J R C U C N C C C R O P C O C C U
A F O F R F P F G F P M F N F L S F J Q R N F N F F A
G R A T G A W E K D G S G J G Q D G G B L C G B C G R
K Z L K B K E K S K A T E B O A R D K A D T K A H K T
I L E R I A O I T T O R I G I I D B I F S I I F A I E
T E N N I S L N R H N O B E N P N A N N E P N Q M N R
R L M L A L O L I L T N L O T L A F L L R L L X P L B
A P H P T M E P K P L G D P R E P T P B I E P T I P A
Q X P L C Q O Q E Q Q P O Q N O Q D R A E A D R O Q C
X Q M J H L N X O U O O L X B N E F X I S Z B S N F K
D B D N E D L O U D T X Y D A L D B D N O O D D O D T
A X A W R A V N T A R D M A F B R A D Y A T A A N X R
H O M E R U N L Y E Q A P E E A E M F E N N S E L E K
Y N F F E Y E Q L Y B E I Y K E A B N Y J G Y Y Q Y B
L L A V I N A T I E R I C G L D L I L D P T U R I N I
O O O O F O L O U O F L S O O L O N E O G Y O M O O C
G U C U A I O U B U L O A D U B U O U U T E U H U A Y
B F A K B B E B Z L J U J B V A B B R B O E B P A B C
Z L Z Z O Z A L A Z P B U N Z T E Z O Z U S Z I Z A L
X N X B X U X B D X G Z M J X T N X B X C Z X T O X E
G M A O M M T M Y G E X P P M E C M A M H K M C K M G
O Y R O Y E Y Y R Y O Y E E Y R P Y F Y D P Y H Y P O
N R R R K R R A E R T A R O R R G R N R O O R E R R C
E E M S E B A E Q M V W L S E E D J E L W T E R Y E O
T Q A Q G O L F K T O U R N A M E N T O N A Q O O L S
K B C K T P A H O C K E Y E K M K K S Z K W K N R I D
```

ARMSTRONG	GOLF	RED SOX
BAMBINO	HOCKEY	SKATEBOARD
BASKETBALL	HOME RUN	STRIKEOUT
BATTER	JUMPER	SUPER BOWL
BICYCLE	LOCKOUT	TENNIS
BRADY	NET	TOUCHDOWN
CHAMPION	OLYMPICS	TOURNAMENT
FIELD GOAL	PATRIOTS	TURIN
FOOTBALL	PITCHER	WORLD SERIES
GOAL	QUARTERBACK	VINATIERI

ANSWERS ON PAGES 335-338.
FOR MORE PUZZLES GO TO
WWW.WORLDALMANACFORKIDS.COM

Transportation

What city had the first subway in the U.S.? page 252

Getting from There to Here
A SHORT HISTORY OF TRANSPORTATION

5000 B.C.
People harness animal-muscle power. Oxen and donkeys carry heavy loads.

3500 B.C.
Egyptians create the first sailboat. Before this, people made rafts or canoes and paddled them with poles or their hands.

983
First locks to raise water level are built on China's Grand Canal. By 1400, a 1,500-mile water highway system was developed.

1450s
Portuguese build fast ships with three masts. These plus the compass usher in an age of exploration.

1681
France's 150-mile Canal du Midi connects the Atlantic with the Mediterranean Sea.

5000 B.C.

3500 B.C.
In Mesopotamia (modern-day Iraq), people invent vehicles with wheels. But the first wheels are made of heavy wood, and the roads are terrible.

800
Fast, shallow-draft longships make Vikings a powerful force in Europe from 800 to 1100.

Around 1000
Using magnetic compasses, Chinese are able to sail long distances in flat-bottomed ships called junks.

1660s
Horse-drawn stagecoaches begin running in France. They stop at stages to switch horses and passengers—the first mass transit system.

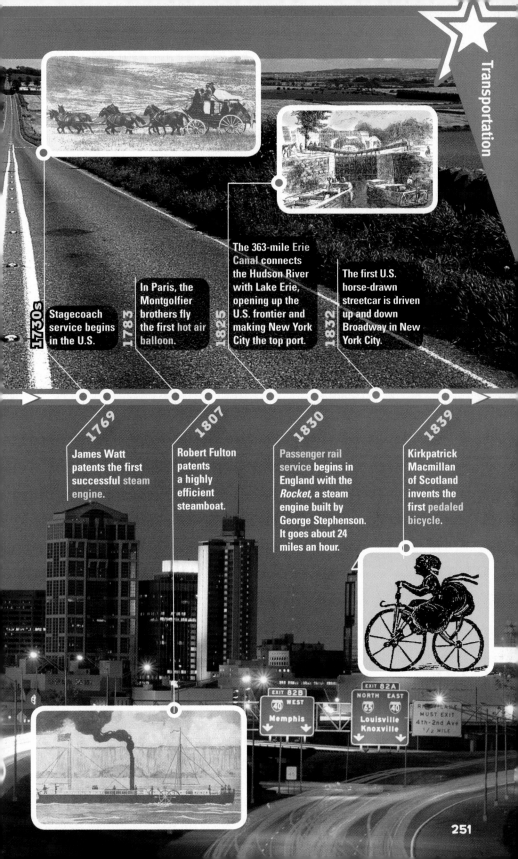

1730s Stagecoach service begins in the U.S.

1783 In Paris, the Montgolfier brothers fly the first hot air balloon.

1825 The 363-mile Erie Canal connects the Hudson River with Lake Erie, opening up the U.S. frontier and making New York City the top port.

1832 The first U.S. horse-drawn streetcar is driven up and down Broadway in New York City.

1769 James Watt patents the first successful steam engine.

1807 Robert Fulton patents a highly efficient steamboat.

1830 Passenger rail service begins in England with the *Rocket*, a steam engine built by George Stephenson. It goes about 24 miles an hour.

1839 Kirkpatrick Macmillan of Scotland invents the first pedaled bicycle.

251

Etienne Lenoir of Belgium builds the first car with an internal-combustion engine.

1862

Transcontinental railroad is completed at Promontory Point, Utah. The Suez Canal opens, saving ships a long trip around Africa.

1869

First practical electric street railway system opens in Richmond, Virginia. Suburbs soon grow around cities as trolley systems let people live farther away from the workplace.

1887

Henry Ford builds the first Model T, a practical car for the general public.

1908

1860s

1863

1873

1897

1903

Paddle-wheel steamboats dominate U.S. river travel.

Using steam locomotives, the London subway (known as the "tube") opens.

San Francisco's cable car system begins service.

The first U.S. subway service begins in Boston. New York City follows in 1904.

At Kitty Hawk, North Carolina, the Wright brothers fly the first powered heavier-than-air machine.

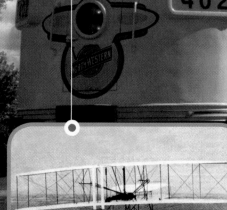

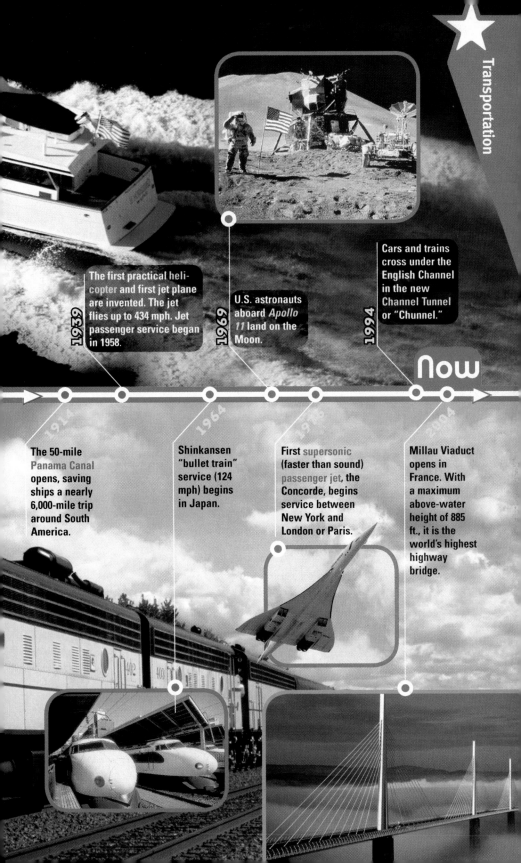

1939
The first practical helicopter and first jet plane are invented. The jet flies up to 434 mph. Jet passenger service began in 1958.

1969
U.S. astronauts aboard *Apollo 11* land on the Moon.

1994
Cars and trains cross under the English Channel in the new Channel Tunnel or "Chunnel."

Now

1914
The 50-mile Panama Canal opens, saving ships a nearly 6,000-mile trip around South America.

1964
Shinkansen "bullet train" service (124 mph) begins in Japan.

1976
First supersonic (faster than sound) passenger jet, the Concorde, begins service between New York and London or Paris.

2004
Millau Viaduct opens in France. With a maximum above-water height of 885 ft., it is the world's highest highway bridge.

WHY IS IT 4 A.M. IN LOS ANGELES WHEN IT'S 7 A.M. IN NEW YORK?

When the sun rises on the east coast, it's still dark in the central states, and the farther west you go, the farther away you are from daybreak. Before the mid-1800s, traveling east or west was so slow that it was possible to use the local time set by each city. But when the railroads came, people could travel hundreds of miles in a day. Organizing a schedule using many different times was nearly impossible. No one could ever agree what time it was! Railroads had to have a system of standard time and time zones. The familiar time zones of Eastern, Central, Mountain, and Pacific were adopted by railroads in the U.S. and Canada in 1883.

Next, 24 international time zones— one for each hour of the day—were established. These begin at the prime meridian, the longitude line passing through Greenwich, England. Halfway around the world, in the Pacific Ocean, is the International Date Line, which roughly follows the 180th meridian and is in the 12th time zone. Cross the line going west, and it's tomorrow. Cross going east, the date is one day earlier.

Pacific Standard Time Mountain Standard Time Central Standard Time Eastern Standard Time Alaska Standard Time Hawaii-Aleutian Standard Time

HOW LONG DID IT TAKE?

What would people from the 1600s, or the 1800s, think if they could come back and look at the world today? They would get lots of surprises. One surprise would be how fast people can travel to distant places.

1911 — The first transcontinental airplane trip, from New York City to Pasadena, California, by C.P. Rodgers, in 82 hours and 4 minutes, air time, over a period of 49 days.

1927 — Charles Lindbergh flew from New York to Paris in 33½ hours. It was the first nonstop flight made across the Atlantic by one person.

1969 — *Apollo 11* took just under four days to reach the moon (about 70 times the distance from London to New York).

1981 — At a speed of about 17,500 miles per hour, space shuttle *Columbia* circled the globe in 90 minutes.

1990 — A U.S. Air Force SR-71 "Blackbird" flew coast-to-coast in 1 hour, 4 minutes, and 20 seconds (at an average speed of 2,124 miles per hour).

1995 — Two Air Force B-1B bombers flew around the world nonstop (refueling in flight) in 36 hours and 13 minutes.

1996 — A British Airways Concorde passenger jet flew from New York to London in 2 hours, 53 minutes.

1999 — Bertrand Piccard and Brian Jones completed the first around-the-world balloon flight in the *Breitling Orbiter 3*. It took 19 days, 21 hours, 55 minutes.

2001 — Steve Fossett sailed across the Atlantic from New York to Cornwall, England. It took 4 days, 17 hours, 28 minutes.

2005 — Steve Fossett became the first person to make a nonstop solo flight around the world without refueling. The trip took 67 hours.

Where is the world's fastest roller coaster? page 259

ROAD TRIP

Wherever you are, there is likely to be a festival, amusement park, historic site, or national park just a short drive away (see pages 256-259). A road trip—short or long—can be lots of fun, with plenty of interesting sights along the way.

The first cross-country drive was made in 1903. H. Nelson Jackson and Sewall K. Crocker (and a bulldog named Bud) drove from California to New York in an early car known as a Winton. There were few roads or bridges in the West, and lots of mud everywhere. The whole trip took 63 days and cost $8,000, including the price of the car. In 1909, Alice Huyler Ramsey became the first woman to drive across the U.S. Her trip from New York to San Francisco took 59 days.

By 1930, there were 23 million cars on the road. More than half of American families owned one. Today in the U.S. there are more cars than licensed drivers. People wanted to see things and go places—especially west. The first coast-to-coast highway was the Lincoln Highway, finished by 1930. The most famous highway was Route 66, completed in 1926, connecting Chicago to Los Angeles. Now called "Historic Route 66," it still has billboards and giant statues advertising its famous hotels, attractions, and restaurants.

A ROADSIDE SAMPLER:
Just a few of the millions of sights across the U.S.!

Carhenge It's not Stonehenge, the famous English monument, but it looks a little like it. Located in Alliance, Nebraska, Carhenge was built by artist Jim Reinders in 1987, out of 38 vintage automobiles. The cars stand like the ancient stones, in a circle 96 feet in diameter.

Corn Palace This huge concrete building in Mitchell, South Dakota, is covered with murals made of corn and other types of grains and grasses. No corny jokes please—they've heard them all here.

Lucy the Elephant She's 115 years old this year. But don't look for her at the zoo. This 90-ton elephant was built out of wood in 1881, and stands 65 feet tall near the beach in Margate, New Jersey.

Winchester Mystery House This spooky, sprawling mansion in San Jose, California, has 160 rooms, 950 doors, and 10,000 windows. Staricases lead into ceilings, windows cut into floors, and one door opens onto an 8-foot drop into a kitchen sink.

Word's Largest Ball of Twine If wacky is your thing, maybe you can get to check out this 18,000-pound ball of twine in Cawker City, Kansas. If you stretched it all out, it would be over 1,300 miles long.

NATIONAL PARKS

The world's first national park was Yellowstone, established in 1872. Today, there are 57 national parks, including one in the Virgin Islands and one in American Samoa. The National Park Service oversees 388 areas in all, also including national monuments, battlefields, military parks, historic parks, historic sites, lakeshores, seashores, recreation areas, scenic rivers and trails, and the White House—84.4 million acres all told! For more information, you can write the National Park Service, Department of the Interior, 1849 C Street NW, Washington, D.C. 20240.

WEB SITE For information on-line, go to http://www.nps.gov/parks.html

ACADIA NATIONAL PARK

In 1913, President Woodrow Wilson set aside 6,000 acres for the park we know today as Acadia. It is the oldest national park east of the Mississippi River. More than two million people visit Acadia each year. The park covers 47,000 acres of the coast of Maine, and includes over 30,000 acres of Mount Desert Island. This wild and rocky coast is a great place to hike and see wildlife. There are 120 miles of hiking trails and 45 miles of gravel trails for bike riding. Moose and bear live there, but you aren't likely to see either. However, on a boat trip to nearby islands you can see seals or black and white puffins. Puffins are distant cousins of the penguins that can swim fast and, unlike penguins, can also fly.

GRAND CANYON NATIONAL PARK

This national park, established in 1919, has one of the world's most spectacular landscapes, covering more than a million acres in northwestern Arizona. The canyon is 6,000 feet deep at its deepest point and 15 miles wide at its widest. Most of the 40 identified rock layers that form the canyon's 277-mile-long wall are exposed, offering a detailed look at the earth's geologic history. The walls display a cross section of the earth's crust from as far back as two billion years ago. The Colorado River—which carved out the giant canyon—still runs through the park, which is a valuable wildlife preserve with many rare, endangered animals. The pine and fir forests, painted deserts, plateaus, caves, and sandstone canyons offer a wide range of habitats.

PETRIFIED FOREST NATIONAL PARK

In northeast Arizona you'll find one of the world's biggest collections of petrified wood—trees that have turned to stone over millions of years. Some of these fossilized logs are 6 feet in diameter and more than 100 feet long. The Painted Desert is also part of this park. This area of rough "badlands" is dry and filled with canyons and flat-topped rock formations called mesas, from the Spanish word for "table." The rocks of the Painted Desert date back to the Triassic Period of 225 to 195 million years ago. The colorful sandstone and mudstone layers are the result of minerals—iron, manganese, and carbon—that formed in the sediment. At least 16 varieties of lizards and snakes make their home in the park's 93,533 acres. The climate can be extreme there, with violent thunderstorms common in the summer.

SHENANDOAH NATIONAL PARK

You are very likely to see a black bear and plenty of deer—maybe even a fox or a wild turkey—in the 200,000 acres of Shenandoah National Park in western Virginia. The area that became the park was a favorite spot of President Hoover, who had his summer White House in the mountains. The famous Skyline Drive runs from Front Royal, Virginia, to the Virginia/North Carolina border. This 105-mile drive along the spine of the Blue Ridge Mountains offers some of the best scenery in the east, especially overlooking the historic Shenandoah Valley. More than a million visitors a year come to the park, many of them in the fall to see the leaves change color. The Appalachian Trail runs 101 miles along the length of the park, and there are some 500 miles of trails all together.

YELLOWSTONE NATIONAL PARK

Located mostly in northwestern Wyoming, partly in eastern Idaho and southwestern Montana, Yellowstone is known for its 10,000 hot springs and geysers—more than anyplace else in the world. Old Faithful, the most famous geyser, erupts for about four minutes every one to two hours, shooting 3,700-8,400 gallons of hot water as high as 185 feet. Other geysers include the Giant, which shoots a column of hot water 200 feet high, and the Giantess, which erupts for over four hours at a time, but only about twice a year. There are grizzly bears, wolves, elk, moose, buffalo, deer, beavers, coyotes, antelopes, and 300 species of birds. The use of snowmobiles in the park has been a big controversy. Some people want to ban them because of noise and air pollution; others disagree. They are allowed now, though their use is somewhat limited.

...ark visitors watch ...ld Faithful erupt.

UNNATURAL WONDERS:
Big City Destinations

You can have fun and learn about different cultures by visiting cities around the world as well as in the U.S. Each city has its own flavor of food, art, architecture, history, and more.

NEW YORK

NEW YORK, NEW YORK Take the elevator to the top of the **Empire State Building** for a bird's-eye view of this huge city. See the dinosaurs at the **Museum of Natural History**. Pet the real live zoo animals in **Central Park** and ride on the carousel. And don't forget the ferry to the **Statue of Liberty** and **Ellis Island**.

LONDON, ENGLAND See the **Tower of London**, a royal fortress that has stood on the banks of the Thames River for over 900 years. It houses the crown jewels, and there is a museum of arms and armor. See all of London from the **Eye**, a 443-foot-high ferris wheel.

LONDON

PHILADELPHIA, PENNSYLVANIA Visit **Independence Hall**, where the Declaration of Independence was adopted and the U.S. Constitution was drafted. Spend time in the **Franklin Institute Science Museum**. And don't forget to have a **"Philly Cheesesteak"** sandwich.

PHILADELPHIA

PARIS, FRANCE A short walk from the medieval cathedral of **Notre Dame** are the lively cafés on the **Left Bank** of the River Seine. After climbing the steps of Sacre Coeur in hilly **Montmartre**, enjoy a boat ride along the **Seine**, or visit the **Eiffel Tower** and get a bird's-eye view of where you've been.

PARIS

NEW ORLEANS, LOUISIANA Settled by the French in 1718, this city on the Mississippi became part of the U.S. with the Louisiana Purchase of 1803. It's world-famous for jazz music, **Mardi Gras**, and foods like **jambalaya** and shrimp gumbo.

NEW ORLEANS

ROME, ITALY Along with the famous **Trevi Fountain**, you'll want to see the **Colosseum** and other historic Roman ruins. At the Vatican, don't miss the **Sistine Chapel**, painted by Michelangelo from 1508 to 1512.

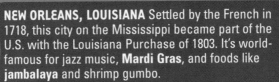

ROME

SAN FRANCISCO, CALIFORNIA Ride the famous cable cars. Tour an old prison on **Alcatraz Island**. See the **Golden Gate Bridge**. And maybe visit the **Ghirardelli Chocolate Factory**! Enjoy the street performers at **Fisherman's Wharf**, where you can also eat seafood and watch the boats on the bay.

SAN FRANCISCO

BEJING

BEIJING, CHINA Dog statues guard the entrance to the **"Forbidden City."** For 500 years only the emperors and persons connected with them were allowed inside. It's the Palace Museum now, open to all. In 2008, the Summer Olympics will be held in China for the first time.

The first amusement parks appeared in Europe over 400 years ago. Attractions included flower gardens, bowling, music, and a few simple rides.

The first real roller coaster in the U.S. was the Switchback Gravity Pleasure Railway. It opened in Brooklyn's Coney Island in 1884 and went all of 6 miles per hour! In 1893, the **George Ferris Great Wheel** was introduced in Chicago. The "Ferris" Wheel weighed over 4 million pounds and stood 264 feet high. It had 36 cars that could hold 60 people each! It revolved about 4 times per hour.

In the 1920s, some of the best **roller coasters** of all time were built—reaching speeds of 60 mph. The Great Depression in the 1930s caused many to close. But nowadays there are plenty of roller coasters that are faster and bigger than ever.

Fabulous Facts

Biggest park: Walt Disney World, Lake Buena Vista, Florida, 28,000 acres

Most rides: 68, Cedar Point, Sandusky, Ohio

Most roller coasters: 16, Cedar Point, Sandusky, Ohio, and Six Flags Magic Mountain, Valencia, California

Oldest Ferris wheel: Wonderland, Gaultier, Mississippi (It opened at Palace Amusements in New Jersey in 1895 and moved to Wonderland in 1990.)

Tallest observation wheel: 443 feet, London Eye (also known as the Millennium Wheel), London, England

WORLD'S FASTEST ROLLER COASTERS*

1. **Kindga Ka:** 128 mph, Jackson, New Jersey
2. **Top Thrill Dragster:** 120 mph, Sandusky, Ohio
3. **Dodonpa:** 107 mph, FujiYoshida-shi, Japan
4. **Superman: The Escape:** 100 mph, Valencia, California
   Tower of Terror: 100 mph, Gold Coast, Australia
5. **Steel Dragon 2000:** 95 mph, Mie, Japan

WORLD'S TALLEST ROLLER COASTERS*

1. **Kindga Ka:** 456 ft, Jackson, New Jersey
2. **Top Thrill Dragster:** 420 ft, Sandusky, Ohio
3. **Superman: The Escape:** 415 ft, Valencia, California
4. **Tower of Terror:** 377 ft, Gold Coast, Australia
5. **Steel Dragon 2000:** 318 ft, Mie, Japan

* Rankings as of early 2005

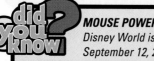

MOUSE POWER. *Hong Kong Disney World is set to open on September 12, 2005. It will be the fifth Disney theme park in the world and the third outside the U.S. Disney also has parks in Paris (Disneyland Paris) and Tokyo (Tokyo Disneyland).*

Kinda Ka reaches top speed 3.5 seconds after the ride begins.

United States

Which state was the last to enter the Union in the 1800s? page 306

FACTS & FIGURES

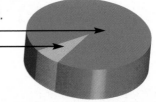

AREA 50 states and Washington, D.C.

LAND	3,537,437	square miles
WATER	181,272	square miles
TOTAL	3,718,709	square miles

POPULATION (MID-2005):
295,734,134

CAPITAL:
Washington, D.C.

LARGEST, HIGHEST, AND OTHER STATISTICS

Sears Tower

Largest state: Alaska (663,267 square miles)
Smallest state: Rhode Island (1,545 square miles)
Northernmost city: Barrow, Alaska (71°17′ north latitude)
Southernmost city: Hilo, Hawaii (19°44′ north latitude)
Easternmost city: Eastport, Maine (66°59′05″ west longitude)
Westernmost city: Atka, Alaska (174°12′ west longitude)
Highest settlement: Climax, Colorado (11,360 feet)
Lowest settlement: Calipatria, California (184 feet below sea level)
Oldest national park: Yellowstone National Park (Idaho, Montana, Wyoming), 2,219,791 acres, established 1872
Largest national park: Wrangell-St. Elias, Alaska (8,323,148 acres)
Longest river system: Mississippi-Missouri-Red Rock (3,710 miles)
Deepest lake: Crater Lake, Oregon (1,932 feet)
Highest mountain: Mount McKinley, Alaska (20,320 feet)
Lowest point: Death Valley, California (282 feet below sea level)
Tallest building: Sears Tower, Chicago, Illinois (1,450 feet)
Tallest structure: TV tower, Blanchard, North Dakota (2,063 feet)
Longest bridge span: Verrazano-Narrows Bridge, New York (4,260 feet)
Highest bridge: Royal Gorge, Colorado (1,053 feet above water)

INTERNATIONAL BOUNDARY LINES OF THE U.S.

U.S.-Canadian border . . . . 3,987 miles
(excluding Alaska)
Alaska-Canadian border . . . . . 1,538 miles
U.S.-Mexican border . . . . 1,933 miles
(Gulf of Mexico to Pacific Ocean)

Atlantic coast . . . . 2,069 miles
Gulf of Mexico coast . . . . 1,631 miles
Pacific coast . . . . 7,623 miles
Arctic coast, Alaska . . . . 1,060 miles

MAPMAKING ODDITY *On many maps, the top of Maine looks like the northernmost point in the U.S. outside of Alaska. But that's an optical illusion. No part of the lower 48 states is above 49 degrees of latitude except a "bubble" on the Minnesota/Canada border. That's the Northwest Angle, a 130-square mile peninsula that juts out eastward from the Canadian province of Manitoba into a lake. It's surrounded by Canadian territory, and belongs to the U.S. because of an error by mapmakers.*

The **Great Seal**

The Great Seal of the United States shows an American bald eagle with a ribbon in its mouth bearing the Latin words *e pluribus unum* (out of many, one). In its talons are the arrows of war and an olive branch of peace. On the back of the Great Seal is an unfinished pyramid with an eye (the eye of Providence) above it. The seal was approved by Congress on June 20, 1782.

THE **FLAG**

1777

1795

1818

The flag of the United States has 50 stars (one for each state) and 13 stripes (one for each of the original 13 states). It is unofficially called the "Stars and Stripes."

The first U.S. flag was commissioned by the Second Continental Congress in 1777 but did not exist until 1783, after the American Revolution. Historians are not certain who designed the Stars and Stripes. Many different flags are believed to have been used during the American Revolution.

The flag of 1777 was used until 1795. In that year Congress passed an act ordering that a new flag have 15 stripes, alternate red and white, and 15 stars on a blue field. In 1818, Congress directed that the flag have 13 stripes and that a new star be added for each new state of the Union. The last star was added in 1960 for the state of Hawaii.

There are many customs for flying the flag and treating it with respect. For example, it should not touch the floor and no other flag should be flown above it, except for the UN flag at UN head-quarters. When the flag is raised or lowered, or passes in a parade, or during the Pledge of Allegiance, people should face it and stand at attention. Those in military uniform should salute. Others should put their right hand over their heart. The flag is flown at half staff as a sign of mourning.

Pledge of Allegiance to the Flag

"I pledge allegiance to the flag of the United States of America and to the republic for which it stands, one nation under God, indivisible, with liberty and justice for all."

THE NATIONAL ANTHEM

"The Star-Spangled Banner" was a poem written in 1814 by Francis Scott Key as he watched British ships bombard Fort McHenry, Maryland, during the War of 1812. It became the National Anthem by an act of Congress in 1931. The music to "The Star-Spangled Banner" was originally a tune called "Anacreon in Heaven."

THE U.S. CONSTITUTION

The Foundation *of* American Government

The Constitution is the document that created the present government of the United States. It was written in 1787 and went into effect in 1789. It establishes the three branches of the U.S. government — the executive (headed by the president), the legislative (Congress), and the judicial (the Supreme Court and other federal courts). The first 10 amendments to the Constitution (the **Bill of Rights**) explain the basic rights of all American citizens.

You can find the constitution on-line at:

WEB SITE http://www.house.gov/Constitution/Constitution.html

The **Preamble** *to the* **Constitution**

The Constitution begins with a short statement called the Preamble. The Preamble states that the government of the United States was established by the people.

"We the people of the United States, in order to form a more perfect union, establish justice, insure domestic tranquility, provide for the common defense, promote the general welfare, and secure the blessings of liberty to ourselves and our posterity, do ordain and establish this Constitution for the United States of America."

THE ARTICLES

The original Constitution contained seven articles. The first three articles of the Constitution establish the three branches of the U.S. government.

Article 1, Legislative Branch Creates the Senate and House of Representatives and describes their functions and powers.

Article 2, Executive Branch Creates the office of the President and the Electoral College and lists their powers and responsibilities.

Article 3, Judicial Branch Creates the Supreme Court and gives Congress the power to create lower courts. The powers of the courts and certain crimes are defined.

Article 4, The States Discusses the relationship of the states to one another and to the citizens. Defines the states' powers.

Article 5, Amending the Constitution Describes how the Constitution can be amended (changed).

Article 6, Federal Law Makes the Constitution the supreme law of the land over state laws and constitutions.

Article 7, Ratifying the Constitution Establishes how to ratify (approve) the Constitution.

Amendments *to the* Constitution

The writers of the Constitution understood that it might need to be amended, or changed, in the future, but they wanted to be careful and made it hard to change. Article 5 describes how the Constitution can be amended.

In order to take effect, an amendment must be approved by a two-thirds majority in both the House of Representatives and the Senate. It must then be approved (ratified) by three-fourths of the states (38 states). So far, there have been 27 amendments. One of them (the 18th, ratified in 1919) banned the manufacture or sale of liquor. It was canceled by the 21st Amendment, in 1933.

The Bill of Rights: *The First Ten Amendments*

The first ten amendments were adopted in 1791 and contain the basic freedoms Americans enjoy as a people. These amendments are known as the Bill of Rights.

1 Guarantees freedom of religion, speech, and the press.

2 Guarantees the right to have firearms.

3 Guarantees that soldiers cannot be lodged in private homes unless the owner agrees.

4 Protects people from being searched or having property searched or taken away by the government without reason.

5 Protects rights of people on trial for crimes.

6 Guarantees people accused of crimes the right to a speedy public trial by jury.

7 Guarantees the right to a trial by jury for other kinds of cases.

8 Prohibits "cruel and unusual punishments."

9 Says specific rights listed in the Constitution do not take away rights that may not be listed.

10 Establishes that any powers not given specifically to the federal government belong to states or the people.

Other Important Amendments

13 (1865): Ends slavery in the United States.

14 (1868): Bars states from denying rights to citizens; guarantees equal protection under the law for all citizens.

15 (1870): Guarantees that a person cannot be denied the right to vote because of race or color.

19 (1920): Gives women the right to vote.

22 (1951): Limits the president to two four-year terms of office.

24 (1964): Outlaws the poll tax (a tax people had to pay before they could vote) in federal elections. (The poll tax had been used to keep African Americans in the South from voting.)

25 (1967): Specifies presidential succession; also gives the president the power to appoint a new vice president, if one dies or leaves office in the middle of a term.

26 (1971): Lowers the voting age to 18 from 21.

The **Executive** Branch

The **executive branch** of the federal government is headed by the president, who enforces the laws passed by Congress and is commander in chief of the U.S. armed forces. It also includes the vice president, people who work for the president or vice president, the major departments of the government, and special agencies. The **cabinet** is made up of the vice president, heads of major departments, and other officials. It meets when the president chooses. The chart at right shows cabinet departments in the order in which they were created. The Department of Homeland Security was created by a law signed in November 2002.

PRESIDENT

VICE PRESIDENT

CABINET DEPARTMENTS

1. State
2. Treasury
3. Defense
4. Justice
5. Interior
6. Agriculture
7. Commerce
8. Labor
9. Housing and Urban Development
10. Transportation
11. Energy
12. Education
13. Health and Human Services
14. Veterans Affairs
15. Homeland Security

HOW LONG DOES THE **PRESIDENT SERVE**?

The president serves a four-year term, starting on January 20. No president can be elected more than twice, or more than once if he or she had served two years as president filling out the term of a president who left office.

WHAT HAPPENS IF THE **PRESIDENT DIES?**

If the president dies in office or cannot complete the term, the vice president becomes president. If the president is unable to perform his or her duties, the vice president can become acting president. The next person to become president after the vice president would be the Speaker of the House of Representatives.

The White House has an address on the World Wide Web especially for kids. It is:

WEB SITE http://www.whitehousekids.gov

You can send e-mail to the president at:

EMAIL president@whitehouse.gov

The White House, home of the U.S. president

PRESIDENTS AND VICE PRESIDENTS OF THE UNITED STATES

PRESIDENT / VICE PRESIDENT	YEARS IN OFFICE
1 George Washington	**1789–1797**
John Adams	1789–1797
2 John Adams	**1797–1801**
Thomas Jefferson	1797–1801
3 Thomas Jefferson	**1801–1809**
Aaron Burr	1801–1805
George Clinton	1805–1809
4 James Madison	**1809–1817**
George Clinton	1809–1812
Elbridge Gerry	1813–1814
5 James Monroe	**1817–1825**
Daniel D. Tompkins	1817–1825
6 John Quincy Adams	**1825–1829**
John C. Calhoun	1825–1829
7 Andrew Jackson	**1829–1837**
John C. Calhoun	1829–1832
Martin Van Buren	1833–1837
8 Martin Van Buren	**1837–1841**
Richard M. Johnson	1837–1841
9 William H. Harrison	**1841**
John Tyler	1841
10 John Tyler	**1841–1845**
No Vice President	
11 James Knox Polk	**1845–1849**
George M. Dallas	1845–1849
12 Zachary Taylor	**1849–1850**
Millard Fillmore	1849–1850
13 Millard Fillmore	**1850–1853**
No Vice President	
14 Franklin Pierce	**1853–1857**
William R. King	1853
15 James Buchanan	**1857–1861**
John C. Breckinridge	1857–1861
16 Abraham Lincoln	**1861–1865**
Hannibal Hamlin	1861–1865
Andrew Johnson	1865
17 Andrew Johnson	**1865–1869**
No Vice President	
18 Ulysses S. Grant	**1869–1877**
Schuyler Colfax	1869–1873
Henry Wilson	1873–1875
19 Rutherford B. Hayes	**1877–1881**
William A. Wheeler	1877–1881
20 James A. Garfield	**1881**
Chester A. Arthur	1881
21 Chester A. Arthur	**1881–1885**
No Vice President	
22 Grover Cleveland	**1885–1889**
Thomas A. Hendricks	1885
23 Benjamin Harrison	**1889–1893**
Levi P. Morton	1889–1893
24 Grover Cleveland	**1893–1897**
Adlai E. Stevenson	1893–1897
25 William McKinley	**1897–1901**
Garret A. Hobart	1897–1899
Theodore Roosevelt	1901
26 Theodore Roosevelt	**1901–1909**
Charles W. Fairbanks	1905–1909
27 William Howard Taft	**1909–1913**
James S. Sherman	1909–1912
28 Woodrow Wilson	**1913–1921**
Thomas R. Marshall	1913–1921
29 Warren G. Harding	**1921–1923**
Calvin Coolidge	1921–1923
30 Calvin Coolidge	**1923–1929**
Charles G. Dawes	1925–1929
31 Herbert Hoover	**1929–1933**
Charles Curtis	1929–1933
32 Franklin D. Roosevelt	**1933–1945**
John Nance Garner	1933–1941
Henry A. Wallace	1941–1945
Harry S. Truman	1945
33 Harry S. Truman	**1945–1953**
Alben W. Barkley	1949–1953
34 Dwight D. Eisenhower	**1953–1961**
Richard M. Nixon	1953–1961
35 John F. Kennedy	**1961–1963**
Lyndon B. Johnson	1961–1963
36 Lyndon B. Johnson	**1963–1969**
Hubert H. Humphrey	1965–1969
37 Richard M. Nixon	**1969–1974**
Spiro T. Agnew	1969–1973
Gerald R. Ford	1973–1974
38 Gerald R. Ford	**1974–1977**
Nelson A. Rockefeller	1974–1977
39 Jimmy Carter	**1977–1981**
Walter F. Mondale	1977–1981
40 Ronald Reagan	**1981–1989**
George H. W. Bush	1981–1989
41 George H. W. Bush	**1989–1993**
Dan Quayle	1989–1993
42 Bill Clinton	**1993–2001**
Al Gore	1993–2001
43 George W. Bush	**2001–**
Richard B. Cheney	2001–

United States

The **Legislative** Branch

CONGRESS

The Congress of the United States is the legislative branch of the federal government. Congress's major responsibility is to pass the laws that govern the country and determine how money collected in taxes is spent. It is the president's responsibility to enforce the laws. Congress consists of two parts—the Senate and the House of Representatives.

THE SENATE

The Senate has 100 members, two from each state. The Constitution says that the Senate will have equal representation (the same number of representatives) from each state. Thus, small states have the same number of senators as large states. Senators are elected for six-year terms. There is no limit on the number of terms a senator can serve.

▲ *The Senate*

The Senate also has the responsibility of approving people the president appoints for certain jobs: for example, cabinet members and Supreme Court justices. The Senate must approve all treaties by at least a two-thirds vote. It also has the responsibility under the Constitution of putting on trial high-ranking federal officials who have been impeached by the House of Representatives.

WEB SITE www.senate.gov

THE HOUSE OF REPRESENTATIVES

▼ *The Capitol, where Congress meets*

The number of members of the House of Representatives for each state depends on its population according to a recent census. But each state has at least one representative, no matter how small its population. A term lasts two years.

The first House of Representatives in 1789 had 65 members. As the country's population grew, the number of representatives increased. Since the 1910 census, however, the total membership has been kept at 435. After the results of Census 2000 were added up, 8 states gained seats and 10 states lost seats.

WEB SITE www.house.gov

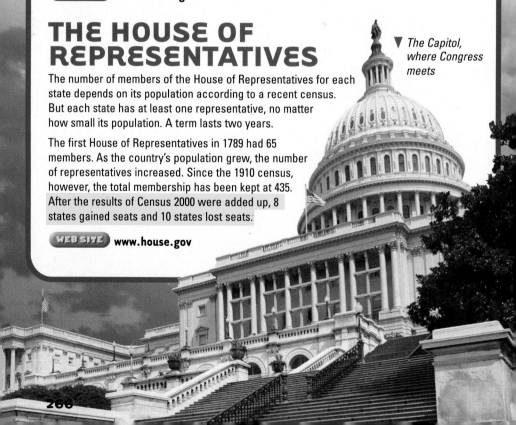

THE HOUSE OF REPRESENTATIVES, BY STATE

Here are the numbers of representatives each state had in 2005, compared with 10 years earlier and 30 years earlier:

	2005	1995	1975		2005	1995	1975
Alabama	7	7	7	Montana	1	1	2
Alaska	1	1	1	Nebraska	3	3	3
Arizona	8	6	4	Nevada	3	2	1
Arkansas	4	4	4	New Hampshire	2	2	2
California	53	52	43	New Jersey	13	13	15
Colorado	7	6	5	New Mexico	3	3	2
Connecticut	5	6	6	New York	29	31	39
Delaware	1	1	1	North Carolina	13	12	11
Florida	25	23	15	North Dakota	1	1	1
Georgia	13	11	10	Ohio	18	19	23
Hawaii	2	2	2	Oklahoma	5	6	6
Idaho	2	2	2	Oregon	5	5	4
Illinois	19	20	24	Pennsylvania	19	21	25
Indiana	9	10	11	Rhode Island	2	2	2
Iowa	5	5	6	South Carolina	6	6	6
Kansas	4	4	5	South Dakota	1	1	2
Kentucky	6	6	7	Tennessee	9	9	9
Louisiana	7	7	8	Texas	32	30	24
Maine	2	2	2	Utah	3	3	2
Maryland	8	8	8	Vermont	1	1	1
Massachusetts	10	10	12	Virginia	11	11	10
Michigan	15	16	19	Washington	9	9	7
Minnesota	8	8	8	West Virginia	3	3	4
Mississippi	4	5	5	Wisconsin	8	9	9
Missouri	9	9	10	Wyoming	1	1	1

Washington, D.C., Puerto Rico, American Samoa, Guam, and the Virgin Islands each have one nonvoting member of the House of Representatives.

Women in Congress

▶ As of January 2005, there were 82 women in Congress (68 in the U.S. House of Representatives and 14 in the U.S. Senate). This is more than ever before.

▶ The first woman elected to the House was Jeannette Rankin (Montana) in 1916. In 1932, Hattie Caraway (Arkansas) was the first woman to be elected to the Senate. Margaret Chase Smith, of Maine, was the first woman elected to both houses of Congress (House in 1940, Senate in 1948).

▶ New York's Shirley Chisholm became the first African-American woman in Congress after being elected to the House in 1968. In 1992, Carol Moseley Braun of Illinois became the first African-American woman elected to the Senate.

▶ In November, 2002, California Representative Nancy Pelosi was selected by her fellow Democrats as their leader in the House of Representatives. This was the highest position in Congress ever held by a woman.

Nancy Pelosi ▶

26

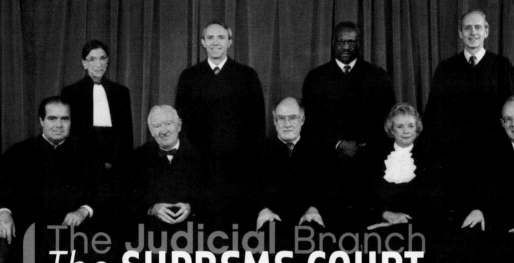

The SUPREME COURT

Above are the nine justices who were on the Supreme Court at the start of its 2004–2005 session. **Back row** *(from left to right): Ruth Bader Ginsburg, David H. Souter, Clarence Thomas, Stephen Breyer.* **Front row** *(from left to right): Antonin Scalia, John Paul Stevens, Chief Justice William H. Rehnquist, Sandra Day O'Connor, Anthony M. Kennedy.*

The highest court in the United States is the Supreme Court. It has nine justices who are appointed for life by the president with the approval of the Senate. Eight of the nine members are called associate justices. The ninth is the chief justice, who presides over the Court's meetings.

WHAT DOES THE SUPREME COURT DO?

The Supreme Court's major responsibilities are to judge cases that involve reviewing federal laws, actions of the president, treaties of the United States, and laws passed by state governments to be sure they do not conflict with the U.S. Constitution. If the Supreme Court finds that a law or action violates the Constitution, the law is struck down.

THE SUPREME COURT'S DECISION IS FINAL.

Most cases must go through other state courts or federal courts before they reach the Supreme Court. The Supreme Court is the final court for a case, and the justices decide which cases they will review. After the Supreme Court hears a case, it may agree or disagree with the decision by a lower court. Each justice has one vote, and the majority rules. When the Supreme Court makes a ruling, its decision is final, so each of the justices has a very important job.

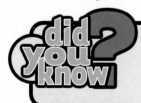

As of early 2005, there had been no change in the justices on the Supreme Court for almost 11 years, since Justice Stephen Breyer joined the Court on August 3, 1994. That's the second longest time this has happened. (The longest time ever was a period of a little over 11 years and 1 month, from February 3, 1812, to March 18, 1823.)

HOW A **BILL** BECOMES A **LAW** ⭐

STEP 1 — SENATORS AND REPRESENTATIVES PROPOSE BILL.

A proposed law is called a **bill**. Any member of Congress may propose (introduce) a bill. A bill is introduced in each house of Congress. The House of Representatives and the Senate consider a bill separately. A member of Congress who introduces a bill is known as the bill's **sponsor**. Bills to raise money always begin in the House of Representatives.

STEP 2 — HOUSE AND SENATE COMMITTEES CONSIDER THE BILL.

The bill is then sent to appropriate committees for consideration. A bill relating to agriculture, for example, would be sent to the agriculture committees in the House and in the Senate. A committee is made up of a small number of members of the House or Senate. Whichever party has a majority in the House or Senate has a majority on each committee. When committees are considering a bill, they hold **hearings** at which people can speak for or against it.

STEP 3 — COMMITTEES VOTE ON THE BILL.

The committees can change the bill as they see fit. Then they vote on it.

STEP 4 — THE BILL IS DEBATED IN THE HOUSE AND SENATE.

If the committees vote in favor of the bill, it goes to the full House and Senate, where it is debated and may be changed further. The House and Senate can then vote on it.

STEP 5 — FROM HOUSE AND SENATE TO CONFERENCE COMMITTEE.

If the House and the Senate pass different versions of the same bill, the bill must go to a **conference committee,** where differences between the two versions must be worked out. A conference committee is a special committee made up of both Senate and House members.

STEP 6 — FINAL VOTE IN THE HOUSE AND SENATE.

The House and the Senate then vote on the conference committee version. In order for this version to become a law, it must be approved by a majority of members of both houses of Congress and signed by the president.

STEP 7 — THE PRESIDENT SIGNS THE BILL INTO LAW.

If the bill passes both houses of Congress, it goes to the president for his signature. Once the president signs a bill, it becomes law.

STEP 8 — WHAT IF THE PRESIDENT DOESN'T SIGN IT?

Sometimes the president does not approve of a bill and decides not to sign it. This is called **vetoing** it. A bill that has been vetoed goes back to Congress, where the members can vote again. If the House and the Senate pass the bill with a two-thirds majority vote, it becomes law. This is called **overriding** the veto.

Elections

On November 2, 2004, President George W. Bush, a Republican, was reelected to another four-year term, defeating Massachusetts Senator John Kerry, a Democrat. President Bush won about 59 million popular votes, or 3 million more than Senator Kerry. But what really mattered was the number of votes he won in the Electoral College (see below). Bush defeated Kerry in 31 states, which gave him 286 electoral votes, 16 more than the 270 he needed to win. Kerry won in 19 states and the District of Columbia, taking in 252 votes.

The map below shows which states Bush won and which states Kerry won. You can see that Kerry did better in the Northeast, the Upper Midwest, and the Far West, while Bush did better in the rest of the country. Only three states, Nevada, Iowa, and New Hampshire supported the candidate of a different party in 2004 than in 2000.

2004 Election
- Won by Bush
- Won by Kerry

The **Electoral College** *State by State*

The Electoral College is not really a college, but a group of people chosen in each state. The writers of the Constitution did not agree on how a president should be selected. Some did not trust ordinary people to make a good choice. So they compromised and agreed to have the Electoral College do it.

The number of electors for each state is equal to the number of senators (2), plus the U.S. House members each state has in Congress. In addition, the District of Columbia has 3 electoral votes. In the early days electors voted for whomever they wanted. In modern times the political parties hold primary elections and conventions to choose candidates for president and vice president. When voters pick candidates of a particular party, they are actually choosing electors from that party. These electors have agreed to vote for their party's candidate, and except in very rare cases this is what they do.

The electors chosen in November meet in state capitals in December. In almost all states, the party that gets the most votes in November wins ALL the electoral votes for the state. In January, the electors' votes are officially opened during a special session of Congress. If no presidential candidate wins a majority of these votes, the House of Representatives chooses the president. This happened in 1800, 1824, and 1877.

Can a candidate who didn't win the most popular votes still win a majority of electoral votes? Yes. That's what happened in 1876, 1888, and again in 2000, when Bush was elected to a first term.

Presidential Puzzlers ★

1 Which president, inaugurated in 1861, was the tallest ever at 6 feet, 4 inches?
A Abraham Lincoln **B** George W. Bush **C** Ronald Reagan **D** George Washington

2 Which president was the first to live in the White House, starting in 1800?
A Woodrow Wilson **B** John Adams **C** Thomas Jefferson **D** George Washington

3 George W. Bush is the second son of a president to be president. Who was the first, starting his term in 1825?
A Grover Cleveland **B** Benjamin Harrison **C** Martin van Buren **D** John Quincy Adams

4 Two men who signed the Declaration of Independence went on to become president. One was John Adams. The other, inaugurated in 1801, was:
A George Washington **B** John Hancock **C** Thomas Jefferson **D** Benjamin Franklin

5 Which president, inaugurated in 1809, was the shortest ever at 5 feet, 4 inches?
A Chester A. Arthur **B** James Madison **C** Bill Clinton **D** James K. Polk

6 Who is the only president to serve more than two terms, starting in 1933?
A George Washington **B** Franklin D. Roosevelt **C** George H.W. Bush **D** Theodore Roosevelt

7 Who was the only president who never married? (He was inaugurated in 1857.)
A James Buchanan **B** Millard Fillmore **C** Calvin Coolidge **D** Herbert Hoover

8 Who was the only president to serve two nonconsecutive (not in a row) terms, one beginning in 1885, the other beginning in 1893?
A Ulysses S. Grant **B** Grover Cleveland **C** Thomas Jefferson **D** Theodore Roosevelt

9 Who was the first president to use the Oval Office, in 1909?
A Andrew Jackson **B** James K. Polk **C** Franklin D. Roosevelt **D** William H. Taft

10 Who was the only president to get married in office? (The ceremony was in 1886.)
A Grover Cleveland **B** Harry S. Truman **C** Abraham Lincoln **D** Lyndon Johnson

11 Which president was the oldest to serve, leaving office at 77 years of age in 1989?
A John Adams **B** Franklin D. Roosevelt **C** Millard Filmore **D** Ronald Reagan

12 Who was the youngest person ever elected president, at age 43 in 1961?
A John F. Kennedy **B** Bill Clinton **C** George Washington **D** George W. Bush

13 Who was the only president also to serve as chief justice of the Supreme Court? (He was inaugurated in 1909.)
A William H. Taft **B** Warren G. Harding **C** Jimmy Carter **D** William McKinley

14 Who was the only president ever to resign from office? (He resigned in 1974.)
A Bill Clinton **B** Abraham Lincoln **C** Andrew Jackson **D** Richard Nixon

ANSWERS ON PAGES 335-338. FOR MORE PUZZLES GO TO
WWW.WORLDALMANACFORKIDS.COM

Presidents of the United States

GEORGE WASHINGTON Federalist Party　　　**1789–1797**
BORN: Feb. 22, 1732, at Wakefield, Westmoreland County, Virginia
MARRIED: Martha Dandridge Custis (1731-1802); no children
DIED: Dec. 14, 1799; buried at Mount Vernon, Fairfax County, Virginia
EARLY CAREER: Soldier; head of the Virginia militia; commander of the
　　Continental Army; chairman of Constitutional Convention (1787)

JOHN ADAMS Federalist Party　　　**1797–1801**
BORN: Oct. 30, 1735, in Braintree (now Quincy), Massachusetts
MARRIED: Abigail Smith (1744-1818); 3 sons, 2 daughters
DIED: July 4, 1826; buried in Quincy, Massachusetts
EARLY CAREER: Lawyer; delegate to Continental Congress; signer of the
　　Declaration of Independence; first vice president

THOMAS JEFFERSON Democratic-Republican Party　　**1801–1809**
BORN: Apr. 13, 1743, at Shadwell, Albemarle County, Virginia
MARRIED: Martha Wayles Skelton (1748-1782); 1 son, 5 daughters
DIED: July 4, 1826; buried at Monticello, Albemarle County, Virginia
EARLY CAREER: Lawyer; member of the Continental Congress; author of the
　　Declaration of Independence; governor of Virginia; first secretary of
　　state; author of the Virginia Statute on Religious Freedom

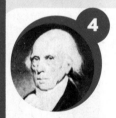

JAMES MADISON Democratic-Republican Party　　**1809-1817**
BORN: Mar. 16, 1751, at Port Conway, King George County, Virginia
MARRIED: Dolley Payne Todd (1768-1849); no children
DIED: June 28, 1836; buried at Montpelier Station, Virginia
EARLY CAREER: Member of the Virginia Constitutional Convention (1776);
　　member of the Continental Congress; major contributor to the U.S.
　　Constitution; writer of the *Federalist Papers*; secretary of state

JAMES MONROE Democratic-Republican Party　　**1817–1825**
BORN: Apr. 28, 1758, in Westmoreland County, Virginia
MARRIED: Elizabeth Kortright (1768-1830); 2 daughters
DIED: July 4, 1831; buried in Richmond, Virginia
EARLY CAREER: Soldier; lawyer; U.S. senator; governor of Virginia;
　　secretary of state

JOHN QUINCY ADAMS Democratic-Republican Party　　**1825–1829**
BORN: July 11, 1767, in Braintree (now Quincy), Massachusetts
MARRIED: Louisa Catherine Johnson (1775-1852); 3 sons, 1 daughter
DIED: Feb. 23, 1848; buried in Quincy, Massachusetts
EARLY CAREER: Diplomat; U.S. senator; secretary of state

7 ANDREW JACKSON Democratic Party 1829–1837
BORN: Mar. 15, 1767, in Waxhaw, South Carolina
MARRIED: Rachel Donelson Robards (1767-1828); 1 son
DIED: June 8, 1845; buried in Nashville, Tennessee
EARLY CAREER: Lawyer; U.S. representative and senator; soldier in the U.S. Army

8 MARTIN VAN BUREN Democratic Party 1837–1841
BORN: Dec. 5, 1782, at Kinderhook, New York
MARRIED: Hannah Hoes (1783-1819); 4 sons
DIED: July 24, 1862; buried at Kinderhook, New York
EARLY CAREER: Governor of New York; secretary of state; vice president

9 WILLIAM HENRY HARRISON Whig Party 1841
BORN: Feb. 9, 1773, at Berkeley, Charles City County, Virginia
MARRIED: Anna Symmes (1775-1864); 6 sons, 4 daughters
DIED: Apr. 4, 1841; buried in North Bend, Ohio
EARLY CAREER: First governor of Indiana Territory; superintendent of Indian affairs; U.S. representative and senator

10 JOHN TYLER Whig Party 1841–1845
BORN: Mar. 29, 1790, in Greenway, Charles City County, Virginia
MARRIED: Letitia Christian (1790-1842); 3 sons, 5 daughters
Julia Gardiner (1820-1889); 5 sons, 2 daughters
DIED: Jan. 18, 1862; buried in Richmond, Virginia
EARLY CAREER: U.S. representative and senator; vice president

11 JAMES KNOX POLK Democratic Party 1845–1849
BORN: Nov. 2, 1795, in Mecklenburg County, North Carolina
MARRIED: Sarah Childress (1803-1891); no children
DIED: June 15, 1849; buried in Nashville, Tennessee
EARLY CAREER: U.S. representative; Speaker of the House; governor of Tennessee

12 ZACHARY TAYLOR Whig Party 1849–1850
BORN: Nov. 24, 1784, in Orange County, Virginia
MARRIED: Margaret Smith (1788-1852); 1 son, 5 daughters
DIED: July 9, 1850; buried in Louisville, Kentucky
EARLY CAREER: General in the U.S. Army

13 MILLARD FILLMORE Whig Party 1850–1853
BORN: Jan. 7, 1800, in Cayuga County, New York
MARRIED: Abigail Powers (1798-1853); 1 son, 1 daughter
Caroline Carmichael McIntosh (1813-1881); no children
DIED: Mar. 8, 1874; buried in Buffalo, New York
EARLY CAREER: Farmer; lawyer; U.S. representative; vice president

14 **FRANKLIN PIERCE** Democratic Party   1853–1857
BORN: Nov. 23, 1804, in Hillsboro, New Hampshire
MARRIED: Jane Means Appleton (1806-1863); 3 sons
DIED: Oct. 8, 1869; buried in Concord, New Hampshire
EARLY CAREER: U.S. representative, senator

15 **JAMES BUCHANAN** Democratic Party   1857–1861
BORN: Apr. 23, 1791, Cove Gap, near Mercersburg, Pennsylvania
MARRIED: Never
DIED: June 1, 1868, buried in Lancaster, Pennsylvania
EARLY CAREER: U.S. representative; secretary of state

16 **ABRAHAM LINCOLN** Republican Party   1861-1865
BORN: Feb. 12, 1809, in Hardin County, Kentucky
MARRIED: Mary Todd (1818-1882); 4 sons
DIED: Apr. 15, 1865; buried in Springfield, Illinois
EARLY CAREER: Lawyer; U.S. representative

17 **ANDREW JOHNSON** Democratic Party   1865–1869
BORN: Dec. 29, 1808, in Raleigh, North Carolina
MARRIED: Eliza McCardle (1810-1876); 3 sons, 2 daughters
DIED: July 31, 1875; buried in Greeneville, Tennessee
EARLY CAREER: Tailor; member of state legislature; U.S. representative;
governor of Tennessee; U.S. senator; vice president

18 **ULYSSES S. GRANT** Republican Party   1869–1877
BORN: Apr. 27, 1822, in Point Pleasant, Ohio
MARRIED: Julia Dent (1826-1902); 3 sons, 1 daughter
DIED: July 23, 1885; buried in New York City
EARLY CAREER: Army officer; commander of Union forces during
Civil War

19 **RUTHERFORD B. HAYES** Republican Party   1877–1881
BORN: Oct. 4, 1822, in Delaware, Ohio
MARRIED: Lucy Ware Webb (1831-1889); 5 sons, 2 daughters
DIED: Jan. 17, 1893; buried in Fremont, Ohio
EARLY CAREER: Lawyer; general in Union Army; U.S. representative;
governor of Ohio

20 **JAMES A. GARFIELD** Republican Party   1881
BORN: Nov. 19, 1831, in Orange, Cuyahoga County, Ohio
MARRIED: Lucretia Rudolph (1832-1918); 5 sons, 2 daughters
DIED: Sept. 19, 1881; buried in Cleveland, Ohio
EARLY CAREER: Teacher; Ohio state senator; general in Union Army;
U.S. representative

CHESTER A. ARTHUR Republican Party   **1881–1885**
BORN: Oct. 5, 1829, in Fairfield, Vermont
MARRIED: Ellen Lewis Herndon (1837-1880); 2 sons, 1 daughter
DIED: Nov. 18, 1886; buried in Albany, New York
EARLY CAREER: Teacher; lawyer; vice president

GROVER CLEVELAND Democratic Party   **1885–1889**
BORN: Mar. 18, 1837, in Caldwell, New Jersey
MARRIED: Frances Folsom (1864-1947); 2 sons, 3 daughters
DIED: June 24, 1908; buried in Princeton, New Jersey
EARLY CAREER: Lawyer; mayor of Buffalo; governor of New York

BENJAMIN HARRISON Republican Party   **1889-1893**
BORN: Aug. 20, 1833, in North Bend, Ohio
MARRIED: Caroline Lavinia Scott (1832-1892); 1 son, 1 daughter
         Mary Scott Lord Dimmick (1858-1948); 1 daughter
DIED: Mar. 13, 1901; buried in Indianapolis, Indiana
EARLY CAREER: Lawyer; general in Union Army; U.S. senator

GROVER CLEVELAND   **1893–1897**
SEE 22, ABOVE

WILLIAM MCKINLEY Republican Party   **1897–1901**
BORN: Jan. 29, 1843, in Niles, Ohio
MARRIED: Ida Saxton (1847-1907); 2 daughters
DIED: Sept. 14, 1901; buried in Canton, Ohio
EARLY CAREER: Lawyer; U.S. representative; governor of Ohio

THEODORE ROOSEVELT Republican Party   **1901–1909**
BORN: Oct. 27, 1858, in New York City
MARRIED: Alice Hathaway Lee (1861-1884); 1 daughter
         Edith Kermit Carow (1861-1948); 4 sons, 1 daughter
DIED: Jan. 6, 1919; buried in Oyster Bay, New York
EARLY CAREER: Assistant secretary of the Navy; cavalry leader in
         Spanish-American War; governor of New York; vice president

WILLIAM HOWARD TAFT Republican Party   **1909–1913**
BORN: Sept. 15, 1857, in Cincinnati, Ohio
MARRIED: Helen Herron (1861-1943); 2 sons, 1 daughter
DIED: Mar. 8, 1930; buried in Arlington National Cemetery, Virginia
EARLY CAREER: Reporter; lawyer; judge; secretary of war

WOODROW WILSON Democratic Party   **1913–1921**
BORN: Dec. 28, 1856, in Staunton, Virginia
MARRIED: Ellen Louise Axson (1860-1914); 3 daughters
         Edith Bolling Galt (1872-1961); no children
DIED: Feb. 3, 1924; buried in Washington, D.C.
EARLY CAREER: College professor and president; governor of New Jersey

29 WARREN G. HARDING Republican Party 1921–1923
BORN: Nov. 2, 1865, near Corsica (now Blooming Grove), Ohio
MARRIED: Florence Kling De Wolfe (1860-1924); 1 daughter
DIED: Aug. 2, 1923; buried in Marion, Ohio
EARLY CAREER: Ohio state senator; U.S. senator

30 CALVIN COOLIDGE Republican Party 1923–1929
BORN: July 4, 1872, in Plymouth, Vermont
MARRIED: Grace Anna Goodhue (1879-1957); 2 sons
DIED: Jan. 5, 1933; buried in Plymouth, Vermont
EARLY CAREER: Massachusetts state legislator; lieutenant governor and governor; vice president

31 HERBERT HOOVER Republican Party 1929-1933
BORN: Aug. 10, 1874, in West Branch, Iowa
MARRIED: Lou Henry (1875-1944); 2 sons
DIED: Oct. 20, 1964; buried in West Branch, Iowa
EARLY CAREER: Mining engineer; secretary of commerce

32 FRANKLIN DELANO ROOSEVELT Democratic Party 1933–1945
BORN: Jan. 30, 1882, in Hyde Park, New York
MARRIED: Anna Eleanor Roosevelt (1884-1962); 4 sons, 1 daughter
DIED: Apr. 12, 1945; buried in Hyde Park, New York
EARLY CAREER: Lawyer; New York state senator; assistant secretary of the Navy; governor of New York

33 HARRY S. TRUMAN Democratic Party 1945–1953
BORN: May 8, 1884, in Lamar, Missouri
MARRIED: Elizabeth Virginia "Bess" Wallace (1885-1982); 1 daughter
DIED: Dec. 26, 1972; buried in Independence, Missouri
EARLY CAREER: Farmer; haberdasher (ran men's clothing store); judge; U.S. senator; vice president

34 DWIGHT D. EISENHOWER Republican Party 1953–1961
BORN: Oct. 14, 1890, in Denison, Texas
MARRIED: Mary "Mamie" Geneva Doud (1896-1979); 2 sons
DIED: Mar. 28, 1969; buried in Abilene, Kansas
EARLY CAREER: Commander, Allied landing in North Africa and later Supreme Allied Commander in Europe during World War II; president of Columbia University

35 JOHN FITZGERALD KENNEDY Democratic Party 1961–1963
BORN: May 29, 1917, in Brookline, Massachusetts
MARRIED: Jacqueline Lee Bouvier (1929-1994); 2 sons, 1 daughter
DIED: Nov. 22, 1963; buried in Arlington National Cemetery, Virginia
EARLY CAREER: U.S. naval commander; U.S. representative and senator

36 **LYNDON BAINES JOHNSON** Democratic Party   1963–1969
BORN: Aug. 27, 1908, near Stonewall, Texas
MARRIED: Claudia "Lady Bird" Alta Taylor (b. 1912); 2 daughters
DIED: Jan. 22, 1973; buried in Johnson City, Texas
EARLY CAREER: U.S. representative and senator; vice president

37 **RICHARD MILHOUS NIXON** Republican Party   1969–1974
BORN: Jan. 9, 1913, in Yorba Linda, California
MARRIED: Thelma "Pat" Ryan (1912-1993); 2 daughters
DIED: Apr. 22, 1994; buried in Yorba Linda, California
EARLY CAREER: Lawyer; U.S. representative and senator; vice president

38 **GERALD R. FORD** Republican Party   1974-1977
BORN: July 14, 1913, in Omaha, Nebraska
MARRIED: Elizabeth "Betty" Bloomer (b. 1918); 3 sons, 1 daughter
EARLY CAREER: Lawyer; U.S. representative; vice president

39 **JIMMY (JAMES EARL) CARTER** Democratic Party   1977-1981
BORN: Oct. 1, 1924, in Plains, Georgia
MARRIED: Rosalynn Smith (b. 1927); 3 sons, 1 daughter
EARLY CAREER: Peanut farmer; Georgia state senator; governor
of Georgia

40 **RONALD REAGAN** Republican Party   1981–1989
BORN: Feb. 6, 1911, in Tampico, Illinois
MARRIED: Jane Wyman (b. 1914); 1 son, 1 daughter
Nancy Davis (b. 1923); 1 son, 1 daughter
DIED: June 5, 2004; buried in Simi Valley, California
EARLY CAREER: Film and television actor; governor of California

41 **GEORGE H.W. BUSH** Republican Party   1989–1993
BORN: June 12, 1924, in Milton, Massachusetts
MARRIED: Barbara Pierce (b. 1925); 4 sons, 2 daughters
EARLY CAREER: U.S. Navy pilot; businessman; U.S. representative; U.S.
ambassador to the UN; CIA director, vice president

42 **BILL (WILLIAM JEFFERSON) CLINTON** Democratic Party 1993–2001
BORN: Aug. 19, 1946, in Hope, Arkansas
MARRIED: Hillary Rodham (b. 1947); 1 daughter
EARLY CAREER: College professor; Arkansas state attorney general;
governor of Arkansas

43 **GEORGE W. BUSH** Republican Party   2001-
BORN: July 6, 1946, in New Haven, Connecticut
MARRIED: Laura Welch (b. 1946); 2 daughters
EARLY CAREER: Political adviser; businessman; governor of Texas

Meet the First Ladies

ABIGAIL ADAMS, wife of John Adams, didn't have much formal education, but she read widely and had strong opinions. The hundreds of letters she wrote to her husband provide a history of life during the Revolutionary era. Besides being the wife of the second U.S. president, she was the mother of the sixth, John Quincy Adams.

ABIGAIL FILLMORE, wife of Millard Fillmore, was a former schoolteacher who started the first library in the White House. After attending the inauguration of her husband's successor, Franklin Pierce, in March 1853, she developed pneumonia, and died several weeks later.

FRANCES CLEVELAND, wife of Grover Cleveland, was the first bride of a president to be married in the White House. With her marriage in 1886, she became the youngest First Lady, at the age of 21. She was known as a delightful hostess. In 1893, she gave birth to Esther Cleveland, the only child ever born to a First Lady in the White House.

ELLEN WILSON, first wife of Woodrow Wilson, was an accomplished painter. Social issues became important to her as First Lady. She worked to improve housing conditions for African Americans in Washington and was a major force behind a slum clearance bill, which Congress passed on August 6, 1914 — the day she died in the White House of a kidney condition called Bright's disease.

GRACE COOLIDGE, the wife of Calvin Coolidge, graduated from the University of Vermont in 1902, and then became a teacher of the deaf. As First Lady, she continued her support for people with disabilities. An animal lover, she had a pet raccoon named Rebecca in the White House. She had a strong interest in baseball and was a devoted fan of the Boston Red Sox.

LADY BIRD (CLAUDIA) JOHNSON, wife of Lyndon Johnson, turned a love of the outdoors into a campaign. She encouraged Americans to beautify their country by planting flowers in many places, even along highways. After leaving the White House, in 1969, she published *A White House Diary*, which provided a record of her years as First Lady.

LAURA BUSH, wife of George W. Bush, was a librarian and teacher. She is interested in books, history, art, and the well-being of children. She and her husband have twin daughters, Jenna and Barbara. Both girls graduated from college in 2004.

United States History

14,000 B.C. — 11,000 B.C. Paleo-Indians use stone points attached to spears to hunt big **mammoths** in northern parts of North America.

11,000 B.C. Big mammoths disappear and Paleo-Indians begin to gather **plants** for food.

After A.D. 500 Anasazi peoples in the Southwestern United States live in homes on cliffs, called **cliff dwellings**. Anasazi pottery and dishes are well known for their beautiful patterns.

After A.D. 700 Mississippian Indian people in the Southeastern United States **develop farms** and build burial mounds.

16,000 B.C. — 12,000 B.C. First people (called **Paleo-Indians**) cross from Siberia to Alaska and begin to move into North America.

9500 B.C. — 1000 B.C. North American Indians begin using **stone** to grind food and to hunt bison and smaller animals.

1000 B.C. — A.D. 500 Woodland Indians, who lived east of the Mississippi River, bury their dead under large **mounds** of earth (which can still be seen today).

700–1492 Many **different Indian cultures** develop throughout North America.

279

Colonial America
and the
American Revolution:
1492-1783

1492
Christopher **Columbus** sails across the Atlantic Ocean and reaches an island in the Bahamas in the Caribbean Sea.

1513
Juan **Ponce de León** explores the Florida coast.

1524
Giovanni da **Verrazano** explores the coast from Carolina north to Nova Scotia, enters New York harbor.

1540
Francisco Vásquez de **Coronado** explores the Southwest.

1565
St. Augustine, Florida, the **first town** established by Europeans in the United States, is founded by the Spanish. Later burned by the English in 1586.

BENJAMIN FRANKLIN (1706-1790)
was a great American leader, printer, scientist, and writer. In 1732, he began publishing a magazine called *Poor Richard's Almanack*. Poor Richard was a make-believe person who gave advice about common sense and honesty. Many of Poor Richard's sayings are still known today. Among the most famous are "God helps them that help themselves" and "Early to bed, early to rise, makes a man healthy, wealthy, and wise."

1634
Maryland is founded as a Catholic colony, with religious freedom for all granted in 1649.

1664
The English seize **New Amsterdam** from the Dutch. The city is renamed New York.

1699
French settlers move into Mississippi and Louisiana.

1732
Benjamin Franklin begins publishing *Poor Richard's Almanack.*

1754–1763
French and Indian War between England and France. The French are defeated and lose their lands in Canada and the American Midwest.

1764–1766
England places taxes on sugar that comes from their North American colonies. England also requires colonists to buy stamps to help pay for royal troops. Colonists protest, and the **Stamp Act** is repealed in 1766.

1607

Jamestown, Virginia, the first English settlement in North America, is founded by Captain John Smith.

1609

Henry Hudson sails into **New York Harbor**, explores the Hudson River. Spaniards settle Santa Fe, New Mexico.

1619

The first African **slaves** are brought to Jamestown. (Slavery is made legal in 1650.)

1620

Pilgrims from England arrive at Plymouth, Massachusetts on the *Mayflower*.

1626

Peter Minuit buys **Manhattan** island for the Dutch from Man-a-hat-a Indians for goods worth $24. The island is renamed New Amsterdam.

1630

Boston is founded by Massachusetts colonists led by John Winthrop.

FAMOUS WORDS FROM THE DECLARATION OF INDEPENDENCE, JULY 4, 1776

"We hold these truths to be self-evident, that all men are created equal, that they are endowed by their Creator with certain unalienable rights, that among these are life, liberty, and the pursuit of happiness."

1770

Boston Massacre: English troops fire on a group of people protesting English taxes.

1773

Boston Tea Party: English tea is thrown into the harbor to protest a tax on tea.

1775

Fighting at **Lexington and Concord**, Massachusetts, marks the beginning of the American Revolution.

1776

The Declaration of Independence is approved July 4 by the Continental Congress (made up of representatives from the American colonies).

1781

British General **Cornwallis surrenders** to the Americans at Yorktown, Virginia, ending the fighting in the Revolutionary War.

The New Nation
1783–1900

1784

The first successful daily **newspaper,** the *Pennsylvania Packet & General Advertiser*, is published.

1787

The **Constitutional Convention** meets to write a Constitution for the U.S.

1789

The new **Constitution** is approved by the states. George Washington is chosen as the first president.

1800

The federal government moves to a new capital, **Washington, D.C.**

1803

The U.S. makes the **Louisiana Purchase** from France. The Purchase doubles the area of the U.S.

THE LOUISIANA PURCHASE

WHO ATTENDED THE CONVENTION?

The **Constitutional Convention** met in Philadelphia in the hot summer of 1787. Most of the great founders of America attended. Among those present were George Washington, James Madison, and John Adams. They met to form a new government that would be strong and, at the same time, protect the liberties that were fought for in the American Revolution. The Constitution they created is still the law of the United States.

We the People

1836

Texans fighting for independence from Mexico are defeated at the **Alamo.**

1838

Cherokee Indians are forced to move to Oklahoma, along "The **Trail of Tears.**"

1844

The **first telegraph** line connects Washington, D.C., and Baltimore.

1846–1848

U.S. war with Mexico: Mexico is defeated, and the United States takes control of the Republic of Texas and of Mexican territories in the West.

1848

The discovery of **gold** in California leads to a "rush" of 80,000 people to the West in search of gold.

1852

Uncle Tom's Cabin is published.

"THE TRAIL OF TEARS"

The **Cherokee Indians** living in Georgia were forced by the government to leave in 1838. They were sent to Oklahoma. On the long march, thousands died because of disease and the cold weather.

UNCLE TOM'S CABIN

Harriet Beecher Stowe's novel about the **suffering of slaves** was an instant bestseller in the North and banned in most of the South. When President Abraham Lincoln met Stowe, he called her "the little lady who started this war" (the Civil War).

1804

Lewis and Clark, with their guide Sacagawea, explore what is now the northwestern United States.

1812–1814

War of 1812 with Great Britain: British forces burn the Capitol and White House. Francis Scott Key writes the words to "The Star-Spangled Banner."

1820

The **Missouri Compromise** bans slavery west of the Mississippi River and north of 36°30′ latitude, except in Missouri.

1823

The **Monroe Doctrine** warns European countries not to interfere in the Americas.

1825

The **Erie Canal** opens linking New York City with the Great Lakes.

1831

The Liberator, a newspaper opposing slavery, is published in Boston.

1869

The **first railroad** connecting the East and West coasts is completed.

1898

Spanish-American War: The U.S. defeats Spain, gains control of the Philippines, Puerto Rico, and Guam.

1858

Abraham Lincoln and Stephen Douglas **debate** about slavery during their Senate campaign in Illinois.

1860

Abraham **Lincoln** is elected president.

1861

The **Civil War** begins.

1863

President Lincoln issues the **Emancipation Proclamation,** freeing most slaves.

1865

The **Civil War ends** as the South surrenders. President Lincoln is assassinated.

1890

Battle of Wounded Knee is fought in South Dakota—the last major battle between Indians and U.S. troops.

CIVIL WAR DEAD AND WOUNDED

The U.S. **Civil War** between the North and South lasted four years (1861-1865) and resulted in the death or wounding of more than 600,000 people. Little was known at the time about the spread of diseases. As a result, many casualties were also the result of illnesses such as influenza, measles, and infections from battle wounds.

United States Since 1900

WORLD WAR I
In **World War I** the United States fought with Great Britain, France, and Russia (the Allies) against Germany and Austria-Hungary. The Allies won the war in 1918.

1903

The United States begins digging the **Panama Canal**. The canal opens in 1914, connecting the Atlantic and Pacific oceans.

1908

Henry Ford introduces the **Model T** car, priced at $850.

1916

Jeannette Rankin of Montana becomes the first woman elected to Congress.

1917–1918

The United States joins **World War I** on the side of the Allies against Germany.

1927

Charles A. **Lindbergh** becomes the first person to fly alone nonstop across the Atlantic Ocean.

1929

A stock market crash marks the beginning of the **Great Depression.**

SCHOOL SEGREGATION
The U.S. Supreme Court ruled that **separate schools** for black students and white students were **not equal.** The Court said such schools were against the U.S. Constitution. The ruling also applied to other forms of segregation—separation of the races supported by some states.

1963

President John **Kennedy** is assassinated.

1964

Congress passes the **Civil Rights Act,** which outlaws discrimination in voting and jobs.

1965

The United States sends large numbers of soldiers to fight in the **Vietnam War.**

1968

Civil rights leader **Martin Luther King Jr.** is assassinated in Memphis. Senator **Robert F. Kennedy** is assassinated in Los Angeles.

1969

U.S. Astronaut Neil Armstrong becomes the **first person** to walk **on the moon.**

1973

U.S. participation in the **Vietnam War ends.**

1974

President Richard **Nixon resigns** because of the Watergate scandal.

THE GREAT DEPRESSION

The stock market crash of October 1929 led to a period of severe hardship for the American people—the **Great Depression**. As many as 25 percent of all workers could not find jobs. The Depression lasted until the early 1940s. The Depression also led to a great change in politics. In 1932, Franklin D. Roosevelt, a Democrat, was elected president. He served as president for 12 years, longer than any other president.

1933
President Franklin D. Roosevelt's **New Deal** increases government help to people hurt by the Depression.

1941
Japan attacks **Pearl Harbor,** Hawaii. The United States enters World War II.

1945
Germany and Japan surrender, **ending World War II.** Japan surrenders after the U.S. drops atomic bombs on Hiroshima and Nagasaki.

1947
Jackie Robinson becomes the **first black baseball player** in the major leagues when he joins the Brooklyn Dodgers.

1950–1953
U.S. armed forces fight in the **Korean War.**

1954
The U.S. Supreme Court **forbids racial segregation** in public schools.

WATERGATE

In June 1972, five men were arrested in the **Watergate** building in Washington, D.C., for trying to bug telephones in the offices of the Democratic National Committee. Some of those arrested worked for the committee to reelect President Richard Nixon. Later it was discovered that Nixon was helping to hide information about the break-in.

1991
The Persian Gulf War: The United States and its allies defeat Iraq.

2000
George W. Bush narrowly defeats Al Gore in a closely fought battle for the presidency.

2004–2005
Bush defeats John Kerry to win new term. Iraq holds free elections.

1979
U.S. **hostages** are taken **in Iran,** beginning a 444-day crisis that ends with their release in 1981.

1981
Sandra Day O'Connor becomes the **first woman** on the U.S. Supreme Court.

1985
U.S. President Ronald Reagan and Soviet leader Mikhail Gorbachev begin working together to **improve relations** between their countries.

1999
After an **impeachment** trial, the Senate finds President Bill Clinton not guilty.

2001
Hijacked jets crashed into the **World Trade Center** and the Pentagon, September 11, killing about 3,000 people.

2003
U.S.-led forces invade Iraq and remove dictator **Saddam Hussein.**

African Americans:
A Timeline

Would you like to learn more about the history of African Americans from the era of slavery to the present? These events and personalities can be a starting point. Can you add some more?

Rev. Dr. Martin Luther King Jr. ▶

1619	First Africans are brought to Virginia as **slaves**.
1831	Nat Turner starts a **slave revolt** in Virginia that is unsuccessful.
1856-57	**Dred Scott**, a slave, sues to be freed because he had left slave territory, but the Supreme Court denies his claim.
1861-65	The North defeats the South in the brutal Civil War; the **13th Amendment** ends nearly 250 years of slavery. The Ku Klux Klan is founded.
1865-77	Southern blacks play leadership roles in government under **Reconstruction**; the 15th Amendment (1870) gives black men the right to vote.
1896	Supreme Court rules in a case called *Plessy versus Ferguson* that segregation is legal when facilities are **"separate but equal."** Discrimination and violence against blacks increase.
1910	W. E. B. Du Bois (1868–1963) founds National Association for the Advancement of Colored People (**NAACP**), fighting for equality for blacks.
1920s	African American culture (jazz music, dance, literature) flourishes during the **Harlem Renaissance**.
1954	Supreme Court rules in a case called ***Brown versus Board of Education*** of *Topeka* that school segregation is unconstitutional.
1957	Black students, backed by federal troops, enter segregated Central High School in **Little Rock**, Arkansas.
1955-65	**Malcolm X** (1925–65) emerges as key spokesman for black nationalism.
1963	**Rev. Dr. Martin Luther King Jr.** (1929–68) gives his "I Have a Dream" speech at a march that inspired more than 200,000 people in Washington, D.C.—and many others throughout the nation.
1964	Sweeping **civil rights bill** banning racial discrimination is signed by President Lyndon Johnson.
1965	King leads protest march in **Selma**, Alabama; blacks riot in **Watts** section of Los Angeles.
1967	Gary, Indiana, and Cleveland, Ohio, are first major U.S. cities to elect **black mayors**; Thurgood Marshall (1908–93) becomes first black on the **Supreme Court**.
1995	Hundreds of thousands of black men take part in **"Million Man March"** rally in Washington, D.C., urging responsibility for families and communities.
2001	**Colin Powell** becomes first African American secretary of state. He is succeeded in 2005 by Condoleezza Rice, an African-American woman.

THEY MADE HISTORY

These African-Americans fought racial barriers to achieve their goals.

FREDERICK DOUGLASS (1817–1895) was an American abolitionist, speaker, and writer who escaped slavery and urged other blacks to try to escape. He worked on the underground railroad and fought for amendments to the U.S. Constitution giving equal rights to blacks.

Frederick Douglass

W.E.B. DU BOIS (1868–1963) was the first black person to earn a doctorate from Harvard University. He helped found the National Association for the Advancement of Colored People (NAACP) and organized meetings that brought together American blacks and Africans. He urged people to see "beauty in black."

MARIAN ANDERSON (1897–1993) was the first African-American to sing with New York's Metropolitan Opera. In 1939 she gave a famous concert at the Lincoln Memorial after being barred from performing at Constitution Hall because of her race.

THURGOOD MARSHALL (1908–1993) became the first African-American justice on the Supreme Court in 1967. In 1954 he had won a historic case before the Court, when it ruled that separate schools for blacks and whites were not equal or legal.

ROSA PARKS (born 1913) is called the mother of America's civil rights movement. When she refused to give up her bus seat to a white man in 1955, blacks in Montgomery, Alabama, started a boycott of the bus system, which led to desegregation of the city's buses.

Rosa Parks

JACKIE ROBINSON (1919–1972) was the first black player in the history of major league baseball. He joined the Dodgers, then in Brooklyn, in 1947. In 1949 he won the National League's MVP award and in 1962 was inducted into the Baseball Hall of Fame.

SHIRLEY CHISHOLM (1924–2005) in 1968 became the first African-American woman ever elected to Congress. In 1972 she also became the first black person, and first woman, to campaign seriously for the presidency.

Shirley Chisholm ▶

MALCOLM X (1925–1965) was a forceful Black Muslim leader who spoke against injustices toward blacks and promoted the idea of black pride and independence. He was assassinated by rivals in 1965. His life story, *The Autobiography of Malcolm X*, helped make him a hero especially among black youth.

REV. MARTIN LUTHER KING JR. (1929–1968) used stirring words, strong leadership, and commitment to nonviolence to help change U.S. history by removing racial barriers for blacks. From the mid-1950s to his assassination in 1968, he was the most influential leader of the U.S. civil rights movement. In 1964 he received the Nobel Peace Prize. His birthday was made a national holiday.

TONI MORRISON (born 1931) was the first African-American to win the Nobel Prize for literature (in 1993). Her writing focuses on the American black experience. Many of her novels have strong women characters, like her 1987 novel *Beloved*, which won a Pulitzer Prize.

CONDOLEEZZA RICE (born 1954) was the first African-American woman to be national security adviser. A close adviser to President George W. Bush, she went on to become the first African-American woman secretary of state in 2005.

Condoleezza Rice ▶

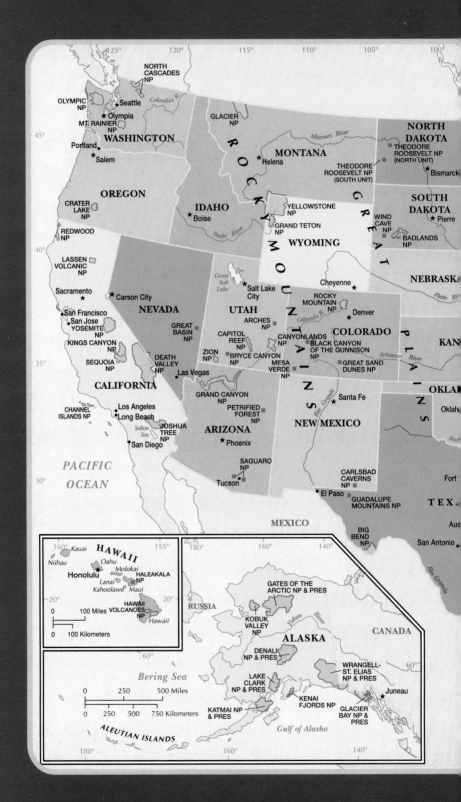

NORTH
CASCADES
NP

OLYMPIC
NP
•Seattle
★ Olympia
MT. RAINIER
NP
WASHINGTON
Portland •
★ Salem

Columbia R.

GLACIER
NP

Missouri River

MONTANA
• Helena

THEODORE
ROOSEVELT NP
(NORTH UNIT)

NORTH
DAKOTA
THEODORE
ROOSEVELT NP
(SOUTH UNIT)
• Bismarck

OREGON

CRATER
LAKE
NP

REDWOOD
NP

IDAHO
★ Boise

Snake River

YELLOWSTONE
NP

GRAND TETON
NP

WYOMING

SOUTH
DAKOTA
★ Pierre

WIND
CAVE
NP
BADLANDS
NP

ROCKY

G
R
E
A
T

LASSEN
VOLCANIC
NP

Sacramento

Great
Salt
Lake

• Salt Lake
City

Cheyenne
★

NEBRASKA

Platte Riv

★ Carson City

NEVADA

San Francisco
San Jose
YOSEMITE
NP
KINGS CANYON
NP

SEQUOIA
NP

DEATH
VALLEY
NP
• Las Vegas

UTAH

ARCHES
NP

GREAT
BASIN
NP

CAPITOL
REEF
NP
ZION
NP
BRYCE CANYON
NP

MESA
VERDE
NP

CANYONLANDS
NP

ROCKY
MOUNTAIN
NP

Colorado R.

• Denver

BLACK CANYON
OF THE GUNNISON
NP

COLORADO

GREAT SAND
DUNES NP

Arkansas
River

KAN

M
O
U
N
T
A
I
N
S

CALIFORNIA

CHANNEL
ISLANDS NP

Los Angeles
• Long Beach

Salton
Sea

JOSHUA
TREE
NP

San Diego

GRAND CANYON
NP

PETRIFIED
FOREST
NP

ARIZONA
★ Phoenix

SAGUARO
NP

Tucson •

Rio Grande

Santa Fe
•

NEW MEXICO

P
L
A
I
N
S

OKLA

Okla

CARLSBAD
CAVERNS
NP
• El Paso
GUADALUPE
MOUNTAINS NP

Fort

T E X A

PACIFIC

OCEAN

MEXICO

BIG
BEND
NP

Aus

San Antonio •

HAWAII
160°
Kauai
155°
Niihau
Oahu
Honolulu
Molokai
HALEAKALA
NP
Lanai
Maui
Kahoolawe
20°
HAWAII
VOLCANOES
NP
Hawaii

0   100 Miles

0   100 Kilometers

180°

160°

140°

RUSSIA

GATES OF THE
ARCTIC NP & PRES

KOBUK
VALLEY
NP

Yukon River

ALASKA

CANADA

DENALI
NP & PRES

60°

WRANGELL-
ST. ELIAS
NP & PRES

60°

Bering Sea

0   250   500 Miles

0   250   500   750 Kilometers

LAKE
CLARK
NP & PRES

KENAI
FJORDS NP

Juneau •

GLACIER
BAY NP &
PRES

KATMAI NP
& PRES

ALEUTIAN ISLANDS

Gulf of Alaska

180°

160°

140°

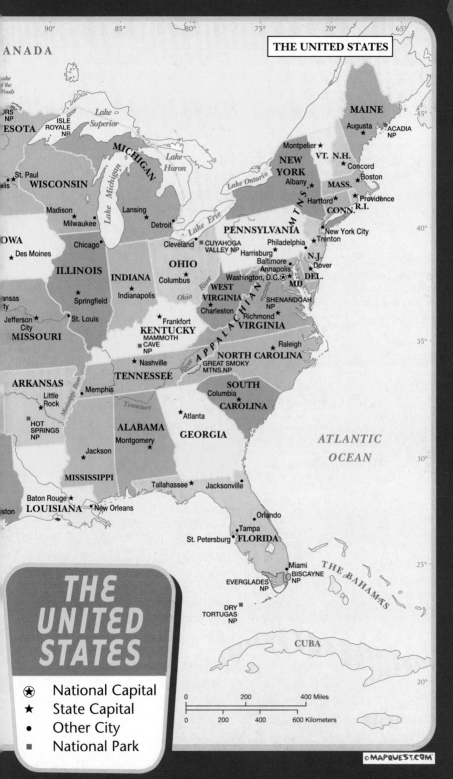

THE UNITED STATES

CANADA

MAINE
Augusta ★
ACADIA NP

Montpelier ★
VT. N.H.
Concord
NEW YORK
Albany ★
MASS.
Boston
Hartford ★
CONN.
Providence
R.I.

ISLE ROYALE NP
Lake Superior
MICHIGAN
Lake Huron
Lake Michigan
Lake Ontario

ESOTA
St. Paul
WISCONSIN
Madison
Milwaukee
Lansing
Detroit
Lake Erie

New York City
Trenton

PENNSYLVANIA
Cleveland
CUYAHOGA VALLEY NP
Philadelphia
N.J.
Harrisburg ★
Baltimore
Dover
Annapolis
DEL.

OWA
Des Moines
Chicago

ILLINOIS
Springfield
INDIANA
Indianapolis
OHIO
Columbus
Ohio River

Washington, D.C.
MD

ansas ty
Jefferson City
St. Louis
MISSOURI

WEST VIRGINIA
Charleston
SHENANDOAH NP

Frankfort
KENTUCKY
MAMMOTH CAVE NP
Nashville
VIRGINIA
Richmond

APPALACHIAN MTNS.

ARKANSAS
Little Rock
HOT SPRINGS NP
Memphis
TENNESSEE
GREAT SMOKY MTNS.NP

NORTH CAROLINA
Raleigh

Tennessee River
Mississippi River

ALABAMA
Montgomery
Jackson
MISSISSIPPI

SOUTH CAROLINA
Columbia

Atlanta
GEORGIA

ATLANTIC OCEAN

ston
Baton Rouge ★
New Orleans
LOUISIANA

Tallahassee ★
Jacksonville

Orlando
Tampa
St. Petersburg
FLORIDA

Miami
BISCAYNE NP
EVERGLADES NP

THE BAHAMAS

DRY TORTUGAS NP

CUBA

90° 85° 80° 75° 70° 65°
45°
40°
35°
30°
25°
20°

THE UNITED STATES

- ⊛ National Capital
- ★ State Capital
- • Other City
- ▪ National Park

0   200   400 Miles
0   200 400   600 Kilometers

©MAPQUEST.COM

HOW the states

ALABAMA comes from an Indian word for "tribal town."

ALASKA comes from *alakshak*, the Aleutian (Eskimo) word meaning "peninsula" or "land that is not an island."

ARIZONA comes from a Pima Indian word meaning "little spring place," or the Aztec word *arizuma*, meaning "silver-bearing."

ARKANSAS is a variation of *Quapaw*, the name of an Indian tribe. *Quapaw* means "south wind."

CALIFORNIA is the name of an imaginary island in a Spanish story. It was named by Spanish explorers of Baja California, a part of Mexico.

COLORADO comes from a Spanish word meaning "red." It was first given to the Colorado River because of its reddish color.

Colorado

CONNECTICUT comes from an Algonquin Indian word meaning "long river place."

DELAWARE is named after Lord De La Warr, the English governor of Virginia in colonial times.

FLORIDA, which means "flowery" in Spanish, was named by the explorer Ponce de León, who landed there during Easter.

GEORGIA was named after King George II of England, who granted the right to create a colony there in 1732.

HAWAII probably comes from *Hawaiki*, or *Owhyhee*, the native Polynesian word for "homeland."

IDAHO's name is of uncertain origin, but it may come from a Kiowa Apache name for the Comanche Indians.

Idaho

ILLINOIS is the French version of *Illini*, an Algonquin Indian word meaning "men" or "warriors."

INDIANA means "land of the Indians."

IOWA comes from the name of an American Indian tribe that lived on the land that is now the state.

KANSAS comes from a Sioux Indian word that possibly meant "people of the south wind."

KENTUCKY comes from an Iroquois Indian word, possibly meaning "meadowland."

LOUISIANA, which was first settled by French explorers, was named after King Louis XIV of France.

MAINE means "the mainland." English explorers called it that to distinguish it from islands nearby.

MARYLAND was named after Queen Henrietta Maria, wife of King Charles I of England, who granted the right to establish an English colony there.

MASSACHUSETTS comes from an Indian word meaning "large hill place."

MICHIGAN comes from the Chippewa Indian words *mici gama*, meaning "great water" (referring to Lake Michigan).

Michigan

MINNESOTA got its name from a Dakota Sioux Indian word meaning "cloudy water" or "sky-tinted water."

MISSISSIPPI is probably from Chippewa Indian words meaning "great river" or "gathering of all the waters," or from an Algonquin word, *messipi*.

MISSOURI comes from an Algonquin Indian term meaning "river of the big canoes."

got *their* names

MONTANA comes from a Latin or Spanish word meaning "mountainous."

Nebraska

NEBRASKA comes from "flat river" or "broad water," an Omaha or Otos Indian name for the Platte River.

NEVADA means "snow-clad" in Spanish. Spanish explorers gave the name to the Sierra Nevada Mountains.

NEW HAMPSHIRE was named by an early settler after his home county of Hampshire, in England.

NEW JERSEY was named for the English Channel island of Jersey.

NEW MEXICO was given its name by 16th-century Spaniards in Mexico.

NEW YORK, first called New Netherland, was renamed for the Duke of York and Albany after the English took it from Dutch settlers.

NORTH CAROLINA, the northern part of the English colony of Carolana, was named for King Charles I.

NORTH DAKOTA comes from a Sioux Indian word meaning "friend" or "ally."

OHIO is the Iroquois Indian word for "good river."

OKLAHOMA comes from a Choctaw Indian word meaning "red man."

OREGON may have come from *Ouaricon-sint,* a name on an old French map that was once given to what is now called the Columbia River. That river runs between Oregon and Washington.

PENNSYLVANIA meaning "Penn's woods," was the name given to the colony founded by William Penn.

RHODE ISLAND may have come from the Dutch "Roode Eylandt" (red island) or may have been named after the Greek island of Rhodes.

SOUTH CAROLINA, the southern part of the English colony of Carolana, was named for King Charles I.

South Dakota

SOUTH DAKOTA comes from a Sioux Indian word meaning "friend" or "ally."

TENNESSEE comes from "Tanasi," the name of Cherokee Indian villages on what is now the Little Tennessee River.

TEXAS comes from a word meaning "friends" or "allies," used by the Spanish to describe some of the American Indians living there.

UTAH comes from a Navajo word meaning "upper" or "higher up."

Utah

VERMONT comes from two French words, *vert* meaning "green" and *mont* "mountain."

VIRGINIA was named in honor of Queen Elizabeth I of England, who was known as the Virgin Queen because she was never married.

WASHINGTON was named after George Washington, the first president of the United States. It is the only state named after a president.

WEST VIRGINIA got its name from the people of western Virginia, who formed their own government during the Civil War.

WISCONSIN comes from a Chippewa name that is believed to mean "grassy place." It was once spelled *Ouisconsin* and *Mesconsing.*

Wyoming

WYOMING comes from Algonquin Indian words that are said to mean "at the big plains," "large prairie place," or "on the great plain."

291

FACTS
About the
STATES

After every state name is the postal abbreviation. The Area includes both land and water; it is given in square miles (sq. mi.) and square kilometers (sq. km.). Numbers in parentheses after Population, Area, and Entered Union show the state's rank compared with other states. City populations are for mid-2003.

ALABAMA (AL) *Heart of Dixie, Camellia State*

Birmingham

Montgomery

POPULATION (2004): 4,530,182 (23rd) **AREA:** 52,419 sq. mi. (30th) (135,765 sq. km.) 🌼 Camellia 🐦 Yellowhammer 🌲 Southern longleaf pine 🎵 "Alabama" **ENTERED UNION:** December 14, 1819 (22nd) ⭐ Montgomery **LARGEST CITIES (WITH POP.):** Birmingham, 236,620; Montgomery, 200,123; Mobile, 193,464; Huntsville, 164,237

⚙ clothing and textiles, metal products, transportation equipment, paper, industrial machinery, food products, lumber, coal, oil, natural gas, livestock, peanuts, cotton

WEB SITE http://www.alabama.gov • http://www.touralabama.org

didyouknow? Huntsville, also known as "Rocket City," is home of NASA's Marshall Space Flight Center, which plays a big role in the U.S. space program.

ALASKA (AK) *The Last Frontier*

Anchorage

Juneau ⭐

POPULATION (2004): 655,435 (47th) **AREA:** 663,267 sq. mi. (1st) (1,717,854 sq. km.) 🌼 Forget-me-not 🐦 Willow ptarmigan 🌲 Sitka spruce 🎵 "Alaska's Flag" **ENTERED UNION:** January 3, 1959 (49th) ⭐ Juneau **LARGEST CITIES (WITH POP.):** Anchorage, 270,951; Juneau, 31,187; Fairbanks, 30,970

⚙ oil, natural gas, fish, food products, lumber and wood products, fur

WEB SITE http://www.state.ak.us • http://www.travelalaska.com

didyouknow? In 1867 the U.S. purchased Alaska from Russia for $7.2 million, or about 2 cents an acre. When Alaska was admitted to the Union as the 49th state in 1959, it increased the area of the U.S. by 20 percent.

ARIZONA (AZ) *Grand Canyon State*

Phoenix ⭐

Tucson

POPULATION (2004): 5,743,834 (18th) **AREA:** 113,998 sq. mi. (6th) (295,253 sq. km.) 🌼 Blossom of the Saguaro cactus 🐦 Cactus wren 🌲 Paloverde 🎵 "Arizona" **ENTERED UNION:** February 14, 1912 (48th) ⭐ Phoenix **LARGEST CITIES (WITH POP.):** Phoenix, 1,388,416; Tucson, 507,658; Mesa, 432,376; Glendale, 232,838; Scottsdale, 217,989; Chandler, 211,299

⚙ electronic equipment, transportation and industrial equipment, instruments, printing and publishing, copper and other metals

WEB SITE http://www.az.gov • http://www.arizonaguide.com

didyouknow? Cut by the Colorado River, the Grand Canyon has an average depth of 4,000 feet for its entire 277 miles. It's 6,000 feet at its deepest point, and ranges from 1 to 15 miles wide.

ARKANSAS (AR) *Natural State, Razorback State*

POPULATION (2004): 2,752,629 (32nd) **AREA:** 53,179 sq. mi. (29th) (137,733 sq. km.) 🌼Apple blossom 🐦Mockingbird 🌲Pine 🎵"Arkansas" **ENTERED UNION:** June 15, 1836 (25th) ⭐Little Rock **LARGEST CITIES (WITH POP.):** Little Rock, 184,053; Fort Smith, 81,562; Fayetteville, 62,078; North Little Rock, 59,687

🔧food products, paper, electronic equipment, industrial machinery, metal products, lumber and wood products, livestock, soybeans, rice, cotton, natural gas

WEB SITE http://www.arkansas.gov • http://www.arkansas.com

did you know? Almost 1 million gallons of water flow out of the springs at Hot Springs every day. Arkansas has the only working diamond mine in North America.

Little Rock ⭐

CALIFORNIA (CA) *Golden State*

POPULATION (2004): 35,893,799 (1st) **AREA:** 163,696 sq. mi. (3rd) (423,971 sq. km.) 🌼Golden poppy 🐦California valley quail 🌲California redwood 🎵"I Love You, California" **ENTERED UNION:** September 9, 1850 (31st) ⭐Sacramento **LARGEST CITIES (WITH POP.):** Los Angeles, 3,819,951; San Diego, 1,266,753; San Jose, 898,349; San Francisco, 751,682; Long Beach, 475,460; Fresno, 451,455; Sacramento, 445,335; Oakland, 398,844

🔧transportation and industrial equipment, electronic equipment, oil, natural gas, motion pictures, milk, cattle, fruit, vegetables

WEB SITE http://www.ca.gov • http://www.gocalif.ca.gov

did you know? The highest (Mount Whitney, 14,494 feet) and lowest (Death Valley, -282 feet) points in the "lower 48" states are only about 85 miles apart in California.

⭐**Sacramento**
San Francisco
Los Angeles
San Diego

COLORADO (CO) *Centennial State*

POPULATION (2004): 4,601,403 (22nd) **AREA:** 104,094 sq. mi. (8th) (269,602 sq. km.) 🌼Rocky Mountain columbine 🐦Lark bunting 🌲Colorado blue spruce 🎵"Where the Columbines Grow" **ENTERED UNION:** August 1, 1876 (38th) ⭐Denver **LARGEST CITIES (WITH POP.):** Denver, 557,478; Colorado Springs, 370,448; Aurora, 290,418; Lakewood, 142,474; Fort Collins, 125,740

🔧instruments and industrial machinery, food products, printing and publishing, metal products, electronic equipment, oil, coal, cattle

WEB SITE http://www.colorado.gov • http://www.colorado.com

did you know? Denver is called the "Mile High City" because of its altitude of about 1 mile (5,280 feet). Nearly twice as high at 10,430 feet, Leadville is the highest incorporated city in the U.S.

⭐ **Denver**
Colorado Springs

Key: 🌼Flower 🐦Bird 🌲Tree 🎵Song ⭐Capital 🔧Important Products

CONNECTICUT (CT) Constitution State, Nutmeg State

Hartford

POPULATION (2004): 3,503,604 (29th) **AREA:** 5,543 sq. mi. (48th) (14,356 sq. km.) Mountain laurel American robin White oak "Yankee Doodle" **ENTERED UNION:** January 9, 1788 (5th) Hartford **LARGEST CITIES (WITH POP.):** Bridgeport, 139,664; New Haven, 124,512; Hartford, 124,387; Stamford, 120,107; Waterbury, 108,130

aircraft parts, helicopters, industrial machinery, metals and metal products, electronic equipment, printing and publishing, medical instruments, chemicals, dairy products, stone

WEB SITE http://www.ct.gov • http://www.ctbound.org

did you know? Many historians believe Connecticut's 1639 constitution was the world's first written constitution and a model for the U.S. Constitution. That's why Connecticut is nicknamed the "Constitution State."

DELAWARE (DE) First State, Diamond State

Dover

POPULATION (2004): 830,364 (45th) **AREA:** 2,489 sq. mi. (49th) (6,446 sq. km.) Peach blossom Blue hen chicken American holly "Our Delaware" **ENTERED UNION:** December 7, 1787 (1st) Dover **LARGEST CITIES (WITH POP.):** Wilmington, 72,051; Dover, 32,808; Newark, 29,821

chemicals, transportation equipment, food products, chickens

WEB SITE http://www.delaware.gov • http://www.visitdelaware.net

did you know? In 1638, people from Sweden settled in Delaware, at Fort Christina (present-day Wilmington). Delaware became the first state when it ratified the U.S. Constitution in 1787.

FLORIDA (FL) Sunshine State

Tallahassee

Jacksonville

Miami •

POPULATION (2004): 17,397,161(4th) **AREA:** 65,755 sq. mi. (22nd) (170,305 sq. km.) Orange blossom Mockingbird Sabal palmetto palm "Old Folks at Home" **ENTERED UNION:** March 3, 1845 (27th) Tallahassee (population, 155,171) **LARGEST CITIES (WITH POP.):** Jacksonville, 773,781; Miami, 376,815; Tampa, 317,647; St. Petersburg, 247,610; Hialeah, 226,401; Orlando, 199,336; Ft. Lauderdale, 162,917

electronic and transportation equipment, industrial machinery, printing and publishing, food products, citrus fruits, vegetables, livestock, phosphates, fish

WEB SITE http://www.myflorida.com • http://www.flausa.com

did you know? In 1565 at St. Augustine, Spain's Pedro Menéndez de Avilés established the first permanent European settlement in what is now the United States—more than 40 years before Jamestown, Virginia.

GEORGIA (GA) *Empire State of the South, Peach State*

★ **Atlanta**

POPULATION (2004): 8,829,383 (9th) **AREA:** 59,425 sq. mi. (24th) (153,910 sq. km.) ❀Cherokee rose 🐦Brown thrasher 🌲Live oak 🎵"Georgia on My Mind" **ENTERED UNION:** January 2, 1788 (4th) ★Atlanta **LARGEST CITIES (WITH POP.):** Atlanta, 423,019; Augusta, 193,316; Columbus, 185,702; Savannah, 127,573; Athens, 102,498

⚙clothing and textiles, transportation equipment, food products, paper, chickens, peanuts, peaches, clay

WEB SITE http://www.georgia.gov • http://www.georgia.org

didyouknow? *Georgia, now the largest state east of the Mississippi River, was first explored by Spain's Hernando de Soto in 1540. The colony of Georgia was founded in 1732.*

HAWAII (HI) *Aloha State*

★ **Honolulu**

POPULATION (2004): 1,262,840 (42nd) **AREA:** 10,931 sq. mi. (43rd) (28,311 sq. km.) ❀Yellow hibiscus 🐦Hawaiian goose 🌲Kukui 🎵"Hawaii Ponoi" **ENTERED UNION:** August 21, 1959 (50th) ★Honolulu **LARGEST CITIES (WITH POP.):** Honolulu, 380,149; Hilo, 40,759; Kailua, 36,513; Kaneohe, 34,970

⚙food products, pineapples, sugar, printing and publishing, fish, flowers

WEB SITE http://www.ehawaiigov.org • http://www.gohawaii.com

didyouknow? *Hawaii is the only state made up entirely of islands. There are eight main islands and 122 islands in all. Kilauea, a volcano on "the Big Island" of Hawaii, has been erupting continuously since 1983.*

IDAHO (ID) *Gem State*

POPULATION (2004): 1,393,262 (39th) **AREA:** 83,570 sq. mi. (14th) (216,445 sq. km.) ❀Syringa 🐦Mountain bluebird 🌲White pine 🎵"Here We Have Idaho" **ENTERED UNION:** July 3, 1890 (43rd) ★Boise **LARGEST CITIES (WITH POP.):** Boise, 190,117; Nampa, 64,269; Pocatello, 51,009; Idaho Falls, 51,507

⚙potatoes, hay, wheat, cattle, milk, lumber and wood products, food products

WEB SITE http://www.idaho.gov • http://www.visitid.org

★ **Boise**

didyouknow? *It's estimated that some 300,000 pioneers crossed southern Idaho on the Oregon Trail between 1841 and 1867. At Three Island Park an annual reenactment is held at the famous Snake River crossing.*

Key: Flower Bird Tree Song Capital Important Products

ILLINOIS

(IL) *Prairie State*

Chicago

Springfield ⭐

POPULATION (2004): 12,713,634 (5th) **AREA:** 57,914 sq. mi. (25th) (149,997 sq. km.) 🌼Native violet 🐦Cardinal 🌳White oak 🎵"Illinois" **ENTERED UNION:** December 3, 1818 (21st) ⭐ Springfield **LARGEST CITIES (WITH POP.):** Chicago, 2,869,121; Aurora, 162,184; Rockford, 151,725; Naperville, 137,894; Joliet, 123,570; Springfield, 113,586; Peoria, 112,907

⚙️industrial machinery, metals and metal products, printing and publishing, electronic equipment, food products, corn, soybeans, hogs

WEB SITE *http://www.illinois.gov • http://www.enjoyillinois.com*

did you know? *Chicago is the nation's third largest city and home of the 1,450-foot Sears Tower, tallest building in the U.S. The world's first skyscraper, the Home Insurance Building, was built there in 1885.*

INDIANA

(IN) *Hoosier State*

Indianapolis ⭐

POPULATION (2004): 6,237,569 (14th) **AREA:** 36,418 sq. mi. (38th) (94,322 sq. km.) 🌼Peony 🐦Cardinal 🌳Tulip poplar 🎵"On the Banks of the Wabash, Far Away" **ENTERED UNION:** December 11, 1816 (19th) ⭐Indianapolis **LARGEST CITIES (WITH POP.):** Indianapolis, 783,438; Fort Wayne, 219,495; Evansville, 117,881; South Bend, 105,540; Gary, 99,961

⚙️transportation equipment, electronic equipment, industrial machinery, iron and steel, metal products, corn, soybeans, livestock, coal

WEB SITE *http://www.in.gov • http://www.enjoyindiana.com*

did you know? *The nickname "Hoosier State" became popular in the 1830s, but the origin of the word "hoosier" is not known.*

IOWA

(IA) *Hawkeye State*

Des Moines ⭐

POPULATION (2004): 2,954,451 (30th) **AREA:** 56,272 sq. mi. (26th) (145,744 sq. km.) 🌼Wild rose 🐦Eastern goldfinch 🌳Oak 🎵"The Song of Iowa" **ENTERED UNION:** December 28, 1846 (29th) ⭐Des Moines **LARGEST CITIES (WITH POP.):** Des Moines, 196,093; Cedar Rapids, 122,542; Davenport, 97,512; Sioux City, 83,876

⚙️corn, soybeans, hogs, cattle, industrial machinery, food products

WEB SITE *http://www.iowa.gov • http://www.traveliowa.com*

did you know? *The eastern and western borders of this state are defined by rivers. The Mississippi River carves out Iowa's eastern border, while the Missouri and Big Sioux rivers form the western border.*

KANSAS (KS) Sunflower State

Topeka ★

Wichita ●

POPULATION (2004): 2,735,502 (33rd) **AREA:** 82,277 sq. mi. (15th) (213,096 sq. km.) 🌻Native sunflower 🐦Western meadowlark 🌲Cottonwood 🎵"Home on the Range" **ENTERED UNION:** January 29, 1861 (34th) ⭐Topeka **LARGEST CITIES (WITH POP.):** Wichita, 354,617; Overland Park, 160,368; Kansas City, 145,757; Topeka, 122,008

⚙cattle, aircraft and other transportation equipment, industrial machinery, food products, wheat, corn, hay, oil, natural gas

WEB SITE http:// www.accesskansas.org • http://www.travelks.org

didyouknow? The Chisholm Trail, used by cowboys to drive cattle from Texas through Indian Territory (now Oklahoma), ended in Abilene, Kansas. Wyatt Earp, marshall of Dodge City, was among the legendary lawmen who kept the peace in rowdy frontier towns along the way.

KENTUCKY (KY) Bluegrass State

★ Frankfort

Louisville ●

POPULATION (2004): 4,145,922 (26th) **AREA:** 40,409 sq. mi. (37th) (104,659 sq. km.) 🌼Goldenrod 🐦Cardinal 🌲Tulip poplar 🎵"My Old Kentucky Home" **ENTERED UNION:** June 1, 1792 (15th) ⭐Frankfort (population, 27,660) **LARGEST CITIES (WITH POP.):** Lexington 266,798; Louisville, 248,762

⚙coal, industrial machinery, electronic equipment, transportation equipment, metals, tobacco, cattle

WEB SITE http:// www.kentucky.gov • http://www.kentuckytourism.com

didyouknow? The 170,000-acre "Land Between the Lakes," located mostly in Kentucky, is a peninsula between Kentucky Lake and Lake Barkley. It has over 300 miles of undeveloped shoreline and 200 miles of scenic hiking trails.

LOUISIANA (LA) Pelican State

POPULATION (2004): 4,515,770 (24th) **AREA:** 51,840 sq. mi. (31st) (134,265 sq. km.) 🌸Magnolia 🐦Eastern brown pelican 🌲Cypress 🎵"Give Me Louisiana" **ENTERED UNION:** April 30, 1812 (18th) ⭐Baton Rouge **LARGEST CITIES (WITH POP.):** New Orleans, 469,032; Baton Rouge, 225,090; Shreveport, 198,364; Lafayette, 111,667

⚙natural gas, oil, chemicals, transportation equipment, paper, food products, cotton, fish

Baton Rouge ★

New ● Orleans

WEB SITE http://www.louisiana.gov • http://www.louisianatravel.com

didyouknow? The state's highest elevation, in northwestern Louisiana, is 535 feet above sea level, and parts of New Orleans are 5 feet below sea level.

Key: 🌼**Flower** 🐦**Bird** 🌲**Tree** 🎵**Song** ⭐**Capital** ⚙**Important Products**

MAINE (ME) *Pine Tree State*

POPULATION (2004): 1,317,253 (40th) **AREA:** 35,385 sq. mi. (39th) (91,647 sq. km.) ✿White pine cone and tassel ♪Chickadee ⬥Eastern white pine ♪"State of Maine Song" **ENTERED UNION:** March 15, 1820 (23rd) ✪ Augusta (population, 18,551) **LARGEST CITIES (WITH POP.):** Portland, 63,635; Lewiston, 35,922; Bangor, 31,550

Augusta ✪

✿paper, transportation equipment, wood and wood products, electronic equipment, footwear, clothing, potatoes, milk, eggs, fish, and seafood

WEB SITE http://www.maine.gov • http://www.visitmaine.com

didyouknow? *Maine is nearly as big as the other 5 New England states (Connecticut, Massachusetts, New Hampshire, Rhode Island, Vermont) combined. Maine harvests about 90% of all U.S. lobsters and blueberries.*

MARYLAND (MD) *Old Line State, Free State*

Baltimore •

Annapolis ✪

✪
Washington, D.C.

POPULATION (2004): 5,558,058 (19th) **AREA:** 12,407 sq. mi. (42nd) (32,134 sq. km.) ✿Black-eyed susan ♪Baltimore oriole ⬥White oak ♪"Maryland, My Maryland" **ENTERED UNION:** April 28, 1788 (7th) ✪Annapolis (population, 36,196) **LARGEST CITIES (WITH POP.):** Baltimore, 628,670; Gaithersburg, 57,365; Frederick, 56,128; Rockville, 55,213; Bowie, 53,660

✿printing and publishing, food products, transportation equipment, electronic equipment, chickens, soybeans, corn, stone

WEB SITE http://www.maryland.gov • http://www.mdisfun.org

didyouknow? *The USS* Constellation, *launched in Baltimore in 1797, was the first ship built for the U.S. Navy. The Navy's last all-sail warship was built in 1854, and also named the* USS Constellation. *It is now an attraction in Baltimore's Inner Harbor.*

MASSACHUSETTS (MA) *Bay State, Old Colony*

Boston ✪

POPULATION (2004): 6,416,505 (13th) **AREA:** 10,555 sq. mi. (44th) (27,337 sq. km.) ✿Mayflower ♪Chickadee ⬥American elm ♪"All Hail to Massachusetts" **ENTERED UNION:** February 6, 1788 (6th) ✪Boston **LARGEST CITIES (WITH POP.):** Boston, 581,616; Worcester, 175,706; Springfield, 152,157; Lowell, 104,351; Cambridge, 101,587

✿ industrial machinery, electronic equipment, instruments, printing and publishing, metal products, fish, flowers and shrubs, cranberries

WEB SITE http://www.mass.gov • http://www.massvacation.com

didyouknow? *Massachusetts is a state of many American firsts: college, Harvard, 1636; post office, Boston, 1639; public library, Boston Public Library, 1653; regularly published newspaper, Boston News-Letter, 1704; lighthouse, Boston Harbor, 1716; subway system, Boston, 1898.*

MICHIGAN (MI) *Great Lakes State, Wolverine State*

POPULATION (2004): 10,112,620 (8th) **AREA:** 96,716 sq. mi. (11th) (250,493 sq. km.) 🌼Apple blossom 🐦Robin 🌲White pine 🎵"Michigan, My Michigan" **ENTERED UNION:** January 26, 1837 (26th) ⭐Lansing **LARGEST CITIES (WITH POP.):** Detroit, 911,402; Grand Rapids, 195,601; Warren, 136,016; Sterling Heights, 126,182; Flint, 120,292; Lansing, 118,379

⚙️automobiles, industrial machinery, metal products, office furniture, plastic products, chemicals, food products, milk, corn, natural gas, iron ore, blueberries

WEB SITE http://www.michigan.gov • http://www.travel.michigan.org

did you know? *From north to south, Lake Michigan is 321 miles long. It is 118 miles across at its widest point, and 923 feet deep at its deepest point.*

Lansing ⭐ Detroit

MINNESOTA (MN) *North Star State, Gopher State*

POPULATION (2004): 5,100,958 (21st) **AREA:** 86,939 sq. mi. (12th) (225,171 sq. km.) 🌼Pink and white lady's-slipper 🐦Common loon 🌲Red pine 🎵"Hail! Minnesota" **ENTERED UNION:** May 11, 1858 (32nd) ⭐St. Paul **LARGEST CITIES (WITH POP.):** Minneapolis, 373,188; St. Paul, 280,404; Rochester, 92,507; Duluth, 85,734

⚙️industrial machinery, printing and publishing, computers, food products, scientific and medical instruments, milk, hogs, cattle, corn, soybeans, iron ore

WEB SITE http://www.state.mn.us • http://www.exploreminnesota.com

did you know? *Minnesota candy maker Frank C. Mars introduced the Milky Way candy bar in 1923, Snickers in 1930, and Three Musketeers in 1937.*

Minneapolis
St. Paul ⭐

MISSISSIPPI (MS) *Magnolia State*

POPULATION (2004): 2,902,966 (31st) **AREA:** 48,430 sq. mi. (32nd) (125,433 sq. km.) 🌼Magnolia 🐦Mockingbird 🌲Magnolia 🎵"Go, Mississippi!" **ENTERED UNION:** December 10, 1817 (20th) ⭐Jackson **LARGEST CITIES (WITH POP.):** Jackson, 179,599; Gulfport, 71,810; Biloxi, 48,972

⚙️transportation equipment, furniture, electrical machinery, lumber and wood products, cotton, rice, chickens, cattle

WEB SITE http://www.mississippi.gov • http://www.visitmississippi.org

did you know? *Stretching for 26 miles, the Mississippi Gulf Coast is the longest man-made sand beach in the world. Elvis Presley, the "King" of rock and roll, was born in Tupelo on Jan. 8, 1935.*

⭐

Jackson

United States

Key: 🌼Flower 🐦Bird 🌲Tree 🎵Song ⭐Capital ⚙️Important Products

MISSOURI (MO) *Show Me State*

POPULATION (2004): 5,754,618 (17th) **AREA:** 69,704 sq. mi. (21st) (180,533 sq. km.) 🌼Hawthorn 🐦Bluebird 🌳Dogwood 🎵"Missouri Waltz" **ENTERED UNION:** August 10, 1821 (24th) ⭐Jefferson City (population 39,079) **LARGEST CITIES (WITH POP.):** Kansas City, 442,768; St. Louis, 332,223; Springfield, 150,867; Independence, 112,079

⚙️transportation equipment, electrical and electronic equipment, printing and publishing, food products, cattle, hogs, milk, soybeans, corn, hay, lead

WEB SITE *http://www.missouri.gov • http://www.missouritourism.org*

didyouknow? *The "boot heel" at the bottom of the state is credited to an influential landowner named John Hardeman Walker. He and other citizens of the area successfully petitioned Congress to be included in the new state of Missouri.*

MONTANA (MT) *Treasure State*

POPULATION (2004): 926,865 (44th) **AREA:** 147,042 sq. mi. (4th) (380,837 sq. km.) 🌼Bitterroot 🐦Western meadowlark 🌲Ponderosa pine 🎵"Montana" **ENTERED UNION:** November 8, 1889 (41st) ⭐Helena (population, 26,353) **LARGEST CITIES (WITH POP.):** Billings, 95,220; Missoula, 60,722; Great Falls, 56,155; Butte, 32,519

⚙️cattle, copper, gold, wheat, barley, wood and paper products

WEB SITE *http://www.discoveringmontana.com • http://visitmt.com*

didyouknow? *Montana's Glacier National Park in the Rocky Mountains preserves more than 1 million acres of land. More than 70 types of mammals live there, including grizzly and black bear, elk, and bighorn sheep.*

NEBRASKA (NE) *Cornhusker State*

POPULATION (2004): 1,747,214 (38th) **AREA:** 77,354 sq. mi. (16th) (200,346 sq. km.) 🌼Goldenrod 🐦Western meadowlark 🌳Cottonwood 🎵"Beautiful Nebraska" **ENTERED UNION:** March 1, 1867 (37th) ⭐Lincoln **LARGEST CITIES (WITH POP.):** Omaha, 404,267; Lincoln, 235,594; Bellevue, 46,734; Grand Island, 43,771

⚙️cattle, hogs, milk, corn, soybeans, hay, wheat, sorghum, food products, industrial machinery

WEB SITE *http://www.nebraska.gov • http://www.visitnebraska.org*

didyouknow? *Arbor Day, the last Friday in April, was first celebrated in Nebraska in 1872, with the planting of more than a million trees*

NEVADA (NV) Sagebrush State, Battle Born State, Silver State

POPULATION (2004): 2,334,771 (35th) **AREA:** 110,561 sq. mi. (7th) (286,352 sq. km.) 🌸Sagebrush 🐦Mountain bluebird 🌲Single-leaf piñon, bristlecone pine 🎵"Home Means Nevada" **ENTERED UNION:** October 31, 1864 (36th) ⭐Carson City (population, 54,311) **LARGEST CITIES (WITH POP.):** Las Vegas, 517,017; Henderson, 214,852; Reno, 193,882

⚙️gold, silver, cattle, hay, food products, plastics, chemicals

WEB SITE http://www.nv.gov • http://www.travelnevada.com

did you know? The famous "Comstock Lode" silver mine was discovered near Lake Tahoe in 1859. In the mid 1870s it yielded $36 million worth of silver ore a year—over $500 million yearly in 2005 dollars. Nevada still produces 40% of all the silver mined in the U.S.

⭐ **Carson City**

Las Vegas •

NEW HAMPSHIRE (NH) Granite State

POPULATION (2004): 1,299,500 (41st) **AREA:** 9,350 sq. mi. (46th) (24,216 sq. km.) 🌸Purple lilac 🐦Purple finch 🌲White birch 🎵"Old New Hampshire" **ENTERED UNION:** June 21, 1788 (9th) ⭐Concord **LARGEST CITIES (WITH POP.):** Manchester, 108,871; Nashua, 87,285; Concord, 41,823

⚙️industrial machinery, electric and electronic equipment, metal products, plastic products, dairy products, maple syrup and maple sugar

WEB SITE http://www.nh.gov • http://www.visitnh.gov

did you know? Revolutionary General John Stark, hero of the 1777 Battle of Bennington, wrote "Live Free Or Die; Death Is Not The Worst of Evils" in an 1809 toast. "Live Free or Die" became the official state motto in 1945.

Concord ⭐

NEW JERSEY (NJ) Garden State

POPULATION (2004): 8,698,879 (10th) **AREA:** 8,721 sq. mi. (47th) (22,587 sq. km.) 🌸Purple violet 🐦Eastern goldfinch 🌲Red oak 🎵none **ENTERED UNION:** December 18, 1787 (3rd) ⭐Trenton **LARGEST CITIES (WITH POP.):** Newark, 277,911; Jersey City, 239,097; Paterson, 150,782; Elizabeth, 123,215; Trenton, 85,314

⚙️chemicals, pharmaceuticals/drugs, electronic equipment, nursery and greenhouse products, food products, tomatoes, blueberries, and peaches

WEB SITE http://www.newjersey.gov • http://www.visitnj.org

did you know? On December 26, 1776, General George Washington and 2,500 men crossed the Delaware River from Pennsylvania and captured Trenton, New Jersey. This battle, along with a victory at Princeton a week later, was a turning point in the American Revolution.

Newark •

⭐ **Trenton**

Key: 🌸Flower 🐦Bird 🌲Tree 🎵Song ⭐Capital ⚙️Important Products

NEW MEXICO (NM) *Land of Enchantment*

Santa Fe ★

● Albuquerque

POPULATION (2004): 1,903,289 (36th) **AREA:** 121,589 sq. mi. (5th) (314,914 sq. km.) Yucca Roadrunner Piñon "O, Fair New Mexico" **ENTERED UNION:** January 6, 1912 (47th) Santa Fe **LARGEST CITIES (WITH POP.):** Albuquerque, 471,856; Las Cruces, 76,990; Santa Fe, 66,476; Rio Rancho, 58,981

electronic equipment, foods, machinery, clothing, lumber, transportation equipment, hay, onions, chiles

WEB SITE http://www.state.nm.us • http://www.newmexico.org

did you know? Carlsbad Caverns National Park contains Lechuguilla Cave, the deepest cave in the U.S. at over 1,570 feet deep. Hundreds of thousands of bats swarm out of the caverns every night to feed on insects.

NEW YORK (NY) *Empire State*

Albany ★

● Buffalo

New York City ●

POPULATION (2004): 19,227,088 (3rd) **AREA:** 54,556 sq. mi. (27th) (141,299 sq. km.) Rose Bluebird Sugar maple "I Love New York" **ENTERED UNION:** July 26, 1788 (11th) Albany (population, 93,779) **LARGEST CITIES (WITH POP.):** New York, 8,085,742; Buffalo, 285,018; Rochester, 215,093; Yonkers, 197,388; Syracuse, 144,001

books and magazines, automobile and aircraft parts, toys and sporting goods, electronic equipment, machinery, clothing and textiles, metal products, milk, cattle, hay, apples

WEB SITE http://www.state.ny.us • http://www.iloveny.com

did you know? New York City was the first capital of the United States. Congress met there from 1785 to 1790, and George Washington was sworn in as president there on April 30, 1789.

NORTH CAROLINA (NC) *Tar Heel State, Old North State*

Raleigh ★

● Charlotte

POPULATION (2004): 8,541,221 (11th) **AREA:** 53,819 sq. mi. (28th) (139,391 sq. km.) Dogwood Cardinal Pine "The Old North State" **ENTERED UNION:** November 21, 1789 (12th) Raleigh **LARGEST CITIES (WITH POP.):** Charlotte, 584,658; Raleigh, 316,802; Greensboro, 229,110; Durham, 198,376; Winston-Salem, 190,299

clothing and textiles, tobacco and tobacco products, industrial machinery, electronic equipment, furniture, cotton, soybeans, peanuts

WEB SITE http://www.ncgov.com • http://www.visitnc.com

did you know? English settlers established a colony on North Carolina's Roanoke Island in 1585, but abandoned it a year later. A second colony was founded in 1587, but had mysteriously disappeared by 1590.

NORTH DAKOTA (ND) *Peace Garden State*

POPULATION (2004): 634,366 (48th) **AREA:** 70,700 sq. mi. (19th) (183,112 sq. km.) 🌹Wild prairie rose 🐦Western meadowlark 🌳American elm 🎵"North Dakota Hymn"
ENTERED UNION: November 2, 1889 (39th) ⭐Bismarck
LARGEST CITIES (WITH POP.): Fargo, 91,484; Bismarck, 56,344; Grand Forks, 48,618; Minot, 35,424

⚙wheat, barley, hay, sunflowers, sugar beets, cattle, sand and gravel, food products, farm equipment, high-tech electronics

⭐Bismarck

WEB SITE http://www.discovernd.com • http://www.ndtourism.com

did you know? The state's nickname is taken from the International Peace Garden, which straddles the boundary between North Dakota and Manitoba in Canada.

OHIO (OH) *Buckeye State*

POPULATION (2004): 11,459,011 (7th) **AREA:** 44,825 sq. mi. (34th) (116,096 sq. km.) 🌹Scarlet carnation 🐦Cardinal 🌳Buckeye 🎵"Beautiful Ohio"
ENTERED UNION: March 1, 1803 (17th) ⭐Columbus **LARGEST CITIES (WITH POP.):** Columbus, 728,432; Cleveland, 461,324; Cincinnati, 317,361; Toledo, 308,973; Akron, 212,215; Dayton, 161,696

Cleveland
Columbus ⭐
Cincinnati

⚙metal and metal products, transportation equipment, industrial machinery, rubber and plastic products, electronic equipment, printing and publishing, chemicals, food products, corn, soybeans, livestock, milk

WEB SITE http://www.ohio.gov • http://www.discoverohio.com

did you know? The Rock and Roll Hall of Fame is in Cleveland, and the Pro Football Hall of Fame is in Canton. Ohio Senator John Glenn, the first American to orbit Earth, in 1962, returned to space in 1998 at the age of 77, the oldest person to fly in space.

OKLAHOMA (OK) *Sooner State*

POPULATION (2004): 3,523,553 (28th) **AREA:** 69,898 sq. mi. (20th) (181,035 sq. km.) 🌹Mistletoe 🐦Scissor-tailed flycatcher 🌳Redbud 🎵"Oklahoma!" **ENTERED UNION:** November 16, 1907 (46th) ⭐Oklahoma City **LARGEST CITIES (WITH POP.):** Oklahoma City, 523,303; Tulsa, 387,807; Norman, 99,197; Lawton, 91,730; Broken Arrow, 83,607

Tulsa
⭐
Oklahoma City

⚙natural gas, oil, cattle, nonelectrical machinery, transportation equipment, metal products, wheat, hay

WEB SITE http://www.youroklahoma.com • http://www.travelok.com

did you know? Oklahoma has produced more astronauts than any other state, including Major General Thomas P. Stafford, Gordon Cooper, Owen Garriott, Shannon Lucid, and William Reid Pogue.

Key: 🌹Flower 🐦Bird 🌳Tree 🎵Song ⭐Capital ⚙Important Products

OREGON (OR) Beaver State

• **Portland**

⭐ **Salem**

POPULATION (2004): 3,594,586 (27th) **AREA:** 98,381 sq. mi. (9th) (254,806 sq. km.) 🌼Oregon grape 🐦Western meadowlark 🌲Douglas fir 🎵"Oregon, My Oregon" **ENTERED UNION:** February 14, 1859 (33rd) ⭐Salem **LARGEST CITIES (WITH POP.):** Portland, 538,544; Salem, 142,914; Eugene, 142,185; Gresham, 95,816

⚙️lumber and wood products, electronics and semiconductors, food products, paper, cattle, hay, vegetables, Christmas trees

WEB SITE *http://www.oregon.gov • http://www.traveloregon.com*

did you know? *The caves in Oregon Caves National Monument, discovered in 1874, are carved out of solid marble. Oregon has the only state flag with different pictures on each side—it has the state seal on the front and a beaver, the state animal, on the back.*

PENNSYLVANIA (PA) Keystone State

Harrisburg
• **Pittsburgh** ⭐
          Philadelphia •

POPULATION (2004): 12,406,292 (6th) **AREA:** 46,055 sq. mi. (33rd) (119,282 sq. km.) 🌼Mountain laurel 🐦Ruffed grouse 🌲Hemlock 🎵"Pennsylvania" **ENTERED UNION:** December 12, 1787 (2nd) ⭐Harrisburg (population, 48,540) **LARGEST CITIES (WITH POP.):** Philadelphia, 1,479,339; Pittsburgh, 325,337; Allentown, 105,958; Erie, 101,373

⚙️iron and steel, coal, industrial machinery, printing and publishing, food products, electronic equipment, transportation equipment, stone, clay and glass products

WEB SITE *http://www.state.pa.us • http://www.experiencepa.com*

did you know? *A turning point in the Civil War, the battle at Gettysburg stopped the second, and last, major Confederate invasion of the North. In 1777-78, George Washington and the Continental Army endured a harsh winter at Valley Forge, where one in ten soldiers died from cold and disease. Valley Forge is now a National Historical Park.*

RHODE ISLAND (RI) Little Rhody, Ocean State

Providence
⭐

POPULATION (2004): 1,080,632 (43rd) **AREA:** 1,545 sq. mi. (50th) (4,002 sq. km.) 🌼Violet 🐦Rhode Island red 🌲Red maple 🎵"Rhode Island" **ENTERED UNION:** May 29, 1790 (13th) ⭐ Providence **LARGEST CITIES (WITH POP.):** Providence, 176,365; Warwick, 87,365; Cranston, 81,679; Pawtucket, 74,330

⚙️costume jewelry, toys, textiles, machinery, electronic equipment, fish

WEB SITE *http://www.ri.gov • http://www.visitrhodeisland.com*

did you know? *Rhode Island is the smallest state in the U.S. Although Rhode Island was the first colony to declare its independence from England in 1776, it was the last of the original 13 colonies to ratify the Constitution (in 1790).*

SOUTH CAROLINA (SC) *Palmetto State*

Columbia

POPULATION (2004): 4,198,068 (25th) **AREA:** 32,020 sq. mi. (40th) (82,931 sq. km.) 🌼Yellow jessamine 🐦Carolina wren 🌲Palmetto 🎵"Carolina" **ENTERED UNION:** May 23, 1788 (8th) ⭐Columbia **LARGEST CITIES (WITH POP.):** Columbia, 117,357; Charleston, 101,024; North Charleston, 81,577; Greenville, 55,926

🔧clothing and textiles, chemicals, industrial machinery, metal products, livestock, tobacco, Portland cement

WEB SITE *http://www.myscgov.com • http://www.discoversouthcarolina.com*

didyouknow? *More battles of the American Revolution were fought in South Carolina than any other colony. The Civil War began in Charleston harbor, with the first shots fired on Fort Sumter in 1861.*

SOUTH DAKOTA (SD) *Mt. Rushmore State, Coyote State*

POPULATION (2004): 770,883 (46th) **AREA:** 77,116 sq. mi. (17th) (199,730 sq. km.) 🌼Pasqueflower 🐦Chinese ring-necked pheasant 🌲Black Hills spruce 🎵"Hail, South Dakota" **ENTERED UNION:** November 2, 1889 (40th) ⭐Pierre (population, 14,012) **LARGEST CITIES (WITH POP.):** Sioux Falls, 133,834; Rapid City, 60,876; Aberdeen, 24,086

⭐ Pierre

🔧food and food products, machinery, electric and electronic equipment, corn, soybeans

WEB SITE *http://www.state.sd.us • http://www.travelsd.com*

didyouknow? *Massive sculptures in the Black Hills include the presidents' faces on Mt. Rushmore and the still-unfinished Crazy Horse Memorial, a mountain carved into the image of the Oglala Sioux chief seated on his horse.*

TENNESSEE (TN) *Volunteer State*

POPULATION (2004): 5,900,962 (16th) **AREA:** 42,143 sq. mi. (36th) (109,150 sq. km.) 🌼Iris 🐦Mockingbird 🌲Tulip poplar 🎵"My Homeland, Tennessee"; "When It's Iris Time in Tennessee"; "My Tennessee"; "Tennessee Waltz"; "Rocky Top" **ENTERED UNION:** June 1, 1796 (16th) ⭐Nashville **LARGEST CITIES (WITH POP.):** Memphis, 645,978; Nashville, 544,765; Knoxville, 173,278; Chattanooga, 154,887

⭐ Nashville
• Memphis

🔧chemicals, machinery, vehicles, food products, metal products, publishing, electronic equipment, paper products, rubber and plastic products, tobacco

WEB SITE *http://www.tennessee.gov • http://www.tnvacation.com*

didyouknow? *The top secret city of Oak Ridge was built for the Manhattan Project, the U.S. government research project (1942-45) that produced the first atomic bomb.*

Key: 🌼Flower 🐦Bird 🌲Tree 🎵Song ⭐Capital 🔧Important Products

TEXAS (TX) Lone Star State

POPULATION (2004): 22,490,022 (2nd) **AREA:** 268,581 sq. mi. (2nd) (695,622 sq. km.) ⚘Bluebonnet ꕤMockingbird ꕤPecan ♪"Texas, Our Texas" **ENTERED UNION:** December 29, 1845 (28th) ★Austin **LARGEST CITIES (WITH POP.):** Houston, 2,009,690; San Antonio, 1,214,725; Dallas, 1,208,318; Austin, 672,011; Fort Worth, 585,122; El Paso, 584,113; Arlington, 355,007; Corpus Christi, 279,208

⚙oil, natural gas, cattle, milk, eggs, transportation equipment, chemicals, clothing, industrial machinery, electrical and electronic equipment, cotton, grains

WEB SITE http://www.texasonline.com • http://www.traveltex.com

didyouknow? The Battle of the Alamo ended March 6, 1836, with the deaths of some 190 defenders against more than 4,000 Mexican soldiers under Santa Anna. On April 28, General Sam Houston defeated Santa Anna at the battle of San Jacinto to win Texas's independence from Mexico.

UTAH (UT) Beehive State

POPULATION (2004): 2,389,039 (34th) **AREA:** 84,899 sq. mi. (13th) (219,887 sq. km.) ⚘Sego lily ꕤSeagull ♣Blue spruce ♪"Utah, This is the Place" **ENTERED UNION:** January 4, 1896 (45th) ★Salt Lake City **LARGEST CITIES (WITH POP.):** Salt Lake City, 179,894; West Valley City, 111,687; Provo, 105,410

⚙transportation equipment, medical instruments, electronic parts, food products, steel, copper, cattle, corn, hay, wheat, barley

WEB SITE http://www.utah.gov • http://www.utah.com

didyouknow? The Great Salt Lake covers an area of about 2,100 square miles, with an average depth of 13 feet. Three rivers carry more than 1.1 million tons of salt into the lake each year.

VERMONT (VT) Green Mountain State

POPULATION (2004): 621,394 (49th) **AREA:** 9,614 sq. mi. (45th) (24,900 sq. km.) ⚘Red clover ꕤHermit thrush ♣Sugar maple ♪"These Green Mountains" **ENTERED UNION:** March 4, 1791 (14th) ★Montpelier (population, 8,026) **LARGEST CITIES (WITH POP.):** Burlington, 39,148; Rutland, 17,103; South Burlington, 16,285

⚙machine tools, furniture, scales, books, computer parts, foods, dairy products, apples, maple syrup

WEB SITE http://www.vermont.gov • http://www.vermontvacation.com

didyouknow? An independent republic from 1777 to 1791, Vermont joined the Union as the 14th state. Until then, its territory had been claimed by both New York and New Hampshire.

VIRGINIA (VA) *Old Dominion*

Alexandria ●
Richmond ☆
● Norfolk

POPULATION (2004): 7,459,827 (12th) **AREA:** 42,774 sq. mi. (35th) (110,784 sq. km.) 🌼Dogwood 🐦Cardinal 🌲Dogwood 🎵"Carry Me Back to Old Virginia" **ENTERED UNION:** June 25, 1788 (10th) ⭐Richmond **LARGEST CITIES (WITH POP.):** Virginia Beach, 439,467; Norfolk, 241,727; Chesapeake, 210,834; Richmond, 194,729; Arlington, 187,873; Newport News, 181,647

⚙transportation equipment, textiles, chemicals, printing, machinery, electronic equipment, food products, coal, livestock, tobacco, wood products, furniture

WEB SITE http://www.virginia.gov • http://www.virginia.org

didyouknow? More U.S. presidents were born in this state than in any other, a total of eight, starting with George Washington.

WASHINGTON (WA) *Evergreen State*

● Seattle
⭐ Olympia

POPULATION (2004): 6,203,788 (15th) **AREA:** 71,300 sq. mi. (18th) (184,666 sq. km.) 🌼Western rhododendron 🐦Willow goldfinch 🌲Western hemlock 🎵"Washington, My Home" **ENTERED UNION:** November 11, 1889 (42nd) ⭐Olympia (population, 43,519) **LARGEST CITIES (WITH POP.):** Seattle, 569,101; Tacoma, 196,790; Spokane, 196,624; Vancouver, 151,654; Bellevue, 112,344

⚙aircraft, lumber, pulp and paper, machinery, electronics, computer software, aluminum, processed fruits and vegetables

WEB SITE http://www.access.wa.gov • http://www.experiencewashington.com

didyouknow? In 1846, the U.S.–Canada border was "cleaned up" by using a line of latitude, the 49th parallel, as the dividing line. This left the town of Point Roberts, on a 5-square-mile tip of a Canadian peninsula, separated from the U.S. mainland.

WEST VIRGINIA (WV) *Mountain State*

⭐ Charleston

POPULATION (2004): 1,815,354 (37th) **AREA:** 24,230 sq. mi. (41st) (62,755 sq. km.) 🌼Big rhododendron 🐦Cardinal 🌲Sugar maple 🎵"The West Virginia Hills"; "This Is My West Virginia"; "West Virginia, My Home Sweet Home" **ENTERED UNION:** June 20, 1863 (35th) ⭐ Charleston **LARGEST CITIES (WITH POP.):** Charleston, 51,394; Huntington, 49,533; Parkersburg, 32,100; Wheeling, 30,096

⚙coal, natural gas, fabricated metal products, chemicals, automobile parts, aluminum, steel, machinery, cattle, hay, apples, peaches, tobacco

WEB SITE http://www.wv.gov • http://www.callwva.com

didyouknow? On Oct. 16, 1859, abolitionist leader John Brown and 18 others seized the federal arsenal in Harpers Ferry in an attempt to end slavery by force. Federal troops captured him and he was put to death in Charlestown later that year.

Key: 🌼Flower 🐦Bird 🌲Tree 🎵Song ⭐Capital ⚙Important Products

WISCONSIN (WI) *Badger State*

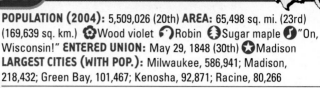

POPULATION (2004): 5,509,026 (20th) **AREA:** 65,498 sq. mi. (23rd) (169,639 sq. km.) 🌼Wood violet 🐦Robin 🌳Sugar maple 🎵"On, Wisconsin!" **ENTERED UNION:** May 29, 1848 (30th) ⭐Madison **LARGEST CITIES (WITH POP.):** Milwaukee, 586,941; Madison, 218,432; Green Bay, 101,467; Kenosha, 92,871; Racine, 80,266

⚙️paper products, printing, milk, butter, cheese, foods, food products, motor vehicles and equipment, medical instruments and supplies, plastics, corn, hay, vegetables

WEB SITE http://www.wisconsin.gov • http://www.travelwisconsin.com

Madison ⭐
Milwaukee

did you know? *Wisconsin, the dairy capital of the U.S., produces more milk than any other state. One of the world's largest air shows takes place every year at the end of July in Oshkosh.*

WYOMING (WY) *Cowboy State*

POPULATION (2004): 506,529 (50th) **AREA:** 97,814 sq. mi. (10th) (253,337 sq. km.) 🌼Indian paintbrush 🐦Western meadowlark 🌳Plains cottonwood 🎵"Wyoming" **ENTERED UNION:** July 10, 1890 (44th) ⭐Cheyenne **LARGEST CITIES (WITH POP.):** Cheyenne, 54,374; Casper, 50,632; Laramie, 26,956

⚙️ oil, natural gas, petroleum (oil) products, cattle, wheat, beans

WEB SITE http://www.state.wy.us • http://www.wyomingtourism.org

Cheyenne ⭐

did you know? *Wyoming boasts the first official national park, Yellowstone, the first national forest, Shoshone, and the first national monument, Devils Tower.*

COMMONWEALTH OF PUERTO RICO (PR)

San Juan ⭐

HISTORY: Christopher Columbus landed in Puerto Rico in 1493. Puerto Rico was a Spanish colony for centuries, then was ceded (given) to the United States in 1898 after the Spanish-American War. In 1952, still associated with the United States, Puerto Rico became a commonwealth with its own constitution. **POPULATION (2004):** 3,894,855 **AREA:** 5,324 sq. mi. (13,789 sq. km.) 🌼Maga 🐦Reinita 🌳Ceiba **NATIONAL ANTHEM:** "La Borinqueña" ⭐San Juan **LARGEST CITIES (WITH POP.):** San Juan, 433,733; Bayamón, 224,915; Carolina, 187,337; Ponce, 185,930

⚙️chemicals, food products, electronic equipment, clothing and textiles, industrial machinery, coffee, sugarcane, fruit, hogs

WEB SITE http://www.gobierno.pr • http://www.gotopuertorico.com

did you know? *Puerto Rico is one of the world's most densely populated islands. La Fortaleza, dating from 1533, is the official residence of the governor, the oldest executive mansion in continuous use in the New World.*

WASHINGTON, D.C. ★
The **Capital** of the **United States**

LAND AREA: 61 square miles **POPULATION (2004):** 563,384
FLOWER: American beauty rose **BIRD:** Wood thrush
WEB SITE http://www.dc.gov • http://www.washington.org

HISTORY Washington, D.C., became the capital of the United States in 1800, when the federal government moved there from Philadelphia. The city of Washington was designed and built to be the capital. It was named after George Washington. Many of its major sights are on the Mall, an open grassy area that runs from the Capitol to the Potomac River.

CAPITOL, which houses the U.S. Congress, is at the east end of the Mall on Capitol Hill. Its dome can be seen from far away.

FRANKLIN DELANO ROOSEVELT MEMORIAL, honoring the 32nd president of the United States, and his wife, Eleanor, was dedicated in 1997. It is outdoors in a parklike setting.

JEFFERSON MEMORIAL, a circular marble building located near the Potomac River. Its design is partly based on one by Thomas Jefferson for the University of Virginia.

KOREAN WAR VETERANS MEMORIAL, dedicated in 1995, is at the west end of the Mall. It shows troops ready for combat.

LINCOLN MEMORIAL, at the west end of the Mall, is built of white marble and styled like a Greek temple. Inside is a large, seated statue of Abraham Lincoln. His Gettysburg Address is carved on a nearby wall.

NATIONAL ARCHIVES, on Constitution Avenue, holds the Declaration of Independence, Constitution, and Bill of Rights.

NATIONAL GALLERY OF ART, on the Mall, is one of the world's great art museums.

NATIONAL WORLD WAR II MEMORIAL, located between the Lincoln Memorial and the Washington Monument at the Mall, honors the 16 million Americans who served during the war. It was dedicated in May 2004.

SMITHSONIAN INSTITUTION has 14 museums, including the new National Museum of the American Indian, the National Air and Space Museum and the Museum of Natural History. The National Zoo is part of the Smithsonian.

U.S. HOLOCAUST MEMORIAL MUSEUM presents the history of the Nazis' murder of more than six million Jews and millions of other people from 1933 to 1945. The exhibit *Daniel's Story* tells the story of the Holocaust from a child's point of view.

VIETNAM VETERANS MEMORIAL has a black-granite wall shaped like a "V". Names of the Americans killed or missing in the Vietnam War are inscribed on the wall.

WASHINGTON MONUMENT, a white marble pillar, or obelisk, standing on the Mall and rising to over 555 feet. From the top, there are wonderful views of the city.

WHITE HOUSE, at 1600 Pennsylvania Avenue, has been the home of every U.S. president except George Washington.

WOMEN IN MILITARY SERVICE FOR AMERICA MEMORIAL, near the entrance to Arlington National Cemetery. It honors the 1.8 million women who have served in the U.S. armed forces.

◀ *Jefferson Memorial*

Weather

What's the highest recorded wind speed? page 312

TAKING TEMPERATURES

There are two main systems for measuring temperature. One is **Fahrenheit** (abbreviated F). The other is **Celsius** (abbreviated C). Another word for Celsius is Centigrade.

Zero degrees (0°) Celsius is equal to 32 degrees (32°) Fahrenheit.

To convert from Celsius to Fahrenheit:
Multiply by 1.8 and add 32.
(°F = 1.8 x °C + 32)
Example: 20° C x 1.8 = 36; 36 + 32 = 68° F

To convert from Fahrenheit to Celsius, reverse the process:
Subtract 32 and divide by 1.8.
Example: 68° F – 32 = 36; 36/1.8 = 20° C

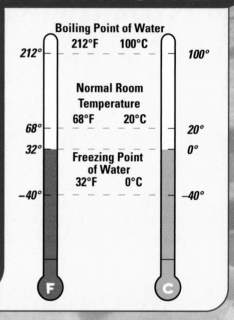

Boiling Point of Water
212°F   100°C

Normal Room Temperature
68°F   20°C

Freezing Point of Water
32°F   0°C

212°	100°
68°	20°
32°	0°
–40°	–40°

F   C

HOTTEST and COLDEST Places in the World

Continent	Highest Temperature	Lowest Temperature
AFRICA	El Azizia, Libya, 136°F (58°C)	Ifrane, Morocco, –11°F (–24°C)
ANTARCTICA	Vanda Station, 59°F (15°C)	Vostok, –129°F (–89°C)
ASIA	Tirat Tsvi, Israel, 129°F (54°C)	Verkhoyansk, Russia, and Oimekon, Russia, –90°F (–68°C)
AUSTRALIA	Cloncurry, Queensland, 128°F (53°C)	Charlotte Pass, New South Wales, –9°F (–23°C)
EUROPE	Seville, Spain, 122°F (50°C)	Ust'Shchugor, Russia, –67°F (–55°C)
NORTH AMERICA	Death Valley, California, 134°F (57°C)	Snag, Yukon Territory, Canada –81°F (–63°C)
SOUTH AMERICA	Rivadavia, Argentina, 120°F (49°C)	Sarmiento, Argentina, –27°F (–33°C)

RECORD TEMPERATURES by State
(THROUGH 2000)

COLDEST TEMPERATURE

HOTTEST TEMPERATURE

State	LOWEST		HIGHEST	
	°F	Latest date	°F	Latest date
Alabama	−27	Jan. 30, 1966	112	Sept. 5, 1925
Alaska	−80	Jan. 23, 1971	100	June 27, 1915
Arizona	−40	Jan. 7, 1971	128	June 29, 1994
Arkansas	−29	Feb. 13, 1905	120	Aug. 10, 1936
California	−45	Jan. 20, 1937	134	July 10, 1913
Colorado	−61	Feb. 1, 1985	118	July 11, 1888
Connecticut	−32	Jan. 22, 1961	106	July 15, 1995
Delaware	−17	Jan. 17, 1893	110	July 21, 1930
Florida	−2	Feb. 13, 1899	109	June 29, 1931
Georgia	−17	Jan. 27, 1940	112	Aug. 20, 1983
Hawaii	12	May 17, 1979	100	Apr. 27, 1931
Idaho	−60	Jan. 18, 1943	118	July 28, 1934
Illinois	−36	Jan. 5, 1999	117	July 14, 1954
Indiana	−36	Jan. 19, 1994	116	July 14, 1936
Iowa	−47	Feb. 3, 1996	118	July 20, 1934
Kansas	−40	Feb. 13, 1905	121	July 24, 1936
Kentucky	−37	Jan. 19, 1994	114	July 28, 1930
Louisiana	−16	Feb. 13, 1899	114	Aug. 10, 1936
Maine	−48	Jan. 19, 1925	105	July 10, 1911
Maryland	−40	Jan. 13, 1912	109	July 10, 1936
Massachusetts	−35	Jan. 12, 1981	107	Aug. 2, 1975
Michigan	−51	Feb. 9, 1934	112	July 13, 1936
Minnesota	−60	Feb. 2, 1996	114	July 6, 1936
Mississippi	−19	Jan. 30, 1966	115	July 29, 1930
Missouri	−40	Feb. 13, 1905	118	July 14, 1954
Montana	−70	Jan. 20, 1954	117	July 5, 1937
Nebraska	−47	Dec. 22, 1989	118	July 24, 1936
Nevada	−50	Jan. 8, 1937	125	June 29, 1994
New Hampshire	−47	Jan. 29, 1934	106	July 4, 1911
New Jersey	−34	Jan. 5, 1904	110	July 10, 1936
New Mexico	−50	Feb. 1, 1951	122	June 27, 1994
New York	−52	Feb. 18, 1979	108	July 22, 1926
North Carolina	−34	Jan. 21, 1985	110	Aug. 21, 1983
North Dakota	−60	Feb. 15, 1936	121	July 6, 1936
Ohio	−39	Feb. 10, 1899	113	July 21, 1934
Oklahoma	−27	Jan. 18, 1930	120	June 27, 1994
Oregon	−54	Feb. 10, 1933	119	Aug. 10, 1898
Pennsylvania	−42	Jan. 5, 1904	111	July 10, 1936
Rhode Island	−25	Feb. 5, 1996	104	Aug. 2, 1975
South Carolina	−19	Jan. 21, 1985	111	June 28, 1954
South Dakota	−58	Feb. 17, 1936	120	July 5, 1936
Tennessee	−32	Dec. 30, 1917	113	Aug. 9, 1930
Texas	−23	Feb. 8, 1933	120	June 28, 1994
Utah	−69	Feb. 1, 1985	117	Jul. 5, 1985
Vermont	−50	Dec. 30, 1933	105	July 4, 1911
Virginia	−30	Jan. 22, 1985	110	July 15, 1954
Washington	−48	Dec. 30, 1968	118	Aug. 5, 1961
West Virginia	−37	Dec. 30, 1917	112	July 10, 1936
Wisconsin	−55	Feb. 4, 1996	114	July 13, 1936
Wyoming	−66	Feb. 9, 1933	115	Aug. 8, 1983

Storm Center

Also called "twisters" and "whirlwinds," tornadoes are the most violent storms on Earth. These rapidly spinning columns of air are often described as "funnel clouds."

Tornadoes form when winds change direction, speed up, and spin around in or near a thunderstorm. They can also spin off from hurricanes. The high winds can cause massive localized destruction, especially from flying debris. Cars can be picked up and blown around!

Tornadoes can come in any month, but are more likely to happen from March through July. They occur most often in Oklahoma, Texas, and Florida, but they can happen in any state. Many strong tornadoes touch down in the central plains of the U.S. This 10-state area, which stretches from north Texas to Nebraska, is called "Tornado Alley."

According to the National Oceanic and Atmospheric Administration's (NOAA) Storm Prediction Center in Norman, Oklahoma, there are an average of 1,200 tornadoes in the U.S. each year. These tornadoes cause an average of 55 deaths and 1,500 injuries a year and more than $400 million in damage.

Tornadoes are measured by how much damage they cause. They are classified on the Fujita scale (at left) and the wind speeds are estimated. If a tornado doesn't hit any buildings, it may not be possible to classify it. Wind speeds have been recorded in weak tornados, but the measuring instruments are destroyed in more violent winds. In May of 1999, portable Doppler Radar measured wind speeds above the ground at 318 mph in an Oklahoma tornado—the highest wind speed ever measured.

TORNADO CATEGORIES:

WEAK
F0: 40-72 mph
F1: 73-112 mph

STRONG
F2: 113-157 mph
F3: 158-206 mph

VIOLENT
F4: 207-260 mph
F5: over 260 mph

U.S. TORNADO RECORDS (since record keeping began in 1950)

YEAR: The 1,717 tornadoes reported in 2004 topped the previous record of 1,424 in 1998.

MONTH: In May 2003, there were a total of 516, easily passing the old record of 399 set in June 1992.

TWO-DAY PERIOD: On April 3 and 4, 1974, 147 tornadoes touched down in 13 states.

For more information on storms and weather, got to the NOAA Education page:
WEB SITE http://www.education.noaa.gov/cweather.html

HURRICANES

Hurricanes are the largest storms. They form over warm, usually tropical, oceans. As the warm seawater evaporates into the air, the pressure drops and winds begin to circulate, creating a huge wall of clouds and rain, wrapped around a calm center called the "eye." As warm, moist air continues to feed the storm, it gets stronger and can spread out to an area 300 miles wide and generate winds as fast as 150 miles per hour or more. In the Pacific Ocean hurricanes are called "typhoons."

Hurricanes can rip trees out by their roots and tear roofs off buildings. The strong winds blowing toward shore create a rise in ocean water called a "storm surge." Combined with heavy rains, this can cause flooding and massive damage.

For the Atlantic Ocean, Caribbean Sea, and Gulf of Mexico, hurricane season runs from June 1 to November 30. About 97% of tropical storms recorded since 1886 have fallen between those dates. Most hurricanes happen in August, September, or October, when the oceans are at their warmest. Very warm, humid air above tropical oceans is the source of energy that drives tropical storms and hurricanes. The water temperature of the ocean needs to be above 80 degrees for a hurricane to start.

Hurricanes are classified into five groups based on wind speed. When steady winds from a tropical storm reach 40 mph, the storm is named. When the maximum sustained winds reach 74 mph, the storm is called a hurricane. Storms in category 3 or higher are considered major hurricanes.

HURRICANE CATEGORIES:

1: 74-95 mph

2: 96-110 mph

3: 111-130 mph

4: 131-155 mph

5: over 155 mph

RECORD YEAR

In 2004, the U.S. was affected by 15 named storms and nine hurricanes. Florida alone was hit by four hurricanes (Charley, Frances, Ivan, and Jeanne). Since record keeping began in 1851, the only other state to be hit by four hurricanes was Texas in 1886. One out every five houses in Florida was damaged by a hurricane in 2004, and over 9 million people were forced to evacuate their homes.

WATCHES & WARNINGS

A "hurricane watch" means that a hurricane could threaten an area in 24 to 36 hours. A "hurricane warning" means that sustained winds of at least 74 mph are expected in 24 hours or less. High water and waves may also be a reason for a warning.

HURRICANE NAMES

Until the 20th century, people named storms after saints. In 1953, the U.S. government began to use women's names for hurricanes. Men's names were added in 1978.

2005 names: Arlene, Bret, Cindy, Dennis, Emily, Franklin, Gert, Harvey, Irene, Jose, Katrina, Lee, Maria, Nate, Ophelia, Philippe, Rita, Stan, Tammy, Vince, Wilma

WEATHER WORDS

barometer An instrument that measures atmospheric pressure. Falling pressure means stormy weather, while rising pressure means calm weather.

blizzard A heavy snowstorm with strong winds that, with blowing snow, make it hard to see.

freezing rain Water that freezes as it hits the ground.

fog Tiny water droplets that float in the air. It's like a cloud formed at ground level.

front Boundary between two air masses.

frost Ice crystals that form on surfaces.

hail Frozen water droplets that keep getting coated with ice until heavy enough to fall to the ground as hailstones.

humidity Amount of water vapor (water in the form of a gas) in the air.

meteorologist A person who studies the atmosphere, weather, and weather forecasting.

precipitation Water that falls from clouds as rain, snow, hail, or sleet.

tornado A violently rotating column of air (wind) that forms a funnel. A tornado can suck up and destroy anything in its path, and also cause severe damage from flying debris.

typhoon A hurricane that forms in the northern Pacific Ocean, west of the International Date Line.

wind chill A measure of how cold it feels when there is a wind. When it is 35°F and the wind is 15 miles an hour, it will feel like 25°F.

Let it Snow!

Snow seems like simple stuff, but it's pretty complicated. When the temperature up in the clouds is below 32° F (0° C), water droplets can freeze into crystals of ice. But there has to be some dust or other tiny particles in the air for the ice to form around. Once there are some ice crystals in the cloud, water vapor can turn directly into ice instead of condensing into water and then freezing (raindrops that freeze on the way down to earth are called ice pellets, or sleet).

Water molecules are made up of one oxygen and two hydrogen molecules. When water starts to freeze, the hydrogen molecules hook together in ways that form six-sided (hexagonal) crystals of ice called "snow crystals." Snowflakes are really many snow crystals stuck together. Snowflakes are usually less than half an inch across, but can be as big as the palm of your hand. The shape snow crystals take depends on the temperature at which they form as they fall through the air. A difference of just one degree can change how one looks. Next time it snows, try to catch a snowflake and see what shape it is.

What is El Niño?

El Niño describes a change in the normal pattern of warm currents in the tropical Pacific Ocean that happens every two to seven years. It is called "El Niño"—a Spanish phrase referring to the Christ child—because fishermen from Peru noticed that the warm waters in their area, indicating the current change, usually came around Christmas.

In a normal year, warm water collects in the western Pacific and cold water rises near South America. But during El Niño, a large zone of warm water collects off the coast of South America (see orange on map). A change in wind patterns is one of the reasons this happens, but scientists still aren't sure of the exact causes.

It is important to study El Niño because it leads to big changes in weather. During El Niño, Australia often has droughts and terrible brushfires. The eastern U.S. gets colder (it snowed in Miami, Florida, in 1977). And in California, coastal storms cause a lot of damage.

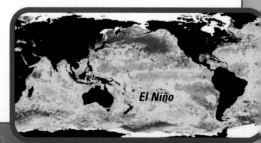

El Niño

Weights & Measures

Which author's name meant two fathoms, or 12 feet? see below

Metrology isn't the study of weather. (That's *meteorology.*) It is the science of measurement. Almost everything you use every day is measured—either when it is made or when it's sold. Materials for buildings and parts for machines must be measured carefully so they will fit together. Clothes have sizes so you'll know which to choose. Many items sold in a supermarket are priced by weight or by volume.

EARLIEST MEASUREMENTS

The human body was the first ruler. An "inch" was the width of a thumb; a "hand" was five fingers wide; a "foot" was—you guessed it—the length of a foot! A "cubit" ran from the elbow to the tip of the middle finger (about 20 inches), and a "yard" was the length of a whole arm.

Later, measurements came from daily activities, like plowing. A "furlong" was the distance an ox team could plow before stopping to rest (now we say it is about 220 yards). The trouble with these units was that they were different from person to person, place to place, and ox to ox.

MEASUREMENTS WE USE TODAY

The official system in the U.S. is the customary system (sometimes called the imperial or English system). Scientists and most other countries use the International System of Units (metric system). The Weights and Measures Division of the U.S. National Institute of Standards and Technology (NIST) makes sure that a gallon of milk in California is the same as one in New York. When the NIST was founded in 1901, there were as many as eight different "standard" gallons in the U.S., and four different legal measures of a "foot" in Brooklyn, New York, alone.

ANCIENT MEASURE

1 foot =
length of a person's foot

12 inches

1 yard =
from nose to fingertip

3 feet or 36 inches

1 acre =
land an ox could plow in a day

4,840 square yards

MODERN MEASURE

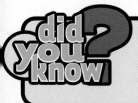

did you know?

HIS NAME WAS A MEASUREMENT. Author Samuel Langhorne Clemens was better known by his pen name, Mark Twain. When he was a riverboat pilot on the Mississippi, water depth was measured by lowering a weight on the end of a knotted cord. "Mark twain" meant "Mark two," for 2 fathoms (12 feet), a safe depth for steamboats.

LENGTH

The basic unit of **length** in the U.S. system is the **inch**. Length, width, and thickness all use the inch or larger related units.

1 foot (ft.) = 12 inches (in.)
1 yard (yd.) = 3 feet = 36 inches
1 rod (rd.) = 5½ yards
1 furlong (fur.) = 40 rods = 220 yards
　　　　　　 = 660 feet
1 mile (mi.) (also called statute mile) =
　　 8 furlongs = 1,760 yards = 5,280 feet
1 nautical mile = 6,076.1 feet = 1.15 statute miles
1 league = 3 miles

AREA

Area is used to measure a section of a two-dimensional surface like the floor or a piece of paper. Most area measurements are given in **square units**. Land is measured in **acres**.

1 square foot (sq. ft.) = 144 square inches
　　　　　　　　 (sq. in.)
1 square yard (sq. yd.) = 9 square feet =
　　　　　　　　　 1,296 square inches
1 square rod (sq. rd.) = 30¼ square yards
1 acre = 160 square rods = 4,840 square
　　 yards = 43,560 square feet
1 square mile (sq. mi.) = 640 acres

CAPACITY

Units of **capacity** are used to measure how much of something will fit into a container. **Liquid measure** is used to measure liquids, such as water or gasoline. **Dry measure** is used with large amounts of solid materials, like grain or fruit. Although both liquid and dry measures use the terms "pint" and "quart," they mean different amounts and should not be confused.

Dry Measure
1 quart (qt.) = 2 pints (pt.)
1 peck (pk.) = 8 quarts
1 bushel (bu.) = 4 pecks

Liquid Measure
1 gill = 4 fluid ounces
1 pint (pt.) = 4 gills = 16 ounces
1 quart (qt.) = 2 pints = 32 ounces
1 gallon (gal.) = 4 quarts = 128 ounces

For measuring most U.S. liquids,
　 1 barrel (bbl.) = 31½ gallons

For measuring oil, 1 barrel (bbl.) = 42 gallons

Cooking Measurements
The measurements used in cooking are based on the **fluid ounce**.
1 teaspoon (tsp.) = ⅙ fluid ounce (fl. oz.)
1 tablespoon (tbsp.) = 3 teaspoons
　　　　　　　　 = ½ fluid ounce
1 cup = 16 tablespoons = 8 fluid ounces
1 pint = 2 cups
1 quart = 2 pints
1 gallon = 4 quarts

VOLUME

The amount of space taken up by an object (or the amount of space available within an object) is measured in **volume.** Volume is usually expressed in **cubic units.** If you wanted to buy a room air conditioner and needed to know how much space there was to be cooled, you could measure the room in cubic feet.

1 cubic foot (cu. ft.) = 12 inches x 12 inches
　　　　　　　　 x 12 inches = 1,728
　　　　　　　　 cubic inches (cu. in.)
1 cubic yard (cu. yd.) = 27 cubic feet

DEPTH

Some measurements of length are used to measure ocean depth and distance.

1 fathom = 6 feet
1 cable = 120 fathoms = 720 feet

WEIGHT

Although 1 cubic foot of popcorn and 1 cubic foot of rock take up the same amount of space, it wouldn't feel the same if you tried to lift them. We measure heaviness as **weight.** Most objects are measured in **avoirdupois weight** (pronounced a-ver-de-POIZ):

1 dram (dr.) = 27.344 grains (gr.)
1 ounce (oz.) = 16 drams = 437.5 grains
1 pound (lb.) = 16 ounces
1 hundredweight (cwt.) = 100 pounds
1 ton = 2,000 pounds (also called short ton)

The METRIC System

The metric system was created in France in 1795. Standardized in 1960 and given the name International System of Units, it is now used in most countries and in scientific works. The system is based on 10, like the decimal counting system. The basic unit for length is the **meter**. The **liter** is a basic unit of volume or capacity, and the **gram** is a basic unit of mass. Related units are made by adding a prefix to the basic unit. The prefixes and their meanings are:

milli- = 1/1,000	deci- = 1/10	hecto- = 100
centi- = 1/100	deka- = 10	kilo- = 1,000

For Example

millimeter (mm)	= 1/1,000 of a meter	milligram (mg)	= 1/1,000 of a gram
kilometer (km)	= 1,000 meters	kilogram (kg)	= 1,000 grams

To get a rough idea of measurements in the metric system, it helps to know that a **liter** is a little more than a quart. A **meter** is a little over a yard. A **kilogram** is a little over 2 pounds. And a **kilometer** is just over half a mile.

 Homework Help Converting Measurements

From:	Multiply by:	To get:	From:	Multiply by:	To get:
inches	2.5400	centimeters	centimeters	.3937	inches
inches	.0254	meters	centimeters	.0328	feet
feet	30.4800	centimeters	meters	39.3701	inches
feet	.3048	meters	meters	3.2808	feet
yards	.9144	meters	meters	1.0936	yards
miles	1.6093	kilometers	kilometers	.621	miles
square inches	6.4516	square centimeters	square centimeters	.1550	square inches
square feet	.0929	square meters	square meters	10.7639	square feet
square yards	.8361	square meters	square meters	1.1960	square yards
acres	.4047	hectares	hectares	2.4710	acres
cubic inches	16.3871	cubic centimeters	cubic centimeters	.0610	cubic inches
cubic feet	.0283	cubic meters	cubic meters	35.3147	cubic feet
cubic yards	.7646	cubic meters	cubic meters	1.3080	cubic yards
quarts (liquid)	.9464	liters	liters	1.0567	quarts (liquid)
ounces	28.3495	grams	grams	.0353	ounces
pounds	.4536	kilograms	kilograms	2.2046	pounds

World History

What ancient people first made silk? page 323

Each of the five sections in this chapter tells the history of a major region of the world: the Middle East, Africa, Asia, Europe, and the Americas. Major events from ancient times to the present are described under the headings for each region.

THE ANCIENT MIDDLE EAST   4000 B.C.–1 B.C.

4000–3000 B.C.
► The world's first cities are built by the Sumerian peoples in Mesopotamia, now southern Iraq.
► Sumerians develop a kind of writing called cuneiform.
► Egyptians develop a kind of writing called hieroglyphics.

2700 B.C. Egyptians begin building the great pyramids in the desert. The pharaohs' (kings') bodies are buried in them.

1792 B.C. Some of the first written laws are created in Babylonia. They are called the Code of Hammurabi.

◄ *Hieroglyphics*

ACHIEVEMENTS OF THE ANCIENT MIDDLE EAST
Early peoples of the Middle East:
► Studied the stars (astronomy).
► Invented the wheel.
► Created written language from picture drawings (hiero-glyphics and cuneiform).
   ► Established the 24-hour day.
      ► Studied medicine and mathematics.

1200 B.C. Hebrew people settle in Canaan in Palestine after escaping from slavery in Egypt. They are led by the prophet Moses.

THE TEN COMMANDMENTS
The Hebrews believed in only one God (monotheism). They believed that God gave Moses the Ten Commandments on Mount Sinai when they fled Egypt.

1000 B.C. King David unites the Hebrews in one strong kingdom.

ANCIENT PALESTINE
Palestine was invaded by many different peoples after 1000 B.C., including the Babylonians, Egyptians, Persians, and Romans. It came under Arab Muslim control in the 600s and remained mainly under Muslim control until the 1900s.

336 B.C. Alexander the Great, King of Macedonia, builds an empire from Egypt to India.

63 B.C. Romans conquer Palestine and make it part of their empire.

Around 4 B.C. Jesus Christ, the founder of the Christian religion, is born in Bethlehem. He is crucified about A.D. 29.

◄ *The pyramids and sphinx at Giza*

THE MIDDLE EAST A.D. 1–1940s

ISLAM: A RELIGION GROWS IN THE MIDDLE EAST 610–632 Around 610, the prophet Muhammad starts to proclaim and teach Islam. This religion spreads from Arabia to all the neighboring regions in the Middle East and North Africa. Its followers are called Muslims.

THE KORAN

The holy book of Islam is the Koran. It was related by Muhammad beginning in 611. The Koran gives

▲ *The Koran*

Muslims a program they must follow. For example, it gives rules about how one should treat one's parents and neighbors.

632 Muhammad dies. By now, Islam is accepted in Arabia as a religion.

641 Arab Muslims conquer the Persians.

LATE 600s Islam begins to spread to the west into Africa and Spain.

711–732 Umayyads invade Europe but are defeated by Frankish leader Charles Martel in France. This defeat halts the spread of Islam into Western Europe.

1071 Muslim Turks conquer Jerusalem.

1095–1291 Europeans try to take back Jerusalem and other parts of the Middle East for Christians during the Crusades.

THE SPREAD OF ISLAM

The Arab armies that went across North Africa brought great change:
- ▶ The people who lived there were converted to Islam.
- ▶ The Arabic language replaced many local languages as an official language. North Africa is still an Arabic-speaking region today, and Islam is the major faith.

Dome of the Rock and the Western Wall, Jerusalem ▼

ACHIEVEMENTS OF THE UMAYYAD AND ABBASID DYNASTIES The Umayyads (661–750) and the Abbasids (750–1256) were the first two Muslim-led dynasties. Both empires stretched across northern Africa, across the Middle East, and into Asia. Both were known for great achievements. They:
- ▶ Studied math and medicine.
- ▶ Translated the works of other peoples, including Greeks and Persians.
- ▶ Spread news of Chinese inventions like paper and gunpowder.
- ▶ Wrote great works on religion and philosophy.

1300–1900s The Ottoman Turks, who are Muslims, create a huge empire, covering the Middle East, North Africa, and part of Eastern Europe. The Ottoman Empire falls apart gradually, and European countries take over portions of it beginning in the 1800s.

1914–1918 World War I begins in 1914. The Ottoman Empire has now broken apart. Most of the Middle East falls under British or French control.

1921 Two new Arab kingdoms are created: Transjordan and Iraq. The French take control of Syria and Lebanon.

1922 Egypt becomes independent from Britain.

JEWS MIGRATE TO PALESTINE Jewish settlers from Europe began migrating to Palestine in the 1880s. They wanted to return to the historic homeland of the Hebrew people. In 1945, after World War II, many Jews who survived the Holocaust migrated to Palestine. Arabs living in the region opposed the Jewish immigration. In 1948, after the British left, war broke out between the Jews and the Arabs.

THE MIDDLE EAST 1940s–2000s

1948 The state of Israel is created.

THE ARAB-ISRAELI WARS Arab countries near Israel (Egypt, Iraq, Jordan, Lebanon, and Syria) attack the new country in 1948 but fail to destroy it. Israel and its neighbors fight wars again in 1956, 1967, and 1973. Israel wins each war. In the 1967 war, Israel captures the Sinai Desert from Egypt, the Golan Heights from Syria, and the West Bank from Jordan.

1979 Egypt and Israel sign a peace treaty, providing for Israel to return the Sinai to Egypt.

THE MIDDLE EAST AND OIL
About 20% of the oil we use to drive cars, heat homes, and run machines comes from the Arabian peninsula in the Middle East. For a brief time in 1973-1974, Arab nations would not let their oil be sold to the United States because of its support of Israel. Many countries rely on oil imports from the region, which has more than half the world's crude oil reserves.

THE 1990s AND 2000s

► In 1991, the U.S. and its allies go to war with Iraq after Iraq invades Kuwait. Iraq is defeated and signs a peace agreement but is accused of violating it. In 2003, the U.S. and Britain invade Iraq and remove the regime of Saddam Hussein. Violence there continues, but millions of Iraqis are able to vote in free elections in January 2005.

► Tensions between Israel and the Palestinians increase, fueled by suicide bombings by Palestinians, and Israeli military actions in the occupied territories. But a change in the leadership of the Palestinians brings hope for peace.

Iraqi Prime Minister Iyad Allawi casts his vote in the election.

ANCIENT AFRICA 3500 B.C.—A.D. 900

ANCIENT AFRICA In ancient times, northern Africa was dominated by the Egyptians, Greeks, and Romans. However, we know very little about the lives of ancient Africans south of the Sahara Desert.

They did not have written languages. What we learn about them comes from weapons, tools, and other items from their civilization that have been found in the earth.

2000 B.C. The Kingdom of Kush arises just south of Egypt. It becomes a major center of art, learning, and trade. Kush dies out around A.D. 350.

500 B.C. The Nok culture becomes strong in Nigeria, in West Africa. The Nok use iron for tools and weapons. They are also known for their fine terra-cotta sculptures of heads. ▼

AROUND A.D. 1 Bantu-speaking peoples in West Africa begin to move into eastern and southern Africa.

50 The Kingdom of Axum in northern Ethiopia, founded by traders from Arabia, becomes a wealthy trading center for ivory.

300s Ghana, the first known African state south of the Sahara Desert, takes power in the upper Senegal and Niger river region. It controls the trade in gold from southern Africa.

660s–900 The Islamic religion spreads across North Africa and into Spain.

900 Arab Muslims begin to settle along the coast of East Africa. Their contact with Bantu people produces the Swahili language, which is still spoken today.

1050 The Almoravid Kingdom in Morocco, North Africa, is powerful from Ghana to as far north as Spain.

1230 The Mali Kingdom begins in North Africa. Timbuktu, a center for trade and learning, is its main city.

1464 The Songhay Empire becomes strong in West Africa. By around 1500, it has destroyed Mali. The Songhay are remembered for their bronze sculptures.

1505–1575 Portuguese settlement begins in Africa. Portuguese people settle in Angola, Mozambique, and other areas.

THE AFRICAN SLAVE TRADE

Once Europeans began settling in the New World, they needed people to harvest their sugar. The first African slaves were taken to the Caribbean. Later, slaves were taken to South America and the United States. The slaves were crowded onto ships and about 10 - 20% died during the long journey. Shipping of African slaves to the United States lasted until the early 1800s.

1652–1835

1 Dutch settlers arrive in southern Africa. They are known as the Boers.

2 Shaka the Great forms a Zulu Empire in eastern Africa. The Zulus are warriors.

3 The "Great Trek" (march) of the Boers north takes place. They defeat the Zulus at the Battle of Bloody River.

1899: BOER WAR The South African War between Great Britain and the Boers begins. It is also called the Boer War. The Boers accept British rule but are allowed a role in government.

1948 The white South African government creates the policy of apartheid, the total separation of blacks and whites. Blacks are banned from restaurants, theaters, schools, and jobs considered "white." Apartheid sparked protests, many of which ended in bloodshed.

1983 Droughts (water shortages) lead to starvation over much of Africa.

THE 1990s AND 2000s
Apartheid ends in South Africa in 1993, and the next year, Nelson Mandela becomes South Africa's first black president. Also in 1994, civil war in Rwanda leads to the massacre of 500,000 civilians. Truces in Angola (1994), and Sudan (2005) help bring an end to long years of civil war. AIDS continues to kill millions of African people each year.

▲ Nelson Mandela

COLONIES win their FREEDOM

Most African countries were once colonies of a European nation such as Britain, France, or Portugal, but later became independent. Here are some that won independence in the 1900s.

Country	Became Independent	From
Egypt	1952	Britain
Morocco	1956	France
Sudan	1956	Britain
Ghana	1957	Britain
Burkina Faso	1960	France
Cameroon	1960	France
Congo, Dem. Rep. of	1960	Belgium
Côte d'Ivoire	1960	France
Mali	1960	France
Niger	1960	France
Nigeria	1960	Britain
Zimbabwe	1960	Britain
South Africa	1961	Britain
Tanzania	1961	Britain
Algeria	1962	France
Uganda	1962	Britain
Kenya	1963	Britain
Malawi	1964	Britain
Angola	1975	Portugal
Mozambique	1975	Portugal

3500 B.C. People settle in the Indus River Valley of India and Pakistan and the Yellow River Valley of China.

2500 B.C. Cities of Mohenjo-Daro and Harappa in Pakistan become centers of trade and farming.

AROUND 1523 B.C. Shang peoples in China build walled towns and use a kind of writing based on pictures. This writing develops into the writing Chinese people use today.

衣
貽
夷

1500 B.C. The Hindu religion (Hinduism) begins to spread throughout India.

AROUND 1050 B.C. Chou peoples in China overthrow the Shang and control large territories.

700 B.C. In China, a 500-year period begins in which many warring states fight one another.

563 B.C. Siddhartha Gautama is born in India. He becomes known as the Buddha—the "Enlightened One"—and is the founder of the Buddhist religion (Buddhism). ▼

551 B.C. The Chinese philosopher Confucius is born. His teachings—especially the rules about how people should treat each other—spread throughout China and are still followed today.

ASIAN RELIGIONS Many of the world's religions began in Asia. Two of the most important were:

► **Hinduism.** Hinduism began in India and has spread to other parts of southern Asia and to parts of the Pacific region.

► **Buddhism.** Buddhism also began in India and spread to China, Japan, and Southeast Asia. Today, both religions have millions of followers all over the world.

320–232 B.C.: INDIA

► Northern India is united under the emperor Chandragupta Maurya.

► Asoka, emperor of India, sends Buddhist missionaries throughout southern Asia to spread the Buddhist religion.

221 B.C. The Chinese ruler Shih Huang Ti makes the Chinese language the same throughout the country. Around the same time, the Chinese begin building the Great Wall. Its main section is more than 2,000 miles long and is meant to keep invading peoples out.

202 B.C. The Han people of China win control of all of China.

ACHIEVEMENTS OF THE ANCIENT CHINESE

► Invented paper.
► Invented gunpowder.
► Studied astronomy.
► Studied engineering.
► Invented acupuncture to treat illnesses.

The Great Wall of China

ANCIENT ASIA A.D. 1-1700s

320 The Gupta Empire controls northern India. The Guptas, who are Hindus, drive the Buddhist religion out of India. They are well known for their many advances in mathematics and medicine.

618 The Tang dynasty begins in China. The Tang dynasty is well known for music, poetry, and painting. They export silk and porcelains as far away as Africa.

THE SILK ROAD

Around 100 B.C., only the Chinese knew how to make silk. To get this light, comfortable material, Europeans sent fortunes in glass, gold, jade, and other items to China. The exchanges between Europeans and Chinese created one of the greatest trading routes in history—the Silk Road. Chinese inventions such as paper and gunpowder were also spread over the Silk Road. Europeans found out how to make silk around A.D. 500, but trade continued until about 1400.

960 The Northern Sung dynasty in China makes advances in banking and paper money. China's population of 50 million doubles over 200 years, thanks to improved ways of farming that lead to greater food production.

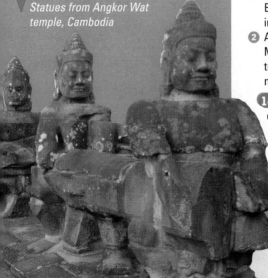

▼ *Statues from Angkor Wat temple, Cambodia*

1000 The Samurai, a warrior people, become powerful in Japan. They live by a code of honor known as Bushido.

1180 The Khmer Empire based in Angkor is powerful in Cambodia. The empire became widely known for its beautiful temples.

1206 The Mongol leader Genghis Khan builds a huge army and creates an empire that stretches all the way from China to India, Russia, and Eastern Europe.

1264 Kublai Khan, grandson of Genghis Khan, rules China as emperor from his new capital at Beijing.

1368 The Ming dynasty comes to power in China. The Ming drive the Mongols out of the country.

1467–1603 WAR AND PEACE IN JAPAN

1. Civil war breaks out in Japan. The conflicts last more than 100 years.
2. Peace comes to Japan under the military leader Hideyoshi.
3. The Shogun period reaches its peak in Japan (it lasts until 1868). Europeans are driven out of the country and Christians are persecuted.

1526 THE MUGHALS IN INDIA

1. The Mughal Empire in India begins under Babur. The Mughals are Muslims who invade and conquer India.
2. Akbar, the grandson of Babur, becomes Mughal emperor of India. He attempts to unite Hindus and Muslims but does not succeed.

1644 The Ming dynasty in China is overthrown by the Manchu peoples. They allow more Europeans to trade in China.

1739 Nadir Shah, a Persian warrior, conquers parts of western India and captures the city of Delhi.

1839 The Opium War takes place in China between the Chinese and the British. The British and other Western powers want to control trade in Asia. The Chinese want the British to stop selling opium to the Chinese. Britain wins the war in 1842.

1858 The French begin to take control of Indochina (Southeast Asia).

1868 The Shogunate dynasty ends in Japan. The new ruler is Emperor Meiji. Western ideas begin to influence the Japanese.

THE JAPANESE IN ASIA Japan became a powerful country during the early 20th century. But it was a small country with few raw materials of its own. In the 1930s, Japan began to invade some of its neighbors. In 1941, the United States and Japan went to war after Japan attacked the U.S. Navy at Pearl Harbor, Hawaii.

1945 Japan is defeated in World War II after the U.S. drops atomic bombs on the Japanese cities of Hiroshima and Nagasaki.

1947 India and Pakistan become independent from Great Britain.

1949 China comes under the rule of the Communists led by Mao Zedong. ▼

CHINA UNDER THE COMMUNISTS The Communist government abolished private property and took over all businesses and farms. Religions were persecuted. Many people were put in jail or executed.

1950–1953 THE KOREAN WAR North Korea, a Communist country, invades South Korea. The U.S. and other nations join to fight the invasion. China joins North Korea. The Korean War ends in 1953. Neither side wins.

Tsunami victims in Indonesia receive aid. ▶

1954–1975 THE VIETNAM WAR The French are defeated in Indochina in 1954 by Vietnamese Communists. The U.S. sends troops in 1965 to fight on the side of South Vietnam against the Communists in the North. The U.S. withdraws in 1973. In 1975, South Vietnam is taken over by North Vietnam.

1972 President Richard Nixon visits China to improve relations.

1989 Chinese students protest for democracy, but the protests are crushed by the army in Beijing's Tiananmen Square.

THE 1990s Japan, South Korea, Taiwan, and some other countries show great strength in the early 1990s, but then have financial trouble. Britain returns Hong Kong to China (1997). China builds its economy, but does not allow democracy.

THE 2000s U.S.-led military action overthrows the Taliban regime in Afghanistan (2001) and seeks to root out terrorists there. North Korea admits it has been developing nuclear weapons, and Iran is believed to be developing them.

A powerful earthquake in the Indian Ocean in December 2004 sets off huge waves (tsunamis) that kills over 160,000 people in Indonesia, Sri Lanka, and other countries.

ANCIENT EUROPE 4000 B.C.–300s B.C.

4000 B.C. People in many parts of Europe start building monuments out of large stones called megaliths. Examples can still be seen today, including Stonehenge in England.

2500 B.C.–1200 B.C.
THE MINOANS AND THE MYCENAEANS

▶ People on the island of Crete (Minoans) in the Mediterranean Sea built great palaces and became sailors and traders.

▶ People in the city of Mycenae in Greece built stone walls and a great palace.

▶ Mycenaean people invaded Crete and destroyed the power of the Minoans.

▲ *Socrates*

THE TROJAN WAR The Trojan War was a conflict between invading Greeks and the people of Troas (Troy) in Southwestern Turkey around 1200 B.C. Although little is known today about the real war, it has become a part of Greek poetry and mythology (see pages 144-145). According to a famous legend, a group of Greek soldiers hid inside a huge wooden horse. The horse was pulled into the city of Troy. Then the soldiers jumped out of the horse and conquered Troy.

900-600 B.C. Celtic peoples in Northern Europe settle on farms and in villages and learn to mine for iron ore.

600 B.C. Etruscan peoples take over most of Italy. They build many cities and become traders.

SOME ACHIEVEMENTS OF THE GREEKS The early Greeks were responsible for:

■ The first governments that were elected by people. Greeks invented democratic government.

■ Great poets such as Homer, who composed the *Iliad*, a long poem about the Trojan War, and the *Odyssey*, an epic poem about the travels of Odysseus.

■ Great thinkers such as Socrates, Plato, and Aristotle.

■ Great architecture, like the Parthenon and the Temple of Athena Nike on the Acropolis in Athens (*see below*).

431 B.C. The Peloponnesian Wars begin between the Greek cities of Athens and Sparta. The wars end in 404 B.C. when Sparta wins.

338 B.C. King Philip II of Macedonia in northern Greece conquers all the cities of Greece.

336 B.C. Philip's son Alexander the Great becomes king. He conquers lands and makes an empire from the Mediterranean Sea to India. For the next 300 years, Greek culture dominates this vast area.

Temple of Athena Nike ▼

The Parthenon

264 B.C.–A.D. 476

ROMAN EMPIRE The city of Rome in Italy begins to expand and capture surrounding lands. The Romans gradually build a great empire and control all of the Mediterranean region. At its height, the Roman Empire includes Western Europe, Greece, Egypt, and much of the Middle East. It lasts until A.D. 476.

▲ *A painting of Jesus Christ*

ROMAN ACHIEVEMENTS

- Roman law. Many of our laws are based on Roman law.
- Great roads to connect their huge empire. The Appian Way, south of Rome, is a Roman road that is still in use today.
- Aqueducts to bring water to the people in large cities.
- Great sculpture. Roman statues can still be seen in Europe.
- Great architecture. The Colosseum, which still stands in Rome today, is an example of great Roman architecture.
- Great writers, such as the poet Virgil, who wrote the *Aeneid.*

49 B.C. A civil war breaks out that destroys Rome's republican form of government.

45 B.C. Julius Caesar becomes the sole ruler of Rome but is murdered one year later by rivals in the Roman army. ▶

27 B.C. Octavian becomes the first emperor of Rome. He takes the name Augustus. A peaceful period of almost 200 years begins.

THE CHRISTIAN FAITH Christians believe that Jesus Christ is the Son of God. The history and beliefs of Christianity are found in the New Testament of the Bible. Christianity spread slowly throughout the Roman Empire. The Romans tried to stop the new religion and persecuted the Christians. They were forced to hold their services in hiding, and some were crucified. Eventually, more and more Romans became Christian.

BYZANTINE EMPIRE, centered in modern-day Turkey, was the eastern half of the old Roman Empire. Byzantine rulers extended their power into western Europe; the Byzantine Emperor Justinian ruled parts of Spain, North Africa, and Italy. Constantinople (now Istanbul, Turkey) became the capital of the Byzantine Empire in 330.

313 The Roman Emperor Constantine gives full rights to Christians. He eventually becomes a Christian himself.

410 The Visigoths and other barbarian tribes from northern Europe invade the Roman Empire and begin to take over its lands.

476 The last Roman emperor is overthrown.

768 Charlemagne becomes king of the Franks in northern Europe. He rules a kingdom that includes parts of France, Germany, and northern Italy.

800 Feudalism becomes important in Europe. Feudalism means that poor farmers are allowed to farm a lord's land in return for certain services to the lord.

▼ *The Colosseum, Rome*

The Temple of Saturn, Rome

EUROPE 800s–1500s

896 Magyar peoples from lands east of Russia found Hungary.

Viking helmet ▼

800s–900s Viking warriors and traders from Scandinavia begin to move into the British Isles, France, and parts of the Mediterranean.

989 The Russian state of Kiev becomes Christian.

1066 William of Normandy, a Frenchman, successfully invades England and makes himself king. He is known as William the Conqueror.

1096–1291 THE CRUSADES In 1096, Christian European kings and nobles sent a series of armies to the Middle East to try to capture Jerusalem from the Muslims. Between 1096 and 1291 there were about ten Crusades. The Europeans briefly captured Jerusalem, but in the end, the Crusades did not succeed in their aim.

One result of the Crusades was that trade increased greatly between the Middle East and Europe.

1215 THE MAGNA CARTA The Magna Carta was a document agreed to by King John of England and the English nobility. The English king agreed that he did not have absolute power and had to obey the laws of the land. The Magna Carta was an important step toward democracy.

1290 The Ottoman Empire begins. It is controlled by Turkish Muslims who conquer lands in the eastern Mediterranean and the Middle East.

1337–1453 WAR AND PLAGUE IN EUROPE

▶ The Hundred Years' War (1337) begins in Europe between France and England. The war lasts until 1453 when France wins.

▶ The bubonic plague (Black Death) begins in Europe (1348). As much as one third of the whole population of Europe dies from this deadly disease, caused by the bite of infected fleas.

1453 The Ottoman Turks capture the city of Constantinople and rename it Istanbul.

1517 THE REFORMATION The Reformation led to the breakup of the Christian church into Protestant and Roman Catholic branches in Europe. It started when the German priest Martin Luther opposed some teachings of the Church. He broke away from the pope (the leader of the Catholic church) and had many followers.

1534 King Henry VIII of England breaks away from the Roman Catholic church. He names himself head of the English (Anglican) church.

1558 The reign of King Henry's daughter Elizabeth I begins in England. During her long rule, England's power grows.

Queen Elizabeth

1588 The Spanish Armada (fleet of warships) is defeated by the English navy as Spain tries to invade England.

◀ *Ottoman Palace of Ciragan, Istanbul*

1600s The Ottoman Turks expand their empire through most of eastern and central Europe.

1618 Much of Europe is destroyed in the Thirty Years' War, which ends in 1648.

1642 The English civil war begins. King Charles I fights against the forces of the Parliament (legislature). The king's forces are defeated, and he is executed in 1649. But his son, Charles II, returns as king in 1660.

Catherine the Great

1762 Catherine the Great becomes the Empress of Russia. She allows some religious freedom and extends the Russian Empire.

1789 THE FRENCH REVOLUTION The French Revolution ended the rule of kings in France and led to democracy there. At first, however, there were wars, much bloodshed, and times when dictators took control. Many people were executed. King Louis XVI and Queen Marie Antoinette were overthrown in the Revolution, and both were executed in 1793.

1799 Napoleon Bonaparte, an army officer, becomes dictator of France. Under his rule, France conquers most of Europe by 1812.

1815 Napoleon's forces are defeated by the British and German armies at Waterloo (in Belgium). Napoleon is exiled to a remote island and dies there in 1821.

1848 Revolutions break out in countries of Europe. People force their rulers to make more democratic changes.

1914–1918 WORLD WAR I IN EUROPE At the start of World War I in Europe, Germany, Austria-Hungary and the Ottoman Empire opposed England, France, Russia, and, later, the U.S. (the Allies). The Allies won in 1918.

1917 The czar is overthrown in the Russian Revolution. The Bolsheviks (Communists) under Vladimir Lenin take control. Millions are starved, sent to labor camps, or executed under Joseph Stalin (1929-1953).

THE RISE OF HITLER Adolf Hitler became dictator of Germany in 1933. He joined forces with rulers in Italy and Japan to form the Axis powers. In World War II (1939-1945), the Axis powers were defeated by the Allies—Great Britain, the Soviet Union, and the U.S. During his rule, Hitler's Nazis killed millions of Jews and other people in what we now call the Holocaust.

1945 The Cold War begins. It is a long period of tension between the United States and the Soviet Union. Both countries build up their armies and make nuclear weapons but do not go to war against each other.

THE 1990s Communist governments in Eastern Europe are replaced by democratic ones. Divided Germany becomes one nation, and the Soviet Union breaks up. The European Union (EU) takes steps toward European unity. The North Atlantic Treaty Organization (NATO) bombs Yugoslavia in an effort to protect Albanians driven out of the Kosovo region.

2002 The euro becomes the single currency in 12 European Union nations.

◄ *Napoleon Bonaparte*

THE AMERICAS 10,000 B.C.–A.D. 1600s

10,000–8000 B.C.
People in North and South America gather plants for food and hunt animals using stone-pointed spears.

Christopher Columbus

AROUND 3000 B.C.
People in Central America begin farming, growing corn and beans for food.

1500 B.C. Mayan people in Central America begin to live in small villages.

500 B.C. People in North America begin to hunt buffalo to use for meat and for clothing.

100 B.C. The city of Teotihuacán is founded in Mexico. It becomes the center of a huge empire extending from central Mexico to Guatemala. Teotihuacán contains many large pyramids and temples.

A.D. 150 Mayan people in Guatemala build many centers for religious ceremonies. They create a calendar and learn mathematics and astronomy.

900 Toltec warriors in Mexico begin to invade lands of Mayan people. Mayans leave their old cities and move to the Yucatan Peninsula of Mexico.

1000 Native Americans in the southwestern United States begin to live in settlements called pueblos. They learn to farm.

1325 Mexican Indians known as Aztecs create huge city of Tenochtitlán and rule a large empire in Mexico. They are warriors who practice human sacrifice.

Mayan pyramid, Yucatan Peninsula, Mexico ▶

1492 Christopher Columbus sails from Europe across the Atlantic Ocean and lands in the Bahamas, in the Caribbean Sea. This marked the first step toward the founding of European settlements in the Americas.

1500 Portuguese explorers reach Brazil and claim it for Portugal.

1519 Spanish conqueror Hernán Cortés travels into the Aztec Empire in search of gold. The Aztecs are defeated in 1521 by Cortés. The Spanish take control of Mexico.

WHY DID THE SPANISH WIN? How did the Spanish defeat the powerful Aztec Empire in such a short time? One reason is that the Spanish had better weapons. Another is that many Aztecs died from diseases brought to the New World by the Spanish. The Aztecs had never had these illnesses before, and so did not have immunity to them. Also, many neighboring Indians hated the Aztecs as conquerors and helped the Spanish to defeat them.

1534 Jacques Cartier of France explores Canada.

1583 The first English colony in Canada is set up in Newfoundland.

1607 English colonists led by Captain John Smith settle in Jamestown, Virginia. Virginia was the oldest of the Thirteen Colonies that turned into the United States.

1619 First African slaves arrive in English-controlled America.

1682 The French explorer Robert Cavelier, sieur de la Salle, sails down the Mississippi River. The area is named Louisiana after the French King Louis XIV.

EUROPEAN COLONIES By 1700, most of the Americas are under the control of Europeans:

Spain: Florida, southwestern United States, Mexico, Central America, western South America.
Portugal: eastern South America.
France: central United States, parts of Canada.
England: eastern U.S., parts of Canada.
Holland: eastern U.S., West Indies, eastern South America.

1700s European colonies in North and South America grow in population and wealth.

1775–1783 AMERICAN REVOLUTION The American Revolution begins in 1775 when the first shot is fired in Lexington, Massachusetts. The thirteen original British colonies in North America become independent under the Treaty of Paris, signed in 1783.

SIMÓN BOLÍVAR: LIBERATOR OF SOUTH AMERICA In 1810, Simón Bolívar began a revolt against Spain. He fought against the Spanish and in 1924 became president of the independent country of Greater Colombia. As a result of his leadership, ten South American countries became independent from Spain by 1830. However, Bolívar himself was criticized as being a dictator. ▶

1810–1910 MEXICO'S REVOLUTION In 1846, Mexico and the United States go to war. Mexico loses parts of the Southwest and California to the U.S. A revolution in 1910 overthrows Porfirio Díaz.

1867 The Canadian provinces are united as the Dominion of Canada.

Becoming Independent

Most countries of Latin America gained independence from Spain in the early 1800s. Some took longer.

COUNTRY	YEAR OF INDEPENDENCE
Argentina	1816
Bolivia	1825
Brazil	1822[1]
Chile	1818
Colombia	1819
Ecuador	1822
Guyana	1966[2]
Mexico	1821
Paraguay	1811
Peru	1824
Suriname	1975[3]
Uruguay	1825
Venezuela	1821

[1]From Portugal. [2]From Britain. [3]From the Netherlands.

1898 THE SPANISH-AMERICAN WAR Spain and the U.S. fight a brief war in 1898. Spain loses its colonies Cuba, Puerto Rico, and the Philippines.

U.S. POWER IN THE 1900s During the 1900s the U.S. strongly influenced affairs in the Americas. The U.S. sent troops to various countries, including Mexico (1914; 1916–1917), Nicaragua (1912–1933), Haiti (1915–1934; 1994–1995), and Panama (1989). In 1962, the U.S. went on alert when the Soviet Union put missiles on Cuba.

1994 The North American Free Trade Agreement (NAFTA) is signed to increase trade between the U.S., Canada, and Mexico.

2001 Radical Muslim terrorists crash planes into U.S. targets, killing about 3,000 people; the U.S. launches a "war on terrorism."

2003 U.S.-led forces invade Iraq and overthrow the regime of Saddam Hussein.

LOOKING BACK

From 2005

10th ANNIVERSARY — 10 YEARS AGO—1995

- A massive car bomb explosion destroyed the Alfred P. Murrah Federal Building in Oklahoma City, OK. The search for survivors lasted 17 days. There were 168 people killed.
- O.J. Simpson, former football star, was found not guilty of the murder of his wife, Nicole Brown Simpson, and a friend of hers, Ron Goldman.
- The Dayton Accords, organized by the United States, ended a war in Bosnia, Croatia, and Serbia that had killed thousands of people.

50 YEARS AGO—1955

- *The Return of the King*, the last book of J.R.R. Tolkien's "Lord of the Rings" trilogy, was published.
- McDonald's founder Ray Kroc opened his first restaurant, in Des Plaines, IL.
- Disneyland opened in Anaheim, CA, and *The Mickey Mouse Club* started on TV.
- The *Sam and Friends* TV show, starring Jim Henson's first muppets, aired in Washington, DC.

100 YEARS AGO—1905

- President Theodore Roosevelt hosted a peace conference that settled a war between Russia and Japan. A year later he won the Nobel Peace Prize for his efforts.
- Albert Einstein, then 26 years old, published some of his key scientific discoveries, including the special theory of relativity.
- The NCAA was formed to organize college sports, and football rules were standardized.

From 2006

10th ANNIVERSARY — 10 YEARS AGO—1996

- Astronaut Dr. Shannon Lucid lived for 188 days in space, setting a record for U.S. astronauts.
- Gary Kasparov, chess champion, faced Deep Blue, a computer that analyzed 100 million chess moves per second. Kasparov won the match, 3 to 1.
- In a three-party election, President Bill Clinton beat Ross Perot and Bob Dole to win a second term.

50 YEARS AGO—1956

- Service on Montgomery, AL, city buses was desegregated after the yearlong Montgomery bus boycott. The Supreme Court had ruled unanimously against state laws requiring segregation on buses.
- A new minimum wage of $1 an hour, up from 75 cents an hour, went into effect.
- Yankee pitcher Don Larsen pitched the only perfect game in World Series history. The Yankees won 2–0. None of the opposing Brooklyn Dodgers made it to first base.

100 YEARS AGO—1906

- A great earthquake, followed by three days of fires, destroyed much of San Francisco (see p. 65).
- Upton Sinclair published *The Jungle*, his novel exposing the abuses and dangers of the American meatpacking industry. In response, Congress passed the Meat Inspection Act and Pure Food and Drug Act banning unsafe food and medicine.
- Brothers Will Keith and John Harvey Kellogg began marketing the cereal they invented, called cornflakes.

WOMEN IN HISTORY

The following women played important roles in shaping some of history's biggest events.

CLEOPATRA (69-30 B.C.), queen of Egypt famous for her association with Roman leaders Julius Caesar and Mark Antony. After her father's death, Cleopatra, at the age of about 17, and her 12-year-old brother Ptolemy jointly ruled and, by custom, were forced to marry each other. A few years later, she was sent away, but came back to rule when Caesar defeated her enemies. For a time, she lived with Caesar In Rome until his assassination in 44 B.C. She later went back to Egypt, where she met and married Antony.

JOAN OF ARC (1412-1431), French heroine and patron saint of France, known as the Maid of Orléans. She led French troops to a big victory over the English in the battle of Orléans (1429), a turning point in the Hundred Years' War. Joan believed she was guided by voices from God, and she dressed like a male warrior. In 1431 she was burned at the stake as a heretic. The Catholic Church later declared her innocent, and she was made a saint in 1920. She is the subject of many monuments, paintings, and works of literature.

SOJOURNER TRUTH (c. 1797-1883), abolitionist and women's rights activist (born Isabella Baumfree). She was raised as a slave on an estate in upstate New York. She escaped in 1826. In 1843, she became a traveling preacher and took the name Sojourner Truth. She traveled widely speaking out against slavery and for women's rights. Her famous speech, "Ain't I a Woman?" was about how women were as smart and strong as men.

Sojourner Truth

ELIZABETH CADY STANTON

(1815-1902), social reformer and leader of the women's rights movement. Along with Lucretia Mott, she organized the first women's rights convention (1848), and won passage of a resolution demanding voting rights for women. She was president of the National Woman Suffrage Association, which she and Susan B. Anthony founded in 1869.

Elizabeth Cady Stanton & Susan B. Anthony

SUSAN B. ANTHONY (1820-1906), social reformer who, with Elizabeth Cady Stanton, led the struggle for women's rights. She was a lifelong campaigner for woman suffrage, but died 14 years before the adoption of the 19th Amendment, which allowed women to vote. She opposed the use of liquor and worked to free slaves. In 1979, the U.S. Mint issued the Susan B. Anthony dollar coin in her honor.

JULIETTE GORDON LOW (1860-1927), founder of the Girl Scouts of the USA. In 1912, a year after meeting Boy Scouts founder Sir Robert Baden-Powell in England, she organized the first Girl Guides troop in the U.S. It had 18 members. The name of the group was changed to Girl Scouts in 1913. She devoted the rest of her life to working with the Girl Scouts. Today there are nearly 4 million Girl Scouts in the United States.

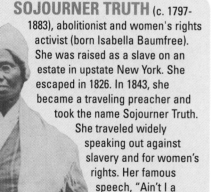

MARIE CURIE

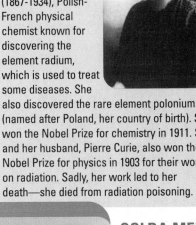

(1867-1934), Polish-French physical chemist known for discovering the element radium, which is used to treat some diseases. She also discovered the rare element polonium (named after Poland, her country of birth). She won the Nobel Prize for chemistry in 1911. She and her husband, Pierre Curie, also won the Nobel Prize for physics in 1903 for their work on radiation. Sadly, her work led to her death—she died from radiation poisoning.

GOLDA MEIR

(1898-1978), Israeli prime minister (1969-1974). She was born in Kiev, Russia, but she and her family emigrated to the U.S. when she was a child. In 1921, she and her husband moved to Palestine (now Israel). She was a signer of Israel's declaration of independence and held several government posts. She came out of retirement at the age of 71 to become prime minister. Her government was known for its open-door policy, which encouraged Soviet Jews to come to Israel.

MARIA TALLCHIEF

(born 1925), the daughter of a chief of the Osage tribe, was one of America's finest ballet dancers. She danced mostly with the New York City Ballet and was famous for the beauty and elegance of her movements. She founded the Chicago City Ballet in 1981 and entered the National Women's Hall of Fame in 1996.

SANDRA DAY O'CONNOR

(born 1930), the first woman Supreme Court justice. She grew up on a ranch in Arizona and became a lawyer. In 1972, while serving in the Arizona state senate, she became the first female state house majority leader in the United States. She later served as a judge. President Ronald Reagan named her to the Supreme Court in 1981.

MAYA LIN

(born 1959), Chinese-American architect and sculptor, who designed the Vietnam Veterans Memorial in Washington, DC, when she was a 21-year-old college student. Her design beat out 1,400 other entries in a nationwide competition. Dedicated in 1982, the wall became one of the most visited sites in Washington.

DR. MAE JEMISON

(born 1956) was the first African-American woman to go into space. She flew on the 1992 space shuttle *Endeavour* as a science mission specialist. She was born in Decatur, AL, and grew up in Chicago. Dr. Jemison is a medical doctor who also has degrees in chemical engineering and African and African-American studies.

ACROSS

1. Ancient people in Italy
7. "Knock, knock." "___'s there?"
8. Egyptian wonders of the world
10. Popular hot English drink
12. American ___. (1775-1783)
13. Precious yellow metal
17. Olden days: Days of ___.
18. It's made from yeast and wheat
19. Trojan Horse or a pirate's fake leg
20. The fifth month
22. Name of people who lived in Mexico long ago
23. I pledge allegiance to the ___
25. World's most populous country
26. It's used to harness oxen
27. A long ___ ago
28. First leader of communist China
32. This group works for a ship's captain
33. Native American people from Guatemala
35. Famous Confederate general
36. Thirteen U.S. states started as these
38. They sailed in long ships
39. A camper might sleep in this
40. Ship's distress signal
43. A map sailors use
44. Home of the Parthenon
45. Muslim holy book
46. Barrier to barbarians in China
47. Yemen is located in the Middle ___

DOWN

1. Oars in a boat help you do this
2. XII compared to IX
3. French dictator ___ Bonaparte
4. The conquistadors came from here
5. Foe of 35 across
6. Male royal leader
7. Angkor ___, ancient Cambodian temple
9. The enlightened One
11. Greek ruler, ___ the Great
14. Bible section prior to Jesus
15. Chinese rulers: Ming ___
16. A limb or a weapon
18. Ancient empire led from Constantinople
19. State, capitol, and president
21. Standing stones in England
23. System serfs lived under
24. Solid water
29. Form of writing or book for a play
30. Stone fortress with moat
31. Island nation, Great ___
33. Not women, but ___
34. Very old
37. ___ before ___ except after C
41. A wound might leave this
42. Opposite of east
44. Hair-styling product

ANSWERS ON PAGES 335-338. FOR MORE PUZZLES GO TO
WWW.WORLDALMANACFORKIDS.COM

Answers

FACES AND PLACES Page 9: 10 YEAR QUIZ

I became the first African-American U.S. Secretary of State in **_2001_**. I am **_Colin Powell_**.

My group first started singing together in **_1996_**. I am **_Justin Timberlake of *Nsync_**.

The first American edition of my novels about muggles and magicians was published in **_1998_**. I am **_J.K. Rowling_**

The same year I started to be "in the middle," I appeared, in a movie with "my dog" **_2000_**. I am **_Frankie Muniz_**.

At age 11, I had just finished my first season of "All That" in **_1997_**. I am **_Amanda Bynes_**.

I made my major-league appearance as a Yankee in **_1995_**. I am **_Derek Jeter_**.

My team won the World Cup in Los Angeles in front of 90,000 fans in **_1999_**. I am **_Mia Hamm_**.

COMPUTER Page 60: WORD *CIRCUIT*

```
C o o k i E n c r y p t i o N e t w o r K e y b o a r D e s k t o P
O                                                                 o
M                                                                 r
P                                                                 t
U                                                                 a
T                                                                 l
E                                                                 a
R  e t n E s a b a t a D a e r h T o o b e R e t n i r P o t p
```

DINOSAURS Page 64: Dino Maze

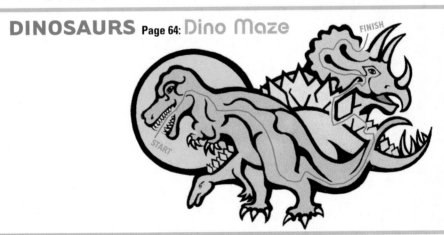

FINISH

START

FASHION Page 83: ThreadbareMaze

Finish

Start

335

LANGUAGE Page 121: Jokes & Riddles

When is the best time of day to go to the dentist? *Tooth-hurty.*

A farmer had 12 cows. All but 9 died. How many cows did he have left? *Nine*

Name the five days of the work week without using Monday, Tuesday, Wednesday, Thursday, or Friday. *The day before yesterday, yesterday, today, tomorrow, the day after tomorrow.*

In what way is the letter "A" and noon exactly the same? *They're both in the middle of day.*

What newspaper did cave people read? *The Prehistoric Times*

What did the boyfriend melon say to the girlfriend melon? *Cantaloupe tonight, Dad has the car.*

Why didn't the skeleton cross the road? *She didn't have the guts.*

I'm the beginning of eternity, The end of space and time, The middle of every buzzing bee, And the end of every rhyme. *The letter "E."*

If 10 robins can catch 10 worms in 10 minutes, how long will it take one robin to catch a worm? *10 minutes*

What starts with a P, ends with an E, and has thousands of letters in it? *Post Office*

Why did Cinderella's soccer team always lose? *Her coach was a pumpkin.*

As I was walking to the mall, I met eight girls, all quite tall. Each tall girl carried a squirrel, except for the one whose hair was in curls. They also came with six young boys, who brought their mothers who carried their toys. How many were going to the mall? *Just me. All the rest were coming from the mall.*

What did the clock do when it was hungry? *It went back "four" seconds.*

What did the mover get when he dropped a computer on his toes? *Megahertz.*

Here's that letter "A" again! How is it like a flower? *Because a "B" is always after it.*

The ancient "Riddle of the Sphinx": *The answer is a man. He crawls on all fours as a baby, walks on two legs when grown, and uses a cane in old age.*

Page 123: Morse Code: A bird that talks in Morse code.

MONEY Page 131: MONEY MATCH UP

Penny—Abraham Lincoln
Nickel—Thomas Jefferson
Dime—Franklin D. Roosevelt
Quarter—George Washington
Half dollar—John F. Kennedy

Dollar coin—Sacagawea
$1 bill—George Washington
$2 bill—Thomas Jefferson
$5 bill—Abraham Lincoln

$10 bill—Alexander Hamilton
$20 bill—Andrew Jackson
$50 bill—Ulysses S. Grant
$100 bill—Benjamin Franklin

Page 131: Bonus Money Questions

The U.S. presidents that appear on both a coin and a bill are? *Jefferson, Lincoln, Washington*

The only three people who appear on money commonly in circulation today who were not U.S. presidents are? *Hamilton, Franklin, Sacagawea*

MOVIES & TV Page 134: 1995 MOVIE QUIZ

1. *Jumanji*
2. *Babe*
3. *The Indian in the Cupboard*
4. *The distance that light travels in one year: 5,880,000,000,000 miles*
5. *The Brady Bunch Movie*
6. *Mighty Morphin' Power Rangers*

NUMBERS Page 193: ROMAN NUMERALS

2005 = *MMV.*

50,000 = *MMMMMMMMMMMMMMMMMMMMMMMMMMMMMMMMMMMMMMMM MMMMMMMMMM*

Page 194: DECIMAL CONVERSIONS

.3 = 3/10, .4 = 2/5, .5 = 1/2, .6 = 3/5

FOR MORE PUZZLES GO TO
WWW.WORLDALMANACFORKIDS.COM

Page 198: TRICKY TRIANGLE

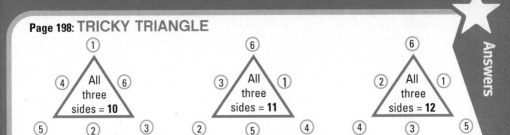

PRIZES Page 205: *MOVIE MARQUEE MAZE*

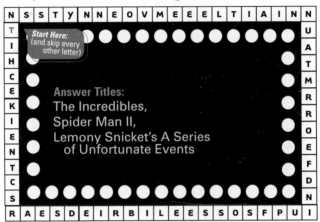

Start Here: (and skip every other letter)

Answer Titles:
The Incredibles,
Spider Man II,
Lemony Snicket's A Series
of Unfortunate Events

SCIENCE Page 219: FIBONACCI PUZZLE

Each number is the sum of the two numbers before it. The next three numbers are 21, 34, 55.

SPACE Page 232: ASTEROID HOPPING

EARTH
JUPITER
MARS
MERCURY
NEPTUNE
PLUTO
SATURN
SUN
URANUS
VENUS

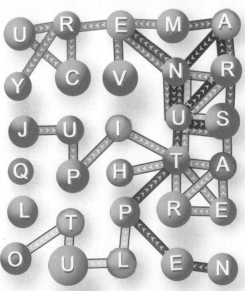

FOR MORE PUZZLES GO TO
WWW.WORLDALMANACFORKIDS.COM

SPORTS Page 249: Sports Word Search

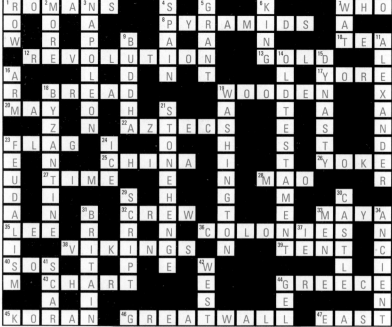

UNITED STATES Page 271: Presidential Puzzlers

1. A: Abraham Lincoln
2. B: John Adams
3. D: John Quincy Adams
4. C: Thomas Jefferson
5. B: James Madison
6. B: Franklin D. Roosevelt
7. A: James Buchanan
8. B: Grover Cleveland
9. D: William H. Taft
10. A: Grover Cleveland
11. D: Ronald Reagan
12. A: John F. Kennedy
13. A: William H. Taft
14. D: Richard Nixon

WORLD HISTORY Page 334: CROSSWORD PUZZLE

FOR MORE PUZZLES GO TO
WWW.WORLDALMANACFORKIDS.COM

INDEX

This product/publication includes images from Artville, ClipArt.com, Comstock, Corbis Royalty-Free, Corel, Digital Stock, Digital Vision, EyeWire, Map Resources, Photos.com, PhotoDisc, Rubberball, which are protected by the copyright laws of the U.S., Canada, and elsewhere. Used under license.

PHOTOGRAPHY: 9: Powell, State Department Photo. Rowling, William De La Hey. Jeter, PHOTO FILE/Landov; all others, AP/Wide World Photos. **10-11:** Lohan, Courtesy of Universal Music Group; Usher, LAFace/Zomba; Clarkson, RCA Records/Photo Kevin Hees; Keys, AP/Wide World Photos. **12-13:** Hughes, LucasFilm Ltd.; *Lemony Snickett*, Courtesy of Paramount Pictures Corporation and Dreamworks LCC. All rights reserved; *Sisterhood*, REUTERS/Fred Prouse/Landov; 'ROBOTS' © 2005 Twentieth Century Fox. All rights reserved. **14-15:** *7th Heaven*, Kwaku Alston; Idol, AP/Wide World Photos; *SpongeBob SquarePants*, © 2005 Viacom International Inc. All rights reserved. Nickelodeon, *SpongeBob SquarePants* and all related titles, logos, and characters are trademarks of Viacom International Inc. SpongeBob SquarePants created by Stephen Hillenburg; Welling, AP/ Wide World Photos. **16-17:** Ohno, Daniel Seurer; All others, AP/Wide World Photos. **18-19:** Brady, MIKE BLAKE/Reuters/Landov; Woods, Jackson, Sorenstam, AP/Wide World Photos; Johnson, REUTERS/Tami Chappell/Landov. **20-21:** Tsunami, REUTERS/Sucheta Das/Landov; Presidents, White House photo by Tina Hager; John Paul II and Benedict XVI, AP/Wide World Photos; *The Gates*, © Edward A. Thomas; dinosaur, reprinted photograph with permission from "Soft-Tissue Vessels and Cellular Preservation in Tyrannosaurus rex." Science, vol. 307, March 25, 2005, p. 1953. 2005 AAAS; Iraq, AP/Wide World Photos. **22-23:** Fossett, Virgin Atlantic; Kwan, AP/Wide World Photos; Arafat and Rabin and Mandela, AP/Wide World Photos; Olsen twins, Getty Images. **34:** Laika, AP/Wide World Photos. **35:** © Kim Johnson. **36:** © Gregory Colbert. **38:** Lincoln, Library of Congress Prints and Photographs Division, Reproduction (P&P P) #LC-USZC4-2439; Lange photo, LOC P&P, #LC-DIG-fsa-8b29516. **39:** Kevin Seabrooke. **41:** Lucid, NASA; Edison, LOC P&P LC-DIG-cwpbh-04043; Cy Young, LOC P&P Baseball Cards from the Benjamin K. Edwards Collection LOT 13163-18, no. 265. **42-43:** Harper Lee, Courtesy of the Mobile Register 2001 © All rights reserved. Reprinted with permission. Photo by Mike Kittrell; McGraw and Jeter, AP/Wide World Photos; Lohan, Courtesy of Universal Music Group; Obama, Courtesy of U.S. Senator Barak Obama; James, LOC P&P #LC-USZ62-3854. **44:** Clinton, United States Senate; Bush daughters, SHAUN HEASLEY/Reuters/Landov; Barton, LOC P&P #LC-USZ62-19319. **45:** Houghton Mifflin Trade and Reference Division. **46-47:** Winn Dixie, © 2005 by Twentieth Century Fox Film Corporation. All rights reserved.; Chasing Vermeer, Scholastic Inc.; Artemis Fowl, Jacket Illustration by Tony Fleetwood. Publisher: Hyperion/Miramax Books; Bud, Not Buddy, Jacket cover from *BUD, NOT BUDDY* by Christopher Paul Curtis used by permission of Random House Children's Books, a division of Random House, Inc.; Chicken Soup, cover artwork by Fred Babb/Cover re-design by Andrea Perrine Brower; Anne Frank, jacket cover from *ANNE FRANK: THE DIARY OF A YOUNG GIRL* by Anne Frank. Used by permission of Bantam, a division of Random House, Inc. **48:** Lewis, Time Life Pictures/Getty Images. **49:** Jim Graham. **50:** Taipei, AP/Wide World Photos. **51:** Elevator buttons, © Aram Schvey; Home Insurance Building, Courtesy of Frances Loeb Library, Graduate School of Design, Harvard University. **52-53:** Kingdom Center, Joseph Poon; Glass House, Ron Blunt; Gherkin, AP/Wide World Photos; Millau, JEAN-PHILLIPE ARLES/Reuters/Landov. **55:** American Camp Association. **56:** Kevin Seabrooke. **59:** Roller Coaster Tycoon, 3, Atari Interactive, Inc. Samsung DVD Jr., courtesy of Samsung Electronics. **60:** Bill Gates, Microsoft Corporation. **61:** fossilized skeleton, Yaoming Hu, Jin Meng/ American Museum of Natural History. **64:** maze, Kerria Seabrooke. **65:** Titanic, LOC P&P #LC-USZ62-90833. **67:** Galveston, LOC P&P #LC-USZ62-56437. **83:** maze, Kerria Seabrooke. **85:** Mr. Potato Head and Matchbox Cars, © Edward A. Thomas. **87:** hand of cards, Aram Schvey. **88:** drawing and photo, Kate Lewis. **97:** LOC P&P #LC-USZ62-354. **98:** Courtesy of USDA. **102:** eye, National Eye Institute, National Institute of Health. **113:** Ash'iya and Maza Maalouf courtesy of Edward A. Thomas. **116:** © Wristies. **126:** D-Day, National Archives. **127-128:** Nickel and Quarter-dollar coin images from the United States Mint. **131:** United States Golden Dollar coin images courtesy United States Mint and used with permission; Hamilton, LOC P&P #LC-USZ62-48272. **132:** Nickelodeon, The Robert Runyon Photograph Collection, (Image #02513), The Center for American History, The University of Texas at Austin. **133:** Shrek 2, Dreamworks S.K.G. American Idol, AP/ Wide World Photos; Home Improvement, Getty Images. **134:** Getty Images. **135:** Sisterhood, REUTERS/Fred Prouser/Landov. Star Wars, Lucas Films, Ltd. **136:** Browing, JACQUELINE BOHNERT. Devon Werkheiser, AP/ Wide World. **137:** Photos by Carolyn Russo/NASM, Smithsonian Institution. **138:** The Children's Museum of Indianapolis. **139:** National Automobile Museum (The Harrah Collection), Reno, Nevada. **141:** Usher/Alisha Keys, MIKE BLAKE/Reuters/Landov; Carey, LEE CELANO/REUTERS/Landov. **143:** Tada! Staff. **147:** LOC P&P #LC-B201-5202-13. **189:** Totem Pole, © Edward A. Thomas; Thorpe, Cumberland County Historical Society. **191:** Courtesy, National Museum of the American Indian, Smithsonian Institution. Photo by R.A. Whiteside. **192:** Mankiller, Fulcrum Publishing; Sequoyah, LOC P&P #LC-USZC4-2566; Sitting Bull, LOC P&P #LC-USZ62-88633. **201:** LOC P&P #LC-B201-5202-13. **202:** Maathai, Ebadi, AP/Wide World Photos; Roosevelt, LOC P&P #LC-USZ62-88633. **204:** Ben Watts. **205:** Kids with kite, Photos.com. **210:** Buddha: © Aram Schvey; Kaaba, AP/Wide World Photos. **218:** Carson, U.S. Fish and Wildlife; Carver LOC #LC-J601-302; Darwin, LOC P&P #LC-USZ61-104. **200:** Lori P. Wiesenfeld. **224:** Whirlpool Galaxy, NASA Goddard Space Flight Center (NASA-GSFC); Wild 2, NASA Jet Propulsion Laboratory (NASA-JPL). **229:** photos, NURC/UNCW; map: Leigh Haeger. **230:** NASA Jet Propulsion Laboratory (NASA-JPL). **232:** NASA/ASSDC. **233:** Red Sox, EPA/JOHN MABANGLO/Landov. **234:** Babe Ruth, LOC P&P #LC-USZC4-7246. **235-241:** AP/Wide World Photos. **243:** Mascots, AP/Wide World Photos. **244:** Didrickson, AP/ Wide World Photos. **245:** REUTERS/Tami Chappell/Landov. **246:** Courtesy of Special Olympics. **247:** AP/Wide World Photos. **249:** Chip Towers, Radi Nabulsi of the University of Georgia Sports Communications Department. **255:** Carhenge, Friends of Carhenge. **256-257:** NPS Photos. **259:** Kingda Ka, Six Flags Theme Parks Inc. **267:** Pelosi, Office of the Democratic Leader Nancy Pelosi. **268:** U.S. Supreme Court, Courtesy of the Supreme Court Historical Society. **272-276:** Washington, Adams, Jefferson, Madison, Monroe, Adams, Jackson, Harrison, Tyler, Pierce, Buchanan, Johnson, Hayes, Arthur, Harrison, McKinley, Roosevelt, Wilson, Harding, Hoover, Roosevelt, Eisenhower, ©1967 by Dover Publications. **273-276:** Van Buren, Polk, Taylor, Fillmore, Lincoln, Grant, Garfield, Cleveland, Taft, Coolidge, Truman, Kennedy, LOC P&P. **277:** Johnson, Lyndon B. Johnson Library; Nixon, LOC P&P; Ford, Courtesy of Gerald R. Ford Museum; Carter, Courtesy of Jimmy Carter Library; Reagan, Courtesy of Ronald Reagan Library; Bush, G., Official White House Photo/LOC P&P; Clinton, Courtesy of the White House; Bush, G.W., Eric Draper-The White House. **278:** Abigail Adams, LOC P&P #LC-USZ62-10016; Frances Cleveland, LOC P&P #LC-USZ62-25797; Grace Coolidge, LOC P&P #LC-USZ62-100816; Abigail Fillmore, Photo courtesy of the Millard Fillmore House Museum, East Aurora, New York; Lady Bird Johnson, LBJ Library Image Archives; Ellen Wilson, LOC P&P #LC-USZ62-25806; Laura Bush, Eric Draper-The White House. **285:** G.W. Bush, Eric Draper-The White House. **286:** King, Lyndon B. Johnson Library. **287:** Chisholm, LOC P&P #LC-U9-25383-33; Douglass, LOC P&P #LC-USZ62-15887; Washington, LOC P&P #LC-USZ62-49568; Rice, U.S. Department of State. **315:** 1 Yard, Timothy Bryk. **318:** Hieroglyphics, © Edward A. Thomas. **320:** Allawi, DoD photo by Staff Sgt. Angelique Perez, U.S. Air Force. **324:** Tsunami, DoD photo by Petty Officer 3rd Class Jacob J. Kirk, U.S. Navy. **326:** Jesus, LOC P&P #LC-USZC2-2971. **328:** Catherine the Great: LOC P&P #LC-USZ62-116782. **329:** Columbus, LOC P&P #LC-USZC4-2920. **331:** Roosevelt, LOC P&P #LC-USZC4-11548; San Francisco Earthquake, LOC P&P #LC-USZ62-123117. **332:** Low, Girl Scouts of the USA; Truth, LOC P&P #LC-USZ62-119343; Jemison, NASA; Stanton & Anthony, LOC P&P #LC-US262-83145. **333:** Meir, LOC P&P #LC-U9-27286-5; Curie, LOC P&P #LC-USZ62-91224.

FRONT COVER: (tl & tr) PhotoDisc, (tc) Ken Graham/Getty Images, (cr) Renee Lynn/Getty Images, (br) Masterfile, (c), Rubber Ball;(bl), EyeWire, (cl), Ron Leighton/Bill Smith Studio, (bg) Nick Gibson/age footstock.

BACK COVER: (cl) Rubber Ball, (tl) Corbis, (c & tr) Corel, (br) PhotoDisc.

INSIDE FRONT COVER: (tl) Artville, (tc) Corel, (tr), Dolores Bego, (c, cr, bl, br & cr), PhotoDisc. **INSIDE BACK COVER:** : (tl, tc & cl), PhotoDisc, (tr) Six Flags Theme Park Inc., (c) mapquest.com, (br & bc) Corel.

The World Almanac For Kids 2006
"WORLD ALMANAC ADVENTURER CONTEST"

Hey Kids Ages 7 to 13! Enter the World Almanac Adventurer Contest!

Ever been to Yellowstone? The Grand Canyon? The next town over? Whether you're traveling across the globe or around the corner, there's always somewhere new to explore. Let us know where you traveled in 2005 and what you learned on your trip. Send us a photo of yourself at the place you visited and write an essay of 250 words or less describing your adventure. Be sure to answer these three questions:

What was the most interesting thing that you did or saw on your trip?
What famous person is from the place you visited?
What is the most notable "roadside attraction" in the place you visited?

The three top winners will have their adventures featured in the *World Almanac For Kids 2007*. The grand prize winner will receive a four-day, all-expense-paid trip for four to New York City and World Almanac headquarters (transportation courtesy of Continental Airlines). The grand prize winner will also be interviewed by our sister company, Weekly Reader, and will appear on the Weekly Reader website. First runner-up will receive a prize package valued at $100, and a second runner up will receive one free copy of the *World Almanac For Kids* for the next three years. Two hundred semi-finalists will receive a World Almanac T-shirt and a stuffed globe.

All entries must be received by February 28, 2006. All entries must include the respondent's name, complete address, age, parent's name, and parent's daytime phone number. Entries should be sent to:

World Almanac for Kids
"World Almanac Adventurer" Contest
512 Seventh Avenue, 21st Floor
New York, NY 10018
Fax: (646) 312-6839
Email: adventurer@waegroup.com

The World Almanac for Kids 2006 "World Almanac Adventurer" Contest Rules: No purchase necessary to enter or win. Purchasing does not improve chances of winning. The World Almanac Adventurer Competition is open to legal residents of the United States who are between the ages of 7-13 at the time of entry. Enter by writing an essay about your trip (250 words or less)that answers the following three questions: 1. What was the most interesting thing that you saw or did on your trip? 2. What famous person is from the place you visited? 3. What is the most notable "roadside attraction" in the place you visited? Also send a photo of yourself at the place you visited.

Entry should be sent by mail, fax, or e-mail together with your printed name, address, ZIP code, and daytime phone number with area code. Entries must be received before 11:59 P.M. EST on February 28, 2006. No other methods of entry are accepted. All entries become the property of World Almanac Education Group and will not be acknowledged or returned. Entries will be judged for originality of content and description. One Grand Prize winner will receive an all-expense-paid trip for four to New York, NY, including transportation (courtesy of Continental Airlines), lodging for three nights, and three meals per day for four days; one first runner up will receive a prize package amounting to $100; one second runner up will receive one World Almanac For Kids for the next three years. Two hundred third runners up will receive a World Almanac For Kids T-shirt and stuffed globe. All taxes on prizes are the responsibility of the winners. Winners will be notified on or about March 15, 2006. Submission of entry constitutes entrant's consent (or that of their parent/legal guardian) to irrevocably assign to World Almanac Books any and all rights to entry, including, but not limited to, intellectual property rights. Acceptance of prize constitutes winners' permission to use their names, likenesses, cities, and states, and to be photographed for advertising and publicity purposes without additional compensation except where prohibited by law. Void where prohibited or restricted by law. All federal, state and local laws and regulations apply. All entries are bound by the Full Rules. To obtain Full Rules, send a self addressed, stamped envelope to the address above.